Answering a Question with a Question

Contemporary Psychoanalysis and Jewish Thought

ACADEMIC
STUDIES
PRESS

Answering a Question with a Question

Contemporary Psychoanalysis and Jewish Thought

Editors

Lewis Aron, Libby Henik

Boston

2010 — תש״ע

Library of Congress Cataloging-in-Publication Data

Answering a question with a question : contemporary psychoanalysis
and Jewish thought / editors, Lewis Aron, Libby Henik.
   p. cm. — (Judaism and Jewish life)
   ISBN 978-1-934843-37-6 (hardback)
   1. Psychoanalysis and culture. 2. Psychoanalysis and religion.
3. Jewish philosophy. 4. Judaism. I. Aron, Lewis. II. Henik, Libby.
   BF175.5.C84A57 2010
   296.3'71 — dc22
                         2010012712

Book design by Ivan Grave

Published by Academic Studies Press in 2009
28 Montfern Avenue
Brighton, MA 02135, USA
press@academicstudiespress.com
www. academicstudiespress.com

In Loving Memory of my Parents
Gertrude and Rubin Aron

May Their Memories Be A Blessing

L.A.

"Livnot U'lhibanot Ba" — "לבנות ולהיבנות בה"

"…we have come … to build and be rebuilt by it."

(from the Zionist song: Anu Banu Artza)

This book is dedicated to the memory of my parents,
Sylvia and Harry Adelman,
who were active in sustaining the nascent
modern Jewish Day School movement,
and in turn, were sustained by it.

L.H.

TABLE OF CONTENTS

3. BIBLICAL COMMENTARY

4. THEORETICAL PAPERS

ACKNOWLEDGEMENT

My thanks to the authors and contributors to this book, many of whom have had a substantial part in my thinking about contemporary psychoanalysis and Jewish thought. As always I want to thank my colleagues at the New York University Postdoctoral Program in Psychotherapy & Psychoanalysis. The "Postdoc" community is the most supportive, productive, challenging, and invigorating psychoanalytic community in the world and I have treasured being a part of the community as a student, graduate, faculty member and as its director.

Special thanks go to my colleague and co-editor Libby Henik who brought consistent energy, intelligence, scholarship, and good sense to this project. Yasher Kochech!

Finally, much thanks and love to my family: my children, Benjamin, Raphi, and Kirya Ades-Aron, and my wife, Jane L. Ades, for their consistent support, encouragement, and love.

L. A.

This is my first venture at editing a book and who better to co-edit with than Lew Aron. Lew was available round the clock to exchange ideas, debate and disagree, and enjoy both the mutuality and the differences in our ideas. I want to thank Lew for inviting me to join him on this important project. Perhaps collaborate more accurately describes the spirit with which Lew made room for me to bring myself to this endeavor, help shape it and find expression in it.

My deepest gratitude to Emily Kuriloff, colleague and friend, with whom I share a love of our psychoanalytic work, a connection to Judaism, the excitement of ideas and the joys of mothering daughters. Emily encouraged me to start writing what I felt passionate about and guided me through the writing and editing process.

A special thanks to Sue Grand, a woman of intellect and grace, who some years ago suggested that I join Lew Aron's reading group and who watched the process of this project unfold, offered support and advice, and delighted with me in this journey.

To my husband Willy and my daughters Erika and Audrey, who have been living with this project and my chapter about Rebecca, to the point that Rebecca is almost considered a third daughter in our family, I want to say thank you for your support, patience and encouragement. My daughters Erika and Audrey should be credited with the title of our book, "Answering a Question with a Question," which they came up with in a brainstorming session around the kitchen table. I also want to thank Erika, a talented editor in her own right, for assisting me in editing my chapter on Rebecca.

To our contributors – Thank you for your enthusiasm and encouragement as this project progressed. I have enjoyed our correspondence and the breadth of your ideas.

L. H.

Our thanks to Chris Bennett for his generosity in allowing us to reproduce *Pharaoh's dream* (see: http://www.chrisbenn.com).

Our experience in publishing with the Academic Studies Press (ASP) has been a pleasure from beginning to end. Much appreciation is due ASP director, Igor Nemirovsky. Special thanks to Series Editor, Simcha Fishbane, who first invited Lew to contribute a volume on contemporary psychoanalysis and Jewish thought to this book series. We have enjoyed working with Sara Libby Robinson, Associate Editor at ASP, and Kira Nemirovsky, Production, ASP. Thank you for helping bring this book to fruition.

L. A., L. H.

PREFACE

The reader will find that the selections collected here are broad and wide-ranging. In compiling this rich collection of essays, a spacious net was cast to bring together the work and thinking of clinical psychoanalysts and scholars from the academic community, both American and international. Our fourteen essays have been divided into four groupings.

1 Historical Overview. We begin with Celia Brickman's "Psychoanalysis and Judaism in Context," a comprehensive overview of the history of scholarship concerned with the Jewishness of psychoanalysis. Brickman follows the developments in psychoanalytic thought regarding religion from Freud onwards (mainly within the Anglo-American psychoanalytic community), and situates psychoanalytic understandings of Judaism within the context of these contributions.

2 Clinical presentations that illuminate various aspects of the therapeutic relationship within a Jewish context. In this grouping Yehoshua Arnowitz's essay "The Jew for Jesus and Other Analytic Explorations of God" invites the reader to sit in as analyst and patient work together in understanding their religious experiences through mutual exploration and creation of meaning. Jill Salberg, in her essay on "Dreams and Competing Authorities" examines Rabbinic and current relational psychoanalytic ideas and controversies in the understanding of dreams and dreamers. Joyce Slochower's paper on "Holding the

Mourner: Jewish Ritual through a Psychoanalytic Lens" deals with therapeutic factors in the non-analytic setting of the Jewish mourning ritual. David M. Goodman, in "Hearing 'Thou Shall Not Kill' When All the Evidence is to the Contrary: Psychoanalysis, Enactment, and Jewish Ethics" explores, through case example and theoretical formulation, the psychoanalytic concept of enactment, wherein analyst and patient are pulled into a relational pattern in which the patient's past traumatic experiences are played out.

3 The third category is that of enriched biblical commentary. Tuvia Peri's paper on "A Freudian and a Kleinian Reading of the Midrash on the Garden of Eden Narrative" demonstrates that we can identify, in midrashic exegesis of the Eden narrative, two interpretive trends which parallel two major psychoanalytic theories: the Freudian theory and the Kleinian theory. Moshe Halevi Spero's essay on "Transformations in the 'Mental Apparatus of Dreaming' as Depicted in the Biblical Story of Joseph" sheds new psychoanalytic light on the biblical episodes of Joseph's relations with his own dreams, the dreams of the ministers and the dreams of Pharaoh. Focusing on certain subtle developments that take place in Pharaoh's experience of dreaming, dream narration, and the role of the person to whom a dream is told, rather than on Joseph's interpretations or the psychosexual meaning of the dream symbols, the author suggests that the Bible has portrayed the development of the mental apparatus of dreaming. Avivah Gottlieb Zornberg's analysis of the life of Moses in "'Let Me See That Good Land:' The Story of a Human Life" combines midrash, literary analysis and psychoanalytic understanding, thereby providing us with a new and deeper understanding of Moses' desires, conflicts and resolution as revealed in his last address to the people [Bnai Yisrael] before his death. There may be no better example of a thinker who raises questions upon questions than Zornberg, difficult, unsettling, and absorbing questions that reflect deeply on the Bible and on human experience.

In "Rebecca's Veil: A Weave of Conflict and Agency," Libby Henik's non-linear reading between Rabbinic exegesis and the psychoanalytic theory of conflict, releases Biblical women from their often one-dimensional, polarized portrayals as either deceitful manipulators or God's instruments into complex agents of intention, choice and multiple life narratives.

4 The final category is devoted to theoretical papers that throw light on historical events, Jewish social/communal behavior and religious ideas and thoughts. In this category we find Lori Hope Lefkovitz's ideas in "'Demand a Speaking Part!': The Character of the Jewish Father" examining the cultural type of the Jewish father from the perspective of critical analysis. Seth Aronson, in his paper "The Problem of Desire: Psychoanalysis as a Jewish Wisdom Tradition" raises and explores the challenging question of whether we can legislate desire in the manner set down in the 10th commandment. Lewis Aron and Karen E. Starr deal with the nature of spiritual transformations in their paper, "'Going Out to Meet You, I Found You Coming Toward Me': Transformation in Jewish Mysticism and Contemporary Psychoanalysis" and how for a richer understanding of transformation, we must not "explain away" spiritual experience in psychoanalytic terms, nor discard psychoanalytic formulations in favor of spiritual metaphors, but rather be willing to play in the possibilities created by opening a dialogue between them. Stephen Frosh's analysis of the social phenomenon of anti-Semitism in "'Foreignness Is the Quality which the Jews and One's Own Instincts Have in Common': Anti-Semitism, Identity and the Other," argues that the connection between the history of psychoanalysis and the centrality to its theoretical foundation in the Jewish practice of interpretation, goes beyond historical accident. The connection with Jewish thinking programmed anti-Semitism into this new 'science,' provoking strong emotions amongst its Jewish and non-Jewish adherents and opponents alike.

Stephen Frosh posits that anti-Semitism is an intrapsychic phenomena which works to preserve the psychic integrity of subjectivity within the consciousness of Western civilizations. By being the embodiment of the 'other,' the Jew preserves the split for Western civilization between what is accepted and disgusted in oneself, between the conscious and unconscious self. Since psychoanalysis is a Jewish discovery and invention, unconscious desires become Jewish, both enticing and dangerous.

The final essay, "A Burning World, An Absent God: Midrash, Hermeneutics, and Relational Psychoanalysis," by Philip Cushman, examines the consequences of the terrorist attack on 9/11 and the rise of religious fundamentalism. From Cushman's perspective, one of the most important features of midrashic practice is its grasp of the primordial entanglements between moral understandings, communal activity, and personal well-being. In particular, the valorization of intertextuality, engaged understanding, the dialectic of absence and presence, and the prohibition against idolatry suggest the kind of psychotherapy that is now referred to as relational psychoanalysis.

L.A., L. H.
January 2010

INTRODUCTION

Lewis Aron, Libby Henik

Early in the history of psychoanalysis, Sigmund Freud wrote one the founding works of the new discipline, a book that was a spin off to his *Interpretation of Dreams*, called *The Joke and Its Relation to the Unconscious*. Freud was stirred to write this book because his friend Wilhelm Fliess had pointed out to him that so many of the dreams he presented included a variety of forms of wit, puns, word play, and humor. Many of the jokes that Freud utilized were Jewish jokes, often jokes that were self-mocking or that ridiculed Eastern European Jewish immigrants. In telling these jokes Freud was both expressing and defending against the anti-Semitism of his time and place. Freud had in fact begun collecting Jewish jokes many years earlier and clearly took pleasure in these jokes. In the introduction to the most recent translation of this work, John Carey (2002) asks why it is that Freud uses the "economic" point of view to explain the functioning of jokes, namely that jokes save energy by defending against more deeply unconscious wishes. Carey argues that not only is the economic point of view a response to Freud's surrounding capitalistic culture, but that it is a specific response to anti-Semitism; "Freud's theory of jokes is itself a kind of joke."

Like the Jewish jokes against Jews that he analyzes, it represents a rejoinder, a pointed response to what he calls, "the manifold and hopeless misery of the Jews'. Since the time of Shylock, and indeed, long before, Jews in Western culture had been traduced and ridiculed. Above all they had been laughed at for their parsimony, the cheese-pairing economies

15

involved in the accumulation of wealth. Freud's reply was to demonstrate that laughter it itself parsimony, a saving of the effort usually spent on emotions and inhibitions. Jewish economies have traditionally been the target of mockery. But the Gentile mockery, when inspected by a great Jewish intellectual, emerges as merely another economy. (Carey, 2002, p. xxvii)

We begin this introduction with the above note because we want to start this book with two jokes, one about Jews and the other about psychoanalysts. What better way to begin a volume that links Contemporary psychoanalysis and Jewish thought? But of course, it is also our way of raising, right from the beginning, that there has always been a link between psychoanalysis and Jewish thought, going back to Freud and the earliest origins and precursors of psychoanalysis. Freud and his circle, the founders of psychoanalysis, were almost exclusively Jewish and the field has remained, in many parts of the world, constituted by large proportions of Jewish practitioners and patients. But let's begin with two jokes:

1. A Jew is asked: "Why do Jews always answer a question with a question?" to which the Jew replies: "What makes you ask?"

2. Two psychoanalysts meet on the street. One asks the other: "How are you?" to which the other analyst replies: "What do you mean by that?"

What is common to these two jokes? Both jokes are rooted in inquiry, reflection, recursiveness, interpretation, meaning, and relational context. These jokes begin to point toward the connection between Jewish thought and psychoanalysis.

From the moment that Freud identified interpretation as his method of creating meaning, psychoanalysis became inextricably linked to, and some may say, a continuation of, Jewish thought. In Jewish tradition it is incumbent upon every generation to attempt to make meaning of its history. However, meaning in Jewish tradition, is co-created within the context of the intersubjective field of a meeting of minds (Aron, 1996). Midrashic inquiry interpreted gaps, contradictions, repetitions and anomalies in sacred text to find new and ever-changing meanings which were then open to scrutiny by successive students and successive generations, who brought their own questions and interpretations, thereby arriving at different meanings and understandings. Past and present influenced each other, bringing new meaning to both. Psychoanalysis, in some respects like the Jewish tradition from which it emerged, represents a body of thought about man's relation to himself and to others and places great value on the influence of memory, narrative, and history in creating meaning within the dyadic relationship of analyst and patient.

Stephen Frosh (2005) suggests that books on psychoanalysis, rather than being shelved in the psychology sections of bookstores and libraries, might be better listed under "Jewish Studies." The element of seriousness in this claim is not just sociological, that the early analysts were almost exclusively Jews, but is rather an assertion regarding the intellectual history of the transmission of ideas, based on the observation that for millennia the main expression of cultural achievement in Jewish life was the continuous argument about the meanings of texts and ongoing debate over the interpretation of words (Frosh, 2005). Interpretation, creating meaning, dialectic, and inwardness were characteristic Jewish concerns.

Harold Bloom (1987) wrote, "Freud's most profound Jewishness, voluntary and involuntary, was his consuming passion for interpretation" (p. 52). It is by now well accepted to think of psychoanalysis, like Judaism and biblical exegesis, as a hermeneutical or interpretive tradition. For psychoanalysts, the rabbinic approach to interpretation should be familiar indeed. David Bakan (1958) persuasively argued that Freud applied to the study of individual behavior the traditional Jewish methodological principle of interpretation, in which every word — even every letter — of the Torah, even the decorative adornments of the letters, even the spaces between letters, was assumed to be meaningful and subject to multiple understandings. For psychoanalysts, the human being, created in the image of God, is like a holy text, subject to ongoing and interminable analysis and interpretation.

In *Answering A Question With A Question: Contemporary Psychoanalysis and Jewish Thought,* the relevance of the Jewish interpretive tradition to the expanding theoretical world of psychoanalysis, and the influence of psychoanalytic orientations regarding the intrapsychic and the interpersonal on Jewish thought are brought together for the first time in the English language. While there have been many articles and books that discuss Freud's Jewish background, much of this material is based on older, more classical versions of psychoanalysis, with a great deal of attention given to Freud's own life and biography and on his intellectual influences, rather than examining more recent, contemporary psychoanalytic perspectives. Mortimer Ostow (1982), who was for decades the preeminent scholar of Judaism and psychoanalysis, edited an important and widely read collection titled *Judaism and Psychoanalysis*, but that collection was written almost exclusively from the point of view of classical American ego-psychology, whereas the present work draws from a much broader and more up to date psychoanalytic field.

In this collection of articles, we have gathered writings, largely, newly written papers prepared specifically for this volume by leading international scholars who share an interest in modern psychoanalysis and Jewish thought. This is the first effort that we know of to bring together scholars, researchers, and clinicians who are addressing the interface of Jewish thought and contemporary psychoanalysis.

Psychoanalysis has influenced many disciplines within the academy and continues to play a significant role in the liberal arts and humanities. Psychoanalysis, however, is not housed within the academy. It is almost universally taught within private institutes established to train clinical therapists. This has led to a major gap, a lack of dialogue between contemporary practicing clinicians and members of other scholarly disciplines. Establishing forums for interdisciplinary dialog is therefore critical. Among the areas most in need of scholarly collaboration and exchange is that of psychoanalysis and Jewish thought.

Freud was concerned, even preoccupied, with the "danger" involved in the psychoanalytic movement "becoming a Jewish national affair" (Klein, 1985, p. xviii). While Peter Gay (1989) may be correct that in many respects Freud was "A Godless Jew," Philip Reiff makes the stronger point that "despite his irreligion," Freud's cultural Jewishness "was more binding than religious orthodoxy" (Gilman, 1993, p. 7). Freud's aim, however, was to invest psychoanalysis with the authority of an objective science, universal in its findings, and to divest it of all traces of Jewishness and particularity. It was Freud's worry that psychoanalysis would be seen as a "Jewish science." that led him to choose a non-Jew, Jung, to lead the movement as his successor. Ironically, Jung would later publicly stress the differences between a Jewish and Aryan psychology and would privately disparage the "essentially corrosive nature" of Freud and Adler's "Jewish gospel" (Gilman, 1993, p. 223). But religious belief was not only taboo among psychoanalysts because of the psychology of religious, ethnic, and racial differences and its role in psychoanalytic history. It also resulted from Freud's view of religion.

Freud viewed religion as an illusion as did analysts following him. Here is a single but poignant illustration: Consider this statement by Otto Fenichel, from his 1939 classic *Problems of Psychoanalytic Technique*, a text that influenced the theory and practice of psychoanalysis for decades — even to our own day:

> It has been said that religious people in analysis remain uninfluenced in their religious philosophies since analysis itself is supposed to be philosophically neutral. I consider this not to be correct. Repeatedly I have seen that with the analysis of the sexual anxieties and with maturing of the personality, the attachment to religion has ended. (p. 89)

Freud's Enlightenment ideal of science saw it as liberating the individual from the illusion of religion. Psychoanalysis offered Truth as replacement for regressive fantasy. Religious belief was "a lost cause," a "childhood neurosis" (1927, p. 53), and Freud paid homage only to "Our god Logos — Reason" (p. 54). Freud was intent to eliminate "the subjective factor," as he called it and Jewishness was definitely a subjective factor. Sander Gillman (1993) has persuasively demonstrated that Freud's goal was to universalize racist characterizations of Jews such that the scientist-analyst was to observe with a neutral, universal gaze, and not with a unique, idiosyncratic, and Jewish one. For psychoanalysis to be an objective science the uniqueness of the individual analyst was not to matter.

Stephen Mitchell's (1993) contemporary revision of psychoanalysis, known as relational psychoanalysis, offered a strong critique of the dichotomizations of fantasy and reality, illusion and rationality, religion and science. For Mitchell, "What is inspiring about psychoanalysis today is not the renunciation of illusion in the hope of joining a common, progressively realistic knowledge and control, but rather the hope of fashioning a personal reality that feels authentic and enriching" (p. 21). With it's goal as the enhancement and revitalization of human experience, and in its primary concern with felt meaning, significance, purpose and value, the sharp division between religion and psychoanalysis diminishes.

In accord with this shift in our view of science and rationality, our contemporary epistemology gives greater recognition to the subjectivity of the scientist and of the psychoanalyst. Today we have reached a point where psychoanalysts can examine their personal perspectives and subjectivities, including their religious beliefs and backgrounds, and examine how this effects their clinical work and theoretical formulations. This shift creates the environment for interdisciplinary dialogue between religious studies, Jewish thought and modern psychoanalysis.

However, this newer welcoming of the analyst's subjectivity and the recognition of the cultural embeddedness of psychoanalytic theory and practice also raises some difficult issues that cannot be ignored as we begin a volume connecting psychoanalysis and Jewish thought. What about Freud's worry that psychoanalysis would be viewed as a "Jewish science?" Are we claiming that that is in fact what it is? And if it is a Jewish science, what is the implication as to its universality? Is the connection between psychoanalysis and Jewish thought simply an historical contingency as it was discovered by a Jew or is it a hermeneutic that is so thoroughly embedded in Jewish thought and culture that they are inseparable? Was Levenson (2001) correct in asserting that Freud wrote Greek, but thought Jewish? Is clinical practice, as he suggests, an exercise in midrash?

Rather than answer this question, we choose to follow Jewish and psychoanalytic tradition, and ask a preliminary question, thus answering a question with a question: Is it possible that it has taken us this long, over a century of psychoanalysis, and more than half a century since the Holocaust, to even begin to "analyze" these questions publicly? Have we reached a point where we can embrace the intersection of psychoanalysis and Jewish thought and culture without making everyone too nervous to continue?

REFERENCES

Aron, L. (1996). *A Meeting of Minds*. Hillsdale, NJ: The Analytic Press.

Bakan, D. (1958). *Sigmund Freud and the Jewish Mystical Tradition*. Princeton, NJ: van Nostrand.

Bloom, H. (1987). *The Strong Light of the Canonical*. The City College Papers, 20:1-77. New York: H. Bloom.

Carey, J. (2002). "Introduction to Sigmund Freud's." *The Joke and Its Relation to the Unconscious*. NY: Penguin Classics, pp vii-xxviii.

Fenichel, O. (1946). "Some Remarks on Freud's Place in the History of Science." *Psychoanal. Quart.*, 15:279-284.

Freud, S. (1927). "The Future of an Illusion." *Standard Edition*, 21, 1-56. London: Hogarth Press, 1961.

Frosh, S. (2005). *Hate and the "Jewish Science."* New York: Palgrave Macmillan.

Gay, P. (1987). *A Godless Jew*. New Haven: Yale University Press.

Gilman, S. L. (1986). *Jewish Self-Hatred: Anti-Semitism and the Hidden Language of the Jews*. Baltimore: John Hopkins University Press.

----------. (1993). *Freud, Race and Gender*. Princeton, NJ: Princeton University Press.

Klein, D. B. (1985). *Jewish Origins of the Psychoanalytic Movement*. Chicago: The University of Chicago Press.

Levenson, E.A. (2001). Freud's Dilemma: On Writing Greek and Thinking Jewish. Contemp. Psychoanal., 37:375-390.

Mitchell, S. (1997). *Influence and Autonomy in Psychoanalysis*. Hillsdale, NJ: The Analytic Press.

Sorenson, R. L. (2000). "Psychoanalytic Institutes as Religious Denominations." *Psychoanalytic Dialogues*, 10:847-874.

Strozier, C. B. (1997). "Heinz Kohut's Struggles with Religion, Ethnicity, and God." In: *Religion, Society and Psychoanalysis*, ed. J. L. Jacobs & D. Capps. Boulder, CO: Westview Press, pp. 165–180.

----------. (2001). *Heinz Kohut: The Making of a Psychoanalyst.* New York: Farrar, Straus, & Giroux.

Yerushalmi, Y. H. (1991). *Freud's Moses.* New Haven, CT: Yale University Press.

1 Historical Context

Psychoanalysis and Judaism in Context *

Celia Brickman

Introduction

When we set out to examine the relationship between psychoanalysis and Judaism, we are confronted with a conundrum: while Freud wrote widely about *religion*, he wrote very little about Judaism per se. Because of the hegemony of Christianity in the religious life of the western world for the past two millennia, the concept of religion itself has generally taken its bearings from Christianity. And because Judaism has always held a particular and necessary place within Christianity — what from a Christian perspective would be called the place of superseded origins — Judaism has often been subsumed as part of so-called "Judaeo-Christian" religious culture, which is then shortened to the seemingly universal term "religion." So, when Freud and other psychoanalysts write about religion, they are generally referring to both Judaism and Christianity (with certain notable exceptions, discussed below). With this common and general use of the term religion, Freud — and his followers — obscure the structural differences between the two religions, as well what we might call the political differences between them — the vast differences in the social and political locations of Christian and Jewish communities and

* A shorter version of this essay was presented at a conference on "Judaism and Psychoanalysis: A Continuing Dialogue" sponsored by the Chicago Institute for Psychoanalysis and the Spertus Institute of Jewish Studies in Chicago on October 5, 2008.

their experiences in European countries leading up to and including the times in which Freud wrote. This use of the term religion also obscures the fact that Jews, unlike Christians, have been understood not only to share a religion, but also a culture and an ethnic identity; and, tellingly, at the time when Freud was writing in particular, to belong to the same race.

In this essay I will trace some developments in psychoanalytic thought from Freud onwards regarding religion in general, limiting myself mainly to Anglo-American contributions, and situating psychoanalytic understandings of Judaism within the context of these contributions. In addition, I hope to show how the ambiguities that reside in Freud's use of the term religion have played out in the differing responses to his writings on religion given by subsequent generations of Jewish and Christian writers.

Freud's critique of religion, and its social & religious context

The biggest affront Freud made to religious believers was to insist that rather than originating in a transcendent reality, religion arises out of human experience, and not only out of human experience, but out of the experience of infancy — the infancy of the individual, and the infancy of humankind. God is none other than the murdered but longed-for father from *Totem and Taboo*; religion is nothing but an illusion held by people who accept the handed-down pieties of tradition rather than thinking for themselves. The illusions of religion compensate for the helplessness of childhood and for the constraints imposed by civilization in adulthood; they belong to an early, narcissistic stage of development and should ideally be outgrown. In *Moses and Monotheism*, Freud's outlook changed somewhat: here he recognized religion as representing the repressed events of a people's history, and he even suggested that Judaism, through its greater resistance to illusions of fulfillment and a greater acceptance of renunciation than is found in Christianity, creates for its members a capacity for greater ethical heights. Nonetheless, when writing his *New Introductory Lectures* in 1933 to recapitulate his life's work (although before he wrote

Moses and Monotheism), Freud stated quite baldly that for psychoanalysis, "Religion alone is to be taken seriously as an enemy." (Freud, 1933, p. 160). Why did Freud take such a strong stand against religion at the same time as he insisted on holding onto his identity as a Jew? Otherwise said, before we consider contemporary psychoanalytic attitudes to Judaism, what did "religion" mean to Freud?

As is well known, Freud was writing at a difficult and tragic time in Jewish history. He was working after a brief period in which the doors to full participation in European social and professional life had opened up to Jews; but a time when those doors were beginning to close and the shadows of anti-Semitism were beginning to lengthen. Freud was a member of a generation of Jewish intellectuals whose families had moved out of the shtetls and ghettos and into cosmopolitan settings, where many of them no longer wished to continue the observances of their fathers and forefathers. For these intellectuals, the secularism that was the promise of much Enlightenment thought and the science that promised progress on all fronts seemed to offer passports out of the denigrated specificity of Judaism and into a universal brotherhood of European humankind. From this vantage point, religion signified the world of Jewish observance that Freud wished to leave behind. But in naming religion as the enemy, Freud was also hoping to point to the Christianity amongst which Jews lived, the Christianity which from its very inception had fostered an antagonistic and persecutory relationship to Judaism, and which had fed into the anti-Semitism that was gaining ground. The hope was, I believe, that without Christianity and without Judaism there would be only Europeans; without religion, there would be only science; and Europe's culture, society and scientific progress would be open to all its citizens.

In addition, in Freud's time Judaism was conceived of not only as a religion but also as a race; and thanks to the widespread nature of Lamarckian ideas at the time, the inferiority that was imputed to the Jews was widely believed to be racially inherited. (Gilman, 1993a, 1993b). Thus when Freud called religion the enemy, religion also signified the racist discourse that marked Jews as innately, i.e. biologically, inferior. Freud was working not only against the binary opposition of Judaism and

27

Christianity, but against that between Jews and "Aryans" as well. The creation of a universal science of the psyche needed to take aim at religion in order to do away with the world of stigmatized religious and cultural differences that were coded as racial and considered to be biologically innate.

In this appeal to a secular and scientific framework that would supersede religious and racial differences, Freud not only participated in, but was an architect of, one of the great theoretical edifices of twentieth century modernity. Modernity — a term that covers a large territory of social, political, and cultural changes — has generally defined itself as something new, in distinction to what it repudiates as the past. For Freud, religion represented the ideologies of this past that modernity was to overcome. While religion in the past may have helped people deal with their distress and helped them answer the question of how to live, it did this, according to Freud, by resorting to illusory and childish answers. Now, psychoanalysis would fulfill a similar function in a manner more suited to the modern age, challenging, rather than accepting, the traditional religious authority of the past. And yet, at the same time, Freud acknowledged on several occasions that he remained Jewish, even if only in ways he could not precisely pinpoint (e.g. Freud, 1913, p. xv).

Psychoanalytic responses to Freud's critique
I: Religion as faith

Within the psychoanalytic community itself, the first generation of psychoanalysts generally followed Freud's view of religion. Indeed, according to Peter Homans, psychoanalysis owed its very origins to the loss of religious faith amongst the first psychoanalysts, and to their creative mourning of that loss (Homans, 1989). Thus mistrust of religion and the psychoanalytic reduction of religion to its component psychological mechanisms was the general rule among the first psychoanalysts. The relationship to religion became one of the central features of the rift between Freud and Jung: while Freud was writing *Totem and Taboo*, arguing for the origins of religion in the primal crime and its echoes throughout the generations, Jung was writing his first major work, *Symbols of Transformation,* in which he argued for a religious impulse within the psyche itself. (Their letters reveal the unraveling of their relationship as they each worked on what were intended to be major contributions to the psychoanalytic understanding of myth and symbols [McGuire, 1988]). Antipathy towards Jung has also played a role in the generalized psychoanalytic mistrust of religion.

In the generation following Freud, Freud's attitude towards religion was in general preserved, at least amongst American psychoanalysts, both classical Freudians and ego psychologists. The idea persisted that religion was an infantile, regressive state, out of which the adult should mature. As but one example: Sara Lawrence-Lightfoot, in her biography of her mother (Dr. Margaret Morgan-Lawrence, one of the first African-American psychoanalysts), reports that training analyst Sandor Rado used to say to his students, "If anyone applies to you to go into analysis and they say they are religious, refuse them because they are too dependent" (Lawrence-Lightfoot, 1988, p. 179).

Yet ever since Freud's time there has developed a wide-ranging literature on the topic of psychoanalysis and religion. Theologians, Jewish and Christian, have made use of psychoanalysis for their religious understandings in spite of Freud's overt stance against religion. Starting with Oscar Pfister, a Protestant minister who was a good friend and staunch supporter of Freud's, several theologians and religious philosophers have managed to assimilate Freud's thought in ways that helped explain and even enlarge their theological beliefs. Bringing psychoanalytic concepts into the purview of their theological outlooks and using them in their pastoral work with their parishioners, Protestant ministers developed the area of pastoral care and counseling, and its younger sibling, clinical pastoral education (the education of hospital chaplains). The renowned theologian Paul Tillich, a major architect of pastoral psychology, saw what Freud called neurosis — including religion as neurosis — as a way of avoiding the full, existential awareness of our radical freedom. Tillich's pastoral psychotherapy owed much to psychoanalysis in how it helped the person confront his anxieties (see Parsons, 2005, p. 7477). In a different vein, the Jewish theologian Richard Rubenstein, having lost his faith after the Holocaust, used Freudian insights to deepen his understanding of Jewish aggadah and legend (Rubenstein, 1968).

In the first generation after Freud both in the United Kingdom and in the United States, there were psychoanalysts who saw no difficulty in reconciling the aims of psychoanalysis and religion. Harry Guntrip (1957), one of the originators of British object relations, and Erich Fromm (1950), Erik Erikson (1959, 1962) and Hans Loewald (1980) in the United States, argued for a positive evaluation of religious life. Erikson, for example, related religion to the human need and capacity to trust, which he saw as emerging in the first of his eight stages of development; and he wrote sympathetic, searching biographies of Luther and of Gandhi. Fromm and Loewald both wrote expansively about psychoanalysis and (various forms of) religion, seeing similarities in their aims.

As time has gone on, this literature has increased, and much of it reflects the contradictions, mentioned above, embedded in the conception of religion used by Freud. Although there are works which escape the following categorization, loosely it can be said that on the one hand there are those who treat Freud's work on religion as a theological challenge, discussing Freud's writings on religion predominantly in terms of faith or the object(s) of faith, even if they attempt to bracket ultimate truth claims (e.g. Milner, 1969; Ricoeur, 1970; Rizzuto, 1979, 1998; Meissner, 1984; McDargh, 1983; Jones, 1991, 1996). Predominantly Christian, these writers want to know whether and how contemporary revisions of psychoanalysis allow for a more positive relationship between psychoanalysis and religious belief than Freud posited. Many of them suggest that post-Freudian readings of psychoanalysis allow a rapprochement between psychoanalysis and religion that was prevented by Freud's scientific, rationalistic and autonomous model of subjectivity.

On the other hand, there has been a body of predominantly Jewish writers who have taken up the issues of psychoanalysis and religion in terms of identity (ethnic, racial, gender) and of interpretation. Rather than focusing on the issue of belief or faith, these writers inquire into the influence of Judaism and Jewish practices on the creation of psychoanalysis, regardless of Freud's claims to scientific neutrality. Some seek parallels between Jewish forms of inquiry and interpretation on the one hand, and those of psychoanalysis on the other; others find embedded in psychoanalytic theory various ways of renegotiating conceptions of Jews current during Freud's time (e.g. Schorske, 1961; Cuddihy, 1974; Robert, 1976; Handelman, 1982; Klein, 1985; Bloom, 1987; Yerushalmi, 1991; Gilman, 1993a, 1993b; Boyarin, 1995, 1998; Bernstein, 1998; Geller, 1997, 2007).

Amongst the first group of those who have attempted to reconcile the insights of psychoanalysis with a theological outlook, the religious philosopher Paul Ricoeur's *Freud and Philosophy* stands out as among the most eminent (Ricoeur, 1971). Ricoeur framed his magisterial interpretation of Freud as a debate between psychoanalysis and the phenomenology of religions: on the one hand, psychoanalysis as a hermeneutics of suspicion that seeks to demystify religious beliefs as illusions, tracing them back to their human and infantile origins; on the other, the phenomenology of religion that seeks "the manifestation and restoration of a meaning addressed to me in the manner of a message" (p. 26). For the believer, the religious symbol refers to divinity, while for the psychoanalyst, the religious symbol refers to infantile longings and illusions. Anticipating Jonathan Lear's claim that the infantile roots of religious symbols need not invalidate the meanings that these symbols come to hold for the adult (Lear, 2005, ch. 7), Ricoeur made the case that symbols are inherently multivalent; that is, they always have more than one level of meaning, and therefore, by their very nature they point simultaneously both backwards towards infancy and forwards towards what lies beyond us, with neither direction annulling the meaning of its opposite. Indeed, religious symbols derive their power and saliency from their ability to condense in themselves both the personal, archeological meanings out of which they have arisen, and the cultural, kerygmatic meanings towards which they gesture. Ricoeur redeems the reductionism with which psychoanalysis had been charged — religion reduced to infantile fantasy — through an appeal to a Hegelian dialectical framework in which the past is only one of two necessary and intertwined steps: the symbol points towards regression

31

and progression simultaneously. Following Ricoeur's line of thought, the anthropologist Gananath Obeyesekere (1990) made use of psychoanalysis for cross-cultural understandings of religion in his ethnographic work in southeast Asia. Obeyesekere built on Ricoeur's dialectic to discern a nuanced relationship, as well as a critical difference, between religious symbol and pathological symptom.

But it was changes in the second and third generations of psychoanalysis in the United Kingdom and the United States — the British school of object relations and in particular the work of D. W. Winnicott, and the work of Heinz Kohut in the U.S. — that opened the door for a more widespread engagement of psychoanalytic writers with the topic of religion as belief and faith. These writers combined clinical and theological concerns to articulate a favorable psychoanalytic view of religion, featuring a framework which foregrounded a psychoanalytic developmental schema (rather than Ricoeur's Hegelian dialectic) together with a re-evaluation of the epistemic value of illusion. Their Anglo-American psychoanalytic perspectives stressed that needs previously seen by the psychoanalytic eye as exclusively infantile were actually on-going throughout the course of life. In addition, these writers reconfigured the damning epithet of religion as "illusory" through Winnicott's well-known concept of transitional space, the relational arena between parent and child in which the first symbolic expressions take place.

As is well known, Winnicott formulated the concept of transitional space as the psychological arena that emerges in early life when the child begins to play by himself, in the reassuring presence of the parent (Winnicott, 1971). Through this play, related to the "fort-da" game Freud observed in his grandson (Freud, 1922), the child negotiates his growing awareness of separation from parental figures; and in this play, the first use of symbols emerges, often in the form of toys. The symbol thus represents the experience of the paradoxical co-existence of union and differentiation — playing alone, but in the presence of the parent — as well as the co-existence of intra-psychic realities and external, objective reality. Winnicott names the product of this transitional activity *illusion*, understood not as a wishful defense against reality, but as part and parcel of how we navigate the relationship between external reality and our inner worlds. Transitional experience is seen as the source of creativity, and of cultural and religious expression throughout life. Many analysts who have contributed to the literature that has made room in psychoanalysis for a position evaluation of religion have been greatly indebted to Winnicott's work.

For many, Winnicott's work took the sting out of Freud's critique of religion as illusion. From this perspective, our representations of God emerge in transitional space, and thus are neither fully internal nor fully external, but rather are expressions of the interaction of the imagination with the reality that confronts us, emerging at least in part out of our capacity to grasp and make sense of the traditions which have been handed down to us. We come to know of God through the language of our religious traditions, which have been given to us; yet each generation renews that language with interpretations it creates.

In addition, the development of self psychology in the United States provided a basis for a response to Freud's view of religion as narcissistic. Freud cast narcissism as an infantile state in which libido is cathected to the self, a stage eventually to be replaced by the development of object love, our love for others. For Kohut, the originator of self psychology, narcissism became reconceived as an ongoing dimension of development that co-exists with the development of object love (Kohut 1977). Kohut saw the needs that arise within the context of early, narcissistic relationships as needs that are never outgrown but continue throughout the course of life, and therefore continue to be met through a range of stage-appropriate objects. The objects (or self-objects) that respond to narcissistic needs may be cultural and religious objects as well as those people of emotional significance to us. In this view, to say that religion meets narcissistic needs is no longer a condemnation, but instead becomes a description that points to the depth of the appeal of religion.

Thus Winnicott and Kohut replaced Freud's emphasis on religion's infantile origins with a developmental framework in which religious experience serves psychological functions throughout the course of a lifetime. Culture and religion no longer are seen to arise out of a primal conflict between child and parent, the repression of which gives rise to symbols that conceal their true origin and meanings by pointing to comforting illusions. The capacity for religious experience — like the capacity for language and culture — is understood to evolve organically, step by step, along with all the other developments of the life span.

Let me pause here to make a few remarks. The writers I have mentioned thus far, and many of the others who have built on their work, have continued to use Freud's undifferentiated term, "religion," with the written or unwritten implication that they are referring both to Judaism and Christianity.[1] Their concern with religion has centered around religious belief, faith, and experience. And the majority of them are or were Christian. Thus the question arises: why have such a preponderance of those who initially took on the challenge of responding to Freud on the question of religion been Christian rather than Jewish, when we know that psychoanalysis has always been disproportionately practiced by Jews; and why have their questions centered around issues of belief, and faith, rather than, say, religious practice or identity?

I believe that this is no coincidence. We know that in general, Christianity stresses belief over practice, while Judaism has traditionally stressed observance of religious practice over belief. (e.g. Dorff, 2000, p. 127). A psychoanalytic explanation of why this should be has been deftly outlined by Robert Paul (1996). Through his close reading of The Book of Exodus alongside Freud's *Moses and Monotheism,* Paul demonstrates that as Freud indicated, the Exodus and the primal murder of the Egyptian pharaoh left in its wake a good amount of unresolved guilt for the Jews. The laws handed down at Mount Sinai organized Jewish society around a network of commandments or *mitzvoth* the observance of which bound up that guilt and made it tolerable. With the advent of Christianity, the sacrifice of Jesus paid back the debt incurred by that foundational murder, and thus observance of the *mitzvoth* was no longer psychologically

---

[1]   The problem with this is illustrated by the quip, "Funny, you don't look Judaeo-Christian to me!"

necessary for those who could *believe* or *have faith* in the redeeming death of Jesus. Thus for Christians, *belief* or *faith* itself became the critical focus of religious life; while *observance, interpretation and identity* remained the critical focus for Jews.

True to this pattern, we see Christian analysts taking up Freud's challenge to religion in terms of the question of belief or faith. Indeed, there is a way in which developments within British object relations and self psychology constitute a kind of "new testament" to the "old testament" of Freud: doing away with the centrality of the primal crime, the Oedipus complex and the law of the father, and bringing the good news that psychoanalysis can indeed — against Freud's intentions — be reconciled with religion.

Furthermore: two of the prominent American psychoanalysts who made significant contributions to forms of psychoanalytic theory more hospitable to religion — Erik Erikson and Heinz Kohut — were both born into and brought up in Jewish families, yet both of them hid their Jewish identity (Strozier, 1997, Gardner, 1999). Thus not only were the majority of the mid-century responses to Freud's critiques made by Christian analysts who responded in terms suited to Christian religiosity, but even some who started out as Jews moved into a Christian framework in their personal lives as well as in their theorizing about religion.

This suggests a second, sociological answer to the question of the preponderance of specifically Christian perspectives on psychoanalysis and religion in this group of mid-century writers. Most analysts who fled Europe in the 1930's to come to Britain or America were Jews, escaping from a Nazi-dominated Europe in which they had feared for their lives on account of their race and religion. Like Freud, they had largely left behind the world of strict Jewish observance. In addition, the enormity of the Holocaust caused a crisis of faith in many of the Jewish circles that survived. Thus, in the postwar years, there was no motivation for a Jewish groundswell of concern over Freud's disdain of religion. Christian analysts have simply not been sufficiently hard-pressed, as part of their understanding of religion, to take the full measure of these issues and in particular, have not taken the full measure of the tragic complexities of the impact of Nazism in their consideration of psychoanalysis' relationship with religion.

The Jewish psychoanalysts who emigrated to Britain and the United States were, I would suggest, more concerned with assimilation into their new, host countries, than in querying Freud's theories of religion. In America, they sought the universal society that Freud had hoped Europe might become; and they strived to adapt to their new homeland, which advertised itself as a haven for all, but whose underlying narratives are, as we know, more than predominantly Christian. Psychoanalysis, presenting itself in the U.S. as a medical science with no overt links to Judaism, was a passport to assimilation into one of the higher and more prestigious ranks of American society.[2] Freud's critique of religion, tied as it was both to the attenuated relationship he had to the world of orthodox observance and to his desire for a universal theory without religious and racial distinctions, served the majority of these émigré psychoanalysts well. Jewish analysts of this generation such as Erich Fromm and Hans Loewald who did develop more affirmative theories of religion, still wrote mainly about "religion" rather than Judaism *per se*.[3] Erikson's work on identity, along with Kohut's work on the self, together with their outlooks on religion, helped remold American psychoanalysis in the image of the American individual, who was conceived in those days to be white, male, and Protestant.

Psychoanalytic responses to Freud's critique II: Critiques of the 'religion as faith' approach

How successful has been the accommodation between psychoanalysis and faith, conceptualized largely in Christian terms, remains open

---

[2] For two different but informative frameworks, see Brodkin, 1998 and Zaretsky, 2004.

[3] Although, as a recent article by Lewis Aron demonstrates, Fromm's analysis of the story of Adam and Eve falls within a quasi rabbinic tradition of interpretation and exhibits certain "characteristically Jewish elements" (Aron, 2005, p. 688).

to question. Elsewhere (Brickman, 2002; 2003, pp. 156-162), I have characterized these attempts as a form of "psychoanalytic functionalism," playing off the mid-century "functionalism" of American anthropology, which had replaced the previous generation's evolutionary outlook with the study of societies in terms of how their constitutive elements facilitated the functioning of the community. Functional anthropology looked at each society as a whole, and asked how its behavior and beliefs helped the whole society function harmoniously.

In a similar manner, a psychoanalytic functionalism does not seek after the evolutionary origins of religion, as Freud did in *Totem and Taboo;* rather, it asks what elements of religion contribute to the self's functioning or well-being. These writers have shifted the focus of their attention from the origins of religion in the primal crime and/or in infantile helplessness, to its function in sustaining the stability and vitality of the self (e.g. Jones, 1991, p. 86; Rizzuto, 1979, pp. 7, 52-3, 89, 180, 202, etc.; McDargh, p. 4; Meissner, pp. 131-32). They ask, in Kohut's words, what it is in religion that "shores up, holds together, makes harmonious, and strengthens the self"? (quoted in Strozier 1997, p. 167).

That religions help sustain the internal coherence of the self is a point Freud readily conceded; but he conceded it as a point which was beside the point. In *Group Psychology and the Analysis of the Ego* (Freud, 1921, p. 142) he stated that

> Even those who do not regret the disappearance of religious illusions from the civilized world of today will admit that so long as they were in force they offered those who were bound by them the most powerful protection against the danger of neurosis. Nor is it hard to discern that all the ties that bind people to mystico-religious or philosophico-religious sects and communities are expressions of crooked cures of all kinds of neuroses.

For Freud, to believe in a positive "god representation," however sustaining this might be, was a "crooked cure" that obscures rather than leads to self-understanding. The fact that religions perform psychological functions that stabilize the individual may itself be seen as part of the problem: their very capacity to fulfill psychological needs for meaning and

37

order makes their followers particularly vulnerable to various authoritarian social and political programs that profit from religious discourse. The emphasis on religion as providing support for the self neglects concern with the believer's attitude towards others. Furthermore, the benevolent tone of the functionalist psychoanalytic approach to religion, like the "high anthropology" of Protestantism which gave birth to the pastoral counseling movement, is at variance with the negating, emptying, and disruptive qualities that can be found in alternative accounts of the sacred. Religion may in some cases satisfy needs; in other cases, however, it may purposefully frustrate them, bringing unrest, disquiet, and even anguish in the search for religious truth (Taylor, 1999; Taussig, 1998; Merton, 1972, pp. pp. 105 & 235). With the functionalist approach to religion, religion itself comes to be seen as a neutral or benign resource from which the self derives sustenance, without regard for the ways in which particular religious beliefs may dispose the self to act towards the other, or may aim at disrupting the self altogether.[4]

In the past few years, psychologist Rachel Blass has come forward with a strong critique of this recent "conciliatory" psychoanalytic stance towards religion, in particular of the use of Winnicott's notion of illusion as a basis for a psychoanalytic re-evaluation of religion (Blass 2004). This usage, she argues, side-steps what she takes to be the crucial issue at stake for Freud (and, by implication, for us): the objective reality of God. If psychoanalysis accepts the value of religion because it now accepts the value of illusion, this denigrates the faith of the believer, who does *not* think s/he is engaging in illusion, says Blass; and it dilutes Freud's theory to an extent that Freud himself would never countenance. Blass sees the developments in psychoanalytic theory as well as in theology that have taken place over the last century as dilutions in both fields of their original, passionate searches for truth.

As I have indicated above, Blass is right to assert that Freud would not be moved by what I have termed the functionalist, and what she

---

[4]   Volkan (1997) and Jones (2002) give psychoanalytic accounts of the negative ramifications of religious identity or belief that move beyond some of these limitations.

has termed the conciliatory, approach to religion. But much as I find limitations in the functionalist approach to religion, I believe her critique gives excessively short shrift to recent developments both in theology and in psychoanalysis, and to the work of Winnicott (before she moves on to a more promising discussion of *Moses and Monotheism*). Blass's emphasis on the need for psychoanalysis to reckon with the fact that for believers, religion is concerned with a God who "is independent of human existence, a God who created and loves humankind" (p. 625) ignores theological developments old and new. Many sophisticated Jewish and Christian theologies eschew notions of an "objective God" out there. Contemporary theologies along these lines developed both in response to the "death of God" that had been brewing in western philosophy for centuries and which was heralded by Nietzsche's pronouncement at the beginning of the twentieth century; and in response to the challenge to theodicy wrought by the Holocaust in the first part of the twentieth century. Many of these theological accounts locate the sacred precisely *within* rather than independent of the realm of human relations[5] Insistence on an objective God "out there" as the only valid object of religiosity also ignores a long history of Jewish and Christian negative theology that has insisted on avoiding any positive enunciation of the characteristics of God in the search for religious truth (the famous "via negativa," of which Maimonides, among others, was a proponent [Fiorenza, 1998]). Against these theological nuances, Blass thinks we should turn to "the large body of traditional believers" (p. 625) for the understanding of religion against which psychoanalysis should measure its critique. While this is indeed the group against which Freud argued in his tracts against religion, to ask us

---

[5] See Taylor (1984) for an elegant explanation of the "death of God" in western philosophy and theology, as well as for the implications of postmodern and poststructuralist philosophies for contemporary theology; and Santner (1990), for a wonderfully lucid examination of postmodernism as an attempt on the part of continental philosophy to come to terms with the Holocaust. The work of the Jewish religious philosopher Emmanuel Levinas, who locates the sacred in "the face of the Other," i.e. within human relationship, continues to be very influential in theological and academic circles.

39

now to limit our understanding of religion to this group alone is akin to asking cultural historians to limit their understanding of psychoanalysis to the "large body of those who have been psychoanalyzed." It is hardly in the interests of deepening our understanding of these two great discursive traditions to ask us to ignore their more learned representatives, and to consider these representatives as somehow pursuing a less "passionate search for truth" (p. 615) than "traditional believers."

Secondly, while Winnicott's deceptively simple prose can be (and has been) hijacked for simplistic understandings of religion, a more generous reading shows him to be doing precisely the kind of work Blass approvingly finds in *Moses and Monotheism*. It is, perhaps, unfortunate that Winnicott chose the word "illusion" to describe transitional phenomena. However, his concept of transitional space is an attempt to describe the way the psyche adjudicates the paradox of union and separation/absence that vexes our relationship with God no less than our relationships with our parents. This paradox is mediated by representations that function as symbols (such as "God") that express both presence and absence (reminiscent of Ricoeur's claim that religious symbols point both to our beginnings and the horizon of our hopes). Most writers who discuss religion in connection with transitional space are careful to emphasize that they are discussing *representations* of God, and thus stick well within the range of the psychic reality that is the province of psychoanalysis (Blass, p. 621). Indeed, Blass's approving citation of Freud's statements in *Moses and Monotheism* which "cannot directly represent the facts, but are not fiction either" (p. 630) corresponds quite closely to Winnicott's description of transitional phenomena about which it cannot be decided: "did you create this object [i.e. is it fiction] or did you find it" [i.e. is it an objective fact]" (Winnicott, p. 96).

Blass finds more favorable grounds for commonality between psychoanalysis and religion in *Moses and Monotheism*. This work permits her to argue that both psychoanalysis and religion pursue the truth but necessarily suffer failure in this pursuit; and that this failure is the common ground on which a productive dialogue can be held. As we will see below, she is not alone in finding this final work of Freud's, so full of unbridled speculation, to be a rich vein to mine for alternative readings of Freud on religion.

Psychoanalytic responses to Freud's critique III: Religion, Psychoanalysis, Feminism

Straddling the ground between Christian and Jewish encounters with Freud on religion is Judith van Herik's *Freud on Femininity and Faith*, which demonstrates the different evaluations Freud eventually accorded to Christianity and to Judaism, respectively (Van Herik, 1982). Seeking neither critique nor mutual accommodation, Van Herik simply demonstrates that Freud identifies instinctual renunciation with the masculine ideals of individual and civilizational progress, while identifying (wish) fulfillment with the feminine (and primitive) limitations of regression and dependency. For Freud, Christianity represents the religion that encourages the wish for the father's guardianship, and thus is regressive and feminine; while Judaism is religion as renunciation which leads to ethical progress, and thus makes a valuable progressive, masculine contribution. (These differences are highlighted in *Moses and Monotheism*.) As Daniel Boyarin (1995, p. 249) has perceptively observed, in this way Freud subverted the centuries-old Christian evaluation of Christianity as the religion of the spirit and Judaism as the religion of the superseded law: Freud contends that it is Judaism which truly represents the apex of morality and thus of spirituality.

This points us in the direction of feminist psychoanalysis and religion, a rich field that owes much to the explorations of recent French feminists but unfortunately lies beyond the scope of this essay. Suffice it to say that these conversations have brought the preoccupations of feminism and psychoanalysis — preoccupations with sexual difference, with Freud's repression/omission/fear of the maternal, preoccupations with the pre-oedipal, the pre-symbolic, and the pre-linguistic registers — to bear upon religious concerns. Luce Irigaray and Julia Kristeva have been influential in this area with work that has pursued the logic that strings together

41

the associations of male/superego/phallus/symbolic order, to emerge on the other side with explorations of forms of female mysticism which exceed and cannot be captured by the Word or the law of the father. These explorations, in turn, generally fall outside of the usual boundaries of Judaism or Christianity, offering outlooks based on a female subjectivity no longer hemmed in by patriarchal tradition. Readers interested in this direction can look not only to the translated works of the above-mentioned authors, but also, among others, to *Speaking the Unspeakable* by Diane Jonte-Pace (2001), which examines counter-narratives in Freud concerning mothers, death, and religion; and *Sensible Ecstasies* by Amy Hollywood (2002), which puts medieval and more recent Christian mysticism into dialogue with contemporary feminist psychoanalytic theory.

Psychoanalytic responses to Freud's critique
IV: Religion as identity, interpretation,
and concern for the other

It took another generation or two after the emigration of psychoanalysts from continental Europe for a significant number of psychoanalysts and scholars to take up the question of Judaism and psychoanalysis on a larger scale. If Freud lived in a time when to be Jewish meant to live under threat and in peril, today, especially in North America, to be Jewish means to have acceded to the highest levels of cultural and material success. Along with this success has come a new interest in Judaism among a new generation of psychoanalysts and scholars no longer constrained by fears associated with exploring the relationship between Judaism and psychoanalysis.

To refer once again to the ambiguity of the term "religion:" the questions raised by many of this new generation of (mainly) Jewish writers about psychoanalysis and religion have been of a very different nature than the questions raised by the Christian analysts mentioned above. These Jewish analysts and scholars are simply not puzzled in the same way that the Christian writers are about "*Why did Freud Reject God?*" to quote the title of a recent book by the Catholic psychoanalyst Ana Maria Rizzuto. If, like Blass, they take up the answers thus far attempted, they question the premises on which these answers have been construed. However, many of them are much more beset with the question of whether, how, and to what degree, Freud's psychoanalysis was influenced by the Judaism he both belonged to but was estranged from. They want to question the received wisdom of Ernest Jones and Peter Gay that Judaism played no role in Freud's creation of psychoanalysis. Rather than accepting an ineluctable antimony between psychoanalysis and religion, they have pursued the continuities between Judaism and psychoanalysis, demonstrating the extent of Freud's involvement with Judaism in his education as a youth, highlighting his participation in societies like the *B'nai Brit* in his adult life, and debating the role of Judaism in the formulation of his ideas (e.g. Klein 1985; Rice 1990; Homans, 1989; Yerushalmi 1991; Bernstein 1998). Rather than posing questions of *faith,* they pose questions of religious *identity* and *practice*: the Jewish identity and practices not only of Freud, but of psychoanalysis itself. Some, like the historian Yosef Yerushalmi (1991), Harriet Lutzky (1989) and Robert Paul (1996), have demonstrated how Jewish myths and themes underlie central psychoanalytic concepts and thus how both Freud and psychoanalysis have been nourished by Jewish tradition. Yet others analyze a spiritual dimension they see already covertly inscribed within Freud's own writings (Santner, 2001; DiCenso, 2001), or they discover resonances between recent developments in relational psychoanalysis and the more mystical dimensions of Jewish thought (Aron, 2005; Starr, 2008).

Focusing on racial, ethnic and gender identity, scholars such as Sander Gilman, Daniel Boyarin, and Jay Geller have examined antisemitic theories of the Jewish body and Jewish sexuality that were in wide circulation in Freud's time, and have analyzed several of Freud's central theories as strategies for counter-acting that discourse (Gilman 1993a; Boyarin 1997; Geller 2007). They have re-introduced the question of the body and its representations in medical and other texts of Freud's time as a topos of religious/racial differentiation, and they have re-conceived Freud's theories of gender and sexuality as creative negotiations of anti-Semitic slurs that had cast male Jews as feminized, gay, and even castrated. According to their theories, the prevailing dichotomy between a superior, masculine, and Christian Aryan, on the one hand, and an

43

transmission of what it means to be Jewish: religion represents authority handed down from the past, but a past that need no longer be overcome: "the past not only subjugates; it also nourishes" (Yerushalmi, 1991, p. 78). Also working closely off of *Moses and Monotheism*, James DiCenso in *The Other Freud* sees Freud's understanding of religious symbols as creatively transforming fixed, self-enclosed psychic structures into more open psychological systems (for instance, a narcissistic system becomes ethically more advanced by becoming more open to others). DiCenso sees in Freud's *Moses* a latent argument for religion as having a dynamic and transformative function with ethically edifying effects.

Thus far, I've drawn a distinction between a largely Christian response to Freud on religion in terms of belief and faith, and a largely Jewish response to Freud on religion in terms of identity and practice. However, in recent years a new wave of Jewish theorists has begun to display an interest in questions of psychoanalysis and Jewish religious faith. Aided by a new generation of Jewish theologians and scholars who have made many Jewish rabbinic and kabbalistic texts available in English for the first time in history, these writers engage with Jewish law, philosophy and Jewish mysticism (e.g. Eigen, 1981, 1998; Spero, 1992; Oppenheim, 2006; Aron, 2004; Starr, 2008). The first salvo from this group came from Michael Eigen, whose 1981 paper examined "the area of faith" in Winnicott, Bion, and Lacan. Eigen, who refers to himself and others who share his interests as "psychoanalytic mystics," practices a religious eclecticism that puts him somewhat outside of the orbit of Jewish religious thought (Eigen, 1998). Nonetheless, he demonstrates his Jewish approach to religion and psychoanalysis by providing a specifically Jewish definition of faith as the experiencing of life "with all one's heart, with all one's soul, and with all one's might" (1998, p. 3). Moshe Halevi Spero (1992) provides a more ambitious model for the mutual accommodation of psychoanalysis and Orthodox Judaism. Just as internalized representations of parents are derived (albeit in distorted fashion) from objectively real parents, Spero suggests that internalized representations of God need not be traced back solely to parental imagos but might very well be derived from an objectively real God. Spero works out a metapsychology based on Halakhah (Jewish law) which he sees as parallel to a psychoanalytic object relations metapsychology, and argues for distinct but overlapping "anthrocentric and deocentric dimensions of psychic experience" (p. 128). Here religious belief is not reduced to psychological developments but interacts and speaks through such developments (although to my mind the theological limitations of casting God as an "object," mentioned on p. 39 above and on p. 47 above, remain).

Other analysts have come to see parallels between Jewish religious and mystical thought and the relational school of psychoanalysis. The relational aspects of the divine, God and Shekhinah, and the mutual responsibility between God and humankind for the redemption of the world that are found in Kabbalistic thought, fit well with this school that stresses the relational and mutual aspects of the psychoanalytic process. These writers have also shifted the emphasis of the analytic enterprise from self-understanding to self-transformation. They see in psychoanalysis the possibility of a transformational encounter which they liken to the transformation promised by mystical experience. They recognize too that the psychoanalytic encounter itself requires a kind of faith — faith that, in the face of the uncertainty, doubt, and even anguish that may be inherent in the psychoanalytic process, the essential aim of freeing someone to develop a capacity for a fuller and richer life will eventually prevail. Faith here is a search for understanding that does not know in advance what its final end will be, as well as an attitude that sees the sacred as an attribute of life around us and between us, demanding to be encountered.

This article would not be complete without reference to the luminous work of Eric Santner in his *Psychotheology of Everyday Life* (2001) which has, to my mind, given the most intricate yet eloquent account to date of the potential interconnections between psychoanalysis and Judaism (and to a lesser extent, to Christianity as well). He has done so by going back to Freud, and juxtaposing his reading of Freud with that of Franz Rosenzweig, the Jewish theologian and philosopher who lived during Freud's time, author of *The Star of Redemption*, and translator, with Martin Buber, of the Hebrew Bible into German. Santner's work breathes life into the complexities of the postmodern sensibility, where "postmodern" implies a critique of the values of progress, wholeness, totality, and mastery that informed the aims of the modern world since the era of the Enlightenment and the Age of Discovery. These values, retrospectively seen from a postmodern position, were ineluctably intertwined with a disavowal of life-forms considered non-normative in racial, ethnic, gender, and sexual terms. Thus the project of modernity was built not only on scientific progress and philosophical enlightenment, but also on various forms of exclusion, colonization, and enslavement of racially and other non-normative forms of human life, culminating eventually in the violence of the Holocaust. Since such qualities as wholeness, totality, and mastery that are based on exclusion of the non-normative other are linked both to the development of modernity as well as to traditional conceptions of God, one can see that questioning these qualities on a philosophical level may eventually entail a theological undermining of traditional conceptions of God (Taylor, 1984; Santner, 1990).

However, as Santner points out, the death of God that has ensued is but the death of an "Elsewhere" or a "beyond" in which to locate the sacred. According to Santner, Freud and Rosenzweig both orient us toward a more immediate and vivifying engagement with the Other in "the midst of life" wherein the sacred lies. Santner shows how Freud and Rosenzweig (along with Levinas) reveal the Jewish message to lie not in traditional notions of an objective God, but, more urgently, in the "blessings of more life" (Bloom, 1987, p. 160, quoted in Santner, p. 26) that emerge when we are freed from our defenses to truly encounter the face — and the unconscious — of our neighbor. For Freud, as for Rosenzweig, our capacity for interpretation often leads to defensive mechanisms which have a life of their own: a mechanical animatedness within the unconscious itself, which Santner describes as an "undeadness" that all too often passes for life itself. Life addresses itself to us in a manner that is greater than our capacity to fully interpret it, always leaving a remainder that is bound up by our idiosyncratic fantasies which support (in distorted fashion) our interpellation into the social and symbolic order. Our participation in the social order enmeshes us, in Buber's terms, in "I — It" relations of commodification that are "undead." Santner reads psychoanalysis, as he does Rosenzweig's philosophy, as aiming to *undo* the unconscious fantasies that adapt us, or bind us, to the status quo, and thus as aiming to convert the structures of undeadness (which are our everyday forms of idolatry) into an "impassioned responsiveness" to the Other in all his or her idiosyncratic singularity. In this way both psychoanalysis and Jewish theology aim to open us up to the "the blessings of more life" right here in the midst of life.

Conclusion

To write about psychoanalysis and Judaism is to wade into the treacherous waters that Freud wished to avoid, where psychoanalysis might be seen as a specifically "Jewish national affair." Yet to ignore the relationship between the two is to ignore resources that have influenced psychoanalysis and that continue to influence many of those who take advantage of this discipline as a form of therapy, theory, or both. Unavoidably, psychoanalysis had a specific provenance. This provenance — the Jewish community of central Europe and the ambivalence towards its religious beliefs and practices that emerged among some of its members prior to and after the rupture of the Holocaust — can be examined both for its historical relevance to the formation of psychoanalysis as well as for on-going similarities between the religious and social practices of Judaism and the therapeutic and theoretical practices of psychoanalysis. This provenance makes psychoanalysis particularly conducive to analogies with Jewish religious thought; however, like any work that endures on the world-historical stage, psychoanalysis cannot be completely reduced to its Jewish influences either in its intent or in its applicability.

While Freud's works mainly argued against religion, the social and political upheavals of the twentieth century have given rise to new sociological realities out of which have emerged new theological formulations that differ in many ways from the belief systems of Freud's time. Over this time psychoanalysis, too, has undergone changes which are best seen, I would argue, as fresh re-readings of Freud rather than as split-off schools of psychoanalysis. Christians and Jews have often asked different questions about, and have therefore found different answers to, the relationship between psychoanalysis and religion. Christian writers have been frustrated by the apparent Godlessness or lack of faith in both Freud and psychoanalysis, and have sought recourse in subsequent readings of psychoanalysis to create a more conciliatory psychoanalytic approach to faith. On the other hand, the inquiry into the relationship between Judaism and psychoanalysis began with questions of the Jewish identity of both Freud and psychoanalysis, and the similarities between Jewish and psychoanalytic practices of interpretation. However, it too has expanded to include issues of spirituality and faith, finding resources not only in relational readings of psychoanalysis but also, latent within the works of Freud himself.

REFERENCES

Aron, L. (2004). God's Influence on my Psychoanalytic vision and values. *Psychoanalytic Psychology*, 21 (3): 442–451.

--------.(2005). The Tree of Knowledge: Good and Evil: Conflicting Interpretations. *Psychoanalytic Dialogues*, 15 (5): 681–707.

Bernstein, R. J. (1998). *Freud and the legacy of Moses*. Cambridge: Cambridge University Press.

Blass, R.B. (2004). Beyond illusion: Psychoanalysis and the question of religious truth. *Int. J. Psycho-Anal.*, 85: 615-634.

Bloom, H. (1987). Freud and Beyond. In: *Ruin the Sacred Truths*, H. Bloom. Cambridge: Harvard University Press. Pp. 143-204.

Boyarin, D. (1998). What Does a Jew Want. In: Christopher Lane, ed., *The Psychoanalysis of Race*. New York: Columbia University Press. Pp. 211-240.

--------. (1995). *Unheroic Conduct: The Rise of Heterosexuality and the Invention of the Jewish Man*. Berkeley: University of California Press.

49

Brickman, C. (2002). Self & Other in the self-psychological approach to religion. In: *Progress in Self Psychology, vol. 18,* ed. A. Goldberg. Hillsdale, N.J.: The Analytic Press, pp. 207-215.

--------. (2003). *Aboriginal Populations of the Mind: Race and Primitivity in Psychoanalysis.* New York: Columbia University Press.

Brodkin, K. (1998). *How Jews Became White Folks and What that Says about Race in America.* New Brunswick, NJ: Rutgers University Press.

Cushman, P. (2007). A Burning World, an Absent God. *Contemporary Psychoanalysis,* 43:1, 47-88.

Cuddihy, J.M. (1974). *The Ordeal of Civility: Freud, Marx, Lévi-Strauss and the Jewish Struggle with Modernity.* Boston: Beacon Press.

DiCenso, J. (1999). *The Other Freud: Religion, Culture and Psychoanalysis.* New York: Routledge.

Dorff, E.N. (2000). Another Jewish View of Ethics, Christian and Jewish. In: *Christianity in Jewish Terms,* ed. Frymer-Kensky, Novak, Ochs, Sandmel, Signer. Boulder. CO: Westview Press. Pp. 127-134.

Eigen, M. (1981/1999). The Area of Faith in Winnicott, Lacan, and Bion. In: *Relational Psychoanalysis: The Emergence of a Tradition,* ed. Mitchell & Aron. Hillsdale, N.J.: Analytic Press. Pp. 1-38.

--------. (1998). *The Psychoanalytic Mystic.* London: Free Association Books.

Erikson, E. (1959/1980). *Identity and the Life Cycle.* New York, W.W. Norton.

--------. (1962). *Young Man Luther.* New York : Norton.

--------. (1969). *Gandhi's Truth: On the Origins of Militant Nonviolence.* New York : Norton.

Fiorenza, F. S. & Kaufman, G.D. (1998). God. In: *Critical Terms for Religious Studies,* ed. M.C. Taylor. Chicago: University of Chicago Press, pp. 136-159.

Freud, S. (1913). *Totem and Taboo.* Standard Edition 13:1-164.

--------. (1921). *Group Psychology and the Analysis of the Ego.* S.E. 18:69-143.

--------. (1922). *Beyond the Pleasure Principle,* S.E. XVIII (1920-1922). Pp. 1-64

--------. (1933). *New Introductory Lectures on Psychoanalysis.* S.E. 22: 5-182.

--------. (1939). *Moses and Monotheism.* S.E. 23:7-137.

Fromm, E. (1950). *Psychoanalysis and Religion*. New Haven, Yale University Press.

--------. (1966). *You Shall be as Gods; A Radical Interpretation of the Old Testament and Its Tradition*. New York: Holt, Rinehart and Winston.

Gardner, H. (1999). The Enigma of Erik Erikson. (Review of Lawrence Friedman, *Identity's Architect*), *New York Review of Books*, 46:11.

Geller, J. (1997). Identifying 'Someone who is himself one of them:' recent studies of Freud's Jewish identity. *Religious Studies Review* 23:4. 323-331.

--------. (2007). *On Freud's Jewish body: Mitigating Circumcisions*. New York: Fordham University Press.

Gilman, S. (1993a). *Freud, Race and Gender*. Princeton: Princeton University Press.

--------. (1993b). *The Case of Sigmund Freud: Medicine and Identity at the Fin de Siècle*. Baltimore, Md.: The Johns Hopkins University Press.

Guntrip, H. (1957). *Psychotherapy and Religion*. New York: Harper.

Handelman, S. (1982). *Slayers of Moses: The Emergence of Rabbinic Interpretation in Modern Literary Theory*. Albany: State University of New York Press.

Hollywood, A. (2002). *Sensible Ecstasies*. Chicago: University of Chicago Press.

Homans, P. (1989). *The Ability to Mourn: Disillusionment and the Social Origins of Psychoanalysis*. Chicago: University of Chicago Press.

Irigaray, L. (1965/1985). La Mysterique. In: Irigaray, *Speculum of the Other Woman*. Trans. G. Gill. Ithaca, N.Y.: Cornell University Press, pp. 191– 202.

Jones, J. W. (1991). *Contemporary Psychoanalysis and Religion: Transference and Transcendence*. New Haven: Yale University Press.

--------. (1996). *Religion and Psychology in Transition: Psychoanalysis, Feminism, and Theology*. New Haven: Yale University Press.

--------. (2002). *Terror and transformation: the ambiguity of religion in psychoanalytic perspective*. New York: Brunner-Routledge.

Jonte-Pace (2001). *Speaking the Unspeakable*. Berkeley: University of California Press.

Klein, D. (1985). *Jewish Origins of the Psychoanalytic Movement.* Chicago: University of Chicago Press.

Kohut, H. (1977). *Restoration of the Self.* New York: International Universities Press.

--------. (1985). Forms and Transformations of Narcissism. In: *Self Psychology and the Humanities,* ed. C. Strozier. New York: W. W. Norton, pp. 97-123.

Kristeva, J. (1983/1987). *Tales of Love.* Trans. L. Roudiez. New York: Columbia University Press.

Lawrence-Lightfoot, S. (1988). *Balm in Gilead: Journey of a Healer.* New York: Penguin Books.

Lear, J. (2005). *Freud.* New York: Routledge.

Loewald, H. (1980). *Papers on psychoanalysis.* New Haven: Yale University Press.

Lutzky, H. (1989). Reparation and Tikkun: A Comparison of the Kleinian and Kabbalistic Concepts. *International Review of Psycho-Analysis,* 16:449-458.

McDargh, J. (1983). *Psychoanalytic Object Relations Theory and the Study of Religion: On Faith and the Imaging of God.* Lanham, New York: University Press of America.

McGuire, W. (1988). ed., *The Freud/Jung Letters,* trans. R. Mannheim and R.F.C. Hull, Cambridge, Mass: Harvard University Press.

Meissner, W.W. (1984). *Psychoanalysis and Religious Experience.* New Haven: Yale University Press.

Merton, T. (1972). *New Seeds of Contemplation.* New York: New Directions.

Milner, M. (1969). *The Hands of the Living God: An Account of a Psychoanalytic Treatment.* New York, International Universities Press.

Obeyesekere, G. (1990). *The Work of Culture: Symbolic Transformation in Psychoanalysis and Anthropology.* Chicago: University of Chicago Press.

Oppenheim, M. (2006). *Jewish Philosophy and Psychoanalysis: Narrating the Interhuman.* London: Lexington Books.

Parsons, W. (2005). Psychology of Religion. In: *The Encyclopedia of Religion,* second edition, ed. L. Jones. Detroit: Macmillan Reference USA.

Paul, R. (1996). *Moses and Civilization: The Meaning Behind Freud's Myth.* New Haven, Conn.: Yale University Press.

Ricoeur, P. (1970). *Freud and Philosophy: An Essay on Interpretation.* New Haven: Yale University Press.

Rice, E. (1990). *Freud and Moses: The Long Journey Home.* Albany: State University of New York Press.

Rizzuto, A. M. (1979), *The Birth of the Living God: A Psychoanalytic Study.* Chicago: University of Chicago Press.

--------. (1998). *Why Did Freud Reject God?* New Haven: Yale University Press.

Robert, M. (1976). *From Oedipus to Moses: Freud's Jewish Identity,* trans. Ralph Manheim. Garden City, NY: Anchor.

Rubenstein, R. (1968). *The Religious Imagination: A Study in Psychoanalysis and Jewish Theology.* Lanham, MD: University Press of America.

Santner, E. (2001). *The Psychotheology of Everyday Life.* Chicago: University of Chicago Press.

--------. (1990). "Postwar/Post-Holocaust/Postmodern". In: *Santner, Stranded Objects: Mourning, Memory and Film in Postwar Germany.* Ithaca, NY: Cornell University Press. Pp. 1–30.

Spero, M. H. (1992). Religious Objects and Psychological Structures: A Critical Integration of Object Relations Theory, Psychotherapy, and Judaism. Chicago: University of Chicago Press.

Starr, K. (2008). *Repair of the Soul: Metaphors of Transformation in Jewish Mysticism and Psychoanalysis.* New York: Routledge.

Strozier, C. (1997). Heinz Kohut's Struggles with Religion, Ethnicity and God. In: *Religion, Society and Psychoanalysis: Readings in Contemporary Theory,* ed. J. L. Jacobs & D. Capps. Boulder, CO: Westview Press. Pp. 165–180.

Taussig, M. (1998). Transgression. In: *Critical Terms for Religious Studies,* ed. M. C. Taylor. Chicago: University of Chicago Press, pp. 349–365.

Taylor, M.C. (1999). Denegating God. In: Taylor, *About Religion.* Chicago: University of Chicago Press. Pp. 29–47.

--------. (1984). Erring: *A Postmodern A/Theology.* Chicago: University of Chicago Press.

Van Herik, J. (1982). *Freud on Femininity and Faith.* Berkeley: University of California Press.

Volkan, V. (1997). *Bloodlines: From Ethnic Pride to Ethnic Terrorism.* Boulder, CO: Westview Press.

Winnicott, D.W. (1971). *Playing and Reality*. London: Routledge.

Yerushalmi, Y. H. (1991). *Freud's Moses: Judaism terminable and interminable*. New Haven: Yale University Press.

Zaretsky, E. (2004). *Secrets of the Soul: A Social and Cultural History of Psychoanalysis*. New York: Knopf.

2 Clinical Presentation

The Jew for Jesus
and Other Analytic Explorations
of God

*Yehoshua Arnowitz**

Introduction

In this article I will examine the ways that I and my patients work together in understanding their religious experiences. Religious experience can be understood from many different theoretical perspectives — Freudian, Kleinian, Ego Psychology, Self Psychology, and Relational to mention a few. The goal of this article is not to reformulate a psychoanalytic theory of religion, but rather to convey a psychoanalytic attitude toward religion — an attitude of mutual exploration and creation of personal meaning.

Despite the seeming conformity of organized religions, each individual experiences his or her God in a highly personal manner formed by early family experiences, relationships, inner needs, fantasies, conflicts — in short the entire fabric of one's intrapsychic world. I will begin by illustrating these points with several clinical vignettes and then conclude with a discussion of the analytic attitude vis-à-vis religion in general and my analytic attitude in particular.

* I would like to thank Professor Emanuel Berman for his help in preparing this article.

The Jew for Jesus

"I have something to ask you and you better answer me and not throw out some psychoanalytic bullshit!" Rachel stormed into my office and threw herself on the couch. She was angry with me and I didn't have the slightest idea why. Bracing myself for a fight, I told her I'd try my best to understand why she was so furious. Somewhat mollified Rachel continued," I need to know something before I say another word to you and if you don't give me a straight answer I'm walking out of here." I waited. "Are you a Jew for Jesus!?"

It was late December, the second year of her analysis. During the previous hour Rachel, a thirty year-old convert to Judaism, had spoken wistfully about her childhood memories of Christmas. As she spoke I was carried away remembering my own boyhood experiences of the holiday season, the attraction I felt to something that was so powerful and at the same time forbidden to me as a Jew. I said something like, "I can see that you have some very good feelings about Christmas. It sounds like a very warm, happy time for you and your family." At the time she seemed to take my comment in stride and I remember congratulating myself that we were finally making room for her non-Jewish past — a subject that she had painstakingly avoided during her first year of analysis. Now, in retrospect, I felt that I had walked into an emotional minefield.

Rachel's European father was an uncircumcised, assimilated Jew who had survived the war by passing as non-Jew. Shortly after the war he met and seduced a young Christian woman, 25 years his junior and reluctantly agreed to marry her when she became pregnant. Rachel, the daughter from this pregnancy, grew up with a sense of herself as the glue that held her parent's marriage together.

Rachel's mother was fearful and anxious, unable to cope with the rigors of married life and motherhood. She had no friends; her husband was her entire life. She was a strict disciplinarian — any disagreement on Rachel's part was met with days of angry silence from her mother. Rachel hated her mother. She experienced her as a competitive older sister and felt triumphant when she and her father would have special time together.

Father was God for Rachel and for her mother as well. Nevertheless, much to her chagrin, her father slept with her mother at night locking Rachel out of the bedroom.

When Rachel was five years old her father began working in another city, returning home only on weekends. Her mother was heartbroken and began to drink to quell her growing anxiety. Rachel became her mother's nursemaid. She would hide the alcohol from her mother, take her to bed when she passed out, and clean up after a long night's drunk. Frantically she would call her father and beg him to come home only to be told that she was a big girl who could take care of herself. Rachel was miserable. She lived for the weekends when her father came home to rescue her but these rescues were more fantasies than reality. In reality her father spent most the weekend watching television or sleeping. As she approached adolescence, Rachel discovered that she could drag her father away from the television by sharing with him intimate details of her adolescent sexual experiences. Eventually her father left mother's bedroom and took to sleeping in the Rachel's bed. Rachel felt triumphant but this triumph was accompanied by a heavy burden of unconscious guilt.

Rachel's only warm childhood memories of her mother were the times that they spent together in church. While mother prayed, Rachel would gaze with delight at the beautiful stained glass windows and the lovely statue of Mother Mary holding baby Jesus.

As opposed to her religious mother, Rachel's father had no connection to Judaism, or to any other religion for that matter. Rachel grew up identified with the spirituality of her mother but she also retained a sense that something else existed, an 'other' that she labeled 'Jew'.

During her late adolescence Rachel met and married an observant Jewish man many years her senior. Without fully considering the consequences she readily agreed to leave her family, her studies, her religion — anything to feel loved by this older Jewish man. She attempted to bury her past and embraced whole heartedly her newfound husband and religion.

Rachel tried to be a good Jew. She had child after child to please both her husband and her God. But underneath this obedience she was terrified and angry — terrified that her husband would leave her, terrified that her newfound God would punish her, angry that her God and her husband 'demanded' such sacrifices. Rachel began to experience intense rage toward her husband and her children. She felt overwhelmed as a mother, overwhelmed as a wife. She eventually became deeply depressed and it was this depression that finally brought her to analysis.

Freud's God

God and religion have been subjects of psychoanalytic inquiry since the beginning of psychoanalysis. Freud's publications on religion span his entire career as a psychoanalyst beginning with *Obsessive Actions and Religious Actions* (Freud, 1907) and *Civilized Sexual Morality* (Freud, 1908) and ending with *Moses and Monotheism* (Freud, 1939) published the year of his death. Over the course of his psychoanalytic career Freud offered several different, yet complimentary ideas about religion.

Freud originally hypothesized that religious rites, like neurotic symptoms are the result of internal compromises between instinctive drives that strive for expression and intrapsychic agencies which, sensing the dangerous consequences of this expression, channel it into a form that is no longer harmful to society.

In *Totem and Taboo* (Freud, 1913), *The Future of an Illusion* (Freud, 1927) and later in *Moses and Monotheism* (Freud, 1939) Freud postulated that God was an outwardly projected object created from man's need for an omnipotent father as well as his guilty murderous wishes toward that father. Thus for Freud, father and God were synonymous and religion, like neurosis, represented mankind's attempts to deal with their conflicting feelings toward their father-God.

As Freud predicted, Rachel modeled her God after her beloved (and unconsciously hated) father. However, her God was not only an oedipal father but rather a rich combination of both mother and father, the Christian and the Jew, each part split off from the other. Consciously Rachel rejected her mother's Christianity and embraced her father's Judaism while unconsciously she identified with her mother's spirituality.

60

Unconsciously Rachel created an idealized version of her father and transformed him into Jesus — a father who did not abandon little girls but rather sacrificed himself for them. Her wishes for her mother's love found their expression in the image of a loving mother Mary who held the baby Jesus. She consciously rejected her mother's God while at the same time she recreated the harsher, punitive aspects of her mother in her Jewish God. This God also contained Rachel's own split-off, projected anger toward her father. Rachel needed to keep her Gods apart in the same way that, as a child, she wished to keep her parents apart. So when her Jewish therapist expressed warm feelings toward Christmas, Rachel was devastated. She attempted to integrate her past and present, the Jew and the Christian, father and mother, in the only way available to her at the time. I had become a Jew who joined forces with her Christian mother. I had joined the enemy — I was a Jew for Jesus!

God in the Transitional Space

Early psychoanalysts, basing themselves on Freud, viewed religion as the societal equivalent of neurosis. The first major opposing viewpoint was that of Winnicott who conceptualized religion as the healthy outgrowth of transitional phenomenon (Winnicott, 1953, 1971). Winnicott's transitional space is a potential space within which the infant can negotiate the difficult task of reconciling subjective experience with objective reality. Within this space there is no need to distinguish between what is internally created and what has been created by the external world; illusion and play reign supreme. Winnicott viewed transitional experiences as the healthy wellspring from which all creativity and culture flow. Religious experiences, in Winnicott's view, are the adult heir to these early transitional experiences.

The Breasts of God

Sam couldn't pray. He knew the words by heart and he set aside special times each day to pray. But he just couldn't bring himself to actually pray.

He described his experience to me: "When I pray I don't just say the words. When I have a good prayer I feel God so close that it's overwhelming. But while I'm praying I become terrified that He will leave me. And then I can't stand myself, I can't stand God. I feel such pain, it's not emotional; it's physical. I'd rather not pray at all than face that pain." As he talked, Sam looked ready to cry — not tears of sadness but tears of frustration, tears of rage. He was angry with God for not allowing him to pray and angry with me for not helping him.

Sam was very passionate about praying. In fact I often wished that he could be a little less passionate about life in general. Unmarried, in his early thirties, Sam would become enamored with a woman and carry on an intense, stormy relationship with her — but only in his fantasies. He would pine for his loved one and experience waves of ecstasy if she happened to say hello to him — but often she barely noticed him. In fact Sam was expert at picking younger, unavailable women who often barely noticed him. Women his own age didn't interest Sam. "I want to be the first, the only love. I won't settle for seconds!"

By this point in our therapy Sam and I had a pretty good picture of his father. Sam's father, like Sam himself, was plagued by intense anxieties and hypochondriac symptoms. He felt mistreated by life and took his resentment out on Sam and on Sam's mother who eventually divorced him. Sam hated everything connected with his father and consciously tried to be as different from his father as possible. Unconsciously Sam was very identified with his father and his distress was palpable when people told him that he looked like his father and even had the same facial expressions as his father.

Based on Sam's life history I expected Sam's God to resemble the harsh paternal God described by Freud. To be sure there were aspects of Sam's God that spoke for his need for a protective, all-knowing father as well as his fears of an over-critical, punishing father. However both Sam's longings toward God and his longings toward women seemed to me to be more connected to wishes for early merging with a mother. Sam's mother, as he presented her in therapy, was an overwhelmed, as-if woman who was preoccupied with order and outward appearances.

She played life by the book and feared making mistakes. Sam had few childhood memories of his mother other than her cleaning, cooking, and fighting with his father.

After this particular hour I found myself musing about the Winnicott's patient (Winnicott, 1960) (p. 592) who commented that a good session was like a good feed. Sessions with Sam seemed just the opposite. At the end of a particularly good session Sam felt deprived and enraged that we had to stop. It was as if I was removing the breast before Sam was finished. This image of an interrupted blissful feed also fit well with Sam's experiences in prayer. Despite the rather sparse picture that I had of his mother, I wondered to myself about another, internal mother who Sam experienced as possessing boundless riches, a mother who frustrated Sam by withholding herself from him. According to Winnicott some infants and mothers fail to create a transitional space either because the mother insists upon offering herself to the infant rather than allow co-creation of the transitional object or because she withdraws abruptly in a manner that is traumatic to the infant. Sam, like the child described by Winnicott (Winnicott, 1971) (pp. 6-7), seemed unable to experience a transitional space within and after the hour — he could only feel soothed by my physical presence.

I shared this metaphor of an interrupted feeding with Sam. He liked it and felt that I had captured the feeling state of his distress. My metaphor became an organizing node for both of us, a way for Sam to put a name to his previously unnamed anxieties and a way for me to be more tolerant of the stresses that I experienced as Sam's therapist. As we continued our explorations together Sam's anxieties became more manageable and gradually he was more able to leave the sessions without intense frustration and rage.

Despite these shifts within Sam and within our relationship, I had a sense of uneasiness. Sam had come to take my metaphor quite literally — as a description of actual early experiences — while I tended to minimize the actual experience of his mother snatching her breast away and to emphasize the feelings of a greedy infant, full of rage, who wanted more of his mother. Nevertheless this metaphor organized Sam and gave meaning to a number of disparate feeling states that had formerly puzzled us. For Sam this was enough.

Over the next several years Sam's religious practices became more regular and he finally met a woman his own age that he liked and genuinely liked him. Around this time his mother came to visit and Sam decided to ask her about his early development. Here is her story: "Actually it's hard for me to remember much about you as a baby. I was terrified all the time; I felt that everything I did was wrong. I had no idea how to be a mother and by the time your brother was born (that was an accident, the last thing I wanted was to be pregnant again) anyway by the time your brother was born I wanted to crawl into a hole and die. I asked my pediatrician "How can I ever feed two babies?" I wasn't breast-feeding, I tried for a while but nothing came of it. Now I can see I was too anxious but then I saw it as another sign of my failure as a mother. Anyway, the doctor told me that I needed to get you on a schedule — that you were too old to eat whenever you wanted. So I started to feed you exactly like the doctor said — regular feedings for regular amounts of time, timed by the clock. I remember you crying when I put you back to bed but the doctor warned me not to spoil you and I listened. Now I'm not sure that I did the right thing. Anyway, it was so long ago. You don't think it had any effect on you ... do you?"

The Development of God

Meissner, a Jesuit and a psychoanalyst, has written extensively on religion from a developmental perspective (Meissner, 1984). Whereas Freud focused solely on the oedipal phase of development, Meissner emphasizes the contribution of each developmental stage to the individual's ongoing experience of God. To give some examples: The young infant's experience of being mirrored contributes to a sense of God as embracing and cherishing. Early idealization of parents is later re-experienced as longings to obtain well being and omnipotence through merging with God. The oedipal child, conflicted by love and fear of his parents, replicates this conflict in his relationship to God. Once the child reaches latency he begins to experience God anthropomorphically; as a man who lives in heaven and has supernormal powers. The adolescent, with his increased ability for symbolic thinking, is able to conceive of God on a more abstract, spiritual level. The adolescent's search for identity causes him to reevaluate religious values and this reevaluation may lead to either belief or disbelief in God. According to Meissner modification of religious experiences continues throughout the life cycle. As death approaches, questions of God's existence return. The dying person may return to the God that he rejected in his youth or may throw out his God for the last time

Thank God I'm an Atheist

When I wondered about Sharon's God she was indignant. "I knew it! I knew eventually you would get to this. You just want to manipulate me, use your psychology to make me a Hozaret BeTushuvah (someone who returns to religious observance). Well, it's not to going to work, you can't trick me!"

Ten years before we met, Sharon had left both her husband and her religion. An intellectually gifted woman, Sharon was born to observant Jewish parents who placed a high value on social conformity. Sharon's brilliance was a mixed blessing to her parents. Her mother, in particular, took great pride in Sharon's intellectual achievements while at the same time she made Sharon feel that her intelligence was a handicap. Mother was constantly instructing Sharon on how to behave, how to think, how to feel. She shouldn't let people know she was so smart; no one would like her. She should be more sociable; no one liked a stick-in-the mud. She shouldn't ask too many questions; no one liked a smart aleck.

Sharon grew up feeling very proud of her mind but along with this pride came the feeling that she was 'all wrong'. She wanted to please her mother but pleasing her mother meant that Sharon had to renounce her own essence. She might have gotten a different view of herself from her father but, unfortunately, Sharon experienced her father as weak and ineffectual. Everything she did was equally wonderful to her father, which left Sharon feeling that his opinion of her was not worth very much at all.

Sharon was a lonely, isolated child. She longed for intimacy while at the same time she was terrified at losing herself in another person. She compensated for her isolation by developing a rich fantasy life. In fantasy Sharon could have relationships which she controlled; relationships where people fit into her and did not demand that she be other than who she really was.

Sharon married at an early age and settled down to bear children. Her husband was a weak, ineffectual man like her father, who kept a safe distance from her emotionally and sexually. Sharon had great difficulties being a mother — she was often angry at her children and frightened by her anger. She felt lost and disconnected from everyone including herself. After almost twenty years of marriage Sharon entered therapy. With the help of her therapist Sharon decided to leave her husband even though this entailed leaving her children as well.

Although Sharon originally consulted me because of migraine headaches, her main unstated difficulty was her extreme social isolation. Sharon lived in a world of fantasized romantic relationships. She would repeatedly attach herself to a highly intellectual, emotionally distant man who was unavailable for a real relationship and then lose herself in fantasies about him. In reality Sharon felt suffocated by other people. Fantasized relationships offered her a sense of closeness without the messy encumbrance of having to actually relate to another person.

By the time we started our work together Sharon had completely rejected her religious past. She ate non-kosher food, worked on Saturday, and ate on Yom Kippur. Knowing this I was surprised when Sharon told me that she didn't like visitors on Saturday. "It's a pain. I have to make sure everything is in order before I open the door. Maybe it's one of my religious neighbors. I don't want them to catch me watching TV." When I wondered about her need to hide her nonobservance, Sharon felt threatened and responded with the angry outburst that I've described above.

66

My curiosity about Sharon's reaction to her neighbors led us to explore her internal God. Sharon's God was an overpowering maternal presence who insisted that Sharon deny her own wants and needs and follow Her religious rules. Sharon needed to maintain a safe emotional distance from her God and thus preserve her independent sense of self. In fact, while consciously a nonbeliever, Sharon unconsciously needed to repeatedly reject her God in order to continually reaffirm her independent existence. Although Sharon consciously denied the existence of God, I wondered about her unconscious longings for a God who could put aside Her rules and accept Sharon as she truly was.

In the midst of our work together Sharon made a dream. In her dream it was Friday afternoon. She was traveling by bus to visit religious relatives and was anxious to get there before the start of the Shabbat. She rang the bell but the driver (who looked a lot like me) would not stop. Eventually Sharon got off the bus and began to walk back to the neighborhood where her relatives lived. As she walked her anxiety disappeared. With a smile, Sharon related how much she enjoyed revisiting the beautiful religious neighborhood where she had lived as a child. I could sense a shift as Sharon spoke. I wondered out loud whether our travels together had allowed Sharon to move past her ancient struggles with her mother and perhaps to even enjoy some aspects of her religious past. It seemed to me that Sharon was beginning to sense the possibility of integrating her religious past without the threat of losing her identity as Sharon.

Recently Sharon and I revisited this phase of our therapy when I asked her permission to use our work together for this article. As we discussed what I would write Sharon insisted that her concerns at the time had nothing to do with God but rather with the ways that she would be perceived by observant people. Nevertheless, while speaking, Sharon mentioned her enjoyment of holiday meals with her friends and informed me that she now treats Saturday as any other day; that she is no longer concerned about how she appears to her neighbors. Although Sharon and I may disagree on the reasons, we do agree that she is now able to enjoy some positive elements of her religious past without fear of losing herself.

God the Object

Ana-Maria Rizzuto has investigated religious experiences from an object relations viewpoint (Rizzuto, 1979, 1998). According to Rizzuto, our internal sense of God is created from multiple internal representations of self and other as they evolve over the life cycle. Some examples: Children who feel accepted and valued by their parents may later incorporate these experiences into a satisfying, mirroring representation of God. Children who do not feel appreciated may need to become godlike themselves as a defense against feeling small and rejected. As the child develops a sense of himself separate from his parents he begins to use fantasy to regulate this sense of self. God coexists alongside imaginary monsters that contain the child's bad feelings about himself as well as fantasized heroes that hold his feelings of goodness and omnipotence. Children fashion their internal image of God on the most important people that they know — their parents. The oedipal child's love and fear of his parents, especially the opposite gender parent, can color his image of God or cause him to repress it entirely. The pubertal child adds intellectual and philosophical aspects to his God representation which increase its richness without significantly altering its emotional meaning to the child.

Throughout the life cycle the God representation continues to evolve: It will have some aspects that are a direct continuation of the parental representations and others that are in opposition to them. Defensive maneuvers can distort the God representation or deny its existence completely. Idealization can reshape it. This representation can regress to an earlier stage of development or be reworked into a less conflictual form. Conscious and unconscious components of this representation can be complimentary or in conflict with each other. An individual's God may coincide with the God of organized religion or it may be at odds with it. Throughout his life, the individual will use, deny, repress, or alter his representation of God but, like all internal representations, it is a permanent part of one's inner world.

Between Heaven and Earth

Another hour. Again I was struggling to stay present as William droned on in his detached way. It wasn't that I disliked William; actually I was quite fond of him. I liked William well enough; but listening to him was like being lost in a dry, emotionless desert. William was unable to tolerate feelings — his own or others. If William felt something during the hour he would get confused and 'forget' what he was talking about. At times he would hastily leave the room to go to the bathroom. Or he would suddenly become overwhelmed with body pains that left no room for anything else. After the fact William would readily agree with me that he must have been anxious, that he was afraid of his feelings, that he needed to keep me at a distance — all in an intellectual manner that destroyed the emotional impact of my words. Even our language was difficult. A native German speaker, William had chosen to conduct the analysis in Hebrew despite his greater comfort with English because, "I don't want you to have an unfair advantage over me. We'll both use Hebrew so we can be equals."

A handsome man in his early fifties, William had consulted me because he felt he was "living along side of life". He was extremely accomplished with advanced degrees from several universities and some successes in business; he was married, he had children — on the surface he seemed well adjusted and successful. But beneath this surface William was miserable. He had never pursued a career related to his studies, his business deals failed as often as they succeeded. People liked him and considered him a friend but William felt distant from everyone. During his mid thirties, William had embraced Orthodox Judaism hoping to find some meaning in his life. But Judaism had become just as sterile as William's other pursuits — he followed the rules of religion with no real excitement or joy.

William's mother was the daughter of a highly successful family who had lost everything when they fled from the advancing Nazis. From early childhood she groomed William, her only son, to be her 'little prince' who would regain the lost glory of her childhood. Although William took great pleasure in pleasing his mother, her admiration came at a price — William felt his that feelings, his accomplishments, even his body did not belong to him; they were his mother's possessions. From an early age William rejected his mother's ownership of him by remaining emotionally detached from himself and from others.

William longed for a strong, powerful father who would rescue him from his enmeshing mother. Unfortunately, rather than share his wife's view of their son, William's father ignored his considerable accomplishments. While his mother saw him as a great leader of men, his father thought that he might be able to manage a shop — if he was lucky. William angrily rejected his father's devaluation while he unconsciously fulfilled his father's predictions. His accomplishments were proof that his father was wrong but he needed his failures in order to stay connected to his father.

Although William and I were slowly gaining an understanding of his inner world, he had an uncanny knack for turning spontaneous moments of emotional understanding into dry, intellectual knowledge that was of little benefit to either of us. And here we were in the midst of still another hour with William speaking of his existential feelings of emptiness and me feeling this for both us. "I'm on Mount Olympus," he declared, "looking down on the mortals below, never part of their world." Suddenly I woke up. Without understanding why, William's metaphor excited me. "William," I asked, "who lives on Olympus?" Uneasily he laughed. "The gods I guess." "So tell me about the gods!" I demanded. Nervously but with growing excitement, William described his childhood fantasy of himself as a Greek god. In William's fantasy the Greek gods were powerful, immortal beings who interacted with humans while remaining aloof from humanity. But the Greek gods were all too human with their intrigues and their defeats. Far above Olympus, was Heaven — home to the most powerful God of all, the God of Judaism. William longed to ascend to Heaven and become one with his omnipotent Jewish God but his terror of losing himself made him flee to Earth. On Earth he found himself a devalued human being and tried to ascend toward Heaven in order to feel worthwhile. "William," I said. "You are caught between Heaven and Earth. You flee from Heaven in order not to be your mother's little prince but fleeing Heaven leaves you a mere mortal, a shop manager. So you stay trapped on Olympus, never able to be God and never able to join the world of us ordinary human beings." As William nodded in agreement I felt that we had touched each other emotionally — and William had not fled the room!

William's God, as S/He emerged in the months that followed, was a rich amalgamate of multiple self and object representations, early identifications, wishes and defenses against those wishes, conflicts, and compromise formations. To describe a few of these aspects: William experienced his Jewish God as an omnipotent mother. He longed to merge with this God but was also terrified of losing himself in Her. Parts of his Jewish God represented the all-powerful father that William longed for as a child but this same omnipotence made God a potent source of disapproval and punishment. Olympus offered William a way out of his many intrapsychic dilemmas. By staying on Olympus, William could avoid competing with his wished-for omnipotent father without becoming a devalued store manager. He remained his mother's 'little prince' while avoiding becoming an adult and fulfilling her dreams. As an Olympian god William denied feeling small and powerless. From Olympus William could stay involved with people while maintaining a safe emotional distance.

This piece of analytic work developed into a seminal experience for both of us. For my part my deepening understanding of the multiple determinants of William's need to be godlike helped me stay connected to him despite the distance that he continued to create. As for William — shortly after this hour William decided to switch the language of our analysis to English because, "I want to reach out to you and make sure you understand me as well as you can." I wasn't quite sure if I had ascended Olympus or if William had begun to descend but I did feel us meeting emotionally in the space between us.

Discussion

A strange thing has happened to psychoanalysis over the last twenty years — it seems to have (re)found religion. Of course religion was never really lost. As Simmonds has documented, psychoanalysts have been wrestling on and off with religion ever since Freud (Simmonds, 2006). However in the last twenty years a wealth of study groups, articles, and books have emerged all treating religion as a serious area of psychoanalytic interest and study. Viewed historically this is a fascinating phenomenon, especially given Freud's undisguised antagonism toward religion. Freud viewed religion as an outdated, irrational form of societal neurosis, maybe even a delusional system, which was in the process of being evolutionarily replaced by rational and scientific modes of relating to the world. If religion, in Freud's view, was an expression of neurotic wishes and fantasies then the role of the psychoanalyst was to expose these infantile wishes for what they were and to 'cure' humanity of its neurosis. Not much room for mutual discussion or admiration in this schema.

A perusal of recent literature leads me to conclude that there is no longer any trend in modern psychoanalysis that does not grapple with religion in a respectful, often complimentary manner. Let me give some examples:

▶ Images of God expressed in the Christian tradition have been seen to correspond with Kleinian internal objects which are formed during various developmental stages. As such these internal objects are subjected to cycles of projection and introjection which mold them and make them potentially useful as well possible loci for internal difficulties (Hyrck, 1997).

▶ The capacity for religious experience is conceptualized as being forged from experiences within the transitional space, an area of illusion where the infant and mother co-create objects without having to ask "Is it real or is it an illusion?" These transitional experiences do not 'go inside' but rather transform and become the seeds of religious and cultural experience. (Winnicott, 1953) (Meissner, 1984)

▶ Experiences of God are seen as changing expressions of various stages of human development, each with their own characteristic wishes, fantasies, and conflicts. An individual's personal religion represents a constantly evolving subjective experience which continues to be transformed throughout the life cycle. (Meissner, 1984) (Fitzgibbons, 1987)

▶ Religion is seen as encompassing a system of internal objects (Rizzuto, 1979). These objects are created and maintained by society and refined over the centuries to meet the needs of humanity. As such, the internal objects of religion not only contain the thoughts, wishes, and fantasies of individual practitioners but also enable humanity as a whole to relate to the larger inhuman matrix in which the human world exists (Black, 1993).

▶ God and religion are conceptualized as beneficial selfobjects (Holliman, 2002). These selfobjects can aid the individual by protecting and bolstering a weak sense of self as well as providing opportunities for transforming normal narcissism into empathic awareness and creativity. The selfobject functions of God and tradition have been cited as one of the factors that allowed some Jews to maintain an intact sense of self despite the inhuman evils perpetrated upon them during the holocaust (Marcus & Rosenberg, 1995).

▶ Jewish influences on relational psychoanalysis have been examined. God's Brit (covenant) with the Jewish people is seen the prototype of an intersubjective relationship that is mutual while remaining asymmetric and unequal. Aspects of this relationship have found their way into the intersubjective view of the analytic relationship (Aron, 2004).

Despite this change in attitude there are some indications that the rapprochement between psychoanalysis and religion is not all it appears to be. LaMothe et al. examined clinical cases presented in psychoanalytic journals and found that in only 2 out of 181 clinical cases was there any attempt to explore and integrate religious experience in the therapy. This finding held true across the entire spectrum of journals regardless of their theoretical orientation (LaMothe et al., 1998). These findings correlate with my personal experience of listening to numerous case conferences and clinical discussions where religion and God seem to have no place in the individual's inner or outer worlds. Simmonds interviewed twenty-five therapists on issues of spirituality and, among other questions, asked how their spiritual sensitivities were addressed in their own therapies. The respondents reported that for the most part their spiritual concerns were either not welcomed by their therapist or viewed as difficulties that required further treatment (Simmonds, 2004). LaMothe and his colleagues discuss how mechanisms of attunement and assertion-recognition may create subtle cues by which the therapist unconsciously shapes material that the individual brings into therapy. In the presence of these cues the patient learns to leave religion and spirituality outside of therapy either as a form of compliance or as a means of protecting vulnerable aspects of him or herself from potential hurt and misunderstanding. Simmond's interviewees confirm that this process actually does occur in the treatment room.

Based on these considerations I can only assume that there must a split between our theoretical knowledge and our clinical practice; that we as therapists must bring some unconscious attitude into the treatment room regardless of our consciously held theoretical beliefs.

So what is this attitude? In my reading the analytic literature I often come across what appears to me to be an unstated attitude of 'this is what it really means' when it comes to religion. I will choose some examples, not to single out any one author but as representatives of this trend. Here is an example from a paper written from an object relations viewpoint "This paper suggests that a religion is ... a socially constructed and maintained system of internal objects, analogous to those spoken of in psychoanalysis. Like analytic internal objects, religious objects have a heuristic function but no material existence. Unlike analytic objects, they are derived from a definite cultural tradition and are elaborated over time to meet the experience of practitioners." (Black, 1993) (p. 625) Here is another quote, this time from the perspective of self psychology "This paper has presented an understanding of religious experience as selfobject experience and as a resource for satisfying selfobject needs. Religious experience can provide compensatory self structure; sustain self-cohesion; enhance development of self structure; and provide opportunities for transformation." (Holliman, 2002) (p. 205) Internal objects and self-objects are part of our created inner world. Although it probably is not the intent of these authors, if this view is taken too literally it would lead us to conclude that man creates God or maybe man and God together co-create God. While the tone of these contributions is respectful, I have a sense that attempts to explain religion and spirituality solely in terms of inner psychological needs could be perceived by our patients as being similar to Freud's reductionist view of religion even if their content is quite different.

What of my own analytic attitude toward religion? Since my attitude as an analyst is the result of who I am as a person, I'll begin by sharing some things about myself. As an Orthodox Jew I've had firsthand experience with the tensions between psychoanalysis and religion that I've been describing in this article. During my training, both as a psychiatrist and later as an analyst, religion was seldom mentioned by my teachers or my supervisors. When religion was discussed it was usually in the context of Freud's antagonistic anti-religious world-view. In this atmosphere I felt uncomfortable sharing my own spirituality. I rarely discussed religion with my colleagues or supervisors even though some of my patients were observant. On the other side of things, within the Orthodox Jewish community psychoanalysis is often viewed with suspicion as a secular religion that preaches permissiveness and atheism. (At social gatherings when someone learns that I am an analyst their next question is often some form of "Do you believe in Freud?"). Within both communities I've experienced considerable dissonance between myself as an observant Jew and myself as a psychoanalyst. Although I've become more comfortable with these different aspects of myself, some of this dissonance has remained. For example while writing this article I've found myself struggling over how much of my personal religious feelings I want to share with the reader.

My analytic attitude toward religion has been greatly influenced by my own relationship with God. Judaism plays an important part in the formal aspects of this relationship. Prayer, learning, mitzvoth, rituals, holidays, customs — all provide a formal structure to my religious experience. Within this structure I relate to God in my own idiosyncratic manner based on who I am as a person. My internal wishes, fantasies, conflicts, the important people in my life — all influence the ways that I experience relationships in general and my relationship to God in particular. My relationship to God is not static — it has evolved as the issues that I grapple with in my life have changed. For instance my experience of God as an adult is far more complex and abstract than the relationship I had with God as a child. Despite my very personal experience of God, I don't assume that God is 'really' anything like my internal experience of Him. In fact, given the limitations imposed by my being human, I don't believe that is possible for me to objectively experience God. Rather than claim objectivity, I am trying emphasize the ways that my subjectivity creates and sustains my relationship to God. This is the attitude that I take with me into the treatment room.

When my patients tell me about their families, their coworkers, and their friends I listen with the understanding that they are sharing with me a picture from their internal world, a picture which might or might not match up with my mental representation were I to actually meet that person. I can never say, "Oh, your mother really was like this" or "Your father really did that to you" — not because it might not be true but because analysis, in my opinion, is about one's subjective truth and how each of us incorporates this truth into our world. I listen in this same way when my patients speak about God. I don't say to myself or to the patient "Oh, God really is like that" nor do I dismiss their God as merely an internal creation serving specific intrapsychic needs. Instead I try to maintain within myself and within the therapy a potential space where I and my patients can explore the ways that their inner world has shaped their subjective experiences of God without being concerned about the objective validity of these experiences.

Empirically, I find that many of my patients do bring their religious and spiritual sensitivities into therapy. Based on the discussion above, I have to assume that I am bringing cues into the therapy which invite my patients to explore their religious feelings. What are these cues? I'll start with my appearance: I wear a knitted kippah and I have a beard. In Israeli society my appearance indicates that I identify with the Zionistic religious stream. This is a rather large and varied group that encompasses a wide range of religious observance. I don't wear a hat and coat which would identify me as coming from the world of Lithuanian yeshiva learning. I don't have a long beard, payot (long sideburns), or wear clothing that would identify me with the Chassidic life style. My office has a mezuzah on the door as is common to many buildings in Israel. People who examine my bookshelf will discover titles like 'The Birth of the Living God', 'A Godless Jew', 'Judaism and Psychoanalysis', and a book on Shabbatai Zvi scattered among books by Freud, Winnicott, and others. If the subject of Jewish learning comes up my patients will realize that I have some knowledge of Jewish texts including the Talmud. I probably use this knowledge to signal certain patients that religion can be a part of our work together. At the same time people who are engaged in full time Torah learning quickly intuit the limits of my knowledge.

My patients react to these clues — each in their own way. For some the Freud books indicate that I am anti-religious and secular; for others the kippah indicates that I am rigid and judgmental — or not rigid enough in the case of some patients. I have been a Jew for Jesus, a bigot, a mystic, an uneducated newly religious Jew, a Torah scholar, and a secular nonbeliever — all to different people and sometimes to the same person at different times. People use me in whatever ways they need in order to work on their own inner issues.

I think that beyond my appearance, my background, and the clues in my office, I also nonverbally convey my own struggles with and (I'd like to believe) integration of some of the issues I've discussed in this article. It's like talking about sex — if I am comfortable, curious, and non judgmental within myself then I communicate this and people eventually feel comfortable enough to bring their private thoughts, feelings, and fantasies into the therapy. The analogy to sex is a good one. In both cases I listen not only for what is being said but also for what is being left out of the therapy room. When religion doesn't enter the therapy, and often it does not, it is usually because these areas are either not particularly meaningful or not excessively troublesome to the individual. Sometimes this omission is defensive and, if so, I ask myself and the patient why they are leaving religion out of the therapy.

I'd like to conclude with one further thought. When I discuss my work with colleagues I often get the response "Well, you can work that way with religion because you're religious yourself." I disagree. I don't believe that my being observant is the main factor in my ability to work in the ways that I've described in this article. My religious observance is often very different from that of my patients who run the entire gamut from ultra-orthodoxy to secular disbelief. Even when the patient's religious background is similar to mine, my God is never the same as his or her God — each of us has our own subjectively experienced God and our individual relationship to that God. I don't believe that the therapist's belief or disbelief is at issue here. What is at issue, in my opinion, is good analytic technique; that is an openness to explore the meanings of God for each person without needing to place either God or the patient within defined framework — be it psychoanalytic or religious. I think that we therapists do this type of open exploration in many areas of our patients' lives but that we sometimes fail to maintain this attitude when it comes to God, religion, and spirituality. This failure can result in the person leaving important aspects of his or her self out of the therapy; an omission which I view as a lost analytic opportunity. I have been fascinated by the wealth of personal meaning contained in my patients' religious experiences. Joint analytic exploration of these meanings has been an extremely rewarding experience for my patients as well as for me both as an analyst and as a human being.

REFERENCES

Aron, L. (2004). *God's Influence on my Psychoanalytic Vision and Values.* Psychoanal. Psychol., 21: 442-451.

Black, D.M. (1993). What Sort of a Thing is a Religion? A View from Object-Relations Theory. *Int. J. Psycho-Anal.,* 74: 613-625.

Fitzgibbons, J. (1987). Developmental Approaches to the Psychology of Religion. *Psychoanal. Rev.,* 74: 125-134.

Freud, S. (1907), Obsessive Actions and Religious Practice. *Standard Edition,* 9. London: Hogarth Press. 1959.

-------. (1908). Civilized Sexual Morality. *Standard Edition,* 9. London: Hogarth Press. 1959.

Freud, S. (1913). Totem and Taboo: Some Points of Agreement between the Mental Lives of Savages and Neurotics. *Standard Edition*, 8. London: Hogarth Press. 1960.

——. (1927). The Future of an Illusion. *Standard Edition*, 21. London: Hogarth Press. 1961.

——. (1939). Moses and Monotheism: Three Essays. *Standard Edition*, 23. London: Hogarth Press. 1964.

Holliman, P.J. (2002). Chapter 12. Religious Experience as Selfobject Experience. *Progress in Self Psychology*, 18: 193-205.

Hyrck, M. (1997). Inner Objects and the Christian Images of God. *Int. Forum Psychoanal.*, 6: 41-43.

LaMothe, R., Arnold, J., Crane, J. (1998). The Penumbra of Religious Discourse. *Psychoanal. Psychol.*, 15: 63-73.

Marcus, P., Rosenberg, A. (1995). The Value of Religion in Sustaining the Self in Extreme Situations. *Psychoanal. Rev.*, 82: 81-105.

Meissner, W. (1984). *Psychoanalysis and Religious Experience*. New Haven: Yale Univ. Press.

Rizzuto, A.M. (1979). *The Birth of the Living God. A Psychoanalytic Study.* Chicago: The Univ. of Chicago Press.

——. (1998). *Why Did Freud Reject God? A Psychodynamic Interpretation.* New Haven: Yale University Press.

Simmonds, J.G. (2004). Heart and Spirit: Research with Psychoanalysts and Psychoanalytic Psychotherapists about Spirituality. *Int. J. Psycho-Anal.*, 85: 951-971.

——. (2006). The Oceanic Feeling and a Sea Change: Historical Challenges to Reductionist Attitudes to Religion and Spirit from Within Psychoanalysis. *Psychoanal. Psychol.*, 23: 128-142.

Winnicott, D. (1953). Transitional Objects and Transitional Phenomena. *Int. J. Psycho-Anal.*, 34: 89-97.

——. (1960). The Theory of the Parent-Infant Relationship. *Int. J. Psycho-Anal.*, 41: 585-595.

——. (1971). *Playing and Reality.* New York: Basic Books.

Dreams and Authoritative Knowledge: Bridging Judaism and Psychoanalysis

Jill Salberg *

I go to sleep at night never quite sure of how it will go. Will it be tranquil, uneventful; or will it be a roller coaster ride, thrilling and terrifying? Sometimes when I dream, I awake in the mornings remembering nothing. Then there are some mornings when I can't shake the dream and it colors my entire day. And yet there are the few times when I am so sorry to have to wake and leave my dream world. I turn over longing to re-enter some delicious place. One night I dreamt of the most beautiful turquoise water I had ever seen, a far deeper and richer color than the Caribbean or the Mediterranean, and everywhere I looked was this water. A long wooden dock, not unlike a boardwalk, extended for hundreds of feet into this sea of aqua Technicolor. I walked down this dock with a kickboard in hand and a pail. The kickboard slipped out of my hand into the water and floated off. There was a swimming lesson going on out in the water and I called out to them to catch the kickboard but they either didn't hear me or just didn't respond. I was saddened by the loss of the kickboard but still had the pail. I woke up and the call of the gorgeous azure water was great. I must return. Why did I have to leave? How do I get back there?

---

* I would like to thank Joseph Katz, for his love of dreams and encouraging me to dream, Rabbi Burton L.Visotzky for introducing me to the wonderment of Midrash, and Rabbi Carol Levithan for her support. Additionally, there are a group of writers and friends, colleagues and cohorts who have read, given feedback and sustained my work through many versions of which I am in their debt.

I have no idea where this sacred sanctuary was or why I felt such a sense of peacefulness and longing to stay.

In this essay I will attempt to think about dreams as bridges between the realms of old and of today, between what the Rabbis felt and believed about dreams, dreamers and interpreters and our contemporary modern psychoanalytic sensibilities. While I do this I hope to hold in mind the experiential aspect of a dream, for that is what we all share. Dreams are 'lived' events reminding us that we are embodied beings who encounter our lives through our senses. Dreams are our thoughts in images. We fall asleep and a personal cinema takes over, often vivid with our hearts racing, our eyes dazzled by amazing colors; or on the other hand the scene can be quite ordinary, unremarkable except for some odd detail. I imagine my Aqua Sea as my unconscious — vast, colorful and slightly dangerous. My longing to return speaks to an ever present yearning to live more fully inside my deepest thoughts and desires. The odd detail of the kickboard and pail are long remembered objects of childhood, my own and my children's. While all is familiar there is also the being disconsolate. I am happy to be at this sea but I've lost my kickboard. The lesson already in progress in the water prevents my call from being heard — have I been overlooked or left behind? Am I to be a student in wait for a teacher, or an experience based self-learner? (I will return to my dream, which I use as a "lived" example, later in this chapter.) In dreams, the familiar and the strange live side by side, we see people we know, people we've never met, and deceased people we love come back to life. Oftentimes we live within the moments of these personal films and at the same time we stand outside as narrator or critic. I am left to wonder why I have shown up and what I am to do now. Is that not how life is, we show up to a world already in progress, how are we to engage? We are the dreamer and the dreamed.

Dreams are mysterious and I assume that as long as humankind has been around so have the dreams of nighttime. They have probably been part of all recorded cultures and religions. And long before neuroscientists and sleep researchers made them objects of scientific inquiry they were considered magical and mystical. My point of entry for this endeavor will start with Biblical references to dreams and dreamers. I will be exploring the evolution of dream interpretation from early Jewish writings to present-day psychoanalytic theory. The universality of a dream life is my particular interest but the uses of that form of communicating and communing with unknown parts of oneself and its broader significance is my destination. I will be tracking who dreams and who has the right to understand their dreams: that is, whose voice becomes authoritative.

Now it is not obvious why a psychoanalyst might consider and utilize Jewish texts or any ancient texts for an understanding of dreams when there has been a great deal written within psychoanalysis on dreams.[1] In fact one might say that Psychoanalysis was born of dreams with Freud's (1900) foundational work *The Interpretation of Dreams*. But if we can agree that dreams are probably as old as humankind then we can also assume that people have always longed to unlock the enigma of what we dream. The writers and redactors of the Biblical text as well as the Rabbis were also interested in trying to understand the purpose of the dream. What I hope to show is not only the differences between ancient and rabbinic approaches to dreams compared to modern psychoanalytic methods but also more interestingly the common concerns that we still share. Further I will be demonstrating that a strikingly similar path in terms of thought was traveled by both the Rabbis and modern psychoanalytic writers, revealing an evolution of ideas that address many of the same questions and concerns.

Biblical Dreams and Dreamers

I want to start not with the better-known biblical dreams of someone like Joseph but the more discrete references we first find to dreams in the biblical text. In doing this I will be focusing our attention on who gets to dream, whose dreams are considered significant and how the nature

---

[1]   Erich Fromm (1951) was one of the early psychoanalysts whose emphasis on culture would be demonstrated in his book on dreams which would include references to Jewish texts, myths and fairy tales of different cultures.

of authority is formulated. If we look in the Biblical text at Num. 12:1-8 we see the first direct reference to the importance of dreams as divine communication. It is here that Miriam and Aaron, in what we might hear as criticism of Moses, ask: "Has the LORD spoken only through Moses? Has he not spoken through us as well?" And the response they receive is clear and direct:

> "Hear these My words: When a prophet of the Lord arises among you, I make Myself known to him in a vision, I speak with him in a dream. Not so with My servant Moses; he is trusted throughout My household. With him I speak mouth to mouth, plainly and not in riddles, and he beholds the likeness of the LORD."

So we are told quite directly that God, the ultimate authority, does speak to Prophets in a dream. The dream is important as divine communication, a prophetic foretelling of the future. Now we understand the import of a Jacob or a Joseph having a dream. They are singled out by God and become vehicles of God's voice to us. Nonetheless, in this biblical text, the importance remains not with the individual but in the content of what is transmitted in the dream, i.e., a narrative unfolding of historical events.

Dreams in the biblical text are important in their historical context and not as entities by themselves or as expressions of an individual's unique nature — our more modern, psychoanalytic understanding. Let's use for an example a little referenced dream of Jacob. Near the end of Genesis Jacob, an old man at this time, learns that his beloved son Joseph — whom he had long thought was dead — is still alive. With great determination he decides that he must travel to Egypt and see his son. Gen. 46:1-4 tells us the following:

> So Israel set out with all that was his, and he came to Beer-Sheba, where he offered sacrifices to the God of his father Isaac. God called to Israel in a vision of night: "Jacob! Jacob!" He answered, "Here." And He said, "I am God, the God of your father. Fear not to go down to Egypt, for I will make you there into a great nation. I Myself will go down with you to Egypt, and I Myself will also bring you back; and Joseph's hand shall close your eyes."

In this dream we learn that God again has "visited" Jacob and confirmed his plan to go to Egypt to see Joseph. Once again God's covenant, promised to the Patriarchs, of "making you into a great nation" is re-affirmed. I will return to this dream later and other elements present within it, but for now, what I want to underscore is the unfolding of historical events that is evident in this recounting. We know what is to follow — that, despite anything to the contrary, God's plan for Jacob/Israel and the nation to follow from him is continuing. To put this in more human terms, Jacob has been reassured.

If we turn now to Deut. 13:2-6 we will see another perspective expressed towards dreams within the Biblical text:

> "If there appears among you a prophet or a dream-diviner and he gives you a sign or a portent, saying, "Let us follow and worship another god" — whom you have not experienced — even if the sign or portent that he named to you comes true, do not heed the words of that prophet or that dream-diviner... As for the prophet or dream-diviner, he shall be put to death; for he urged disloyalty to the Lord your God."

The view in Deuteronomy is that dreams and those who speak about dreams are to be considered false prophets and should not be believed or followed. What is explicit here is that these people will urge you to worship other gods and are not to be trusted. This is a new development, a warning that not all dreams and dreamers are alike, exactly the view we will hear from the writings of the Prophets themselves. Now we are to understand that "True Prophets of God" have visions or hear God speak to them, but no longer in dreams. There is a shift now and a beginning of uncertainty as to the nature of authority. Here we have the beginnings of what I want to call "competing authorities." The warning is to be wary of people claiming authority that is not theirs to claim, due to a lack of authenticity — no credentials from God.

Take a look at one of the writings of the Prophet, Jeremiah 23: 25-28:

> "I have heard what the prophets say, who prophesy falsely in My name: "I had a dream, I had a dream." How long will there be in the minds of the prophets who prophesy falsehood — the prophets of their own deceitful minds — the plans to make My people forget My name, by means of the dreams which they tell each other, just as their fathers forgot My name because of Baal? Let the prophet who has a dream tell the dream; and let him who has received My word report My word faithfully! How can straw be compared to grain? — says the Lord."

The Prophets are clearly stating for us that dreams are *never* prophecy. The text shows us that a distinction is being drawn between someone who dreams and a Prophet who has received God's word. Within this distinction is a shift from the image that might appear in a dream to the word, the text of the dream. How are we to understand this change in format of divine transmissions, and does it suggest a shift in the nature of authority?

These two texts, Deuteronomy and Jeremiah, are telling us that the dreams of the Israelites, the ordinary individuals, are not trustworthy sources of divine communication. What is the danger of considering these dreams as having any importance? To allow for thoughtful contemplation of personal dreams would have been giving them a magnitude, a value that could suggest authority. It became untenable to think that dreams were divinely given, not only because we all dream but additionally because of the difficulty in finding a definitive meaning that all could discern. Imagine everyone interpreting the authority of divine word in his or her dreams? Chaos might ensue; interpretation and authority would need to be reckoned with. In this way the Prophets understood the ambiguity and the power of dreams and share with the writers of Deuteronomy the clear belief that prophecy cannot and does not appear within a dream. Obviously in this context my own opening oceanic dream would be of no consequence. Of course psychoanalysts are particularly interested in the meaning of dreams and, not unlike the writers of the biblical text, believe that one's dream seem to be bringing to us messages from afar. The issue of concern for the Prophets was very much one of authority, specifically the authority to speak and consequently to be listened to and followed.

Rabbinic Concerns

With the destruction of the Second Temple the pre-exilic Israel era, ruled by Kings who were guided by prophets speaking the word of God came to a close. No longer would the authoritative message come from a charismatic person who had direct contact with God. The early Rabbis believed that God's divine message was now embedded within text. While God's revelation to Moses at Sinai was considered the giving of the law *with* the text, future generations would find God and revelation *within* the written word. Exegesis became the vehicle of this revealed word with the Rabbis deciding what was authoritative as text and how to interpret it.

Within the Babylonian Talmud (Bavli), Chapter IX: Berakoth we find a loosely based pastiche of sayings on dreams. However, when more fully considered there seem to be three broad categories within the writings. The first part of the text has general pithy statements as to the importance of dreams such as:

> "R. Hisda said: Any dream which is not interpreted is like a letter which is not read."
> "R. Berekiah said: While a part of a dream may be fulfilled, the whole of it is never fulfilled."

These two quotes reflect an attitude towards dreams that both acknowledge their importance in one's life and also the difficulty in comprehending what they might mean. Clearly dreams are now valued and understood to have significance. The first statement by R. Hisda implies a need for interpretation by likening it to a written document, such as a letter, the dream then becomes a kind of text. Given this conceptualization of dreams *as* a form of text I believe it suggests the Rabbi's gave serious contemplation of dreams since the interpreting of text is of the highest value for the Rabbis. Further quotes suggest even more:

> 55a: Rav Judah also said in the name of Rav: There are three things for which one should supplicate: a good king, a good year, and a good dream. These things depend directly upon the will of God.
> A prophet that hath a dream let him tell a dream: and he that hath My word let him speak My word faithfully. What hath the straw to do with the wheat, saith the Lord. What is the connection of straw and wheat with a dream? The truth is, said R. Johanan in the name of R. Simeon b. Yohai that just as wheat cannot be without straw, so there cannot be a dream without some nonsense.

The first statement is very much in line with what I have said earlier, dreams are important and their value is the dream's connection to God. In the second example, we are told not to be put off if there is a little nonsense in our dreams, for even wheat comes from unusable parts of the straw. Nonsense? Unusable bits of straw? What have the Rabbis in mind with these analogies? I believe they were struggling with the very problems of interpretation and meaning. What if something makes no sense in a dream, how then are we to understand it? This begins to approach our modern, perhaps psychoanalytically inflected experience of our own dreams. They have important information for us to know about our interior lives. Separating the wheat and straw, by which the Rabbis mean the knowable from the unknowable, is a significant part of the task of interpretation. And continuing:

> R. Hisda also said: Neither a good dream nor a bad dream is ever wholly
> fulfilled. R. Hisda also said: A bad dream is better than a good dream.
> R. Huna said: A good man is not shown a good dream, and a bad man is not
> shown a bad dream. (Footnote in Soncino translation reads: Rashi reads:
> A good man is shown a bad dream and a bad man is shown a good dream.
> The purpose is to turn the good man to repentance and to give the bad man
> his reward in this world.)

Here we are indebted to Rashi whose exegetical talents help us to see that the relevance of the qualitative aspects of our dreams are also linked to God. One way to understand the mood or tenor of the dream is to think in terms of what the dream is attempting to accomplish in terms of reflecting on our behavior. If we think of the Prophets as warning us that it was our sinful or disobedient behavior towards God and God's laws that led to our punishment from God (think enslavement, suffering, exile) then the path is clear. If we repent, offer true *teshuvah* and turn to God, then there is return. Bad dreams become important as personal messages regarding repentance. So far, all of these points, to my mind, anticipate a Freud, a modern emphasis on the psychological understandings of our innermost thoughts and feelings. They also suggest a complexity to understanding authoritative knowledge. Rashi is counseling us to read *against* the text in that we need to understand contextually a "good or bad" dream.

There are also stories about the Rabbis as dream-interpreters and a group of independent interpreters known as oneirocritics. Within this third section is a long story about a Rabbi referred to as Rava and the dream-interpreter Bar Hedya. The story of Bar Hedya, one of those free-lance dream interpreters, tells us that he would give a good interpretation when paid a fee and a bad one when not paid. And within this story lies what I believe is the heart of the Bavli's dream-book agenda. If dreams are prophetic messages from God, as some were considered like the dreams of Jacob and Joseph in the Biblical text, then how are the Rabbis to deal with dreams in their current, post-prophetic time? As Ken Frieden (1990) states, "Berakot implicitly depicts a contest between conflicting schools of interpretation. At one extreme is the belief that dreams literally prophesy future events; at another extreme is the view that dreams do not bear meaning until interpreted (p. 92)." We now have levels of competing authorities. The first is where dreams derive from; the second is who has the authority to interpret dreams.

Another quote, Berakoth 55b: "All dreams follow the mouth" expresses yet another aspect of the central idea at issue in this text. The Rabbis took this to mean that the outcome of a dream was somehow a direct result of the interpretation. Following an hermeneutic device often used to interpret text, the Rabbis put two statements together — a dream is like a letter and all dreams follow the mouth — and conclude that a dream is to be treated as a text and therefore analogous to Scripture. This is not a huge leap since the Rabbis were already engaged in a similar enterprise, i.e. interpreting oral Torah and written Torah, Scripture and commentary. But not just anyone could interpret scripture. Consequently the same specialized guild, i.e. Rabbis who interpret text, should be the ones to interpret dreams. In fact they were already interpreting dreams within Scriptural text so it was already part of their providence. We can now see how an independent group of dream interpreters would be of some great concern to the Rabbis. Clearly this left the Rabbis deeply ambivalent about dreams. Having established their own authority as the prime interpreters of revelation they now seem to need to dis-empower the outside guild of dream interpreters. But the Rabbis still need to account for the fact that everyone does dream. Even the Rabbis themselves must have been dreaming. The logic follows that if everyone has dreams then they can't all be having prophetic ones.

Consequently, dreams can only be a small part of prophecy, one-sixtieth according to Berakoth.

What of the dreams that disturb and unsettle us? I believe that the Rabbis have always at some level been concerned with healing. It is therefore interesting to find that within the liturgy of the Birkat Kohanim, the Priestly Blessing recited on the three festival Hagim and the High Holy Days, the following personal supplication may be spoken softly by a congregant during the blessing:

> "Master of the world, I am Yours and my dreams are Yours. I have dreamed a dream but I do not know what it indicates. May it be Your will, Hashem my God and the God of my fathers, that all my dreams regarding myself and regarding all of Israel be good ones — those I have dreamed about myself, those I have dreamed about others, and those that others dreamed about me. If they are good, strengthen them, fortify them, make them endure in me and in them like the dreams of the righteous Joseph. But if they require healing, heal them like as the waters of Marah were healed by Moses, our teacher, and as Miriam was healed of her leprosy and Hezekiah of his sickness, and the waters of Jericho by Elisha. So may You transform all of my dreams regarding myself and regarding all of Israel for goodness. May you protect me, may you be gracious to me, may You accept me. Amen."

This verse is footnoted in the Artscroll Siddur stating, "Between the verses of Birkat Kohanim it is customary to recite a supplication regarding dreams. The currently prevalent version of this supplication is virtually unchanged from the text appearing in the Talmud where it appears with the following introduction: If one had a dream but is uncertain whether the dream forebode good or evil let him stand before the *Kohanim* at the time they spread their hands in blessing, and let him say, Master of the world! I am Yours and my dreams are Yours..." (Berachoth 55b). The Rabbis' interest and serious concern for people whose dreams were disturbing found a way into the liturgy. This suggests to me an acknowledgement and concern by the Rabbis that dreams could be profoundly disturbing and render people in a state of disease with a need for comfort and to be blessed.

The rest of the dream-book, with its key-symbol approach reveals their attitude towards these 'lesser in importance' dreams. What we see is a concern for the distress and anxiety caused in the dreamer by the content of their dreams. By comparing certain dream events to scripture the Rabbis find a way to diffuse personal anxiety, a kind of therapeutic stance. Despite the Rabbis wanting to provide comfort, there is an inevitable tension created between the Rabbis' concerns over authority issues and their humanitarian or healing desires. Put another way, their concerns are between what is truth and what is curative, not so foreign a concept, and one which is found in contemporary psychoanalytic concerns.

Medieval Rabbinic Dream Writer

Rabbi Solomon Almoli, born in Salonika in 1486, was a Spanish Rabbi and physician who lived in Constantinople and believed that dreams contained the voice of divine guidance helping ordinary men and women navigate their personal lives in accordance with God's plan. He drew heavily from both Scriptural and Talmudic sources as well as the Zohar. From the Zohar he quotes:

> "Come and see: there is nothing which comes to the world without having been announced in a dream or by means of a messenger, as it was taught: Everything is announced in Heaven before it comes to the world; from there it spreads throughout the world and is given over by a messenger, as is written: "The Lord God does nothing without revealing His secret to His servants, the prophets — at the time when there were prophets. And even when prophetic inspiration is lacking, there are "Sages who are superior to prophets, and even when no dream is granted, matters are revealed and ordained through the birds of heaven." (15th/16th cent./1998, p. 5)

Although Almoli was going against the talmudic notion that God's prophetic relationship with humanity ended with the exile after the destruction of the Second Temple, he supports his dream theory by relying on the Kabalistic idea that during sleep the soul rises up to heaven and 'amuses' itself with God. (Also see Covitz, 1990; and Harris, 1994.)

Dreaming can be seen as play — attempts, in the Kabbalistic world, at drawing oneself closer to God. What has changed here is the locus of authority. Almoli no longer has to contend with competing guilds. The authority of the Rabbis has long been established as to text, laws and Jewish life. But it is equally important to consider this text in terms of its historical context. The more pressing issues arise from being a diasporic nation, subject to the will and whim of other prevailing powers and kings. Almoli was writing during the post-expulsion from Spain time frame. In many ways his thinking may bear an imprint of the Inquisition, most notably a sense of helplessness and insecurity over one's fate. It is within this context that Almoli is attempting to empower dreamers to be able to read their own dreams.

Looking back over the collective writings from Jewish sources we see an interest and concern with dreams: where do they come from; how do we interpret their meaning and is only one meaning correct; who has claim to being a dream interpreter and how will the interpretation affect the dreamer? There is a tension between the need to relieve the dreamers' anxiety and the need for clear authority. The theme of competing authorities keeps circulating around anxiety with dreams as the medium. Evidently dreams were considered important experiences that cried out to be understood. Additionally they became the vehicle through which other concerns were addressed, i.e., the anxieties of the dreamer and of the Rabbis. Lastly, the question of what kind of knowledge (and here I am thinking of exegetical interpretative information or a kind of consoling, easing of anxiety) and who contains it seems to be of great concern.

Psychoanalysis, Freud And Dreams

Within his magnum opus, *The Interpretation of Dreams* (1900), Freud was insistent that his approach to dreams countered the approach that had been adopted by the ancients. To interpret dreams psychoanalytically Freud shifted knowledge onto the dreamer, albeit an unknowing kind of knowing. It is our unconscious mind that creates and writes the dream while disguising its true meaning from our conscious psyche.

Dreams derive from our most hidden wishes, the very ones we harbor and conceal from ourselves. It is the work of the dreamer to speak about her associations to the dream, to freely entertain all thoughts in connection to the dream. The analyst, in a style of listening that Freud termed "evenly hovering attention," can begin to discern in the manifest content of the dream what is disguised, a defense against knowing the true wish embedded within the dream's latent content. Hidden wishes could be known and unlocked from behind the defense fortress. These secret desires could be linked to a conscious idea or event and help to produce the layers of meanings in a dream. Freud compared this to "the *entrepreneur*, who, as people say, has the idea and the initiative to carry it out, [but] can do nothing without capital; he needs a capitalist. . .who provides the psychical outlay for the dream... *a wish from the unconscious*" (p. 561). Freud believed that if this could be made conscious and we could learn what our deepest longings were along with dismantling the defenses we erect to protect ourselves from knowing what we desire, we could be cured of our neuroses.

I believe that Freud's groundbreaking work was undertaken as a result of a personal loss of authority. In the 1880's, Freud had befriended Josef Breuer, an older Viennese physician, who had discovered with his patient Anna O what they termed "the talking cure." Breuer shared this case information with Freud who started using some of Breuer's techniques under Breuer's tutelage. But the two men did not agree on the aetiology of the neuroses and the collaboration eventually ended. Freud had been insisting on a sexual basis and was especially keen on developing a theory that would include both pathology and normality — a continuum of mental functioning. Breuer did not agree with Freud's early sexual theories and by the time the two had published their important work, *Studies in Hysteria* (1895), they parted company. Shortly after this in the fall of 1896 Freud's father, at age 81, passed away, sending Freud into a deep depression.[2] So here we have two losses of authority figures for Freud — his own father

---

[2] For a fuller discussion of Freud's ambivalent relationship with his father see Salberg, 2007.

and Breuer, the older Viennese father-figure physician who had mentored him, loaned him money when Freud could ill afford things, and helped launch Freud's private practice. I want to draw attention to the twofold aspects of loss, the person of a father and a father-figure and additionally, the loss of authority. It was out of this state of mourning and melancholia that memories, dreams and associations flowed and were written down by Freud as he embarked on a path to cure his depression with an "analysis", a self-analysis to be precise. Much of this was then written about in letters to his new close confidante Wilhelm Fliess, a Berlin physician and perhaps a new father substitute. Freud often used his own dreams to illustrate his theories and to demonstrate how dreams are a portal to unconscious material via further associative elaborations.

I turn now to a dream that Freud reported both in a letter to Wilhelm Fliess and later in *The Interpretation of Dreams*. In the letter, he tells Fliess of his father's death, and reported both the effect on him and a dream:

> "By one of the obscure routes behind the official consciousness the old man's death affected me deeply. I valued him highly and understood him very well indeed, and with his peculiar mixture of deep wisdom and imaginative light-heartedness he meant a great deal in my life. By the time he died his life had long been over, but at a death the whole past stirs within one. I feel now as if I had been torn up by the roots. . . I must tell you about a very pretty dream I had on the night after the funeral. I found myself in a shop where there was a notice up saying:

> You are requested
> to close the eyes.

> I recognized the place as the barber's to which I go every day. On the day of the funeral I was kept waiting, and therefore arrived at the house of mourning rather late. The family were displeased with me, because I had arranged for the funeral to be quiet and simple, which they later agreed was the best thing. They also took my lateness in rather bad part. The phrase on the notice-board has a double meaning. It means "one should do one's duty towards the dead" in two senses — an apology, as though I had not done my duty and my conduct needed over-looking, and the actual duty itself. The dream was thus an outlet for the feeling of self-reproach which a death generally leaves among the survivors." (pp.170-171)

Freud tells us in his letter to Fleiss that he is quite shaken by his father's death, "I feel now as if I had been torn up by the roots" and then he mentions the dream. Uprootedness is a state of upheaval that leaves one feeling exposed to one's core, an utter rootlessness. The dream opens with the signpost words, "You are requested to close the eyes" and Freud acknowledges the duty one is to perform towards the dead. I want to suggest that this moment of deracination echoes the moment of terror and anxiety with which we all approach loss, particularly parent and child. The death of his father Jacob sends Freud into a deep depression. It is a loss and upheaval that he had not anticipated and was unprepared for.

Now let's recall the earlier dream of Jacob, the biblical patriarch, which contains very similar language: "and Joseph's hand will close your eyes." I will not be suggesting that Freud was familiar with this biblical verse, although he might have been. I am more struck by the resonance between Freud's experience of his father's death and his understanding of showing filial respect, and the biblical story in which Joseph is also to respect and honor Jacob's death. No doubt this is an important Jewish cultural value: for a son to honor his father's death and to show respect by closing the eyes. I believe that it is not only respect that is embedded within these stories and dreams but also the symbolic act of the son supplanting the father's authority in the act of closing the father's eyes. It is the son who now can *see* and be the one who knows.

Additionally, there is great anxiety surrounding the loss of parental authority by the son, as well as the parent's fears in approaching death. Jacob of the Biblical text had long believed his son was dead. In learning of the truth that Joseph is still alive, Jacob is both eager to see him and to behold him before dying. In some way Jacob knows that to see Joseph again may be his *dying wish* and it is therefore with trepidation that he sets out for Egypt. Seeing Joseph then becomes fraught with anxiety and problematic. To see him has been a longed for wish but to be with him ushers in the end of his life, a terrible irony. It is in this state of mind that Jacob goes to sleep and God visits with him in a dream. One way to interpret this visit is that God is concurring that this is the path to be followed, re-establishing God's authority in a moment of anxiety. Additionally God is reassuring Jacob that he will not be alone. First I will accompany you and then for your final journey out of life, Joseph will accompany you. Two aspects of fatherhood are present in this dream: authority as in knowledge, specifically of the future, and a kind of authority that can provide comfort.

Perhaps this is a way to understand Freud's dream as well. He too thought he had been prepared for the inevitable death of his father. He remarks that his father was elderly and his health had been failing for some time. In many ways Freud sounds like the triumphant Oedipal son who has already replaced his father in the position of familial authority. But he was unprepared for the unconscious resonance, upheaval and the extirpation caused by his father's death. In fact a week later he writes again to Fliess and re-iterates, "By the time he died, his life had long been over, but in [my] inner self the whole past has been reawakened by this event. I now feel quite uprooted." (p. 202) We may ask, what gets awakened for Freud or for any of us when we lose a parent? Certainly a great many things but foremost may be a loss of the original authority figure in all its dimensions, both illusory and real. This loss ushers in uncertainty as the inevitable moving up of a generation that is to replace the parental figures and become the new authority.

In many ways, interestingly, Freud's conception of mind is based on a particular notion of authority and perhaps uncertainty. We are not really masters of our own minds because we are ruled by unconscious passions and wishes that we cannot let ourselves know we have. We erect sentinels, a kind of "in house" authority or guard. Adam Phillips picked up on the illogical nature of Freud's enterprise when he wrote, "Freud, after all, had done a very paradoxical thing: he invented a form of authority, the science of psychoanalysis, as a treatment that depended on demolishing forms of authority." (p. 30) While apparently shifting the emphasis of 'knowing' onto the dreamer, who was to produce the associations, which would unlock the dream, Freud ultimately located the authority of interpretation within the analyst and analytic theory. And so his very act of demolishing authority simultaneously re-instates it. Bollas (1996) also believed that Freud was unwittingly setting up a paradox; "Even though Freud privileged the analyst's interpretation of meaning, his fascination with dream contents and the matrix of unconscious material and his fidelity to the process of free association meant that at no point in his writings did his belief in his interpretive truths ever displace a method that would always undermine him." (p. 3)

Competing Authorities and The 'Relational Turn'

Within contemporary psychoanalysis there has been a debate as to what is the actual authority of the analyst. Friedman (1996) makes an interesting point regarding Freud's belief on what constituted analytic authority. On the one hand Freud likens the trust in the analyst to what one feels towards a beloved parent and on the other hand the analyst has knowledge about how the mind operates. Thus, Friedman sees the debate as focusing on whether the analyst is a fact-based authority or whether the influence and authority of the analyst flows out of the relationship. The traditional analytic point of view, well articulated and elaborated by Brenner (1976) and Arlow (1986) maintained that Freud's theory of pathology — that conflicts over sexual and aggressive wishes in childhood produce defenses and therefore symptoms in patients — would lead the analyst to "know" how to interpret and cure the patient. This classical point of view, which even contemporary Freudians are less inclined to hold fast to, put forth a hierarchical model that placed the analyst in the powerful position of absolute knowledge. It was the analyst whose theories informed what dynamics were to be found once the patients' resistance, defenses and ultimately character analysis were traversed. The Holy Grail was the unconscious, the land of sexual and aggressive impulses. And the patient was to submit or surrender to this process, i.e., the will and authority of the analyst and the analysis. Rebellion to this authority was seen as resistance, an impasse or, even worse, a flight from the analysis.

Are there competing authorities and can they all be true? This is the very same question debated regarding dreams by the Rabbis in the Talmud using Biblical texts and reconsidered within the medieval era using Kabbalistic ideas. Embedded in Jewish writings was an awareness of some of this very complexity involved with the question of authority and authority figures. Are they — be it a prophet, a sage, a dream interpreter, Rabbi or analyst — in possession of ultimate truths or is it the reassurance inherently within certain relationships that are helpful and curative? Today, in our psychoanalytically postmodern infused world, this question is still relevant. In the past ten to fifteen years within the contemporary psychoanalytic literature we find this question asked in some form by analysts across diverse theoretical lines. Attempts by Relational and Interpersonal analysts to address this paradox began with looking at the subtle ways that both analyst and analysand mutually influence each other and the absolute inter-subjectivity of the analytic encounter (See Aron, 1991; Renik, 1993; Ogden, 1994; Hoffman, 1996; Mitchell, 1997; and Benjamin, 2004; to name a few). The "relational turn" (Rubin 1996; Mitchell 1999), as it has been referred to, ushered in a movement from authoritative hierarchical models for the analysis toward a more mutual, co-construction of an analysis. Mitchell (1997, 1998) felt that the relational approach altered how we understand what exactly the analyst could be an authority on. He further believed that the goal of analysis is to help someone to understand the ways in which their felt victimhood (and sense of lack of authority) included their own participation. In expanding the ways in which someone begins to understand their life, and their relationships with the people within their life, Mitchell noted that we were expanding a person's capacity for personal agency, a kind of self-authorization. In doing this, the patient and the analyst are co-creating new meaning and a new understanding of the patient's life narrative. This approach differs and inevitably competes with the authoritative stance of classical theory where the contents of the unconscious are known and need to be interpreted and made conscious to free the patient from repeating unconscious dynamic patterns.

Perhaps nowhere in an analysis is this question more at issue than with dreams and their interpretation. Dreams had long been considered the gold standard in analysis and perceived to be directly created by the unconscious mind. The concurrently long held belief was that the accuracy of an interpretation was crucial. But is it? Greenberg (1999) argues that as early as 1931 the analytic world was attempting to understand how accurate one needed to be. He uses Glover's 1931 paper on "The Therapeutic

Effect of Inexact Interpretation" as a key example of a beginning shift from analytic authority as truth/fact based to authority based in the relationship. Greenberg further argues that each analytic dyad is unique and will create its own set of meanings that come out of the relationship that is forged, worked on and negotiated between the two participants. If the emphasis shifts from an authoritative "knowing" the contents and structure of mind to a belief that a particular dyad will work on a capacity to reflect on their relationship, then doesn't it follow that the patient can come to "know" their own mind perhaps as well as or better than the analyst? Mitchell (1998) strongly argues that, "the analytic process is about expanding and enriching the patient's experience of his own mind and facilitating his capacity to generate experience that he finds vitalizing and personally meaningful. From this perspective, arriving at a "best guess" decoding of the dream is neither possible nor desirable; what is important is engaging him about the dream in a way that sparks and quickens his own analytic interest in himself." (p. 24)

This more relational approach might focus the analyst to ask the patient what state of mind they were in within the dream, or what they thought got solved within the dream and where the disruption lies. We invite the patient to become both curious and engaged in their own dream, believing that they know a great deal more about the dream's meaning than they even suspect. Returning to my own dream with some of these ideas in mind I recalled that when, as a child, I had been sent to sleep-away camp and was struggling with learning many activities, swimming was crucially one of them. I was a reluctant, perhaps fearful swimmer and so to help in learning my parents had engaged the waterfront counselor for private lessons, which I was to receive during rest hour. I remembered that I would walk down to the waterfront, with nary a person around, everyone back in their bunks while I approached the lake, maybe even with a kickboard in hand. So far the dream structure recreates what I know; the manifest level is uneventfully the same. We might even call this the 'dream text'. Only in the dream the instructor is already in the water teaching someone else. This bit begins to enter less conscious territory. I have an older sister who had previously gone to sleep away camp and was already a far more accomplished athlete and camper than I. Growing up I was often aware of feeling unsure if I could compete with her: to my eyes, she seemed perfect, athletic and adept. Again the dream is structured in a way that recapitulates aspects of my life. But I lose the kickboard in the dream while still holding the pail. This interests me as something different now and my curiosity is piqued, and to quote myself, "I am saddened by the loss of the kickboard but still have the pail." How am I to understand this, what we could now consider a subtext in the dream?

I push myself to expand what seems like a simple dream. A kickboard reminds me of swim lessons and doing laps in a pool, but the pail reminds me of play. When my own children were little we often summered by a beach and I would spend many afternoons building sand castles and filling moats with water. Ah, the multiple uses of a pail, and the singular use of a kickboard. The next question I ask myself is why now, why remember these things at this point in time? What does this have to do with my current life, in other words, what is my emotional context for this dream? I had this dream during a time when I was busily preparing a paper for professional presentation, and working on a personal memoir piece about my grandparents. My sense is that this was an intense time of internal work and also my personal psychoanalytic form of play. The dream suggested the way for me to be writing; not the tried and true kickboard laps across the pool style but a livelier sandcastle approach. The dream also is reminding me not to be a student of a teacher but to self-authorize, to find my own way in the water. I concur with Mitchell when he wrote, "I am offering a view of the analyst's knowledge and authority that portrays the analyst as an expert in collaborative, self-authorizing self-reflection, in developing useful constructions for understanding the analysand's experience." (p. 227) In terms of dream interpretation I would now say, we 'the dreamers', have become our own authorities.

Using another example of a contemporary analyst influenced by Kohut's work on the self, Fosshage (1988) sees dreams in terms of their function in organizing ideas and balancing feelings. For him, dreams directly reveal, through affects, metaphors and themes the dreamer's immediate concerns. In this way images are chosen for their *evocative* power. Dreams are a way of thinking; they are thoughts in images working on the issue or problem one is struggling with at that moment in their life.

Similar to this line of thinking of the evocativeness of dreams Blechner (2001), an Interpersonal analyst, believes that the very essence of a dream is a kind of meaning that doesn't have to be communicated verbally. He writes, "In my view, dreams allow us to express literally unspeakable thoughts, thoughts that cannot be expressed in words because we do not have the words to say them." (p. 25) Blechner sees Sandor Ferenczi, a contemporary of Freud's who experimented with mutual analysis with one of his patients, as the first person to suggest that a patient's dream could illuminate what the analyst is feeling. Blechner furthers this idea by suggesting that patients are unconsciously communicating thoughts and feelings about their analyst and directed to the analyst in their dreams, a kind of supervision of the analyst. These may be thoughts the patient cannot directly say to the analyst about mistakes, flaws or even appreciation of the analytic work.

Bromberg (2006) sees the analytic function regarding dreams slightly differently: "When a patient brings in a dream, the analytic task is to enable him to bring in the dreamer." (p. 38) He sees dreams as quite like dissociated self- states and works with dreams in an experience near way. He wants to allow for the possibility of the dreamer to enter the dream, as in Winnicott's (1951) notion of a transitional space, in an affectively alive way, while at the same time making it safe to begin to inhabit feelings and affects that have been too overwhelming for the person to symbolize in language. The dream presents them as dissociated aspects of self, alternate self-states with differing moods and affects that hold the possibility of being known by the waking self. The analyst, in Bromberg's sense, is helping the patient to self-authorize and develop a fluidity between self-states allowing for greater authenticity.

Many contemporary analysts would agree with the conception that there is a mutual process that occurs within the analytic work (See Aron, 1996). Given this, our own conception of analytic theory — and the use to make of it — has to shift as well. Aron (1998) believes that our analytic theoretical knowledge needs to provide simultaneously two paradoxical things. It needs to be able to provide the analyst with new ways of understanding the patient's material, be it dreams, associations or what occurs within the analytic relationship. But concurrently it also needs to organize and focus our thinking. He writes, "theory serves a paradoxical function: it both narrows and focuses, and it expands and opens options. To put the matter differently, I am suggesting that theory serves a self-organizing function for the analyst." (p. 208) I would expand this to include the patient's use of the analyst. One of the benefits of analysis is often the use of the analyst as simultaneously an object of transference or an old object which limits and focuses what the patient feels towards the analyst and a realization that the analyst is a new object who can expand what the patient feels is possible both for themselves and within a relationship. Both of these aspects suggest an organizing aspect of the relationship and a shifting relationship to knowledge.

Conclusion

Despite the clear differences between early Jewish writings on dreams and modern psychoanalytic conceptions of dreams and mind it is quite fascinating to see that the early Rabbis foreshadowed current Relational psychoanalytic ideas and controversies. The earliest debates concerning the authority of interpretation originated in rabbinic writings on textual analysis and dreams. Until Freud it was believed that dreams resulted from external forces, most specifically communication from God. Freud radically changed this view when he argued that dreams were the result of unconscious wishes, internal feelings that we are unaware of but operate nonetheless. Despite having moved the location of the origination of the dream from externally to internally generated, Freud still keeps authoritative knowledge external to the dreamer by placing it within the analyst or theory. The more contemporary analytic writers have moved the location of knowledge and authority regarding dream interpretation from the analyst, to the analytic dyad and even as far as positing that the patient may be a knowing authority of the analyst's unconscious. Contemporary analysis sees the goal of psychoanalysis as empowering the patient to become their own authority. I have attempted to trace this trajectory and elucidate the conflicting ideas. I don't know if we can ever land on one side or the other regarding fact based or relationship based authority. Perhaps we don't need to decide but accept that both are always in play. Not only are there multiple meanings to any dream, but multiple approaches to interpreting and making use of the dream material.

I return to my aqua sea ready to dive in and play. In my dream the image of the Technicolor water was pre-eminent. Not only was it everywhere as far as the horizon but the compelling quality of the color, the sereneness of the setting and the sense of peacefulness added to my sense of longing upon waking. In many ways these are primordial waters for me. My early family life is represented, my personal struggles, both psychological and physical, as well as my current challenges. The aqua water became a metaphor, a place of enormous possibility — swimming represented the challenge and the pail symbolized play. But what else is here? Can we ever definitively know what a dream means? How do we ever know what is truth and what is disguise? We, and here I mean both the moderns and the sages and Rabbis, are haunted by these questions and still continue to struggle with answers. I take one more dip into my dream sensing the refreshing and restoring warmth of the aqua sea over my entire body. I know that these are creative waters which, when found, offer me vistas and a sense of peacefulness while inventing challenges for me to meet.

REFERENCES

Almoli, Rabbi Shelomo (15th/16th cent./1998). *Dream Interpretation From Classical Jewish Sources*, translated by Yaakov Elman (1998). Hoboken: KTAV Publishing House, Inc.

Arlow, J. A. (1986). The relation of theories of pathogenesis to psychoanalytic therapy. In: *Psychoanalysis, the Science of Mental Conflict*, ed. A. D. Richards & M. S. Willick. Hillsdale, NJ: Analytic Press, pp. 49-63.

Aron, Lewis (1991). "The Patient's Experience of the Analyst's Subjectivity." *Psychoanalytic Dialogues*, 1:29-51.

----------. (1996). *A Meeting of Minds: Mutuality in Psychoanalysis*. Hillsdale, NJ: The Analytic Press.

----------. (1998). "Clinical Choices and the Theory of Psychoanalytic Technique:

Commentary on Papers by Mitchell and Davies." *Psychoanalytic Dialgues*: 8:207-216.

Benjamin, Jessica (2004). "Beyond Doer and Done to: An Intersubjective View of Thirdness." *The Psychoanalytic Quarterly*, 73:5-46.

Blechner, Mark (2001). *The Dream Frontier*. Hillsdale, NJ: The Analytic Press.

Brenner, Charles (1976). Psychoanalytic Technique and Psychic Conflict. New York: International University Press.

Bromberg, Philip (2006). *Awakening the Dreamer: Clinical journeys*. Mahwah, NJ and London: The Analytic Press.

Bollas, Christopher (1996). "Figures and Their Functions: On the Oedipal Structure of a Psychoanalysis." *The Psychoanalytic Quarterly*, 65, (1), 1-20.

Covitz, Joel (1990). Visions of the Night: A Study of Jewish Dream Interpretation. Boston & London: Shambhala.

Fosshage, James (1988). "The Organizing Functions of Dream Mentation." *Contemporary Psychoanalysis*, 33, 3:429-358.

Freud, Sigmund (1895). Studies on Hysteria. In: J. Strachey (Ed. & Trans.), *The standard edition of the complete psychological works of Sigmund Freud* (Vol. 2). London: Hogarth Press.

----------. (1900). The Interpretation of Dreams. In: J. Strachey (Ed. & Trans.), *The standard edition of the complete psychological works of Sigmund Freud* (Vol. 4 & 5). London: Hogarth Press.

----------. (1954). *The Origins of Psycho-Analysis: Letters to Wilhelm Fliess, Drafts and Notes: 1887-1902*. Edited by Marie Bonaparte, Anna Freud and Ernst Kris. New York: Basic Books.

----------. (1896). *The Complete Letters of Sigmund Freud to Wilhelm Fliess: 1887-1904*. Edited by J. M. Masson. Cambridge, MA: Belknap Press, Harvard University Press.

Frieden, Ken (1990). *Freud's Dream of Interpretation*. Albany, NY: State University of New York Press.

Friedman, Lawrence (1996). "Overview: Knowledge and Authority in the Psychoanalytic Relationship." *The Psychoanalytic Quarterly*, 65, (1): 254-265.

Fromm, Erich (1951). *The Forgotten Language: An Introduction to the Understanding of Dreams, Fairy Tales and Myths*. New York: Grove Press.

Glover, E. (1931). "The Therapeutic Effect of inexact Interpretation: A contribution to the Theory of suggestion." *International Journal of Psycho-Analysis*, 12:397-411.

Greenberg, Jay (1999). "Analytic Authority and Analytic Restraint." *Contemporary Psychoanalysis*, 35, (1), 25-41.

Harris, Monford (1994). *Studies in Jewish Dream Interpretation*. Northvale, New Jersey and London: Jason Aronson Inc.

Hoffman, Irwin (1996). "The Intimate and Ironic Authority of the Psychoanalyst's Presence. *The Psychoanalytic Quarterly*, 65:102-136.

Mitchell, Stephen (1997). *Influence and Autonomy in Psychoanalysis*. Hillsdale, New Jersey and London: The Analytic Press.

----------. (1998). "The Analyst's Knowledge and Authority." *The Psychoanalytic Quarterly*, 67:1-31.

----------. (1999). "Attachment Theory and the Psychoanalytic Tradition: Reflections on Human Relationality." *Psychoanalytic Dialogues*, 9:85-107.

Ogden, Thomas (1994). *Subjects of Analysis*. Northvale, NJ: Aronson.

Phillips, Adam (1995). *Terrors and Experts*. London: Faber & Faber.

Renik, Owen (1993). "Analytic Interaction: Conceptualizing Technique in the Light of the Analyst's Irreducible Subjectivity." *The Psychoanalytic Quarterly*, 62:553-571.

Rubin, J.B. (1996). "Psychoanalysis is Self-Centered." *Journal of the American Academy of Psychoanalysis*, 24:633-648.

Salberg, Jill (2007). "Hidden in Plain Sight: Freud's Jewish Identity Revisited." *Psychoanalytic Dialogues*, 17:197-217.

Winnicott, D. W. (1951). Transitional objects and transitional phenomena. In: *Playing and Reality*. New York: Basic Books, 1971.

Holding the Mourner: Jewish Ritual through a Psychoanalytic Lens

Joyce Slochower

*In memory of my father, Harry Slochower
and my mother, Muriel Zimmerman
and with gratitude to Minyan M'at, Sharon Penkower Kaplan,
and my children, Jesse, Alison and Avi*

This essay addresses the potential presence of therapeutic factors in a non-analytic setting. It first took shape when I sat *shiva* for my father and discovered its therapeutic power. When my mother died more than a decade later, I was again surprised by the power of Jewish mourning ritual in helping me live through and gradually integrate her loss. Those two experiences come together in this essay.

Filtering these experiences through the lens of my psychoanalytic sensibility, I have formulated an understanding of their therapeutic function that organizes around the role of affective resonance and illusion. This theme, variously described, is most commonly subsumed under the psychoanalytic concept of "holding." Holding here has a meaning that goes well beyond what meets the eye, and in order to explicate its many dimensions, I take a brief detour into its history before considering how *shiva* ritual reflects this theme.

105

The Winnicottian Vision

Early psychoanalytic thinkers (especially Freud and Klein) emphasized the power of sexual and aggressive drives in development with an emphasis on the oedipal period. The baby's drives were either met or frustrated; parental care was assumed to balance (i.e. gratify and frustrate), more or less effectively, the press of these internally derived drives. The (paternal) analyst aimed to explicate the patient's unconscious conflicts, studying free associations and offering interpretations aimed at deepened insight. The analyst was believed to remain more or less "outside" the emotional fray of back and forth interaction with the patient. If the analyst were to have a strong counter-transference response to a patient, she should analyze it privately in order to return to a stance of neutrality and objectivity.[1]

A strikingly different perspective on both child development and psychoanalysis took shape among British Object Relations theorists beginning in the late 1940's. Winnicott (1958; 1965; 1971) and his colleagues made a passionate case for an alternate psychoanalytic sensibility. Rejecting the presumption that early development is primarily drive derived and that parental impact can be understood in these terms, they turned instead to the pre-Oedipal period, arguing persuasively for the centrality of need over that of desire. The baby has basic needs that, if unmet, will result not in frustration or fixation but instead in the break-up of a sense of inner continuity, which Winnicott called "going on being." Development proceeds relatively smoothly only when the mother holds the infant "well enough;" during the earliest months, frustration is assimilated simply as failure and is not ego strengthening but disorganizing. Only later will the infant be able to absorb and react non-traumatically to the experience of being failed ("dropped").

Winnicott emphasized the 'actual' mother's capacity to protect the infant from disruptive environmental impingements while sidelining

---

[1]   Throughout this essay, I use the pronoun "she" to refer equally to male and female individuals.

the power of the drives. The metaphor of holding describes both actual physical holding and symbolic holding — the protective (maternal) function. This now familiar view of the mother's role had a powerful effect on the psychoanalytic world and through it, an entirely different metaphor of the analytic function gradually coalesced. Vulnerable patients, like infants, require holding within a safe, non-impinging setting in order to work through early trauma and access "true self" experience. The analyst's job with these patients is to minimize disruptions while remaining emotionally resonant, present, parental.

The Winnicottian role, then, was less to interpret than to symbolically provide. Within this protected setting, the capacity to contact and elaborate on affective memory and experience would be deepened. Early trauma could be re-contacted and worked through, allowing the patient to move beyond the "frozen failure situation." These ideas represented a ground-breaking departure from the paternal metaphors that dominated early psychoanalytic thinking. If the analyst symbolically can become the mother, the possibility of reworking early trauma is enormously increased; what cannot be remembered can be re-experienced and then repaired; the patient can, in fact, be a baby again, but with a better, more responsive mother.

The analytic holding function is a complex but idealized one. Unlike more active interpretive or confrontational work which involves communicating understanding to the patient, holding requires that the analyst attempt to contain her understanding, sometimes for long periods. This therapeutic vision also assumes that the analyst has the ability and willingness to remain emotionally present in the face of a wide range of difficult emotional states. Multiple metaphors have been invoked to describe this therapeutic capacity: Providing an environmental mediator (Spitz, 1956), background of safety (Sandler, 1960), extra-uterine matrix (Mahler, 1968), basic unit (Little, 1981), protective shield (Khan, 1963), emotional container (Bion, 1962; 1963) and transformational object (Bollas, 1987). Central to all is the analyst's capacity for containment wherein counter-transference is managed internally and not expressed directly or via interpretation.

But the concept of psychoanalytic holding did not remain unchallenged for long. Beginning in the 1970's, feminist and American relational thinking emerged on the theoretical scene, critiquing this idealized vision of analyst as nurturing maternal object. Feminists (e.g. Bassin et al, 1994; Benjamin, 1988; Chodorow, 1978) reminded us that even mothers are incapable of anything close to perfect affective responsiveness. They argued persuasively for the inclusion of non-resonant maternal subjectivity in our construction of motherhood. Psychoanalytic writers (including Mitchell, 1988; Aron, 1991; Tansey, 1992, Burke, 1992 and others) picked up this theme and applied it to the treatment situation. The essential problem was this: If maternal subjectivity is ubiquitous, often at odds with the baby's emotional needs in ways that interfere with her holding capacity, how can the analyst, less connected to her patient than the mother is to her baby, possibly sustain this level of therapeutic responsivity or consistently set her separate experience aside (Kraemer, 1996)? How can she empty herself of herself?

A collision gradually took shape between the vision of a maternal (psychoanalytic) environment and one grounded in the actuality of analytic (and feminist) subjectivity. Increasingly, contemporary psychoanalytic theorists rejected the Winnicottian ideal as infantilizing of the patient and illusory in its depiction of therapeutic capacity. Very much influenced by these two opposing schools of thought, I (Slochower, 1991; 1996a; 1996b; 1999; 2005; 2006a; 2006b) attempted to address and resolve this apparent collision of ideas by reformulating the notion of holding within a relational framework. Affirming the ubiquity of the analyst's subjectivity in the treatment relationship, I revised the therapeutic shape of holding by considering how it is experienced by both patient *and* analyst. I rejected the assumption that the analyst can sustain an emotionally resonant stance by fully containing her subjectivity and simply "being there" for the patient. By including the analyst's subjectivity within the treatment matrix, I shifted the notion of holding away from an idealized one-person model toward a relational (two person) one.

During moments of holding, the analyst "brackets" her subjectivity. By bracketing, I allude to a therapeutic position that simultaneously includes the analyst's struggle to contain her separate (and often disjunctive) experience while underscoring the patient's need, at certain times, for a space within which her affect state is accepted more than challenged. But the analyst doesn't bracket alone: the patient participates in sustaining the holding experience by bracketing particularly disturbing aspects of the analyst's separateness. In this sense, holding is co-constructed by the dyad.

Where Winnicott considered holding to be a necessary treatment technique only for very vulnerable regressed patients, I extended its scope by suggesting that holding is ubiquitous (though not always central) in the treatment of a wide range of difficult emotional states *other* than dependence. Holding emerges as figure rather than ground at those times when the reality of the analyst's separate subjectivity *consistently disrupts* inner process and cannot be worked with or worked through. These disruptions can occur when patients are flooded with intense affects like hate, envy and self involvement, all states that evoke anything *but* a maternal response in the analyst. At these moments, the patient's emotional need collides with (i.e., feels highly emotionally disjunctive, or 'out of sync') with the therapist's separate affect state.

> *Whatever its affective ambience*, holding involves the mutual establishment, by patient and analyst, of a temporary *illusion of analytic attunement*. The analyst *seems to* remain evenly and consistently present, intact, and available to the patient. While the analyst *may* represent a maternal, nurturing figure, it is also possible that an illusion of attunement will organize around the patient's experience of the analyst as non-retaliatory, alive and firm, consistently able to recognize and tolerate her patient's intense and toxic affect states (Slochower, 2005, p. 35).

Holding and *Shiva*

I have experienced both sides of the holding process, as patient and as analyst. I know something about its therapeutic potential from my own treatment and also about the feeling of strain that can accompany my struggle as analyst to sustain a holding position in work with difficult patients. But holding is essentially a metaphor that psychoanalysis has borrowed from life. The human need for the illusion of (parental) attunement is ubiquitous, taking a variety of forms that reflect individual need as well as socio-cultural idiosyncrasies.

Because I came to conservative Judaism in adulthood, I knew little about *shiva* ritual from the inside; in fact, it was not until my own father died that I experienced these rituals first hand. I did, however, know enough to dread sitting *shiva*. I wanted to be alone with my family and closest friends and did not welcome the prospect of an onslaught of visitors or the awkwardness of *shiva* ritual. Yet to my surprise, I was profoundly moved by nearly every detail of the *shiva* experience. To have people — some of whom I did not even know — come just to be with me, to listen more than talk while they tolerated my tears, reminiscences, self reproaches and even my (not always so funny) jokes, was extraordinarily moving and felt deeply healing.

It was some time after *shiva*'s end that I realized that I had felt held in ways strikingly reminiscent of the psychoanalytic holding environment. I began to think about how most of the very detailed laws and traditions of Jewish mourning represent both a culturally derived pre-psychoanalytic therapeutic response to the bereaved individual, and an intuitive understanding of *shiva*'s emotional impact on the community. That understanding extends beyond the mourner's obvious need for nurturance and support, and reflects the paradoxical aspects of intimacy and strain inherent in the analytic interchange (Winnicott, 1971; Modell, 1990). Following a brief review of the mourning process and the traditions of *shiva*, I address the impact of *shiva* on both mourner and caller as it mirrors the complex dynamics of holding within a relational psychoanalytic model.

Loss and Mourning

The death of a loved one is always a profound and wrenching experience. Such loss, whether expected or not, whether dreaded or wished for, contains a traumatic element. This is, of course, especially so when the loss is of a central and irreplaceable relationship. Grief creates a state of psychic aloneness and intensifies our need for connectedness. On one level, our personal relationship with the deceased is profoundly different from anyone else's; on another, we may feel deeply linked both to others who share the loss and more broadly, to those who have known grief at another time.

The psychoanalytic literature has normalized the complexity of the mourning experience, making room for the enormous individual variation in its shape and depth (see Siggins, 1966, for a review of this literature). Immediately following a death, the mourner is often in shock — flooded by painful feelings and memories, grief and helpless. A sense of despair, a desire to withdraw from the world, are common reactions. The mourner may reject offers of comfort *or* turn to others with appeals for help, literal or symbolic. Psychoanalytic theorists note that anger is a normal part of the mourning process, and may be directed toward the deceased, who is sometimes unconsciously reproached for having abandoned the bereaved.

The dynamics of mourning are often likened to depressive process. Freud (1917) described mourning as a "normal" variant of depression. Loss triggers painful feelings of dejection and results in a temporary absence of interest in the outside world, a diminished capacity to love and an inability to engage in everyday activities. Freud believed that mourning allowed the individual's emotional attachment (libido) to slowly and painfully detach from the lost loved one. Klein (1975) underlined the inevitable guilt and fear of retaliation following such loss.

> The poignancy of the actual loss of a loved person is … greatly increased by the mourner's unconscious phantasies of having lost his internal 'good' objects as well. He then feels that his internal 'bad' objects predominate and his inner world is in danger of disruption… Fears of being robbed and punished by both dreaded parents — that is to say, feelings of persecution — have also been revived in deep layers of the mind … I should say that in mourning the subject goes through a modified and transitory manic-depressive state and overcomes it (1975, p. 353).

111

Other early psychoanalytic writers (e.g. Abraham, 1924; Bibring, 1953 and Jacobson, 1957) linked normal mourning to neurotic depression by emphasizing the mourner's experience of lowered self-esteem and her struggle with ambivalence toward the deceased. Later writers believed that rather than detaching emotionally from the deceased, the mourner deals with the pain of loss by introjecting the relationship, allowing it inner, if not actual psychic continuity.

To some extent, then, the mourner may contend with feelings of abandonment, grief, guilt, hatred and self-hate, even feelings of triumph over the dead person. Avoidance is also part of mourning, as the mourner attempts to sidestep its inevitable pain. Of course, the intensity of an individual's mourning will depend on the nature of the mourner's relationship to the deceased, the relative emotional health of the mourner, and the circumstances of the death. The affective tone of the mourning process will be shaped by the relative presence of feelings of abandonment, relief, guilt, rage, etc. In mourning as in depression, the mourner may need to resolve guilt feelings toward the deceased and perhaps a sense of responsibility for the death. Winnicott (1958) understood the source of these feelings to be the destructive wishes that inevitably accompany loving.

Death in Jewish Tradition

All cultures recognize the mourner's need to express respect for the dead person and grief at the loss (see Mandelbaum, 1959, for a discussion of the social function of funeral rites in some other societies). But psychoanalysts do not often explore the dynamic function of these kinds of religious rituals because of the heavy ideology with which they are laden. Mourning ritual carries specific beliefs about the meaning of death, the relationship to the dead, and the location of the dead vis-à-vis the living (see Ashenburg, 2002 for a discussion of mourning ritual across history and culture).

Some aspects of Jewish laws and traditions pertaining to death and *shiva* have their origins in the Biblical period (cf. Gen. 50:15; Lev. 10:20;

Amos 8:10); many were developed during the Rabbinic period (Kraemer, 2000). These laws are most complex; they address not only the mourner's and community's behavior during the week of *shiva*, but from the moment of death and for up to eleven months after burial. Only a broad outline of these customs will be described here. (See Lamm, 1988, for a full and detailed discussion of the laws of Jewish mourning and references to relevant texts).

It is mainly within religious Jewish communities that the laws of mourning are scrupulously observed. Although secular Jews have incorporated some aspects of *shiva* ritual into mourning observance, these rituals are often followed in a truncated or perfunctory way. This should not be particularly surprising. Death continues to be a subject that is treated gingerly by contemporary culture, very much reinforcing our natural discomfort with facing such pain. It often seems easier to simply get on with life and relegate traditional mourning observance to an earlier time and social structure. The mourner may view as excessively restrictive and time consuming the requirement to set aside a full 7 days during which to withdraw from the world and face the loss, particularly when the emotional function of *shiva* seems obscure or foreign.

Jewish tradition describes five stages of mourning, each with its own laws and customs. It should be noted that one sits *shiva* only for parents, siblings, children, and spouse. These relationships are deemed the most central and least replaceable in life, and thus deserving of a formal mourning. The first stage of mourning (*aninut*) begins with death and lasts until burial. The mourner's loss is first concretized in the custom of *keriah*. Either at the moment of death or at the funeral, a tear is made in the mourner's outer garment, which is worn throughout the week of *shiva*. This dramatic act of ripping reenacts the mourner's torn state and represents a symbolic separation from the world, a separation that is reinforced in multiple ways across the *shiva* week.

Most of the laws concerning this period involve honoring the deceased. From the moment of death, the body is watched (guarded), and shortly before burial it is bathed, dressed, and placed in a casket, sometimes by members of the mourner's own community. Burial itself is designed in such a way that its impact is stark; an unadorned wooden casket (or, in Israel, a shroud without a casket) is used; at the cemetery the coffin or shroud is covered with earth by the mourner(s), members of the mourner's family and by the community. During this phase, all social amenities as well as most positive religious requirements (i.e. laws pertaining to religious acts of ritual observance such as reciting prayers) are suspended. Every attempt is made to shorten this period by arranging that burial take place as soon as possible so that mourning itself can begin. This is considered both respectful of the deceased and in the best interests of the mourner.

Shiva formally begins when the mourner returns home from the cemetery. The mourner washes her hands prior to entering the home (this symbolizes a cleansing following contact with death). Mirrors (traditionally associated with vanity) are covered. A symbolic meal of condolence is traditionally provided by the community, not by the mourner, and includes foods associated with life, such as bread and hard-boiled eggs. A memorial (yahrzeit) candle is lit; it will burn for the shiva period.

Ordinarily, shiva lasts for seven days but excludes Shabbat, which the mourner, with the community, is expected to observe. During the week of shiva, the mourner ordinarily remains at home (but may travel to the shiva house if she cannot reside there). The laws of shiva dramatically disrupt ordinary social behavior for both mourner and visitor. These disruptions are both awkward and, I believe, therapeutically central. They establish powerful barriers against superficial social interchange and prescribe behaviors that 1) symbolically express the mourner's state of grief and 2) symbolically separate the mourner from the community. For example, the mourner wears the same (torn) garment and does not wear leather shoes (traditionally associated with comfort and vanity).[2] The study of Torah is forbidden as such study is believed to bring joy. The mourner refrains from shaving, using cosmetics, cutting hair, or engaging in sexual relations. She doesn't bathe (though

---

[2] Actually, these prohibitions originally involved wearing shoes of any kind, and sitting anywhere other than the floor. The ancient mourner was thus placed in close emotional and literal proximity to the deceased (Tractate Semachot, 6:1).

exceptions are made for those who find this restriction very difficult). The mourner is free to walk, stand, lie, or sit, but only on a low stool or chair.[3]

Throughout the week of shiva, the mourner's basic physical needs are attended to by others; traditionally the community provides food for the mourner, who is forbidden to serve others or engage in household tasks. Whenever possible, prayer services are held in the home, allowing the mourner to say *kaddish* there. Thus, the mourner is freed from all social obligations and invited into a space that provides few distractions from the actual process of mourning.

Visitors to the mourner operate under similarly unusual rules. A *shiva* call (visit) is considered its own good deed and obligation *(mitzvah)*. In traditional settings such calls are paid by most of the mourner's community, whether or not they were personally involved with the deceased or with the mourner. Callers generally come unannounced at any time during the day or evening; thus, for much of the day, the mourner is not alone, but in the presence of others whose sole purpose is to provide comfort.

The mourner is not expected to rise, greet or otherwise entertain the caller. In fact, callers are not supposed to greet the mourner but rather to wait for the mourner to speak. By creating space for the mourner to use as she sees fit, the caller provides an opportunity (but not a requirement) for the mourner to speak about the loss, share memories of the deceased, or avoid the subject of loss altogether. At different times the mourner may be engaged in conversation of more or less emotional depth or may simply sit silently with the caller(s).

There is perhaps no form of *shiva* more powerful than when a silent mourner is allowed to remain so in a roomful of silent visitors. It requires that the caller contain the anxiety and social awkwardness of such moments and allow the mourner simply to remain in her own private space while acting as a witness. This process bears a striking parallel to the therapeutic function created by the analyst's capacity to remain present as the patient elaborates on interior experience (Slochower, 1999).

---

[3] Contrary to popular belief the chair need not be hard or uncomfortable. Instead, this low seat symbolizes the mourner's lowered emotional state.

The caller, who is not expected to stay long, does not say good-bye, and, instead, utters a traditional phrase, "May God comfort you among the mourners of Zion and Jerusalem." Others make statements like "may we only meet at happy occasions *(simchas)*," emphasizing the profound disruption that death has caused while also alluding to the possibility that life will again bring joy. The mourner does not respond to the caller's statement with a farewell greeting and remains seated, i.e., remains the mourner and resists the pull to enter into the role of host.

On the morning of the seventh day, the mourner is traditionally escorted on a short walk, a symbolic re-entry into the world outside the home. At this point, the mourner "gets up" from *shiva* and resumes daily life in most respects; however, during the subsequent thirty days, *(shloshim)* certain activities (such as attending parties, concerts, etc.) designed to bring joy are curtailed or avoided altogether. Many male mourners also refrain from shaving throughout *shloshim*. This represents a most powerful and visible expression of the mourner's state of bereavement. And in the instance of a parent's death (a loss lacking the possibility of even partial replacement), for a full eleven months, many male mourners (and increasingly, female mourners as well), continue to concretely acknowledge their loss by saying *kaddish* in synagogue daily and also limiting social activities and participation in festivities.[4]

The Psychological Function of *Shiva*

The laws of *shiva* are most complex; I have detailed only their broadest outline here. Although I have some ideas about the psychic impact of this process, it is important to note that because *shiva* occurs within a social

---

[4] It should be noted that the custom of reciting the Mourner's *Kaddish* daily is, as with all public prayer, viewed as an obligation incumbent only on men within the orthodox tradition. In recent years, however, many women have taken on this ritual in both more and less traditional communities. The recitation of *Kaddish* during the 11 months after a death can represent a powerful symbol of the mourning process that continues, even as the mourner progressively returns to everyday activities. If the female mourner feels deprived of this opportunity, her own mourning process may be truncated.

rather than an analytic context, its psychological impact on the individual mourner is to some extent impenetrable. Certainly, my own response to each *shiva* was highly subjective, colored by my relationship with my parent and my idiosyncratic response to these traditions. Despite these caveats, I believe that useful inferences can be made concerning the therapeutic impact of *shiva* rituals.

From the moment of each parent's death, I felt both profoundly alone and aware of the protective function of my community. As my family and I dealt with arrangements at the funeral home, I was moved to tears by the sight of a synagogue member with whom I was only slightly friendly acting as "*shomer*" — watching over my father's body until the actual burial. At my mother's funeral, especially dear friends prepared the body. Knowing that their caring hands had bathed and readied her body for burial transformed a traumatic process into one of comfort, wherein I felt not utterly alone but symbolically protected by others who were not themselves grieving but who were aware of my grief. At the cemetery, I stood among my children and dearest friends as the burial service was directed by someone I knew cared about me.

There was something both raw and compelling as the unprettified pine casket was covered with earth by my family and friends, who encouraged me to take as long as I needed filling in the grave (and ignored the funeral director's pressure to finish up). The possibility of denying death was absent and its shock was intense. I then returned home to find a meal laid out for me and my family. Having anticipated that I would not want food, I was moved to tears by the beautifully prepared meal (one of many to follow) that had been left for me — to eat or not as I chose. It was provision without expectation of acknowledgement — a symbolic holding.

As I remained at home for the week, I continued to be the recipient of this kind of holding. I was both protected from and deprived of the external distractions that might be viewed as relieving the pain of loss; I neither worked, nor shopped, cooked for myself or my family, etc. Yet I was far from alone; a stream of *shiva* callers appeared who set aside their own concerns and allowed me to talk about my father (and later, my mother) when I needed to, and about other things when I did not. They

117

came and left unrequested and thus freed me from the burden of having to ask for company that I did not always know I needed; at the same time, they made it possible for me to retreat in privacy when I wished to do so.

Some *shiva* callers were close friends or relatives; many were more casual acquaintances. I was surprised to find myself deeply moved by a stranger's visit — the mother of a friend of my eldest son's — who came, sat, and when I looked inquiringly at her, identified herself and said no more. She, like most of those who paid *shiva* calls, made it possible for me to talk, to stay with the feelings of loss as long as I needed to. They rarely interrupted me to share similar experiences of their own; they never changed the subject. Their farewell greeting offered the comfort of community ("May God comfort you among the mourners …") as did the silent hugs, and even the awkward apologies of those unable to recite the somehow difficult phrase. Intention mattered more than form.

Together, these farewells reconnected me to my living family, reminding me that I was not alone in the experience of loss. We would all suffer painful losses, but we would also celebrate together at bar and bat mitzvahs, weddings, the arrival of new babies. Hope was affirmed but not used to negate pain. I emerged from this very intense week of remembering exhausted but relieved. My recovery did not end there, but was steady, supported in part by my engagement with other post-*shiva* rituals of memorialization (Slochower, 2006b) and the love of family and friends.

Taken together, *shiva* ritual interferes with the denial of death. Grief (whether felt or unfelt at any moment) is multiply embodied: the mourner's shoes, clothing, lowered chair, unadorned skin, etc., underscore her state of mourning and interfere with the possibility of "putting on a face" (false self) to the world. Yet very little was expected of the mourner: I received callers' visits and farewells in silence. Although I found this prohibition to be awkward, it had a profoundly therapeutic impact. The custom requiring that the caller wait for me to speak first, strikingly akin to the opening of a therapy session, placed the affective tone and content of the conversation in my hands and made it harder for any of us to escape into social convention.

It is not only the mourner who is forced to face death during *shiva*. The caller is also confronted with her own experienced or anticipated losses. Yet within the *shiva* setting, there is little room for her. Instead, the *shiva* caller is expected to temporarily set aside personal concerns, troubles and joys, and discomfort about the *shiva* call itself, in order to provide a space for the mourner. This emotionally protective setting is remarkably reminiscent of the therapeutic holding environment (Winnicott, 1964). But during *shiva*, it is the community of callers rather than a single individual, that supports this process. Like the parent or analyst whose protective presence permits a sense of "going on being," the *shiva* caller acts as a witness for the mourner but tries not to intrude on the mourner's experience with her own agenda, allowing the mourner to be the single subject in the mourning context. Within this space, the mourner is free to experience and express a wide range of emotional states without attending to the reactions or needs of the caller. The mourner is, in a sense, permitted to use people within the community without regard for their own needs (i.e. ruthlessly).

The repeated expression of intense and painful feelings of loss may provide the deeply grieving mourner with a non-regressive opportunity (Modell, 1988) to work through painful feelings in the presence of the (m)other (Winnicott, 1958) who acts as witness but usually not as a participating subject. Like other therapeutic experiences, *shiva* ritual permits the mourner to use people within that community "ruthlessly" (Winnicott, 1965; 1965c; 1971), for the mourner is not expected to be able to shift out of her own frame, i.e., to engage in mutuality (Aron, 1996; Benjamin, 1995).

Shiva in an Intersubjective Context

Even those who are familiar with *shiva* tradition frequently struggle with the obligation to pay such calls. It is far from easy to tolerate the tension and social awkwardness associated with death, to face the pain of a grieving other, and to encounter what may be an unfamiliar set of people and traditions. To enter a *shiva* house and not to greet anyone, to sit in silence (often among a group of strangers) waiting to be acknowledged, can be an intensely uncomfortable experience. It can leave the caller wanting to fade away, to leave as quickly as possible, even not to have come at all. To further complicate matters, the interpersonal nature of the *shiva* call means that the caller inevitably will be affected by variations in the mourner's own emotional state in a context that requires containment more than expressiveness.

The holding function of *shiva* thus exists in tension with the caller's own feelings. Yet, inevitably, the caller carries her personal relationship with the mourner as well as potential social anxieties or preoccupations that may be evoked by the experience of paying such a call. Even more than the mother or the analyst who attempts to hold the patient, the *shiva* caller exists as a subject in a situation that leaves little room for her separate needs. To the extent that the visitor has failed to assimilate her own feelings about death, *shiva* ritual confronts her with a range of difficult and un-metabolized affect states connected with anticipated deaths in her own life, or those that occurred long ago. But the visitor is expected *not* to express or enact those feelings in a way that would pull the mourner out of her own state of grief.

The *shiva* caller's struggle both to contain *and* use her own subjectivity will be shaped by the intersection and collision (Slochower, 2006) of the caller and mourner's feelings and personal styles. When the mourner's grief is palpable, for example, the caller is acutely confronted with the subject of loss. The caller may feel moved and caring of the mourner, intensely anxious, awkward or even burdened by the mourner's need. Differences between the mourner's feeling state, expressive style and that of the caller will alternately intensify or minimize felt pressure on the caller. In addition, the caller's memory (or anticipation) of her own losses may resonate or clash with the mourner's, leaving the caller more or less able to provide a holding function. If the caller chooses to share her own memories, however, the mourner may be left feeling deeply understood and held. At times, the caller's expressiveness may function as an affective interference (impingement), derailing the mourner's inner process much as the analyst's expression of her subjectivity can sometimes derail the patient.

I have suggested that analytic holding can be therapeutically essential in work around issues other than dependence. These include self involvment, ruthlessness, and rage. In a similar way, the holding function of *shiva* may be essential at precisely those times when the mourner seems *not* to be acutely grieving. For despite our focus on grief during *shiva*, mourners typically shift among a range of affect states and degrees of interpersonal relatedness across the *shiva* week. The need to defend against grief will at times appear as a flat focus on the self or on external or trivial matters, accompanied by an apparent disinterest in and imperviousness to the caller. The mourner may behave as if nothing is wrong, as if the *shiva* call were, in fact, a social visit. It can be difficult to remain emotionally available to a mourner who appears at best oblivious to the purpose of the caller's presence. The caller may feel emotionally obliterated, useless, or awkward. As the caller's sense of empathy atrophies, she may feel relief (at the absence of emotional pressure), bored, shut out, even judgmental of the mourner's apparent lack of grief. These reactions very much parallel the analyst's feelings in work with narcissistic patients (Modell, 1976). Yet *shiva* tradition requires that the caller remain with the mourner, and not demand that the mourner change, i. e. express real feelings.

A different set of emotional challenges emerge when the mourner's own feelings about the death are complex and involve guilt about past actions or inactions, feelings of hatred toward the dead person, etc. (cf. Klein, 1975). Here, the mourner is likely to experience expressions of concern ambivalently. The caller's caring can intensify the mourner's guilt about felt failures vis-à-vis the deceased or, alternatively, enrage the mourner by its inadequacy in the face of loss. The mourner may react to the caller with irritation or respond with anger or guilt to expressions of sympathy. In such a context, the caller, like the analyst working with an angry or self-blaming patient, contends with feeling unhelpful, unappreciated, or even hurtful to the mourner. The pull to withdraw out of annoyance or anxiety about the usefulness of the *shiva* call may be strong, colliding with the requirement to remain emotionally present for the mourner.

When the emotional experience of mourner and caller are resonant, the holding function of the *shiva* call will feel relatively organic to both parties.

When, however, the caller contends with the press of her own disjunctive subjective state, there is likely to be a stronger sense of tension between the press to hold and to express. The caller's capacity to sustain awareness of this double demand and to negotiate internally with herself will shape the degree to which she successfully provides a holding experience for the mourner.

Paradoxical Aspects of the *Shiva* Call

The analytic relationship is unlike anything else in ordinary social experience; it is both "real" and "unreal", requiring that analyst and patient tolerate paradox without challenging it edges. For example, the analyst's genuine caring for the patient exists in tension with the fact that she gets 'paid to care'. The therapeutic interplay between the two involves an ongoing mix of different levels of experience and reality within a transitional space (Winnicott, 1971; Modell, 1990; Pizer, 1992). If this space is to function therapeutically, both patient and analyst must be able to suspend disbelief and tolerate these contradictory dimensions without collapsing either the potential or limits of the analytic situation.

In similar ways, *shiva* creates an extra-ordinary social situation, a kind of transitional space characterized by paradox. For a limited and circumscribed time and in a fixed setting, the *shiva* caller functions in a highly specific, rather artificial way with a person temporarily in need. Within that context, the *shiva* caller provides a therapeutic presence for the mourner who is buffered from the pressures and distractions of the "real" world. Yet the caller, even more than the analyst, cannot possibly know what the mourner's internal world is like, and may not even be personally involved with the mourner. Like the analytic setting (which occurs in a fixed place and time), the boundary around the *shiva* experience is quite rigid and artificial. But unlike the analytic process, the conclusion of the *shiva* week marks the absolute end of the caller's responsibility toward the mourner. Like patient and analyst, the mourner and caller do not ordinarily challenge the meaningfulness of *shiva*. Instead, the mourner also brackets awareness of this reality, implicitly agreeing not to challenge the illusion of attunement characteristic of this transitional space and instead, to tolerate its ambiguities.

When *Shiva* Fails

Like any therapeutic process, *shiva* sometimes fails to provide a holding function because either the mourner or the community cannot tolerate the emotional strain inherent in the holding process. This is particularly likely when the mourner's community is unaware of or uncomfortable in following the *shiva* ritual. I vividly remember a *shiva* when those present (who were unfamiliar with these traditions) sat in strained silence interspersed with small talk and self-conscious political comments as they ate a meal provided by the family. The mourner's grief had no place in this context, and *shiva* provided no relief at all. Mourner and callers colluded to avoid addressing death and thus prevented the loss from being integrated. All too often, I have seen this happen even in observant contexts. When the caller, even if well versed in *shiva* ritual, is unable to tolerate its impact, she may use jokes or small talk to sideline the mourner's grief.

At other times, however, it is not the community's emotional limitations that fail the mourner, but instead the traditions of *shiva* themselves that fail to hold. *Shiva* observance is limited to four types of relationship (parent, spouse, sibling and child). It excludes loved ones who fall into different relationship categories and also excludes infants under 30 days of age.[5] Parents who have lost a newborn are left bereft of rituals with which to mourn this acutely traumatic loss, as are those who lose loved ones whose relationship falls outside a culturally prescribed role set.[6]

The holding function of shiva is also ritually interrupted by *Shabbat*. On that day (requiring communal observance), the mourner may leave the

---

[5] This is probably because high infant mortality rates in ancient cultures made this such a frequent event.

[6] Some individuals choose to voluntarily "take on" *shiva* observance when it is not mandated.

house and attend synagogue. This break in the intensity of mourning may be extremely difficult for the traumatized mourner, or alternatively, may be a relief. Shabbat may begin to draw the mourner back into life, much as a small disruption in holding can facilitate an integrative process in a patient.

More problematic are those instances when a death coincides with a major holiday (*Yom Tov*) that (depending on precisely when the actual mourning begins) cancels or postpones the *shiva* period. In these situations, the mourner's need to grieve is overridden by the community's need for ritual observance as well as by religious beliefs about the obligation to celebrate the holiday with joy. If this failure in adaptation to the mourner's needs was preceded by a period of good-enough holding, it may be strengthening rather than traumatic. But when *shiva* is cut off in its early stages or canceled altogether, it is likely that the mourner will be failed in a major way. It is only, perhaps, the most religious mourners who can suspend or bracket their grief because of the obligation to celebrate a religious holiday. More typically, holding fails here, and the mourner is left to cope with being dropped, left traumatically unprotected in ways that delay or prevent a full working through of the loss. I have worked with several patients who had this reaction to a death that was not marked by *shiva* observance, in contrast to their fuller mourning process where death was followed by *shiva*.

Protection of the Caller in *Shiva*

The laws of *shiva*, then are designed for the protection of the mourner and place considerable strain on the caller. It can be quite difficult for people who are not psychologically trained to tolerate the range of feelings evoked by a mourner. The laws of *shiva* do, however, take this vulnerability into account by protecting the *shiva* caller in ways similar to the protection provided the analyst by therapeutic parameters.

Shiva calls are short, ordinarily paid not more than once by any individual. Instead, the mourner's larger community takes on this obligation. The holding function thus falls lightly on its individual members and the community of callers, to some extent, hold each other. In some respects, the caller is provided the same protections inherent in the structured analytic hour. Although the caller allows the mourner to set the tone and content of the conversation, it is the caller, not the mourner, who sets the time of her call and of its termination, retaining, perhaps, the potential to express hatred in this way (Winnicott, 1949). In fact, it may be that the limits placed on the mourner's needs are actually what permit the community to tolerate the very great demand that is made of it during the period of *shiva* observance.

On the seventh day of *shiva*, the mourner must "get up," whether she is emotionally ready to or not, freeing the caller from further obligation. Because *shiva* is interrupted by *Shabbat* and cancelled by major holidays, the community's desire to remain involved in life, in joyous or religious events is reaffirmed, and this desire supersedes the needs of the individual mourner. Like the analyst who ends sessions and takes vacations despite the patient's need for treatment, *shiva* laws place the mourner's needs within a larger context — that of the community need.

It is, of course, not uncommon that the practice of *shiva* fails to hold the mourner, because either the mourner or the community cannot tolerate the discomfort it generates. Clearly, *shiva* cannot provide a holding experience in the absence of some degree of cohesive community, yet this is absent for too many. What is nevertheless compelling is the power of *shiva* ritual to meet an individual's temporarily intense need for a holding experience in its varied aspects while still protecting the larger group. These laws are in many ways a brilliant pre-psychoanalytic adaptation to universal human need, reflecting the capacity of society to temporarily hold its members while at the same time ensuring that the community remains a going concern.

REFERENCES

Abraham, K. (1924). A Short Study of the Development of the Libido: Viewed in the Light of Mental Disorders. In: *Selected Papers on Psychoanalysis* London: Hogarth.

Aron, L. (1991). The Patient's Experience of the Analyst's Subjectivity. *Psychoanal. Dial.*, 1:29-51.

----------. (1996). *A Meeting of Minds: Mutuality in Psychoanalysis*. Hillsdale, NJ: The Analytic Press.

Ashenberg, K. (2002). *The Mourner's Dance*. Toronto: Macfarlane Walter & Ross.

Balint, M. (1968). *The Basic Fault*. London: Tavistock.

Bassin, D., Honey, M. & Kaplan, M. M. (eds.) (1994). *Representations of Motherhood*. New Haven, CT: Yale Univ. Press.

Benjamin, J. (1988). *The Bonds of Love: Psychoanalysis, Feminism and the Problem of Domination*. New York: Pantheon.

----------. (1995). *Like Subjects, Love Objects*. New Haven, CT: Yale University Press.

Bibring, E. (1953). The Mechanism of Depression. In: P. Greenacre (ed.), *Affective Disorders*. New York: International Universities Press, pp. 14-48.

Bion, W. R. (1962). *Learning from Experience*. London: Heinemann.

----------. (1963). *Elements of Psycho-Analysis*. London: Heinemann.

Bollas, C. (1987). *The Shadow of the Object*. New York: Columbia University Press.

Bowlby, J. (1980). *Loss: Sadness and Depression*. New York: Basic Books.

Burke, W. F. (1992). Countertransference Disclosure and the Asymmetry/ Mutuality Dilemma. *Psychoanal. Dial.*, 2:241-271.

Chodorow, N. (1978). *The Reproduction of Mothering*. Berkeley: University of California Press.

Freud, S. (1917). Mourning and Melancholia. *Standard Edition*. 14 London: Hogarth.

Jacobson, E. (1957). Denial and Repression. *J. Am. Psychoanal. Assoc.* 5:61-92.

Khan, M. (1963). The Concept of Cumulative Trauma In: *The Privacy of the Self*. New York: International Universities Press, 1974, pp. 42-58.

Klein, M. (1975). *Love, Guilt and Reparation*. New York: Delta.

Kraemer, D. (2000). *Meanings of Death in Rabbinic Judaism*. London: Routedge.

Kraemer, S. (1996). "Betwixt the Dark and the Daylight" of Maternal Subjectivity: Meditations on the Threshold. *Psychoanal. Dial.*, 6:765-791.

Lamm, M. (1988). *The Jewish Way in Death and Mourning*. New York: Jonathan David.

Little, M. (1981). *Transference Neurosis and Transference Psychosis: Toward a Basic Unity*. New York: Jason Aronson.

Mahler, M. (1968). On Human Symbiosis and the Vicissitudes of Individuation. *J. Am. Psychoanal. Assoc.* 15:740-763.

Mandelbaum, D. G. (1959). Social Uses of Funeral Rites In: Feifel, H. (ed.) *The Meaning of Death*. New York: McGraw-Hill, pp. 189-217.

Mitchell, S. (1988). *Relational Concepts in Psychoanalysis*. Cambridge: Harvard University Press.

Modell, A. H. (1975). A Narcissistic Defense Against Affects and the Illusion of Self Sufficiency. *Int. J. Psychoanal.* 56:275-282.

--------. (1976). The Holding Environment and the Therapeutic Action of Psychoanalysis. *J. Am. Psychoanal. Assoc.* 24:285-307.

--------. (1988). The Centrality of the Psychoanalytic Setting and the Changing Aims of Treatment. *Psychoanal Q.*, 57:577-596.

--------. (1990). *Other Times, Other Realities: Toward a Theory of Psychoanalytic Treatment*. Cambridge: Harvard University Press.

Pizer, S. A. (1992). The Negotiation of Paradox in the Analytic Process. *Psychoanal. Dial.* 2:215-240.

Sandler, J. (1960). The Background of Safety. *Int. J. Psychoanal.* 41:352-356.

Siggins, L. D. (1966). Mourning: A Critical Survey of the Literature. *Int. J. Psychoanal.* 47:14-25.

Slochower, J. (1991). Variations in the analytic holding environment. *Int. J. Psychoanal.* 72:709-718.

127

----------. (1996a). *Holding and Psychoanalysis: A Relational Perspective.* Hillsdale, NJ: The Analytic Press.

----------. (1996b). Holding and the evolving maternal metaphor. *Psychoanal. Rev.,* 83: 195-218.

----------. (1999). Interior Experience in Analytic Process. *Psychoanal. Dial.,* 9: 789-809.

----------. (2005). Holding: Something Old and Something New. In: Aron, L., & Harris, A., (Eds.) *Relational Psychoanalysis,* Volume II. Hillsdale, NJ: The Analytic press, pp. 29-50.

----------. (2006a). *Psychoanalytic Collisions.* Hillsdale, NJ: Analytic Press.

----------. (2006b). Beyond the consulting room: Ritual, mourning and memory. In: R. Curtis (Ed.) *On Deaths and Endings.* New York: Routledge. Pp. 84-99.

Spitz, R. (1956). Countertransference. *J. Am. Psychoanal. Assoc.* 4:256-265.

Tansey, M. J. (1992). Psychoanalytic expertise. *Psychoanal. Dial.,* 2:305-316.

Winnicott, D. W. (1949). Hate in the Countertransference. *Int. J. Psychoanal.* 30:69-74.

----------. (1958). The Capacity to be Alone. In: *The Maturational Processes and the Facilitating Environment.* New York: International Universities Press.

----------. (1965). The Theory of the Parent-Infant Relationship. In: *The Maturational Processes and the Facilitating Environment.* New York: International Universities Press.

----------. (1971). *Playing and Reality.* New York: Basic Books.

Hearing "Thou Shall Not Kill" When All the Evidence is to the Contrary: Psychoanalysis, Enactment, and Jewish Ethics

David M. Goodman

> To recognize the Other is to recognize a hunger.
> To recognize the Other is to give.
>
> *Emmanuel Levinas*

Introduction

Looking over my client's chart, I read the same disturbing comments that many of these files had. "Sexually molested by grandfather." "Ritually beaten by his alcoholic father before the abandonment." "Mother in and out of jail — can't keep the needle out of her arm." "Major behavioral and emotional disturbance and difficult to manage." "Several psychotropic medications already administered by the age of 7, with minimal benefit."

After fourteen foster home placements, John[1] had finally been plopped into a residential treatment facility (at the age of 7). It was here that I met him in the special education classroom. He was bright, creative, moody, and energetic. About three months into his time in my classroom, we had several consecutive weeks of exciting progress. His math lessons were coming along with lightning speed. Also, his warmth and ability to

---

[1]   The name "John" is used to protect the confidentiality of the client.

connect were becoming more evident — he was starting to attach after a very rough start. He was beginning to tell the residential staff that I was his favorite.

One afternoon, I was kneeling next to John's desk working on a complicated math problem with him. As had become commonplace, he was elated at his ability to master the equation and would grin wildly at my encouragement. The moment came quickly, with no premeditation, no preparation, and no warning. As I looked down at his page to scribble a note, I felt a fist come across my face and heard the loud crack of his knuckle bones against my cheek bone. I felt a sharp pain and my eyes teared up immediately. Shock and anger exploded into my consciousness and my body flooded with powerful instinctual reactions. Protect self. Fight back.

What took place next remains seared into my mind. I looked up at John, his face a foot and a half away from mine. His chest was heaving, his eyes were filled with tears. But besides this, there was a look of desperate expectation. His eyes exclaimed, "Hit me! Push me! Shove me away! Hate me! I am truly intolerable, unlovable, and disgusting... I just proved it!"

This story is emblematic of particular types of encounters with clients in psychotherapy. Unlike young children, adults often cloak their fear, angst, and brokenness in more hidden and "sophisticated" forms. Years of socialization allow adults to find less obvious means of expressing their fears, repeating their pain, and reliving their pasts. However, in these moments, the message to the therapist is the same: "Thou *shall* commit murder."

The Jewish continental philosopher, Emmanuel Levinas, argued that the face of the Other exclaims the opposite command, "Thou shall *not* kill." But what if this command is buried so far beneath one's lived experience to the contrary that it is no longer recognizable? What if, instead, the face of the Other pulls for, tugs at, and screams out to be murdered, strangled, debased, and reduced? What if one's 'way of being' in the world knows nothing but the renunciation of life, worth, and love?

These movements in the relationship between the therapist and the client will be explored with Levinas as a guide. Based on his Lithuanian Jewish roots and complex philosophical system, Levinas makes clear the ethical context of relationships and I will extrapolate that ethic to therapy. From this frame, it is understood that the psychological violence of which the client is a victim becomes the responsibility of the therapist. I will map the complexity of this arrangement by considering the concept of enactment, a psychoanalytic notion that past and present violence endured by the client can become calcified into current relational patterns which lure others (including the therapist) into participating in this reductive violence. My thesis is that enactment needs an ethical frame. Psychoanalysts delineate the processes involved in enactment and merely assume an ethical response by the therapist. On the other hand, Levinas is most articulate about the ethical frame but less clear about the developmental and psychological processes involved in enactment. Conversation between the two might be fruitful. *First*, I will briefly explain the psychoanalytic concept of enactment. *Second*, I will explore the enactment process through Levinas' ethical lens, with particular emphasis upon inherent Jewish dimensions in his thought. Considering Levinas' concepts of radical responsibility, expiation, and surrender, I conclude by arguing that the therapist is uniquely situated to recognize and respond to the Other's commandment "Thou shalt not kill," allowing for an interruption of violence and the development of new and ethical relational possibilities.

Enactment in Psychological Perspective: Relationship and Repetition

Ultimately, Freud and Levinas agree that within the interhuman and intersubjective space — in the presence of an-other — time is curved upon itself. The present moment is not merely *now* nor the accumulation of the past. Rather, it is folded upon itself. It is the past alive in the present. It is the ancient in the new. Time is not a synchronic succession, but rather lapses upon itself, so that every moment is infused with the past as though it was present. Clearly, the impact of the intersubjective upon time and what is meant by the "past" mean very different things for Freud and Levinas. However, I suggest that a conversation between Levinasian thought and the psychoanalytic concept of enactment may provide a needed ethical enrichment of psychoanalytic language. The importance of developing an understanding of psychology as a "moral discourse" has been argued extensively elsewhere (Browning, 1987; Cushman, 1995; Richardson, Fowers, & Guignon, 1999; Rieff, 1987, 2006, Tauber, in press; Taylor, 1989).

For Freud, and the psychoanalytic tradition that followed in his wake, persons are understood to relate to others out of reminiscence of their past relationships. More specifically, past relations are transferred upon and re-lived within present relations. Thus, the present other is encountered as a repeated experience of a past attachment figure, or an amalgam of figures and experiences; this is called transference. Transference is not merely a cognitive phenomenon, it is an embodied and lived experience (Freud, 1914/1958). It is not a memory based on past experience, but rather a present interrupted and shaped by a lived remembering without memory — that is, the process is unconscious (Freud, 1914/1958; Ginot, 2007; Goodman & Grover, 2008). Freud (1914/1958) writes, "[W]e may say that the patient does not *remember* anything of what he has forgotten and repressed, but *acts* it out. He reproduces it not as a memory but as an action; he *repeats* it, without, of course, knowing that he is repeating it" (p. 150).

As the client acts out the past in the present relationship, the therapist finds him or herself activated and unconsciously responds out of his or her own relational past; this is called counter-transference. Ultimately, the combined effect of the transference and counter-transference is an "interplay" (Maroda, 1998, p. 517) that is referred to in psychoanalytic literature as *enactment*. Enactment is a concept that describes the *folding over* of the past upon the present within the inter-subjective space between the therapist and client. It is the unconscious dance of two psyches, a tug and pull of affective histories and unresolved traumas.

Enactment is not a monolithic term with a clear meaning in psychoanalysis. It has evolved and taken many shapes and forms (Aron, 2003; McLaughlin, 1991). Furthermore, there have been and are differing opinions in the psychoanalytic literature about the dangers and benefits of enactment (Chused, 1991; Gabbard, 1995). For some analysts, enactment is the very grist wherein transformation takes place. It provides access to lived patterns and inter-subjective space in a way that bears significant substance and meaning. At worst, enactment represents a re-traumatizing of the client wherein the therapist is not functioning out of intention or volition, but rather is "acting out" of his or her own elicited psychic material.

Thus described, it is hard to imagine that enactments can be considered therapeutic or good. However, some important contemporary psychoanalytic motifs need to be understood before making this determination. In a recent panel discussion, Nancy McWilliams (2008) explained that contemporary psychoanalysis *assumes* that therapists will wound their clients and that this is integral in the process of healing. Her point, in short, is that entering into the mire of lived relationship and the covert patterns repeated there inevitably leads to re-creating wounding experiences, to enactments (Aron, 2003; Gabbard, 1995; Hirsch, 1994; Maroda, 1998). Without this risk, therapy remains too buoyant and consciousness oriented. To encounter the client — the other before us — requires a level of exposure and proximity that precedes and violates intelligibility, active consciousness, and intentionality. Our controls, in this space, escape us (at least in part). Stephen Mitchell (1988) elaborates this point when he claims that

> Unless the analyst affectively enters the patient's relational matrix or, rather, discovers himself within — unless the analyst is in some sense charmed by the patient's entreaties, shaped by the patient's projections, antagonized and frustrated by the patient's defenses — the treatment is never fully engaged, and a certain depth within the analytic experience is lost. (p. 293)

In lived relationship, we engage one another a few steps apart from conscious reflection. Levinas mirrors this assertion when he writes, "Consciousness is always late for its meeting with the close other" (quoted in Smith, 2005, p. 229).

That both therapist and client live out of alluring patterns from their pasts is part of the process of therapeutic engagement. Maroda

(1998) provides helpful nuance when she reminds about the danger of "counter-transference dominance" in enactments (p. 522). She states that for enactments to be therapeutically useful, "In general, one can safely say that the goal should be that more of the patient's past be re-created than the analyst's, and even more important, that the patient have every opportunity to safely work through these events within the boundaries of the analytic relationship" (p. 530). Nonetheless, the therapist *is* a partner in enactment; he or she is an "enactor" (Hirsch, 1994). There has been a growing recognition that the analyst cannot remain a "blank slate" or uninvolved member of the dyad. Over the past couple of decades, conversations in relational schools of psychoanalysis have called for a "two person psychology" rather than the "one person psychology" that had preceded it (Aron, 1996). The inter-subjective space is understood to be jointly constructed.

Other than the sheer inevitability of enactment in lived relationship, what are its therapeutic benefits or possibilities? One answer to this question involves the belief that enactments provide an opportunity for communication beyond words and outside of signification. I will briefly address this point to set the stage for an engagement with Levinas' thought.

Enactments are moments of profound vulnerability for patients. They are engaged in an expression without exact words or clear symbolization; a sacred whisper of need. Without awareness, clients are welcoming the therapist into a space outside of the safety of the known. In these contexts, the client has little means of communicating except through "acting out" or eliciting an alteration in the relationship itself. Pulling for some patterned way of being/feeling is the only mode of expression that the client can access.

In this way, enactments are a kind of pre-verbal communication of a client's vulnerability and wounds. In therapy, the client "cannot escape from this compulsion to repeat; and in the end we understand that this is his way of remembering" (Freud, 1914/1958, p. 150). Clients "act out" (in the sense that Freud understood it) to communicate that which has not been formulated, processed, or placed into other modes of expression (Stern, 2003). Reductive transferential pulls are communications (Boesky, 1982, p. 46) that may be "impossible to communicate through verbal description" (Chused, 1991, p. 637). That is, they cannot be expressed directly. However, the unconscious and preverbal quality of an enactment does not minimize its felt reality for either patient or analyst. "During an enactment, the patient has a conviction about the accuracy of his perceptions *and* behaves so as to induce behavior in the analyst which supports his conviction" (Chused, 1991, p. 617). This can be done with words, gestures, a certain form of presence, or an absence (Gabbard, 1995; Ginot, 2007). It is an embodied expression that attends to both "word and deed" without dichotomizing them (Aron, 2003, p. 624).

Returning to John's story may illustrate this first point concerning the vulnerability in enactment. Upon being struck, without thinking, I wanted to kill, hurt, and yell. My automatic response was "natural" and based out of my own physiological reactivity and threat response. Immediately, I no longer wanted to work with John. I was ready to abandon our work together and abandon him. He had violated the most basic building block in our relationship: respect. My immediate desire was to push away and punish him for this violation. If he could not respect me, then I would abandon him. This seemed basic. However, why was there this emphasis upon "respect"? Is that merely a causal derivative of a natural self-protective process? There is much more behind this than appears at the surface. In terms of my own history, after my mother passed away from cancer when I was 16, my father abandoned me. The word "respect" or, more clearly, his need to feel respected was frequently his rationale for leaving. This was confusing and profoundly wounding as a well-behaved teenage boy. My dad's rigid, warped, and self-aggrandizing need for respect from his adolescent son, as the basic condition of love, remained a wound that carried with me into a variety of future relationships. Now, here it was again with John. However, this time I was the perpetrator. Just as I was abandoned around "respect," I was about to do the same to John. Without respect, my love for him was threatened. At a deep level, he had violated my conditions of love for him. He had successfully elicited one of my ongoing unconscious struggles and a complex vein in my convoluted history. Chronology and lived relationship at that present moment were pregnant with both of our pasts.

Complexly and simultaneously, my internal experience mirrored and paralleled John's emotional needs at that moment. This was his communication. He exposed his wounds by offering me a chance to become his abusive father, the absent mother, the invasive grandfather, and the inconsistent foster home care-takers. In order to remain within a world that was slightly predictable and tolerable, he needed to live out a repetition of what he had known (Boesky, 1982). Sameness is safe and works smoothly within the implicit grooves that we all readily live out. It is not that John wanted me to reject him and abuse him. In this case, it was John's unconscious means of protecting himself from the terror of something unknown: trust, connection, and love. We had become quite close and this was intolerable. Also, the enactment was his means of bringing me into his experience, his internal conflicts, and his relational history. It was the only way he knew how to share his past. It was, simultaneously, a means of expressing, remembering, and protecting. And, in this instance, his way of bringing me into his experience was by inciting my places of pain and pushing me beyond the functions of my consciousness.

In many ways, the therapist's psyche is borrowed by the client so that he or she can communicate and express broken processes, unconscious stuck points, and unformulated wounds (Stern, 2003). For wounded clients, suffering is lived in the raw, not subject to conscious or rational engagement alone. They play out and repeat painful interactions in current relationships. In this way, enactments serve as arrows pointing toward a previous place of murder: "Injustice took place, here!" But the "here," is confused, something lived both then and now and many times in between. In this way, enactments provide a venue for the expression of deep relational pain and are locations of profound vulnerability for clients. My next step is to place this clinical and theoretical issue in conversation with Levinas' Jewish ethics.

Enactment from a Jewish Ethical Perspective

> We are created by another's love and create
> ourselves by accepting the burden of this love
> and its obligations…Before philosophy, there is
> responsibility.
>
> *Rabbi Ira Stone*

Levinas and Jewish Ethics

Emmanuel Levinas is frequently referenced alongside of Franz Rosenzweig and Martin Buber as one of the most influential Jewish thinkers of the twentieth century (Putnam, 2008). His impact on Western philosophy, religious studies, and recent psychological theories and practices has been immense and continues to grow rapidly. In recent years, there has been a significant amount of interest in the interchange between Levinas and psychoanalytic theory, as evidenced by a special issue of *Psychoanalytic Review* in August 2007 and several books exploring the relation between Levinas' thought and contemporary psychoanalysis (Alford, 2002; Marcus, 2008).

Levinas was a Jewish, Lithuanian ethicist, continental philosopher, and Talmudic commentator whose primary concern was the phenomenological fabric within the ethical relation of the self and the Other (Goodman, 2009). Losing the majority of his family in the *Shoah* and spending five years of his life in a German prisoner camp (Malka, 2006), Levinas' trenchant critiques of his philosophy teachers — Husserl and Heidegger — bore a distinctive emphasis: radical ethics. Cohen (1994) paints a broad picture of the impact that the events of World War II had upon Levinas' subsequent thought. He stated,

> Then and henceforth Levinas would propound an ethical and dialogical metaphysics grounded in a careful phenomenological description of the human situation in both its individual and social moments. From the pain, horror, and confusion of political, social, and ethical upheavals on a scale unprecedented in European history, Levinas would forge a philosophy grounded in the highest demands of personal ethics and social justice. From the unparalleled extremity and incongruous juxtaposition of this historical and historic contrast of good and evil, war and peace, culture and

137

> barbarism, justice and injustice, Levinas created a philosophy infused with the highest moral teachings of Judaism. (p. 119)

Levinas critiqued Western philosophy for its ethical impoverishment and egoist accounts of human relation (Levinas, 1969). Ultimately, he called for "ethics as first philosophy," hoping to supplant the detached rationalities of Western thought with a radical recognition of the otherness of the Other and the inexhaustible responsibility that comes with this alterity (Levinas, 1985). His sources for this critique were distinctively Jewish.

Though Levinas' philosophical writings are categorized within the continental and phenomenological philosophical traditions, his emphasis upon ethics, goodness, and holiness are distinctively Jewish in shape. It is true that Levinas, himself, rejected the description of his work as Jewish philosophy or Jewish thinking. And, for a variety of reasons, Levinas "has been read as a philosopher, while the Jewish dimension of his thought has largely been ignored, or honored by a mention and then ignored" (Gibbs 1992, p. 10; see also Arnowicz, 1994; Cohen, 1994; Putnam, 2002; Tauber, 1998). However, many recent scholars have come to understand Levinas' resistance to these labels as a natural outgrowth of the context within which he was writing. For instance, Gibbs (1992) describes the anti-Semitic and post-religious intellectual atmosphere of France in Levinas' day. Also, Levinas' was wary of the way that philosophy was quickly discarded and de-legitimized when it was labeled as "theology" (Ford, 1996, 1999; Purcell, 2006). Jean Halperin explains this as well when he writes that Levinas

> wanted to be understood and perceived as a thinker, period. But he could not deny that his thinking, taken as a whole, was in reality often read as Jewish thinking. Because it was entirely inspired by this Jewish education, this ahavat Israel, this Jewish knowledge that he had always possessed. When you open *Totality and Infinity* or *Otherwise than Being* or *The Humanism of the Other*, you will find phrases or paragraphs without references and without footnotes, but which, while reading them, you can feel are fundamentally Jewish thoughts that are being presented by Levinas in his philosophical works. (as cited in Malka, 2002/2006, p. 139)

138

Cohen (1994) wrote, "Those who are familiar with the many layers and the long history of Jewish thought will see in Levinas's philosophy not only a thought in dialogue with the whole history of philosophy but a thought at the same time thoroughly consonant with many of Judaism's most significant beliefs and practices" (p. 122).

Levinas' frequent allusions to Scripture, placement of the Other's needs and vulnerability as primary, use of religious terminology (glory, expiation, substitution, Divine, transcendent, God, election, holiness, etc.), indebtedness to Rosenzweig, positioning of the self as *hineni* ("here I am"), and even his central argument concerning ethics as being more appropriately understood as holiness (Levinas, 2004) require his work to be understood from the Lithuanian Jewish context out of which it arose. Additionally, Levinas' concern to make the particularity of Jewish ethics a universal challenge to human persons emerges from a long tradition within Judaism that spans back to Philo (Cohen, 2003). This drive to universalize Judaism was a prominent feature of European Jewry. For Levinas, it was a critical project wherein justice might be restored to the world order. As such, there is a clear messianic eschatology throughout his texts (Gibbs, 1992; Lesser, 1996; Levinas, 1976/1990; Ward, 1996). Cohen (1994) writes, "His work shows, then, to what extent Jewish sources can be made vital to global 'Western' civilization" (p. 127). This lays the foundation for his translation work between Western philosophy and Jewish ethics.

Levinas' project, in short, was a conversation between his Hebraic thought and the dominant vein of Western philosophy (which is arguably Greek). Levinas understood his thought to be a translation of a biblical (or ethical) perspective into and through Greek thought and sensibilities (i.e., academy, sciences, Western philosophy) (Aronowicz, 1994; Cohen, 1994; Gibbs, 1992; Goodman, 2009; Putnam, 2002). That is, he described his work as a continuation of the Septuagint (Levinas, 1986; Stone, 1998). It is my hope that this translation project can be extended into contemporary psychoanalytic theories and practices. That is the impetus of this piece.

The possible implications of Levinas' thought upon psychoanalysis are manifold, despite the fact that Levinas' interaction with psychoanalytic theories was minimal and largely negative (Cohen, 2002; Hutchens, 2007). However, recent appropriators of Levinas' thought to psychoanalytic theory have creatively considered some of the kindred points of connection and possible places of constructive critique (Alford, 2002, 2007; Atterton, 2007; Cohen, 2002, 2005; Gans, 1996; Kunz, 1998; Marcus, 2007, 2008).

Particularly pertinent to the topic of enactment is Levinas' sensibility concerning the needs and vulnerability of the Other. Hilary Putnam (2002) claims that an essential "human truth" in Hebrew scripture is "that every human being should experience him/herself as *commanded* to be available to the neediness, the suffering, the vulnerability of the other person" (p. 48). This is a core feature of Levinas' thought. Furthermore, Levinas understood the Torah's commandments to be most poignantly encountered in the vulnerable expression of the Other. For Levinas, the face of the Other bears a trace of the Divine that simultaneously represents the plight of the most destitute and a calling from on high. The face of the Other is a "glorious abasement" (Levinas, 1969, p. 251) that demands of me an inexhaustible responsibility. Levinas (1988/2007) writes,

> There is the possibility of a responsibility for the alterity of the other person, for the stranger without domicile or words with which to converse, for the material conditions of one who is hungry or thirsty, for the nakedness of the defenseless mortal. Where is the person who would not come toward me in that essential misery, whatever countenance they may put on? The other, the one separated from me, outside the community: the face of the person who asks, a face that is already a request... In that weakness there is the commandment of a God or an authority, and, despite all they say, there is a renouncing of the force of constraint. And from that moment forth, in this self persevering in being, there emerges mercy and the overturning of beings' tautology of pure 'being *qua* being.' (p. 119)

The Other comes to me naked and hungry, and my responsibility is to these needs, before anything else. Levinas maintains that this is meant to be concrete and not abstract. That is, one is to take the food from his or her own mouth and offer it to the Other (Levinas, 1981). My very selfhood and identity is contingent upon this responsiveness (Levinas, 1981). Israel's identity as God's people (as the prophets Isaiah and Jeremiah remind) was contingent upon their responsiveness to the widow, the orphan, the stranger, and the alien in the land. Inasmuch as Israel forgot or neglected this command, they were exiled and estranged from their identity. Levinas maintained that the self is only a self "insofar as the self is for-the-other" (Cohen, 2002, p. 42). Inasmuch as the self is unresponsive to the Other's needs, it remains trapped and chained within itself, suffocating (Levinas, 1981). For Levinas, the self is a moral exchange, ethical interchange, and substitution for another (Cohen, 2002; Edelglass, 2006; Gantt & Williams, 2002; Levinas & Robbins, 2001). The Torah and its commandments, encountered in the face of the other, are the wellspring of Levinas' corpus. "Here the face of the other speaks God's word and reveals the law to me. Levinas radicalizes a certain relationship to the law in Judaism" (Robbins, 1991, p. 143).

By introducing Levinas' thought into the rich psychoanalytic dialogue around the transforming power of enactment, my hope is that psychoanalytic discourse might be enriched with Jewish ethical thought.

Levinas and Enactment

Lewis Aron, a leading psychoanalyst at NYU, recalls that,

> In his Clinical Diary, Ferenczi (1932) asserted that, as the analysis of a traumatized patient progressed, the analyst would unavoidably "have to repeat with his own hands the act of murder previously perpetrated against the patient" (p. 52). Ferenczi claimed that it is the intensity of the interpersonal experience that is transformative and that what differentiates analysts from others is their commitment to face honestly and acknowledge their role and participation in these enactments without hiding their complicity from their patients. (2003, p. 624)

This statement bears a profound Levinasian ethic, recognizing the sacredness of the Other's vulnerability and the therapist's responsibility for these wounds. Though this statement calls for the analyst to be honest and acknowledge his or her responsibility, there is a paucity in explicit ethical language. In describing the process of enactment, psychoanalysts assume that the therapist recognizes his or her role to care for the client and seek a non-hostile way of being with the client. On what is this ethical injunction grounded? That is less clear in the literature than the articulation of the nuts and bolts of the enactment process. For that reason I turn to Levinas for his ethical perspective grounded in the face of the other and the injunction of sacred texts.

In an earlier work, Alvin Dueck and myself conceived the role of the therapist/analyst (from a Levinasian perspective) in the following way:

> For Levinas, in an encounter with a client, we have before us an individual exposed, nude, vulnerable, and with a history of being psychologically murdered. In seeing the face before us, we lay down our lives before the patient. We expiate for the murders performed. We are responsible for the defacing of his or her soul, the smearing of the trace of God. We are party to this violence, and must disabuse ourselves any illusions to the contrary. We now sit with the broken, persecuted state of the other and experience with them in the pangs of exposure. We are responsible for this drama of self-mutilation, and we are not finished with our "duty" until the other has been emptied of the terror. (Dueck & Goodman, 2007, p. 612)

This will be further developed here.

To understand how enactments allow something new to develop that interrupts the violence of the client's lived experience warrants a deeper examination of Levinas' ethical concepts of radical responsibility, expiation, substitution, and guilt. Levinas claims that we are responsible for the wrongs done to the Other. We are responsible for the murders performed upon him or her. Even if we are not party to the initial moment of terror — even if our hand was not the tool of abuse — this guilt still rests upon us. Jeffrey Kosky (2001) writes, "The self is an expiation, a martyr, and even a *Sacrifice*, insofar as it sacrifices all concern for itself in responsibility for every other, to the point of expiating for the fault of others" (p. 154). One of Levinas' favorite quotes came from Dostoyevsky: "We are all responsible for everyone else — but I am more responsible than all the others" (Levinas, 1986, p. 31). Levinas used this Dostoyevsky quote numerous times throughout his writings. We are hostage and live in apology under the burden of this inexhaustible responsibility.

Enactment is a specific and concrete illustration of how therapists enter into and are responsible for the continued violence against their clients. As persons engaged in relationship with our clients — within the morass of the inter-subjective space — my past and the client's past are folded into an inscrutable "entanglement" (Ginot, 2007, p. 317). Consciousness is eclipsed in the cloud of enactment. Without clarity at its onset, the client invites us into perpetration of violence. The therapist finds him or herself enticed toward particular feelings and forms of action. Ultimately, as I live in this allurement and act out of this place, I become complicit in continued violence against my client. As my psyche carries some of the expression of the Other — the Other alive in my flesh (Levinas, 1981) — I become identified with the negligent, hateful, lustful, and violent figures who torment my client. My identity *is*, in part, drawn to reduction, totalization, egoism, defensiveness, protection, complacency, and even murder. In being radically exposed to a client's needs, desires, and history the therapist's psyche is truly persecuted and pulled to its extremes. Rage. Hate. Eros. Love. Affection. Madness. With John, I immediately wanted to strike back or yell. At the very least, I wanted to withdraw from the relationship and abandon him without looking back. These thoughts and reactions were my own, but they were also extensions of his past (and perpetually present) psychic trauma. I became responsible for his trauma and guilty of its continuation.

However, this is not the end of the story. The therapist's psyche can be a gift (Marion, 2003/2006), if it receives the client's message and responds, ultimately, without violence. Substitution takes place as the therapist's psychic protection is "denucleated" and he or she becomes hostage to the client's terror. The therapist's passivity (defined as Levinas would) means offering the flesh of one's body and the content of one's psyche to the needs of the Other. With John, my instinctual responses to either push away/withdraw (i.e., flight) or strike back/punish (i.e., fight) must become secondary to my love for him. The "murderousness of my natural will" (Levinas, 2004, p. 75-76) must be called into question by a history more fundamental than the client's accumulation of violent experiences and my patterned reactions. This requires a passivity and kenotic stance that allows for the possibility of recognizing this claim and responsibility (Dueck & Goodman, 2007). It means that I, as therapist, must hollow out and witness the Other *in* my own sameness. I must call into question my tendencies and activities and sacrifice their primacy for the client. As Levinas (1981) beautifully wrote, it is a moving "from the outrage undergone to the responsibility for the persecutor and in this sense from suffering to expiation for the other" (p. 111). This sometimes takes on the need for uncomfortable self-disclosure (Ginot, 2007; Sorenson, 2004) and entering into the "cloud of unknowing" where one's footholds are not as clear.

Expiation takes place when, instead of or in spite of "acting out" upon this highly affected state, the therapist retains an attunement to what Levinas calls an immemorial history. Levinas refers to this as the "past on the hither side of every present" (Levinas, 1981, p. 12). When the therapist remains committed to a history not remembered through experience, violence is closed down. It is here, in this primordial level of relation, that I (the therapist) can hear the command "Thou shall not kill," despite all evidence to the contrary.

Behind the repeated pattern that is comfortable and begged for, we witness the request that this mundane story might have a different ending. Behind John's desire for me to hit him back is the desire for caress (Levinas, 1969). His yearning for a dad who did not beat him is resident in his provocation. It is a perverted and distorted means of requesting love — it contraindicates love. But, this is the potential gift of therapy. I must watch for the contraindications that might lead me into harm, hatred, and violence. From these calls to murder I must witness the prior claim that the Other has upon me, a claim behind my client's history and my own proclivities, a sacred claim that is witnessed most poignantly in this vulnerability of the client.

The therapist's psyche is a gift in that he or she takes responsibility for his or her murderousness. The violence resident in the acting and reacting cycle is interrupted in this substitution and radical responsibility. Violence is not allowed to remain ultimate. The therapist lives out of an alternate ethic, one of non-possessive and primordial love. Hospitality and welcome replace murder and violation. Gentleness stands in the place of violence. This is where expiation for the other takes place. A new ending to the narrative is formed based on a different ethic.

Conclusion

Levinas states that the face of the Other bears the command "You shall not kill," however, within the therapy hour, clients often pull for old patterns of being killed. They often live out of choreographed histories from which they cannot find escape. Despite this, hopefully, the therapist maintains a deeper sensibility, a remembering of the more primordial calling of the face. Despite the *said*, found within the words and behaviors that pull for enactment, the *saying* demands a reversal of history, a reversal of this natural course toward reactive violence (Levinas, 1981). We raise the knife, but, hopefully, recognize this posture before the blade falls. Behind the client's blatant "murder me" we hear him or her whisper, "please do not kill me." We witness in the face a more original calling.

As John's eyes watered and my face reddened, I was stunned by the look of expectation and terror upon his face. My rage went from boil to simmer. My mind raced to understand what had just befallen me *and* us. We had become close, too close, intolerably close. We had passed the thresholds that he had come to know. He needed to push me back, keep me from moving into the tender areas where I could hurt him. He would hurt me first, assuring for himself some degree of control and comprehension around how and why I would hurt him back. If he brought it about, then my violence toward him was predictable and known. In sensing this, I also found myself growing in compassion and empathy for this protected place that he had just shown me. It was the most primal of communications. He had expressed what he could find no other way to express. He lived it and forced me to live it with him. We sat, looking one another in the eyes, for about 30 seconds before words came to me. "John, why did you do that? It really hurt. I don't understand." His breathing remained shallow and rapid. A droplet rolled down his right cheek. "I thought we were working well together and enjoying the work. Was I wrong?" His shoulders shrugged and then returned to their tense posture. I rubbed my cheek bone. "I don't understand what's going on. Are you as confused as I am?" He remained quiet but seemed to loosen up a bit as my tone became even softer. "I'm going to take some space and take some deep breaths so that I can get myself back together a bit. But, I will be back in 5 minutes so that we can take another pass at the math problem we were working on. If you want to talk with me about this, I am happy to talk about it anytime. I'm here, okay?" John slowly nodded, looking a bit bewildered. I stood up and worked to center myself at my desk, still within John's eye sight. Five minutes later, I returned to his desk and we carried on as though nothing had happened. Since he was seven, I respected his inability to really address and consider what happened. Much of it could not be symbolized or verbalized. But our relationship from this point on had a different quality: it somehow felt more real. He had communicated with me and I had listened. He had asked to be killed and I had heard his deeper request. I had not struck back or abandoned. No perfect ending, but we both witnessed something new and good.

It is fair to argue that this story ends without a true enactment coming to pass. Though John's transference and "acting out" elicited a profound intrapsychic response in myself that linked up to my unconscious processes around abandonment and respect, I *did not* strike him back, punish him, or abandon the relationship. My impulse to react ended up being short-circuited before it was enacted. Chused (1991) states,

> In the best of all possible worlds, an analyst is sensitive to his patient's transference, as expressed in either words or actions, but does not act. Sympathetic with a patient's pitiful state, he does not nurture; temporarily aroused by a patient's seductive attacks, he does not counterattack. An analyst contains his impulses, examines them, and uses the information gained to enrich his interpretive work. This best of all possible worlds is the ideal, something we strive for, but often fail to achieve. In the second best possible world, where most of us dwell, an analyst reacts to his patient — but catches himself in the act, so to speak, regains his analytic stance, and in observing himself and the patient, increases his understanding of the unconscious fantasies and conflicts in the patient and himself which have prompted him to action." (p. 616)

My understanding of why *this* story ends "in the best of all possible worlds" is because of John's age. The look on his seven-year-old face, the tears in his eyes, the history in his chart, and the linkage between his lost childhood and my own allowed me a sensitivity that I otherwise might not have had in other situations and with other clients. Seeing a small child expressing his wounded past through violent action felt far more obvious (and less layered and hidden) than my work with so many adults. The complexity of enactments with adults frequently muffles the "thou shall not kill" far more effectively. It may not be until one is in the center of an enactment or even fully on the other side of an enactment that it begins to make some sense or emerge as a meaningful expression or relational possibility. And, sometimes it comes to neither. John's story seemed like a particularly poignant illustration mainly because of the palpability of the tension between the commands of "thou shall kill" and "thou shall *not* kill" resident in his actions.

Enactments are a reliving of past experience that produce possibilities of deeper entrenchment (eliciting murder yet again) or reparative relation (violence interrupted). In relationally and ethically oriented psychotherapy, what "patient and analyst do to and with each other" (Aron, 2003, p. 625) remains the emphasis. Healing and transformation are understood to come from ongoing collaborative witnessing of relational patterns and implicit processes, in the heat of their manifestation. This provides both an "opportunity for meaning and symbolization" (Ginot, 2007, p. 325; see also Bromberg, 1998; Lyons-Ruth, 2003) and reparative ethical experience. A different ending is forged to an otherwise infinitely repeated narrative of violence. Substitution and expiation allow for these possibilities.

Enactment allows for a dialogical and midrashic transformation (Cushman, 2007). It is a lived, breathed, and embodied experience of something new, something ethical, and of non-possessive love. From a Levinasian frame, it is the meeting of sacred vulnerability and sacred responsiveness. The Divine is invited into this space.

REFERENCES

Alford, C. F. (2002). *Levinas, the Frankfurt school, and psychoanalysis.* Middletown, CT Wesleyan University Press.

--------. (2007). Levinas, Winnicott, and therapy. *Psychoanalytic Review,* 94: 529-551.

Aron, L. (1996). *A meeting of minds: Mutuality in psychoanalysis.* Hillsdale, NJ: The Analytic Press.

--------. (2003). The paradoxical place of enactment in psychoanalysis: Introduction. *Psychoanalytic Dialogues,* 13(5): 623-632.

Aronowicz, A. (1994). Translator's introduction. In E. Levinas' *Nine Talmudic Readings* (pp. ix-xxxix). Bloomington, IN: Indiana University Press.

Atterton, P. (2007). 'The talking cure': The ethics of psychoanalysis. *Psychoanalytic Review,* 94: 553-576.

Boesky, D. (1982). Acting out: A reconsideration of the concept. *Int. J. Psycho-Anal,* 63: 39-55.

Bromberg, P. (1998). *Standing in the spaces: Essays on clinical process, trauma, and dissociation.* Hillsdale, NJ: Analytic Press.

Browning, D. S. (1987). *Religious thought and the modern psychotherapies: A critical conversation in the theology of culture.* Philadelphia: Fortress Press.

Burggraeve, R. (2007). *The wisdom of love in the service of love: Emmanuel Levinas on justice, peace, and human rights.* Milwaukee, WI: Marquette University Press.

Chused, J. F. (1991). The evocative power of enactments. *Journal of the American Psychoanalytic Association,* 39: 615-640.

Cohen, R. (1994). *Elevations: The height of the good in Rosenzweig and Levinas.* Chicago, IL: The University of Chicago Press.

--------. (2002). Maternal psyche. In: E. Gantt & R. Williams (Eds.), *Psychology for the other: Levinas, ethics and the practice of psychology* (pp. 32-64). Pittsburgh, PA: Duquesne University Press.

--------. (2003). Translator's introduction. In: E. Levinas' *Humanism of the Other* (pp. vii-xliv). Chicago, IL: University of Illinois.

--------. (2005). Review of 'On escape.' *European Journal of Psychotherapy, Counselling, and Health,* 7: 109-115.

Cushman, P. (1995). *Constructing the self, constructing America: A cultural history of psychotherapy.* Garden City, NY: DaCapo Press.

--------. (2007). A burning world, an absent God: Midrash, hermeneutics, and relational psychoanalysis. *Contemporary Psychoanalysis,* 43: 47-87.

Dueck, A., & Goodman, D. (2007). Expiation, substitution, and surrender: Levinasian implications for psychotherapy. *Pastoral Psychology,* 55 (5): 601-617.

Edelglass, W. (2006). Levinas on suffering and compassion. *Sophia,* 45: 43-59.

Ford, D. (1996). On substitution. In S. Hand (Ed.), *Facing the Other: The ethics of Emmanuel Levinas.* Richmond, United Kingdom: Curzon Press.

--------. (1999). *Self and salvation: Being transformed.* Cambridge, England: Cambridge University Press.

Freud, S. (1958). Remembering, repeating, and working-through. In J. Strachey (Ed. & Trans.), *The standard edition of the complete psychological works of Sigmund Freud, Vol. 12* (pp. 147-156). London: Hogarth Press. (Original work published 1914)

Gabbard, G. O. (1995). Countertransference: The emerging common ground. *International Journal of Psychoanalysis,* 76: 475-485.

Gans, S. (1996). Levinas and Freud: Talmudic inflections in ethics and psychoanalysis. In S. Hand (Ed.), *Facing the other: The ethics of Emmanuel Levinas* (pp. 45-61). Richmond, England: Curzon Press.

Gibbs, R. (1992). *Correlations in Rosenzweig and Levinas.* Princeton, NJ: Princeton University Press.

Ginot, E. (2007). Intersubjectivity and neuroscience: Understanding enactments and their therapeutic significance within emerging paradigms. *Psychoanalytic Psychology,* 24: 317-332.

Goodman, D. (2010). Emmanuel Levinas. In: D. Leeming, K. Madden, & S. Marlan's (Eds.) *Encyclopedia of Psychology and Religion* (pp. 512-515). Springer Online Reference.

Goodman, D. & Grover, S. (2008). Hineni and transference: The remembering and forgetting of the other. *Pastoral Psychology,* 56: 561-571.

Hirsch, I. (1994). Countertransference love and theoretical model. *Psychoanalytic Dialogues,* 4(2): 171-192.

Hoffman, M. (in press). Redemption of the sins of our fathers in the therapy room: Enactment, rupture and repair in psychoanalytic thought. *Journal of Philosophy and Christianity*.

Hutchens, B. C. (2007). Is Levinas relevant to psychoanalysis? *Psychoanalytic Review*, 94: 595-616.

Kosky, J. L. (2001). *Levinas and the philosophy of religion*. Bloomington, IN: Indiana University Press.

Kunz, G. (1998). *The paradox of power and weakness: Levinas and an alternative paradigm for psychology*. New York: State University of New York Press.

Lesser, A. H. (1996). Levinas and the Jewish ideal of the sage. In: S. Hand (Ed.), *Facing the Other: The ethics of Emmanuel Levinas* (pp. 141-152). Cornwall, United Kingdom: Curzon Press.

Levinas, E. (1969). *Totality and infinity: An essay on exteriority* (A. Lingis, Trans.). Pittsburgh, PA: Duquesne University Press. (Original work published 1961)

--------. (1981). *Otherwise than being: Or, beyond essence* (A. Lingis, Trans.). Boston Hingham, MA: M. Nijhoff.

--------. (1986). Dialogue with Emmanuel Levinas. In: R. Cohen (Ed.), *Face to Face with Levinas* (pp. 13-33). Albany, NY: SUNY Press.

--------. (1989). *The Levinas reader* (S. Hand, Ed. & Trans.). Cambridge, MA: Blackwell Publishers.

--------. (1990). *Difficult freedom: Essays on Judaism* (S. Hand, Trans.). Baltimore, MD: The Johns Hopkins University Press. (Original work published 1976)

--------. (1999). *Alterity and transcendence* (M.B. Smith, Trans.). New York: Columbia University Press. (Original work published 1995)

--------. (2004). Emmanuel Levinas: Ethics of the Infinite. In: R. Kearney (Ed.), *Debates in continental philosophy: Conversations with contemporary thinkers* (pp. 65-84). New York: Fordham University Press.

--------. (2007). *In the Time of the Nations* (M. B. Smith, Trans.). New York: Continuum. (Original work published 1988)

Lyons-Ruth, K. (2003). Dissociation and the parent-infant dialogue: A longitudinal perspective from attachment research. *Journal of the American Psychoanalytic Association*, 51: 883-911.

Malka, S. (2006). *Emmanuel Levinas: His life and legacy* (M. Kigel & S. Embree, Trans.). Pittsburgh, PA: Duquesne University Press. (Original work published 2002)

Marcus, P. (2007). 'You are, therefore I am.' Emmanuel Levinas and psychoanalysis. *Psychoanalytic Review, 94*: 515-527.

--------. (2008). *Being for the Other: Emmanuel Levinas, ethical living, and psychoanalysis.* Milwaukee, WI: Marquette University Press.

Marion, J.-L. (2006). *The erotic phenomenon* (S. Lewis, Trans.). Chicago, IL: University of Chicago Press. (Original work published 2003)

Maroda, K. (1998). Enactment: When the patient's and analyst's past converge. *Psychoanalytic Psychology, 15*: 517-536.

McLaughlin, J. T. (1991). Clinical and theoretical aspects of enactment. *Journal of the American Psychoanalytic Association, 39*: 595-615.

McWilliams, N. (2008, August). *Conversation Hour: Rediscovering the Common Ground of Psychoanalysis and Humanistic Psychology.* Paper presented at the annual meeting of the American Psychological Association (APA). Boston, MA.

Mitchell, S. A. (1988). *Relational concepts in psychoanalysis: An integration.* Cambridge, MA: Harvard University Press.

Olthuis, J. H. (2001). *The beautiful risk: A new psychology of loving and being loved.* Grand Rapids, MI: Zondervan.

Purcell, M. (2006). *Levinas and theology.* New York: Cambridge University Press.

Putnam, H. (2002). Levinas and Judaism. In S. Critchley & R. Bernasconi (Eds.), *The Cambridge companion to Levinas* (pp. 33-62). New York: Cambridge University Press.

--------. (2008). *Jewish philosophy as a guide to life: Rosenzweig, Buber, Levinas, Wittgenstein.* Bloomington, IN: Indiana University Press.

Richardson, F. C., Fowers, B. J., & Guignon, C. B. (1999). *Re-envisioning psychology: Moral dimensions of theory and practice.* San Francisco, CA: Jossey-Bass Publishers.

Rieff, P. (1987). *The triumph of the therapeutic: Uses of faith after Freud.* Chicago, IL: The University of Chicago Press.

--------. (2006). *My life among the deathworks: Illustrations of the aesthetics of authority.* Charlottesville: University of Virginia Press.

Robbins, J. (1991). *Prodigal son/ elder brother: Interpretation and alterity in Augustine, Petrarch, Kafka, Levinas.* Chicago, IL: The University of Chicago Press.

Smith, M. B. (2005). *Toward the outside: Concepts and themes in Emmanuel Levinas.* Pittsburgh, PA: Duquesne University Press.

Sorenson, R. L. (2004). *Minding spirituality.* Hillsdale, NJ: The Analytic Press.

Stern, D. B. (2003). *Unformulated experience: From dissociation to imagination in psychoanalysis.* Hillsdale, NJ: The Analytic Press.

Stone, I. F. (1998). *Reading Levinas / Reading Talmud: An introduction.* Philadelphia: The Jewish Publication Society.

Tauber, A. (1998). Outside the subject: Levinas's Jewish perspective on time. *Graduate Faculty Philosophy Journal, 20/21,* 439-459.

--------. (in press). *Freud, the reluctant philosopher.* Princeton, NJ: Princeton University Press.

Taylor, C. (1989). *Sources of the self: The making of the modern identity.* Cambridge, MA: Harvard University Press.

Ward, G. (1996). On time and salvation: The eschatology of Emmanuel Levinas. In: S. Hand (Ed.), *Facing the Other: The Ethics of Emmanuel Levinas* (pp. 153-172). Cornwall, United Kingdom: Curzon Press.

3 Biblical Commentary

A Freudian and a Kleinian Reading of the Midrash on the Garden of Eden Narrative

Tuvia Peri

The well known narrative of the sin and punishment of Adam and Eve in the Garden of Eden (Genesis 2-3) has been the subject of a number of psychoanalytic studies. Spero (1996) conceptualized Eden as signifying of the development of internalization of symbolic language. Osman (2000) understands the narrative as epitomizing an archaic version of the Oedipus complex in which progressive growth, with separation and individuation of the young, is experienced as perilous — not only to them, but also to their procreators. Similarly, Loewald (1979), in his discussion of Oedipus, perceives the guilt in Eden as originating in the emancipation and individuation process of the young. Burston (1994) argues that the fall narrative of Genesis 2-3 represents the implicit or unconscious model for Freud's early version of infantile sexual researches in the quest for sexual knowledge, where the child's disposition to truth, aversion to deception, and willingness to rebel are in conflict with the father's authority expression.

Aron (2005) discusses two interpretations of the Eden story: those of psychoanalyst Erich Fromm and Talmudic scholar and philosopher Rabbi Joseph B. Soloveitchik. Fromm champions freedom and valorizes rebellion, interpreting the story not as a "fall" but as a step forward towards independence, autonomy, and attainment of reason and wisdom. With the help of the snake, man rebels against a dominating God. Soloveitchik advocates the surrender and submission to God and his law as the basis for inter-subjectivity and mutuality in human relationships. He interprets the Eden narrative as a "fall": the failure to surrender to God's prohibition and reduction of the desire for the other to the sheer delight of possession. The snake represents the will to dominate and to exploit, especially through sexuality and seduction. Adam and Eve feel ashamed because of their attitude of depersonalization and ruthless exploitation, where sexuality is imbued with the quest for power.

Israeli philosopher Shalom Rosenberg (personal communication, 2004) based his interpretation of the Eden narrative on Freud's classic structural model. In it, the narrative symbolizes the inner struggle between the id (serpent), the ego (Adam and Eve), and the superego (God). Early psychoanalysts interpreted the story in accordance with the Myth of Oedipus, understanding the story as a myth describing the struggle between the man and his father over the mother. The fact that the man was created out of "*adama*" (earth), possibly a feminized version of the name "Adam", was seen as supporting the notion that Adam actually had sexual contact with his mother (Roheim, 1940; Burston, 1994).

Freud, in a letter to Jung (Burston, 1994),[1] was critical of the use of the Eden narrative, or the "Apple story" as he called it, as a subject for psychoanalysis or as a source of support for psychoanalytic ideas:

> You have asked me for an example of my objections to the most obvious method of exploiting mythology. I shall give you an example I used in the debate. Fräulein Spielrein had cited the Genesis story of the apple as an instance of woman seducing man. But in all likelihood the myth of Genesis is a wretched, tendentious distortion devised by an apprentice priest, who as we now know stupidly wove two independent sources into a single narrative (as in a dream). It is not impossible that there are two sacred trees because he found one tree in each of the two sources. There is something very strange and singular about the creation of Eve. — Rank recently called my attention to the fact that the Bible story may quite have reversed the original myth. Then everything would be clear; Eve would be Adam's

---

[1]   Dated December 17, 1911.

mother, and we should be dealing with the well known motif of mother incest, the punishment for which, etc. (p. 210)

While I agree with Freud's assertion that the Biblical narrative has a dreamlike quality, his disparaging remarks are difficult to comprehend as the conclusions of an analyst. As Aron (2005) wrote:

> As psychoanalysts we might think of how differently each of us might interpret this story if we heard it as the dream of one of our patients. Buber demonstrates how dreamlike is the scene in which Eve and then Adam eat the forbidden fruit. How would we interpret this dream? Interpretations inevitably reflect the subjective world of the interpreter, of the analyst. (p. 720)

Freud's derogatory remarks on the Genesis narrative seem to express his attitude, at that phase of his life, to the Jewish tradition in general and to the Hebrew Bible specifically (For a discussion of Freud's evolving attitude toward the Bible and his own Jewishness, see: Ostow, 1989; Yerushalmi, 1993; Aron, 2005; and Salberg, 2007). Obviously, Freud was unable at this phase of his life, to accept the advice that his father's, Jacob, offered in the poignant Hebrew inscription in the Philippson Bible presented to him for his 35th birthday in 1891: "…This Book of Books is a spring which the sages dug and (from it) the legislators learned knowledge and judgment… And I called it 'Spring up, o well — sing to it'…" (Ostow, 1989, pp. 483-484)

The source critical, psychoanalytic, and philosophic interpretations mentioned above are creative, exciting and inspiring, yet remain, to some extent, "emotionally distant" or "experience distant". Their very profundity places them beyond the easy grasp of the Bible's audience. These interpretations, therefore, lack the ability to explain the enormous appeal of the Eden narrative for Jews, Christians, and others for several millennia. As Ellens (1997) wrote:

> Genesis 2:25-3:24 is one of those stories that carries with it such archetypical quality that we sense at once that it touches, at the center, a generic truth of obvious human history and of vital personal experience, even though it has no literal root in historical events…It is an intensely pathetic story of loss,

grief, guilt, and shame which is, in the end, more true about our humanness than mere historical reporting could ever possibly be. (pp. 222, 228)

I believe that the influence and attraction of this narrative for such a wide audience over such a long period of time is rooted the fact that it treats basic human drives and experiences in a manner that remains accessible and "not in heaven".

In this essay I will interpret the Eden narrative through the eyes of the reader or educated listener and follow his associations and understanding of the story. I will use intertextual association to similar Biblical phrases and motifs as a primary exegetical tool. These associations may lead us to more than a single interpretation, and I acknowledge that no interpretation using this method is ever truly complete. However, this represents a similar type of analysis that psychoanalysts employ in the interpretation of a patient's dream.[2]

Additionally, intertextual interpretation of the Bible is a characteristic feature of midrashic literature.[3] The Midrashim, compiled in the early centuries of the Common Era, are collections of the Biblical interpretation and exegesis of the Ancient Rabbis. They characteristically offer a range of viewpoints and interpretations of Biblical narratives, and the Eden narrative is no exception. An additional point of resemblance between the midrashic and psychoanalytic interpretive traditions is noted by Aron (2005):

> It is by now well accepted to think of psychoanalysis, like Judaism and biblical exegesis, as a hermeneutical or interpretive tradition. The Jewish interpretive tradition is radically open. The compilers of the midrashic collections — and there have been numerous anthologies over many

---

[2] As opposed to the approaches outlined above, the approach presented here seeks to locate psychological depth in the literary composition of the text itself: a fact which makes this approach more accessible to the educated consumer of the Bible from both the textual and technical vantage points. Regarding the Bible's strategies for addressing an audience consisting of both the uneducated and the elite, see Sternberg, 1987, 48-56.

[3] For an introduction to midrash which emphasizes its intertextual aspects, see Boyarin, 1990.

centuries — were quite comfortable presenting a range of interpretive options without suggesting any single definitive, monolithic, or authoritative reading of the biblical text...The mark of a Talmudic scholar is the ability to read and analyze the text and to explain both sides of any rabbinic disagreement by offering imaginative and compelling reasons for both sides of an argument. (pp. 681-682)

In this work I would like to argue that it is possible to trace, in the vast amount of midrashic material on the Eden narrative, two lines of interpretation which correspond to two of the major classical psychoanalytic theories about the nature of humanity, namely the Freudian and Kleinian approaches. These two readings of the narrative place the sex drive and envy, respectively, at the center of human will and drive.

The text of the Bible lends itself to different interpretations by blurring details and leaving gaps: Why was eating from the Tree of Knowledge so terminally bad? What motivated the serpent, Eve, and Adam to disobey God and eat from the tree? Why were Adam and Eve frightened and ashamed after they ate from the tree? Is there any *quid pro quo* in the punishments meted out at the end of the narrative? A detailed textual analysis of this dreamlike narrative, as well as an understanding of certain midrashic statements through Freudian and Kleinian lenses, may clarify some of these perplexing questions.[4]

The Freudian reading of the text

Throughout this work, "Freudian theory" will refer to the central role of the sex drive and the Oedipus complex in understanding human behavior and development. The Oedipus complex has been reinterpreted several times throughout the history of psychoanalysis (see Loewald, 1979; Blass, 2001; Ogden, 2006). This work relates to the classical version of the Oedipus complex, as summarized by Ogden (2006) as follows:

---

[4] For the reader's convenience, I have provided the full text of Genesis 2-3 as an appendix.

1. All of human psychology and psychopathology, as well as all human cultural achievements, can be understood in terms of urges and meanings that have their roots in the sexual and aggressive instincts.

2. The sexual instinct is experienced as a driving force, beginning at birth and elaborated sequentially in its oral, anal and phallic components in the course of the first five years of life.

3. Of the multitude of myths and stories that human beings have created, the myth of Oedipus, for psychoanalysis, is the single most important narrative organizing human psychological development.

4. The triangulated set of conflictual, murderous, and incestuous fantasies constituting the Oedipus complex is 'determined and laid down by heredity' i.e. it is a manifestation of a universal, inborn propensity of human beings to organize experience in this particular way. (p. 652)

The sexual interpretation of the Eden story has a long history, beginning in the apocryphal literature and becoming the dominant Christian interpretation, especially in Augustine's theological writings. This interpretation acquired dominance despite the fact that the sexual character of the sin is not explicit in the narrative text. The story recounts God's prohibition of the fruit of the Tree of Knowledge and Adam and Eve's transgression of that prohibition. Although "eating of the forbidden fruit" has acquired a connotation of sexual unfaithfulness, this association is itself the product of a long Jewish and Christian interpretive tradition.

The sexual character of the sin in Eden, and specifically the Oedipal, triangular relationship between Adam, Eve and the Serpent is the subject of a significant number of midrashic statements which address a particular gap in the narrative:

> "And the woman said to the snake..." and where was Adam during this conversation? Abba Halfon b. Korya said: "He had engaged in 'the way of the land' (a euphemism for sexual intercourse — T.P.) and then fallen asleep". (Gen. Rabbah Ch. 19)[5]

---

5 Translations of the Biblical text generally follow the new Jewish Publication Society translation of the Tanakh (1987). Translations of other Rabbinic texts are my own.

An analogous interpretation addresses the somewhat different problem which disturbed the scholars:

> "And they were not ashamed. Now the serpent was more subtle..." It would have been quite sufficient for Scripture to say: "and the Lord God made for the man and his wife garments of skin" (Gen. 3:21). Rabbi Joshua b. Korha said: "It informs us why that wicked one pushed sin on them. Since he saw them engaged in the way of the land, he lusted after her". (*Ibid.* 18)

These two interpretations share a very strong common feature, namely, that the immediate background and cause for the fall was sexual intercourse between Adam and Eve. The serpent watched them in their shameless naiveté and was aroused. While Adam took his post-coital nap, the serpent took the opportunity to tempt Eve. The similarity of this scene to the Freudian "primal scene" is salient.

To trace the textual sources of the vision described in the midrash, we must consider the narrative from its beginning in the previous chapters. In contradistinction to Christian exegeses of the narrative, the midrash is unequivocal that Adam and Eve had a sexual life prior to the fall and that sexual life was part of their duty in God's world (Boyarin, 1995; Shulman, 2003). The verses in the first description of creation explicitly charges man to procreate:

> And God created man in His own image, in the image of God created He him; male and female created He them. God blessed them; and God said to them: 'Be fertile and increase, fill the earth'.... (Gen. 1:27-28)

Similarly, Gen. 2:24, which describes man and woman cleaving to each other and becoming "one flesh" is understood by the Rabbis to refer to either union through sex or through child bearing. The corollary to this assertion, that the Bible views man's companionless state as being unnatural or unfulfilled, finds midrashic expression as well:

> "This one at last" — Rabbi Elazar said: what is the meaning of "This one at last is bone of my bone and flesh of my flesh"? This indicates that Adam copulated with every living animal, but it did not satisfy him until he copulated with Eve (b. Yevamot 63a).

161

The context of this verse is God's statement (Gen. 2:18) that "It is not good for man to be alone" and the subsequent (2:19-20) trial and failure to find an appropriate "helper". Rabbi Elazar's statement actually implies that the serpent, the creature whose shrewdness was matched only by man, was rejected by Adam as a potential mate. This lays the groundwork for a competitive triangle for the right to be man's helper. In fact, a midrash explicitly indicates the serpent's competition with man, including his wish to replace Adam as Eve's husband:

> Rabbi Issi and Rabbi Hoshaya said in the name of Rabbi Hiya Rabbah: God said four things to the snake: I created you to be king of all beasts, but you did not want it — "more cursed shall you be..."; I created you to walk upright like man but you did not want it — "on your belly shall you crawl"; I created you to eat prepared foods like man but you did not want it — "dirt shall you eat"; you wished to kill Adam and marry his wife — "I will put enmity between you and the woman" (Gen. 3:14-15). (Gen. Rabbah Ch. 20)

Having established the background of the serpent's motivation, we now turn to his methods. Several Talmudic and midrashic statements explicitly indicate that the nature of the encounter between Eve and the serpent was sexual:

> Rabbi Yohanan said: When the serpent copulated with Eve he injected pollution into her. (b. Yevamot 103a; Avoda Zara 22b; Shabbat 146a)

> "The woman replied: 'The serpent duped me (hishi'ani) and I ate" (Gen. 3:13) What is meant by "hishi'ani"? It indicates that the snake copulated with Eve and injected her with pollution. (Gen. Rabbah [Buber] 3:12)[6]

> "And from the fruit of the tree in the middle of the garden..." (Gen. 3:3): Rabbi Zeira taught — "the fruit of the tree" refers to man, who is compared to a tree, as it says "for man is the tree of the field" (Deut. 20:19). "In the middle of the garden" refers to woman, who is compared to a garden, as it says "A garden locked is my own, my bride" (Song 4:12) — it says "garden"

---

6   Rashi to Shabbat 146a presents a version of this midrash and suggests that its understanding is based on the linguistic connection between the *hapax legomenon* "hishi'ani" and "nisu'in", the Hebrew word for marriage which shares the same root.

instead of "woman" because it prefers clean speech — just as a garden is sown with seeds and subsequently grows and produces, so, too a woman is sown with seed, becomes pregnant, and gives birth after intercourse. The serpent-rider [a reference to a Satan-like entity — T.P.] copulated with her and she conceived Cain. Later, Adam copulated with her and she conceived Abel, as it says (Gen. 4:1) "Adam knew his wife Eve". (Pirkei de-Rabbi Eliezer Ch. 21)

In addition to its radical claims about the paternity of Cain, this midrash reads the garden descriptions of Genesis against the erotic garden imagery of the Song of Songs. Although it refers specifically to a text that symbolically relates to the beloved woman's virginity ("a garden locked... a fountain locked, a sealed-up spring"), the very fact that the midrash reads the Song of Songs as an inter-text of the Genesis narrative suggests a strong sexual element in the latter. The Song of Songs frequently uses garden imagery, and especially the eating of fruit, as a metaphor for sexuality and woman's body:

> Your stately form is like the palm, your breasts are like clusters. I say:
> "Let me climb the palm, let me take hold of its branches; Let your breasts
> be like clusters of grapes, your breath like the fragrance of apples'.
> (Song 7:8-9)

A close reading of the Eden narrative can offer several other subtle indications of its sexual themes, which may have also informed these midrashic interpretations. First, it makes constant reference to Adam and Eve's nakedness — four times in this narrative (Gen. 2:25; 3:7; 3:10; 3:11). This fact is compounded by the fact that this root ("*arum*") appears nowhere else in the Torah with its meaning of "nakedness". Furthermore, the serpent, the boldest phallic symbol in the narrative, is also described as "*arum*", and immediately after the term's first appearance with regard to Adam and Eve, but in the meaning of "subtle" or "cunning": "Now the serpent was more subtle..." (Gen. 3:1). Considering the phallic associations of the serpent, and in light of the insinuation of its nakedness/ cunning immediately prior to its meeting Eve in the garden, the reader is led to the notion that the narrative implies sexual content.

163

Although the exact nature of Adam's sin is never specified in this line of interpretation, it seems to be related to some type of illicit sexual activity. The midrash does, however, supply Eve's motivation for sharing the forbidden fruit with Adam, again introducing the triangle associated wither the Oedipal scene:

> Rabbi Simlai said: She approached him in a calculating manner. She said: "What do you think, that I will die and another Eve will be created for you? 'There is nothing new under the sun' (Eccl. 1:9).
> (Gen. Rabbah Ch. 19)

In describing the cognitive and emotional process that Eve underwent before eating the forbidden fruit, the text provides a direct inside view of her attraction to the fruit: "The woman saw that the tree was good for eating and a delight to the eyes" (Gen. 3:6). The Hebrew word used for "delight", "ta'avah", has a salient connotation of lust — for food in the biblical context (e.g., Num. 11:4), and for sex in the later Rabbinic and Modern Hebrew context. Considering that "eating", as will be discussed below, is often used as a euphemism for sex in the Bible, the reader is led to understand Eve's inability to resist the serpent's temptation sexually.

Two central themes of the Eden narrative are "knowledge" and "eating", both of which have a sexual association in the Bible and have a subtle effect on readers familiar with Biblical narrative. The motif of "knowledge" appears five times in this narrative (Gen. 2:17; 3:5, twice; 3:7; 3:22). Three appearances relate directly to the nature of the transgression: "The tree of knowledge of good and bad" (2:17); "and the eyes of both of them were opened and they knew that they were naked" (3:7); "now that man has become like one of us, knowing good and bad" (3:22). The term appears again in as the first word in the next episode, but denoting sex "Adam knew his wife Eve, and she conceived and bore Cain" (4:1). This same sense of the familiar "knowledge in the biblical sense" is employed again later in the same chapter (4:25), prior to the birth of Seth. Thus, the "knowledge" motif contains both explicit and implicit sexual connotations.

Similarly, the motif of "eating" has a subtle sexual association in the Bible. The boldest example, which also resonates against the Eden narrative, is from Proverbs 30:20: "Such is the way of an adulteress: She eats, wipes her mouth, and says 'I have done no wrong.'" We have already addressed the eroticism of the fruit-eating imagery of the Song of Songs. The Rabbis also frequently used "eating" or "eating bread" as a euphemism for sexual relations.[7] Thus, we may safely assume that for many readers, the idea of "eating from the forbidden tree" carried euphemistic overtones of sexual misconduct.

The final indication that the forbidden fruit refers to sexual misconduct is the use of the word "*immah*" (together with her) when describing Eve giving the fruit to Adam (Gen. 3:6). This word, in the vast majority of its appearances in the Torah, connotes a sexual relationship. For example, in the narrative of Joseph and Potiphar's wife, we read: "And as much as she coaxed Joseph day after day, he did not yield to her request to lie beside her, to be with her ("*immah*")" (39:10).

Taken together, these associations make it quite clear that the sexual interpretation of the text is based on a series of associations and subtle indications in the narrative itself.

Castration

The association to the Oedipus myth is based not only on the triangular sexual situation, but also by the appearance of castration-like symbols in the story. The punishment imposed on the serpent was midrashically interpreted in the following dramatic way:

"On your belly shall you crawl" (3:14) — when God said "on your belly shall you crawl" to him, the ministering angels descended and amputated his arms and legs, and his voice could be heard to the ends of the world. (Gen. Rabbah Ch. 20)

---

[7] Regarding "eating bread", see: b. Sanhedrin 75a, Yoma 18b, Yevamot 37b, Exod. Rabbah (Vilna) Chapter 1. Regarding "eating" in general, see: Ketubot 64b, Yoma 75a. See also: Boyarin, 1995, p. 72.

In addition to this concrete description of the demotion of the serpent from being the greatest (3:1) to being the least (3:14) of God's creatures, the Rabbis also suggested that Adam's stature suffered as a result of his sin, to the point where he could hide in the brush: "'And Adam and his wife hid' (Gen. 3:8) — Rabbi Eibo said: 'His stature was downgraded to 100 cubits'" (Gen. Rabbah Ch. 19). In addition to these associations, we may add the "fiery, ever-turning sword" (Gen. 3:24) that guards the entrance back to the garden and which seems to symbolize the constant threat of castration that looms for those who fail to follow God's prohibitions. Taken together, the association of these statements to the castration anxiety of the Oedipal Complex in Freud's theory is bold and surprising.

The Aftermath of the Sin

Following the sin, the narrative describes the reactions of the various parties, further reinforcing a sexual interpretation of the episode. The original couple reacted to their sin as follows: "Then the eyes of both of them were opened and they knew that they were naked; and they sewed together fig leaves and made themselves loincloths" (3:7). The scene of Adam and Eve covering their genitalia with fig-leaf loincloths, hiding in the trees, and fearful of God was definitely understood as the result of severe guilt and fear aroused by the sin committed by violating God's prohibition against sexual misconduct. At the end of the narrative, God himself prepared leather garments to clothe their bodies (3:21). Had the scene been merely one of eating a forbidden fruit, we would more reasonably expect that they cover their mouths!

The punishment of Eve is also more readily understandable as a *quid pro quo* for a sexual sin: "To the woman he said: 'I will make most severe your pangs in childbearing; in pain shall you bear children. Yet your urge shall be for your husband, and he shall rule over you" (3:16). A sexual sin causes a curse of painful childbirth, itself the outcome of a sexual relationship. The curse also has a second part: a change nature of the relationship between a woman and her husband. The fulfillment of the woman's desire for her husband will depend on him; she will lose her ability to satisfy her sexual needs autonomously and even her personal independence, as she will be ruled by her man.

Avot de-Rabbi Natan, a homiletic collection from the 3rd Century C.E., explicitly reads the curse and pain of womanhood in a sexual context:

> Eve was cursed with ten curses at that moment, as it says: "I will make most severe your pangs in childbearing; in pain shall you bear children. Yet your urge shall be for your husband, and he shall rule over you". These are the two flows of blood — the painful blood of menstruation and the painful blood of virginity. "In childbearing" refers to the pain of pregnancy. "In pain shall you bear children" is straightforward. "Yet your urge shall be for your husband" teaches that a woman desires her husband when he goes on a journey. "And he shall rule over you" — in that a man may make a verbal proposition, but a woman may only proposition in her heart, enveloped as though in mourning, imprisoned, and excommunicated.

Adam's transgression remains unclear in this line of interpretation, his curse is consequently not specifically interpreted. It is possible, however, that the curse of toiling in an unyielding land is intended to exhaust him through hard labor in the fields, keeping his mind off of sex.

In sum, it is possible to identify, in the biblical account of and midrashic statements about the Eden narrative, a Freudian reading characterized by the following three themes: A. The sexual character of the sin in Eden; B. The triangular situation, parallel to the Oedipal scene, in which the sin occurred; C. The motif of castration as a punishment for sexual misconduct. I wish to argue that, although not specified straightforward in the text, the reader of the text is inspired by these central motifs and attracted by its relevance to his own life and to his constant fight with his own powerful desires.

The Kleinian Reading

The second interpretation suggests reading the Eden narrative in light of Kleinian psychoanalytic theory and demonstrates the possibility of identifying midrashic views that parallel central concepts in the Kleinian approach, and that it is possible to trace the roots of this exegesis back to the Biblical text itself. The central elements of Kleinian theory that the reading will refer to are: the centrality of envy as the most powerful force driving human behavior; excessive splitting between good and bad objects and between good and bad parts of the self as the main organizing principle of the world by the human baby or during adult life; and development towards the "Depressive Position" as a necessary personal developmental phase in order to be able to love and to admire another person or heavenly entity. In my analysis, I will primarily use Klein's seminal work *Envy and Gratitude* (1957), which summarizes her later and most developed theoretical formulations.

Klein believes that envy is a constitutional and congenital human drive:

> Envy is the angry feeling that another person possesses and enjoys something desirable — the envious impulse being to take it away or to spoil it. Moreover, envy implies the subject's relation to one person only and goes back to the earliest exclusive relation with the mother". (p. 180)

In the following, I will argue that envy of God and his creativity and omnipotence drive Adam and Eve to their sin. The notion that man envies God may sound implausible, yet, a recently published statement of the eminent late nineteenth and early twentieth century Rabbi Avraham Yizhak Kook (2005) seems to elaborate a similar notion:

> There is an evil impulse hidden deep in the recesses of the soul — a bone-decaying envy that enfeebles and darkens any idea of light. Envy is strange. Many are not aware of it because several factors prevent language from expressing it, but it is there, slumbering in the recesses of the recesses of the human soul. It is sometimes made manifest in various forms, aside from its true form, in the manner of all effects of jealousy, which are always cloaked in a foreign garment and always bear a foreign name. This strange envy is the envy of God; man is envious of God's infinite happiness, of his absolute perfection. (I:129)

Klein's (1957) description of the envy towards the first object, the mother and her breast, for her creativeness and for the good milk she possesses, may explain what led Adam and Eve to their transgression:

My work has taught me that the first object to be envied is the feeding breast, for the infant feels that it possesses everything he desires and that it has an unlimited flow of milk, and love which the breast keeps for its own gratification. This feeling adds to his sense of grievance and hate, and the result is a disturbed relation to the mother. (p.182)

The envious and destructive attitude towards the breast underlies destructive criticism which is often described as 'biting' and 'pernicious'. It is particularly creativeness which becomes the object of such attacks. (p. 201)

The idea that envy is the root drive leading to Adam and Eve's transgression, and may explain the serpent's motivation as well, may be identified in a series of midrashic statements whose roots can be traced to the biblical narrative itself.

The boldest expression of this motif is found in the serpent's words trying to convince Eve to eat from the forbidden tree. He first denies the threat of death would she eat of the fruit (Gen. 3:4) and then adds: "but God knows that as soon as you eat of it your eyes will be opened, and you will be like God, who knows good and bad"(3:5).

The serpent argues that God does not want humans to acquire the ability to discern good and evil, and thereby attain stature similar to his. To use Klein's terminology, he owns good milk (God, the good breast) but he wants to keep it for himself and deny it to man. This conversation is expanded and dramatized midrashically, calling greater attention to the theme of envy:

Rabbi Joshua of Sakhnin said in the name of Rabbi Levi: [The serpent] began slandering his creator. He said, "[God] ate from this tree and created the world, and then told you not to eat from the tree so that you would not eat from it and create more worlds, because every craftsman hates those who practice the same craft. Rabbi Judah b. Simon says: [The snake argued as follows:] "Everything that was created later rules over that which was created earlier...you were created last to rule over everything. Eat quickly so that he does not create more worlds that will rule over you." This is what is meant by "and the woman saw that it was good" — she saw that the serpent's words made sense. (Gen. Rabbah Ch. 19)

In this text, the serpent invested a lot of effort to convince the woman that there was actually no good reason for God's prohibition except for his ambition to be the sole creator and ruler of the world. In the last part of his comment, the serpent mentions the fact that those creatures created last dominate those which were created earlier and urges Eve to put an end to this cycle by eating from the tree. It is obvious that the serpent, the shrewdest of all wild beasts, is projecting his own feelings after being dominated by humans who were created after him. The insult may even be deeper: Adam man had actually preferred the companionship of God's newest creature, woman, over the serpent, who was rejected along with all other living beasts (Kass, 2003):

> The Lord God formed out of the earth all the wild beasts and all the birds of the sky and brought them to Adam to see what he would call them; and whatever Adam called each living creature, that would be its name. Adam gave names to all the cattle and to the birds of the sky and to all the wild beasts; but for Adam no fitting helper was found (Gen. 2:19-20). (p. 81)

Moreover, the Rabbis visualized the primordial serpent as a humanoid creature: walking erect, possessing language, and highly intelligent. Perhaps they view the serpent in this manner in order to make his envy of man more plausible:

> Rabbi Hoshaya Rabbah said: [The serpent] stood erect and had legs...Rabbi Simon b. Elazar said: He was like a camel. He deprived the world of much good, for had it not been for [the sin and punishment], a person could have sent merchandise with [a serpent] and he would have gone and returned.

The following midrashic statements explicitly detail the cognitive and emotional processes the serpent underwent upon comparing his own stature to man's:

> Rabbi Judah b. Beteira says: Primordial Man was reclining in the Garden of Eden, and the ministering angels were roasting meat and chilling wine for him. The serpent came, saw [man's] great honor, and became jealous of him... what calculation did the evil serpent make at that moment? "I will go kill Adam, marry his wife, become king over the entire world, walk upright, and eat all of the world's delights (Avot de-Rabbi Natan Ch. 1).

Although the last paragraph also seems to include an Oedipal perspective of the serpent wishing to take Adam's wife as his own, the Kleinian component of an envious wish to become human, walk erect, and rule the world remains prominent.

Immediately thereafter, the woman eats of the tree. I would like to suggest that her inability to resist the serpent's arguments is not only due to her envy of God, who created her and the universe, but also due to her envy of Adam, because of his close contact with God. After all, Adam received direct communication from God (2:16-17), whereas he did not speak directly to Eve until after her sin. The Midrash insinuates this line of thought while offering an alternative solution to the problem, mentioned above, of Adam's whereabouts during the serpent's conversation with Eve: "Our Rabbis said: [God] took [Adam] around the whole world and instructed him: 'This is good for planting trees; this is good for planting grain'" (Gen. Rabbah Ch. 19). Eve, left behind, may have been driven by her bitter envy to act out and to rebel god's prohibition:

> There is a direct link between the envy experienced towards the mother's breast and the development of jealousy. Jealousy is based on the suspicion of and rivalry with the father, who is accused of having taken away the mother's breast and the mother. This rivalry marks the early stages of the direct and inverted Oedipus complex, (Klein, 1957, p. 195)

In this narrative, envy is not an exclusively human phenomenon. After cursing Adam and Eve, God expels them from the Garden of Eden. The rationale offered is strikingly similar to the serpent's assertion.

> God said, "Now that man has become like one of us, knowing good and bad, what if he should stretch out his hand and take also from the tree of life and eat, and live forever! (Gen. 3:22).

Surprisingly, the biblical narrative ascribes envy to God himself in his wish to prevent mankind from attaining immortality.[8] The Midrash dramatizes this image:

---

8 For a broader discussion of the notion of God's envy of man, see Liebes, 1994.

It can be compared to a king and a general who were in a carriage together, and the countrymen wished to call the king "His Majesty", but they did not know which one was which. What did the king do? He pushed him out of the carriage so that all would know that he is the general. So, too, when God created the first man, the ministering angels mistook him and wished to call him the Holy One. What did God do? He put him to sleep so they knew that he was human, and told him that he is dust and would return to dust. (Gen. Rabbah 6:10)

In this line of reasoning, the Eden narrative perceives "envy" as the major force driving the world. Its centrality is expressed so that even God is in some way driven by this drive.

A major change is perceived in the garden after the sin: from a harmonious world before the sin, where relationships between God, man, woman, and all living creatures are characterized by friendship, tranquility, and prosperity to a world dominated with fear, guilt and shame. Coexistence, between man and woman, human and animal, creature with Creator, deteriorates into mutual blame and enmity to the point of attempts to kill each other:

"I will put enmity between you and the woman, and between your offspring and hers; they shall strike at your head, and you shall strike at their heel." And to the woman he said "I will make most severe your pangs in childbearing; In pain shall you bear children. Yet your urge shall be for your husband, and he shall rule over you"…"Cursed be the ground because of you; by toil shall you eat of it all the days of your life. Thorns and thistles shall it sprout for you. By the sweat of your brow shall you get bread to eat". (Gen. 3:15-19)

From the Kleinian perspective this is the result of envy.

Strong envy of the feeding breast interferes with the capacity for complete enjoyment, and thus undermines the development of gratitude. There are very pertinent psychological reasons why envy ranks among the seven 'deadly sins'. I would even suggest that it is unconsciously felt to be the greatest sin of all, because it spoils and harms the good object which is the source of life. This view is consistent with the view described by Chaucer in *The Parsons Tale*: "It is certain that envy is the worst sin that is; for all other sins are sins only against one virtue, whereas envy is against all virtue and against all goodness". The feeling of having injured and destroyed the primal object impairs the individual's trust in the sincerity of his later relations and makes him doubt his capacity for love and goodness (Klein, 1957, p. 188).

Melanie Klein (1957) explicitly relates to the narrative of Genesis 2-3 as a fundamental expression of what excessive envy may lead to:

> The spoiling of creativity implied in envy is illustrated in Milton's *Paradise Lost* where Satan[9], envious of God, decides to become the usurper of Heaven. He makes war on God in his attempt to spoil the heavenly life and falls out of Heaven. Fallen, he and his other fallen angels build Hell as a rival to Heaven, and become the destructive force which attempts to destroy what God creates. This theological idea seems to come down from St Augustine, who describes Life as a creative force opposed to Envy, a destructive force. (p. 201).

In this perspective envy mobilizes the serpent (Satan) to tempt Adam and Eve to disobey God's prohibition and, ultimately, to destroy the peaceful existence of the world. The guilt, fear, and shame that follow the transgression of Adam and Eve is thus understood as originating in the feeling that they harmed or destroyed the wonderful world that God created. I would even suspect that Klein herself, while elaborating on the sources of shame and guilt, was aware in some way of the similarity between the mental processes that she was thoroughly developing and the story of the Eden:

> It is my hypothesis that one of the deepest sources of guilt is always linked with the envy of the feeding breast, and with the feeling of having spoilt its goodness by envious attacks (p. 194).

> Jealousy is felt to be much more acceptable and gives rise much less to guilt than the primary envy which destroys the first good object (p. 197).

---

[9] Satan and the serpent are closely related or even identical in the Christian literature and in the apocrypha (see Shulman, 2003, pp. 40-43).

173

The fear of God experienced after the sin, is thus interpreted as the result of projecting inner aggression onto the good object and thus experiencing him as a persecutor.

> It appears that one of the consequences of excessive envy is an early onset of guilt. If premature guilt is experienced by an ego not yet capable of bearing it, guilt is felt as persecution and the object that rouses guilt is turned into a persecutor (p.193).

Accordingly, Adam blames God for giving him the woman as an excuse for his own transgression (Gen. 3:12).

The midrash understands the serpent's punishment as a *quid pro quo* response to its sin:

> Rabbi Issi and Rabbi Hoshaya said in the name of Rabbi Hiya Rabbah: God said four things to the snake: I created you to be king of all beasts, but you did not want it — "more cursed shall you be..."; I created you to walk upright like man but you did not want it — "on your belly shall you crawl"; I created you to eat prepared foods like man but you did not want it — "dirt shall you eat"; you wished to kill Adam and marry his wife — "I will put enmity between you and the woman" (Gen. 3:14-15). (Gen. Rabbah Ch. 20)

The serpent, who wished to become a human-like creature, is deprived even of his special status in the world of the animals, and is humiliated by being forced to crawl and to eat dust. The man and the woman are banished form the Garden of Eden, from the proximity to God which have fostered notions of becoming God-like. The curses placed upon man and woman may be explained in this vein as well in that it touches their most precious quality: creativity. The woman's ability to create new life is now seriously limited, both by becoming dependant on her husband to conceive, and by suffering the pain and sorrow of pregnancy and childbirth. The man's creativity is severely limited in that he must labor hard and invest a lot of sweat before producing bread, and even then he will have no guarantee that the land will produce for him.

Finally, the last verse of God's curse makes it abundantly clear to Adam that he is no God and is far from ever becoming Godlike: "For dust you are, and to dust you shall return" (Gen 3:19). This very sad and painful moment for mankind will allow for the possibility, by accepting the new conditions, of gratitude and admiration for the creativity of others.

Splitting and the Depressive Position

A central concept in Klein's (1957) theory is the use of splitting as an organizing principle that the baby and the adult uses to keep its relationship with important objects stable. The split begins with splitting the mother's breast to a good one and a bad one, and later to splitting between good and loved objects to bad and hated objects, and between the good and bad parts of the self:

> An element of frustration by the breast is bound to enter into the infant's earliest relation to it, because even a happy feeding situation cannot altogether replace the pre-natal unity with the mother...
>
> Together with happy experiences, unavoidable grievances reinforce the innate conflict between love and hate, in fact, basically between life and death instincts, and result in the feeling that a good and a bad breast exist. As a consequence, early emotional life is characterized by a sense of losing and regaining the good object (pp. 178-179).

The story of the garden contains the deviation between the good symbol, God, and the bad symbol, the serpent. In their relationship with each other, Adam and Eve go through transformations beginning with being good objects to each other up to the level of leaving their families of origin and becoming one flesh, to becoming envious and destructive towards each other, the woman failing the man and then the man blaming her in front of God. Finally they become again a loving couple having children while the split continues to exist in their struggle for dominance and in their first two sons, Cain and Abel. The image of God himself oscillates between him being good and supportive to being jealous, persecutory, and punishing. There appears to be remarkable similarity between Klein's former paragraph and the symbolic description of the life in the garden before and after the sin.

A more subtle split is found in the manner in which the narrator deploys the various names of God. It is well known that there are two quite different descriptions of the creation story. One appears in Genesis 1 and the other in Genesis 2. This doublet has received much attention from biblical exegetes, ancient and modern (Shulman, 2003; Aron, 2005). One of the main differences, noted already in midrashic interpretations, is that whereas Genesis 1 refers to God as "Elohim", Genesis 2 primarily refers to "YHWH Elohim". In the midrashic economy, the name "Elohim" refers to God's attribute of justice, whereas YHWH represents God's compassion. The Rabbis explain the transition from Genesis 1 to Genesis 2 by positing that in order for the world to survive, God had to temper his justice with a measure of mercy:

> "YHWH Elohim" — This can be compared to a king who had empty flasks. The king thought, "If I put hot water in them, they will burst. If I put cold water in them, they will snap." What did he do? He mixed hot with cold and but them in, and they held. So, too, God said: "If I create the world with mercy, there will be an abundance of sin. If I create it with strict justice, it will not withstand it. Therefore, I will create it with both justice and mercy, and hopefully it will hold" (Gen. Rabbah Ch. 12).

The prohibition against eating from the Tree of Knowledge was given to Adam in Genesis 2:16, which uses the name "YHWH Elohim", which represents the combination of the attributes of justice and mercy. In the dialogue between the serpent and Eve, the serpent slightly but significantly modifies the command, attributing it to "Elohim" (Gen. 3:1, 3:5), and Eve actually reflects this assertion back to it (3:2). Throughout the remainder of Chapter 3, the dual attribution of "YHWH Elohim" appears, possibly expressing the need for God's mercy to enable the survival of humankind after the sin.

I assert that the text insinuates that the serpent and Eve apply a mechanism similar to the splitting process described by Klein. By attributing to their creator the bad aspect of the split, his attribute of the strict, merciless law, their infidelity becomes possible. They become suspicious of God's intentions and project their own envy onto him. By perceiving God in his "bad" name as strict and merciless, the woman is persuaded that God wants to keep the wonderful and delighting fruit for himself.

The narrative concludes tragically at the end of Chapter 3. Adam and Eve have been cursed by God and banished from the Garden of Eden. The Hebrew root "*etzev*", meaning sadness, pain, or depression, appears three times in the curses, twice in the curse of Eve ("I will make most severe your pangs ['*itzvonekh*'] in childbearing; In pain ['*be-etzev*'] shall you bear children" — 3:16) and once in the curse of Adam ("Cursed be the ground because of you; by toil ['*be-itzavon*'] shall you eat of it all the days of your life" — 3:17). The creativity of woman — giving new life — and of man — producing from the ground — would both now come at the cost of pain and sadness.

Only after this sad acknowledgement is Adam able to control his envy and to acknowledge his wife's important role as a mother: "Adam named his wife Eve because she was the mother of all the living" (3:20). In the very next verse, we again encounter God's generosity: "And the Lord God made garments of skins for Adam and his wife, and clothed them" (3:21). To use Kleinian language, Adam, humanity, must reach a "depressive position" in which he becomes aware of his envy and it's vicissitudes. Only then will he be able to love and admire his wife, to become creative, and to have children with her.

The completion of this process, in my view, is the hope that emerges after the birth of their first son and the ability of humanity to thank and admire God for his part in the new creation: "The man knew his wife Eve, and she conceived and bore Cain, saying 'I have gained a male child with the help of the Lord'" (4:1). The similarity between this part of the narrative and Klein's (1957) description of the depressive position and its role in human development is striking.

> When the infant reaches the depressive position, and becomes more able to face his psychic reality, he also feels that the object's badness is largely due to his own aggressiveness and the ensuing projection. This insight, as we can see in the transference situation, gives rise to great mental pain and guilt when the depressive position is at its height. But it also brings about feelings of relief and hope, which in turn make it less difficult to reunite the two aspects of the object and of the self and to work through the depressive position. This hope is based on the growing unconscious (p. 195).

177

Conclusion

I have attempted to demonstrate that we can identify, in midrashic exegesis of the Eden narrative, two interpretive trends which parallel two major psychoanalytic theories: the Freudian theory and the Kleinian theory. I have also traced some of the sources for these two ways of reading in the biblical text itself and in its intertextual associations. Aron (2005), in his discussion of Fromm's and Soloveitchik's interpretations of the story wrote:

> These two interpretations of the story of the Garden of Eden are irreconcilable. Each explains some aspects of the story meaningfully and leaves other aspects less well explained. Each puts some features into the foreground and leaves other aspects of the story in the background. (p. 702)

Similarly, our two ways of reading the narrative do not exhaust or fully integrate all of its detail, leaving it open for further study and interpretation.

I tried to read the story as a dreamlike narrative, avoiding forced source critical modifications to fit other myths or theoretical positions. Early psychoanalyses of this narrative commonly employed these methods (Freud, 1917; Reik and Rank, as cited in Shulman, 2003). I preferred to accept the version of the text that stood before the rabbis of the midrash and subsequent generations of Jewish exegetes.

Even assuming the validity of these findings, what is their significance? They may represent commonalities of human thought even with a gap of a continent and more than a millennium. Alternatively, it is possible that the parallels cataloged here indicate a common root or source which influenced both midrash and psychoanalysis — perhaps ancient Greece. Greek mythology influenced Western culture in general and psychoanalytic circles in particular. The same is true for the world of the ancient Rabbis who produced the midrash (Lieberman,1994).

A third possibility is that these midrashic and talmudic texts influenced Freud and Klein through the Jewish education they were exposed to in their early years. It is quite certain that Freud knew more about Judaism than he was ready to admit (Ostow, 1989). Furthermore, the resemblance between Freudian and talmudic analysis is widely discussed (Aron, 2005; Salberg, 2007).

I believe that the introduction of psychoanalytic insights into the study of the Bible and of the midrash has the potential to enrich their study and to enable new and deep interpretations of both of them. The Freudian and Kleinian perspectives suggested in this work open the way for introduction of further psychoanalytic developments in the study of sexuality, the Oedipus complex, envy, and the paranoid and depressive positions for the understanding of the Eden narrative. Studies like Loewald's (1997) and Ogden's (2006) may add to the understanding of the story of Eden through the perspective of intergenerational conflicts. Aron's study of Fromm's and Soloveitchik's interpretations, which demonstrates the utilization of intersubjective insights into the interpretations of the Eden story, represents another good model for future studies.

Finally, I would like to entertain the notion that reading the biblical Eden narrative has something to contribute to psychoanalytic theory. The proposed readings of the Eden narrative have a positive contribution to make for our field. I am referring to the central importance of hope in psychodynamic and psychoanalytic therapy.

Psychoanalysis seems to have a complicated attitude towards hope. While lying at the center of any psychotherapeutic endeavor, the concept of hope is treated hesitantly. For example:

> Traditionally, hope has been linked with fantasy and illusion as essentially regressive tendencies...To Boris (Harold Boris 1976, following Klein and Bion), the analytic process represents the relinquishment of hope and precipitation of a crisis of despair (Mitchell, 1993, p.205).

Hope is perceived as being defensive or neurotic and as opposed to the cool, rational, and realistic view expected in psychoanalytic therapy. It is perceived as being opposed to Freud's statement: "our best hope for the future is that intellect — the scientific spirit, reason — may in the process of time establish a dictatorship in the mental life of man" (Freud, 1933, p.171). Nevertheless, it is difficult to understand Freud's "evenly-suspended attention" or Bion's suggested listening "with no memory and no desire"(Bion, 1967) without the hope that the patient's associations will result in fruitful and significant material for the benefit of the patient.[10]

In the aftermath of the sin, the "eyes of both [Adam and Eve] were opened" (Gen. 3:7). In the Freudian reading, they became aware of the intensity of the sexual drive, and in the Kleinian reading, they realized the destructiveness of their own envy. At the same time, in both readings, they acquired new productivity and creativity that were to serve them in their monumental task of repairing the world. Consequently, the Eden narrative, and especially the situation in Eden before the sin, has become, in Western culture, a symbol of hope for a better future. Human redemption is often expressed as a return to Edenic conditions. The fact that humanity experienced a world of peaceful existence between man, woman, God, and nature signifies that it is possible for humanity to recover that existence.

In contrast with the Freudian and Kleinian theories, which demand that the patient reconcile unfulfilled desires and live with a certain level of pain, envy, and jealousy, the Bible tells us that humanity can strive for a better world. The prophet Isaiah expressed his hope for the future ingathering of exiles and ultimate redemption in one of the only places where the Bible explicitly invokes Eden:

> Truly the Lord has comforted Zion, comforted all her ruins; He has made her wilderness like Eden, her desert like the Garden of the Lord. Gladness and joy shall abide there, thanksgiving and the sound of music (Isa. 51:3).

---

[10] For further discussions of the issue of hope, see: Mitchell, 1993, pp. 202-231; Figuerdo, 2004.

REFERENCES

Aron, L. (2005). The Tree of Knowledge: Good and Evil, Conflicting Interpretations. *Psychoanal. Dialogues*, 15(5):681–707.

Bion, W. (1967). Notes on Memory and Desire. *Psychoanal. Forum*, 2:271-286.

Blass, R. (2001). The Teaching of the Oedipus Complex: On Making Freud Meaningful to University Students by Unveiling his Essential Ideas on the Human Condition. *Int. J. Psychoanal.*, 82:1105-1121.

Boyarin, D. (1990). *Intertextuality and the Reading of Midrash*. Bloomington: Indiana University Press

-----------. (1995). *Carnal Israel: Reading Sex in Talmudic Culture*. Berkeley: University of California Press.

Burston, D. (1994). Freud, the Serpent, and the Sexual Enlightenment of Children. *Int. Forum Psychoanal.*, 3:205-218.

Ellens, H. (1997). A Psychodynamic Hermeneutic of the Fall Story: Genesis 2:25–3:24: through a psychological lens. *Pastoral Psych.*, 45:221-236.

Figuerdo L. (2004). Belief, Hope and Faith, *Int. J. Psychoanal.*, 85:1439–53.

Freud, S. (1995). *New Introductory Lessons in Psychoanalysis*. New York: Norton.

Kass, L. (2003). *The Beginning of Wisdom: Reading Genesis*. New York: Free Press.

Klein, M. (1957). *Envy and Gratitude*. Alameda: Tavistock.

Kook, A., *Semonah Kevatzim*. Jerusalem: [Mishpachat ha-mechaber] (Heb.).

Lieberman, S. (1994). *Hellenism in Jewish Palestine*. New York: JTS.

Liebes, Y. (1994), God's love and envy, *Dimui* 7 (Heb.).

Loewald, H. (1979). The waning of the Oedipus complex, *J. Am. Psychoanal. Ass.*, 27:751-775.

Mitchell A. (1993). *Hope and Dread in Psychoanalysis*. New York: Basic Books.

Ogden, T. (2006). Reading Loewald: Oedipus reconceived, *Int. J. Psychoanal.*, 87:651–66.

181

Osman, M. (2000), The Adam and Eve Story as Exemplar of an Early-Life Variant of the Oedipus Complex, *J. Am. Psychoanal. Ass.*, 48:1292-1325.

-----------. (1989). Sigmund and Jakob Freud and the Philippson Bible — (with an analysis of the birthday inscription), *Int. Rev. Psychoanal.*, 16:483-492.

Roheim, G. (1940). The Garden of Eden, *Psychoanal. Rev.*, 27: 1-26.

Salberg, J. (2007). Hidden in plain sight: Freud's Jewish identity revisited, *Psychoanal. Dialogues*, 17:197-217.

Shulman, D. (2003). *The Genius of Genesis.* Bloomington: iUniverse.

Spero, M. (1996). Original Sin, the Symbolization of Desire, and the Development of the Mind: A Psychoanalytic Gloss on the Garden of Eden, *Psychoanalysis and Contemporary Thought*, 19:499-562.

Sternberg, M. (1987). *The Poetics of Biblical Narrative.* Bloomington: Indiana University Press.

Tanakh- The Holy Scriptures: The New JPS Translation (1985). Philadelphia: JPS.

Yerushalmi, Y. (1993). *Freud's Moses: Judaism Terminable and Interminable.* New Haven: Yale University Press.

APPENDIX

Text of Genesis 2:15-3:24

1917 Translation of the Jewish Publication Society

Genesis Chapter 2

15 And the LORD God took the man, and put him into the garden of Eden to dress it and to keep it. **16** And the LORD God commanded the man, saying: 'Of every tree of the garden thou mayest freely eat; **17** but of the tree of the knowledge of good and evil, thou shalt not eat of it; for in the day that thou eatest thereof thou shalt surely die.' **18** And the LORD God said: 'It is not good that the man should be alone; I will make him a help meet for him.' **19** And out of the ground the LORD God formed every beast of the field, and every fowl of the air; and brought them unto the man to see what he would call them; and whatsoever the man would call every living creature, that was to be the name thereof. **20** And the man gave names to all cattle, and to the fowl of the air, and to every beast of the field; but for Adam there was not found a help meet for him. **21** And the LORD God caused a deep sleep to fall upon the man, and he slept; and He took one of his ribs, and closed up the place with flesh instead thereof. **22** And the rib, which the LORD God had taken from the man, made He a woman, and brought her unto the man. **23** And the man said: 'This is now bone of my bones, and flesh of my flesh; she shall be called Woman, because she was taken out of Man.' **24** Therefore shall a man leave his father and his mother, and shall cleave unto his wife, and they shall be one flesh. **25** And they were both naked, the man and his wife, and were not ashamed.

Genesis Chapter 3

1 Now the serpent was more subtle than any beast of the field which the LORD God had made. And he said unto the woman: 'Yea, hath God said: Ye shall not eat of any tree of the garden?' **2** And the woman said unto the serpent: 'Of the fruit of the trees of the garden we may eat; **3** but of the fruit of the tree which is in the midst of the garden, God hath said:

Ye shall not eat of it, neither shall ye touch it, lest ye die.' **4** And the serpent said unto the woman: 'Ye shall not surely die; **5** for God doth know that in the day ye eat thereof, then your eyes shall be opened, and ye shall be as God, knowing good and evil.' **6** And when the woman saw that the tree was good for food, and that it was a delight to the eyes, and that the tree was to be desired to make one wise, she took of the fruit thereof, and did eat; and she gave also unto her husband with her, and he did eat. **7** And the eyes of them both were opened, and they knew that they were naked; and they sewed fig-leaves together, and made themselves girdles. **8** And they heard the voice of the LORD God walking in the garden toward the cool of the day; and the man and his wife hid themselves from the presence of the LORD God amongst the trees of the garden. **9** And the LORD God called unto the man, and said unto him: 'Where art thou?' **10** And he said: 'I heard Thy voice in the garden, and I was afraid, because I was naked; and I hid myself.' **11** And He said: 'Who told thee that thou wast naked? Hast thou eaten of the tree, whereof I commanded thee that thou shouldest not eat?' **12** And the man said: 'The woman whom Thou gavest to be with me, she gave me of the tree, and I did eat.' **13** And the LORD God said unto the woman: 'What is this thou hast done?' And the woman said: 'The serpent beguiled me, and I did eat.' **14** And the LORD God said unto the serpent: 'Because thou hast done this, cursed art thou from among all cattle, and from among all beasts of the field; upon thy belly shalt thou go, and dust shalt thou eat all the days of thy life. **15** And I will put enmity between thee and the woman, and between thy seed and her seed; they shall bruise thy head, and thou shalt bruise their heel.' **16** Unto the woman He said: 'I will greatly multiply thy pain and thy travail; in pain thou shalt bring forth children; and thy desire shall be to thy husband, and he shall rule over thee.' **17** And unto Adam He said: 'Because thou hast hearkened unto the voice of thy wife, and hast eaten of the tree, of which I commanded thee, saying: Thou shalt not eat of it; cursed is the ground for thy sake; in toil shalt thou eat of it all the days of thy life. **18** Thorns also and thistles shall it bring forth to thee; and thou shalt eat the herb of the field. **19** In the sweat of thy face shalt thou eat bread, till thou return unto the ground; for out of it wast thou taken; for dust thou art, and unto dust shalt thou return.'

20 And the man called his wife's name Eve; because she was the mother of all living. **21** And the LORD God made for Adam and for his wife garments of skins, and clothed them. **22** And the LORD God said: 'Behold, the man is become as one of us, to know good and evil; and now, lest he put forth his hand, and take also of the tree of life, and eat, and live for ever.' **23** Therefore the LORD God sent him forth from the garden of Eden, to till the ground from whence he was taken. **24** So He drove out the man; and He placed at the east of the garden of Eden the cherubim, and the flaming sword which turned every way, to keep the way to the tree of life.

Transformations in the 'Mental Apparatus of Dreaming' as Depicted in the Biblical Story of Joseph

Moshe Halevi Spero

> Psycho-analysis has restored to dreams the importance which was generally ascribed to them in ancient times, but it treats them differently. It does not rely upon the cleverness of the dream-interpreter, but for the most part hands the task over to the dreamer himself by asking him for his associations to the separate elements of the dream.
>
> *Sigmund Freud (1923 [1922], p. 240-241)*

> The dream is not a fiction taken for reality; it is the odyssey of a consciousness dedicated by itself, and in spite of itself, to build an only unreal world.
>
> *Jean-Paul Sartre (1940, p. 206)*

This composition sheds new psychoanalytic light on the biblical episodes of Joseph's relations with his own dreams (Gen. 38:1-11), the dreams of the ministers (Gen. 40:1-23), and the dreams of the Pharaoh of Egypt (Gen. 41:1-32).[1] Contrary to all preceding studies, this essay does

---

[1] A brief but important historical clarification is in order. In the *Five Books of Moses*, the various pharaohs that are associated with Abraham, Joseph, and Moses are unnamed, whereas the opposite is the case in the later books of the *Prophets* and *Writings*. The protagonist of the *Genesis* episode, familiar to us only by the title Pharaoh (the Hebrew *Fangr'o* is the cognate of the two Egyptian words *per 'aa*, "the Great House" or palace), was most probably not a pharaoh *per se* although he was certainly a monarch. Indeed, in Islam's *Al Qur'an* version of the story of

not focus on Joseph's interpretations *per se* (seven thin kine swallowing seven fat kine = seven years of plenty followed by seven years of famine), or the psychosexual meaning of the dream symbols *per se* (e.g., dread of oral engulfment, phallic anxieties, etc.). Instead, we will be concerned with certain subtle developments that take place in Joseph's and Pharaoh's experience of dreaming and dream narration, most of which circle around the particular Hebrew interjective adverb *hē'ney,* "Behold!" By close reading, I will show that a crucial *representational transformation* takes place in Pharaoh's understanding of his dream *prior* to Joseph's famous "wise" socioeconomic declaration, and that Joseph's essential contribution lies not so much in the final interpretation he offers but rather in what he does *not do.* This transformation disposes Pharaoh to "accepting" Joseph's subsequent suggestions. Overall, the developments suggest that the Bible has given us a portrait of the maturation of the mental apparatus of dreaming.

My approach requires that we recast the several subsections of the story of Joseph, leading up to the dream of Pharaoh, as a mythic structure (see Lévi-Strauss, 1958), a highly condensed psychological story that captures and frames crucial developments that take place *within the mind* that bear upon the capacity to experience dreams as dreams. Of course,

---

Joseph (*Sura Yusuf,* 12), Joseph's ruler is referred to as *mal'eq* (Hebrew cognate *mel'ekh*) and not as *Fer'angwn,* Arabic for Pharaoh. This is no accident. The use of the title "Pharaoh" seems to have begun just prior to the period of Moses (the New Kingdom ca. 1553-1292 BCE). Joseph's life and the events of *Genesis,* 41, however, belong somewhere in the Second Intermediate Period *ca.* 1674-1553 BCE, corresponding to the 13th through 17th dynasties of the alien shepherd kings, the *Heqa-khaswt* or Hyksos, who in ancient writings are never referred to as *per 'aa.* Overall, the evidence suggests that Joseph's kingly dreamer was the great warrior Sesostris (Sen'u'sret) II (1897-1878 BCE) and that Joseph's status as vizier may have extended into the brief reigns of the next two rulers (see Aling, 2003; Osman, 1987, pp. 29-30; Rice, 1999, p. 222; Rohl, 1995; Vermes, 1973). We do not know when the anachronistic use of the title Pharaoh entered the biblical text, or why might such an apparent error have been required (see Coats, 1992, p. 980 and Odelain & Seguineau, 1981, p. 270). However, assuming that the Bible is also Moses's chronicle, it is probable that he simply used the title that was well-established during his own experience with Pharaohs Seti and Ramases II. I will follow convention and refer to Joseph's client as Pharaoh.

I fully respect the religious view that the biblical story of Joseph transcribes an historical event regarding the interactions among actual personalities and the moral implications of these interactions. However, here I will look upon the textual details as if they were themselves components of a specific kind of dream — a dream that represents the way in which a prototypic mind becomes aware of its own internal dreamer ("Pharaoh"), censor (the "cup bearer"), and internal interpreter ("Joseph").

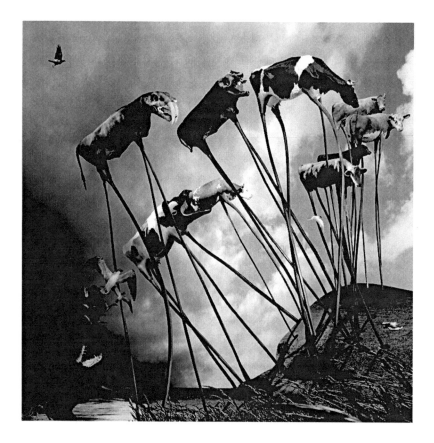

Pharaoh's dream by: **www.chrisbenn.com**

II

Space does not permit an exhaustive review of the literature on the dream episodes of *Genesis* 38, 39, and 41 — including Joseph's dreams and his interpretations of the dreams of others — but the student eventually confronts a dilemma that can be summarized as follows.

Classical Judaic commentary, beginning with the midrashic and Talmudic period through the mediaeval period of biblical glosses and contemporary modern religious scholarship, picks up on scores of prosodic details and chiastic patterns in these texts which are yoked to ethicomoral instruction and to theologically-oriented understandings of God's role in the development of history.[2] It is much harder to find a deep analysis of Joseph's dreams or the Pharaoh's dreams as lawful *psychological* structures in their own right. There is no appreciation of Joseph's grasp of Pharaoh's dream experience as an expression of a certain kind of psychodynamic relationship between the two men.[3] Yet it is difficult to truly problematize this kind of text and enter into the minds of the protagonists if one is too

---

[2]   In *Al Qur'an* (*Sura* 12: 43-57), the story of Joseph or *Yusuf* appears with many interesting variations. Four examples will suffice: (a) The narrative itself is leaner overall (28 verses as opposed to the Bible's 88 verses), and lacks the many digressions and gaps that characterize the biblical version. (b) The king's dream is told only once, in a version even sparser than the first version that appears in the Bible (hence, the king utters none of the qualitative exclamations we find in the second narration in the Bible). (c) The magicians declare the dream "confused." (d) The cup bearer, once he is liberated, makes no declaration of repentance but brings the king's dream to the still imprisoned Yusuf for his interpretation. The successful interpretation motivates the king to investigate the circumstances of Yusuf's incarceration and only then is Yusuf freed. The brevity of the Qu'ranic text dulls the unconscious psychological draw of the story which, of course, depends upon the uneven and uncanny irritating textual terrain (see Kaltner, 2003).

[3]   Aviva Gottleib Zornberg (1995, pp. 286-288; 2009), a bible scholar whose work uniquely straddles the psychological dimensions revealed by the biblical text, appreciates Joseph's special struggle with loss, oblivion, and absence — which explains his sensitivity to the meaning of the "disappearance" of the fat cows in Pharaoh's dream — but she does not discuss the dream process and its evolution.

189

prone to resolve all of the story's aporia, pleonasms, and other textual peculiarities by appealing to providential intent.[4]

The scientific literature that discusses the biblical and rabbinic perspectives on dream psychology in general also neglects the kinds of developments I will underscore here.[5] When it does touch on Joseph's management of dreams, it seems primarily interested in socio-historical aspects of the story, the mantic-propitiatory function of dreams, the semiotic meanings of the dream figures (the sheaves, the seven kine, the Nile, etc.), and Joseph's Mesopotamian-bred skill at manipulating the manifest content in Pharaoh's dreams (e.g., $she'va_{ng}$ = 7; $so'va_{ng}$ = plenty) for his own political ends. There is awareness of a certain maturation in Joseph's approach to the sensitivities of the dreamer — from Joseph's narcissistic bandying of his early dreams before his brothers and father, his more chaste and empathic role with the dreams of his ministerial fellow prisoners, to his dramatic coup with Pharaoh's dream — but I have not found any discussion of the kind of empathic bridge that takes place when a narrator insists upon telling a dream to a specific listener.

The psychoanalytic literature itself also does not take us too far, emphasizing psychosexual themes within the dream content as opposed to the dream *process* (Berger, 1981; Kelman, 1986; Lauer, 1913; Lorand, 1957; Lowinger, 1908; Wax, 1998, 1999).[6] Indeed, note a significant irony: Freud

---

[4] In this analysis, I make no reference to providential or divine intentions or interventions, my personal orthodox Jewish commitments notwithstanding. Although I do not discount this dimension, its putative role is not necessary for a fuller understanding the phenomena in question. At the same time, a psychological-naturalistic understanding does *not* contradict the theological dimension which speaks in terms of the need for divine intentions and interventions throughout history in general and this story in particular. Elsewhere I present a metapsychology that might integrate and "contain" both the scientific and religious dimensions of this kind of approach to mental experience in theoretical as well as clinical applications (Spero, 1992, 2010).

[5] See Chiel (2005); Gimani (1997); Harris (1994); Klein (1997); Noegel (2001); Spero (1980); Turner (1997); Zeitlin (1975-1976); Zeligs (1974, pp. 76-79).

[6] Kelman's (1986) thesis is that Joseph sensed, upon hearing the Pharaoh's dream and his memory of the king's attitude toward the ministers, that Pharaoh tended to replace the well-favored with the lowly, and used this as a stepping stone to dare suggest that a wise man be selected to "replace" the king himself

himself, arguably the "Joseph" of the modern era, has almost nothing to say about these crucial biblical texts (cf. 1900, p. 97).[7] Given Freud's intense personal ambivalence about Judaism and his dread that psychoanalysis be deemed a "Jewish science" or an art of divination — and bearing in mind his pervasive anxiety about intellectual priority, specifically as concerned his views on dreaming[8] — we might understand his need to distance himself from the concrete methods of symbol "translation" of the great biblical diviner. Most likely, Freud regarded Joseph's type of interpretation as a classic example of *anagogic* dream interpretation — the pragmatic or moralistic "over-interpretations" or explanations that some of Freud's contemporaries viewed as a dimension distinct from the psychosexual dimension that Freud considered primary — and, hence, an incomplete or non-psychoanalytic level of interpretation (1900, p. 523-524). And yet, the biblical episode to be investigated is actually a prime

---

in the task of preparing for the coming drought. The following statement by Kelman is memorable, "What was prophetic about [Joseph's approach to] Pharaoh's dreams was not that he predicted harvests correctly, but that he harvested predictions correctly" (p. 309).

[7] In *The Interpretation of Dreams*, Freud (1900, p. 4 n2) refers to two older collections of dream symbolisms by Jewish scholars: Amram (1901) and Almoli (1516 [1998]) — these are, respectively, Nathan ben Hayim Amram (1805-1870), the Palestinian bible scholar, and Solomon Almoli (died *ca.* 1530), the great Spanish scholar and physician from Constantinople. As Freud revised his bibliography over the years, he added reference to studies by Lauer (1913) and Lowinger (1908). None of these authors took advantage of the complexities of the episode under study here, and Freud does essentially nothing with their writings.

Freud does acknowledge a certain kinship to Joseph, but — not unlike Joseph's own incarceration in a deep vault at his brothers' hands — it is buried in a footnote (1900, p. 484, n2): "It will be noticed that the name *Josef* plays a great part in my dreams [refers *infra* to pp. 137-8]. My own ego finds it very easy to hide itself behind people of that name, since Joseph was the name of a man famous in the Bible as an interpreter of dreams." Freud's only other known reference to Joseph is in a letter to Thomas Mann (Freud, 1936, pp. 432-434), in which Freud speculates whether the Joseph myth or personality might shed light on certain aspects of Napoleon's personality. Yet there is no discussion of the relationship between dreams, dream interpretation, and Joseph's life.

[8] This can be seen in some of Freud's own remarks concerning scientific priority and his theory of dreams and free associations (e.g., Freud, 1900, pp. 100, 378; 1922, 1923) (see also Sands, 1999).

example of the relationship between the dream wish and what Freud called the "conditions of representability" that constitute the dream structure.

To be sure, numerous methodological difficulties confront any kind of psychological analysis of the minds of ancient subjects, historical or mythological, since we must employ social, interpersonal, and intra-psychic theories or laws whose veridicality may not stretch beyond cultural and historical boundaries.[9] Some writers are hesitant to do much with the biblical dream due to the assumption that the biblical character had not yet achieved a mature level of self-reflection, introspection, or a capacity for "inward talking" that would be needed in order to justify discussion of a sophisticated dreaming process. Nili Shupak (2006, p. 106), for example, takes it for granted that the dream in the Bible was understood as caused solely by external forces — gods, the dead, demons — and as *not* stemming from an internal psychic reality as maintained by modern psychology. However, in view of considerable evidence for an introspective mind in the Bible (such as Gen. 17:17, 18:12; cf. Lurie, 2000; Niehoff, 1992; Oppenheim, 1966; Smith, 1998),[10] we can assume that the biblical dream ought to evince equal sophistication.

---

[9] The field of psychohistory — which is generally considered to have begun with Erik H. Erikson's *Young Man Luther* (1958) — grapples with these issues (see Anderson, 1981; Cocks & Travis, 1987; de Mause, 1975, 1982; Wallace, 1985), and limits of space forbid taking these up here. But I should say this, echoing Helmut Raguse's (1996) recently emphasis: psychoanalysis no longer sets out to uncover hidden meanings inherent in a text, including the biblical text, but rather to construct new meanings on the basis of the pragmatics of oral or written speech and its intended effect. Thus, among the conditions that permit psychological analysis across time is the evidence of highly idiosyncratic quirks or patterns within certain dense contexts that have never been adequately explained, or are even completely ignored, by previous commentaries, and which 'suddenly' become comprehensible by contemporary lights. Additionally, we are likely to be on the right course toward sensing the openness of an ancient text or behavior to contemporary understandings when we notice that the text or behavior was considered anomalous or radical by the biblical actors themselves (see Izenberg, 1975; Rollins, 2008).

[10] Without doubt, a full disconnection from the notion of the biblical dream as a form of divine message should not be expected within Jewish literature.

I will adopt an alternate approach that imagines the drama of the biblical characters as an analogue to the dynamic process that takes place among various object representational states within a single mind.[11] In this approach, we would bypass the analysis of the actual conflict between two actual historic persons — say, the twin brothers Jacob and Esau — and focus instead on the portrait of the capacity to internalize the tension between superego idealizations, on the one hand, and raw aggressive impulses, on the other hand. For me, the inter-subjective ("actual") and the intra-psychic are dual and intersecting tracks, though I tend to emphasize the intra-psychic. Therefore, as we proceed stepwise through the interactions between Joseph, his brothers and other protagonists, and his and their dreams, I will first portray the development of dream interpretation as depicted *within* the story and then I will underscore the analogous changes that are taking place within the "apparatus of dreaming" in a single prototypical mind.

III

Let us begin our exploration by stating a commonplace. Freud did not discover the dream nor was he the first to suggest that dreams beg to be interpreted. Most readers are familiar with the Talmud's pithy insistence that "a dream that is not interpreted is like a letter that is not read" (*Bra'khot*, 55*b*). Similar appreciation was expressed in ancient Greek and later Arabic medicine (MacKenzie, 1965; von Grunebaum & Caillois, 1966). Freud was also not the originator of the idea that dreams express the dreamer's wishes and fears, as opposed to being wholly "prophetic" messages,

---

Nevertheless, a special emphasis on the role of the dreamer's imaginative faculty does begin to take place around 1100 CE (see Brill, 2000).

[11]   This approach does not discontent the possibility that these stories are also narrative renditions of historical events of some kinds. But it has been argued that historical consciousness achieves its zenith only when concrete narration has surrendered to the gradual inclination of the human mind toward myth and symbolization (for fuller discussion, see Spero, 1996).

warnings, or omens from malign or benevolent external sources (see Isaiah 29:8). But he was the first to comprehend that the deeper meaning of a dream is conveyed *not only* by the symbolic-like images and emotionally evocative manifest story-form in which the dream is enveloped (*verhüllt*). Far more important is the quality of the representational structure that holds the components of the dream together and enables a bit of repressed desire to gain accessibility, providing a semi-coherent impression that an impossible wish has been momentarily fulfilled.

But the full import of Freud's thinking did not emerge until more than half a century after the publication of *The Interpretation of Dreams* (1900). Whereas it was once considered sufficient to know that the capacity to dream, and to dream productively, is one of the basic functions of the mind, it has gradually become more clear *that in order for daily experience to be entertained at all by the mind, to be "mentalized," it must at some point be dreamed.*[12] That is, in order for mental experience to achieve sentience at any given time it has to be washed through dream-quality processes which operate constantly, whether or not we are conscious of dreaming. Otherwise, we probably would remain incapable of truly knowing whether we are awake, asleep, hallucinating or accurately perceiving.

This theoretical perspective bears directly on Pharaoh's and Joseph's dreams. Some have said that the term *dream* applies only to one that can be told, that militates to be told, for it is only in that manner that the intense, quasi-psychotic processes that create the dream finally achieve containment. Malcolm (1959) states that although there are unmistakable differences between dreaming and the waking impression *that one has dreamed,* the sole criterion for asserting the existence of a dream is the dreamer's waking account of the dream. That is, a dream that cannot be reported has for all intents and purposes not occurred, other than on some simple electrical "brain" level of no corroborative value at all.[13] Cecily

---

[12]   Since Bion (1962, 1963, 1965) first suggested this notion, it has been brought forward by Meltzer (1983), Grotstein (1979, 2000), Ogden (2003), and most recently, on a level of great complexity, by Cesar and Sara Botella (2005).

[13]   To help appreciate this point, I assure the reader that we all experience a knee-jerk protest against Malcom's and de Monchaux's view: "Yes, of course *reporting*

de Monchaux (1978) takes this further and states that unless dreaming is a subordinate function, it ceases to be of any use to the ego, since the ego is limited to three-dimensions (plus time).[14] By "subordinate function" she means to say that (1978, p. 203),

> the dream must have fewer dimensions than waking experience, rather as a drawing, a sculpture, a poem, or a film must have fewer dimensions than the natural event to which it bears some relation in its creator's life.

In other words, all perception, all symbolization, necessarily abstracts a great degree of the total amount of stimuli around us (including stimuli that emanate from within). Yet a dream does this to an even greater degree, and this is among the reasons why we have learned to generally *differentiate* "dreaming" from what we call conscious experience. In psychoses, traumatic confusion, and borderline states, this sense of dream *containment* and "tellability" is lost or degraded, although in the hands of especially gifted people, artists, mystics, or patients in psychoanalysis, this kind of "loss" or dedifferentiation can be put to good use.

Generally speaking, in order to ensure that a dream offers a subset of phenomenological experience that is smaller than the ego's overall experience of things, dreaming relies upon a restricted sense of time (e.g.,

---

a dream is a very significant element of the process, but whilst dreaming during the night *I was after all engaged in some very special mental process called dreaming, was I not?!"* Engaged in a mental process, yes; *dreaming,* not quite. After much philosophical and neuro-physiological debate on the matter (cf. Dennett, 1976), it seems inescapable that the true self-assessment that we have dreamed requires that we awaken and report something that is either logically impossible (e.g., "I dreamed I saw a thin ear of corn consume a fat ear of corn!") or known to be impossible by exterior criteria (e.g., Pharaoh's wife testifies that the king never left her side, the Nile being a 3 hour ride by chariot from their palace!). Hence, to state "I dreamed such and such" is to be conscious and aware of a proviso: "and such and such could not possibly have happened, *despite my very strong sense that that is nevertheless exactly what I experienced."* Until such a discrimination can be seized — as it usually is, by almost every dream dreamed by normal people under average conditions, *and as it was not,* at first, by Pharaoh — what we experience ("during the night") is very simply a full-fledged hallucination, just as Freud originally argued.

[14] Analogous to the approach carefully worked out by Matte-Blanco (1975, 1988; see Rayner, 1995).

many events are depicted as if occurring simultaneously), condensation of the number and role of images, and repetition (Matte-Blanco, 1975, pp. 400-421). In dreams, for example, either-or distinctions are abandoned and the principle of logical exclusivity is surrendered (i.e., in a dream, a thing *can be* equal to its negative, and part and whole need not be discriminated). The function of dreaming, then, is to find pictorial ways to express infinite dimensions in a manner that can be somewhat tolerated and somehow understood, if only partially, by the ego whose perspectives are limited to three dimensions. Every dream is a hyper-space which can never be totally experienced within the limited space of the ego, although we can have momentary experiences of this "impossible" tension. These experiences can be pleasurable or terrifying, and are always uncanny. Dream *reporting* that manages to not draw too close to the ego's general conscious-style and logically-framed mode of thought enables the dream to retain its original uncanny quality and affords the dreamer a continued relationship with that special quality of experience as well.

Two critical corollaries attend this view. First, the subsequent telling of the dream, under ideal conditions, is no less a component of the dream itself than the original act or state of dreaming. Second, the dream process itself *can be continued and extended* during the telling in a manner that is also no less significant than whatever "actually" transpired during sleep. One of the traits that distinguish a "good" psychoanalytic process is the ability to foster a salutary transition from *dreaming* to *the dream-like quality of the clinical narrative as a whole.* Under less than optimum conditions, this inherent capability of the analytic process is experienced by a patient (or, via countertransference, by an analyst) as threatening and is resisted. In the classical view, the analyst facilitated emotional enlightenment by virtue of his knowledge of dream processes and his grasp of dream symbols. In the contemporary view, which I am adopting in order to fully understand *Genesis,* 41, greater weight is placed on the analyst's sensitivity to the patient's transference perception of the analyst and how this influences the shape and quality of the dream. In a very important sense, many dreams do not require an interpreter as such; the interpretation is latent, wedded to the structure of the dream. Instead, the dream requires *conditions for suitable narration* that enable the ego to experience in conscious, articulate terms those fleeting states of desire to which it had attempted to give form and figure in a less conscious state.

IV

Let us now reconsider the earlier episodes in Joseph's life reported in Gen.38:1-11 and Gen.39:3-19 and ask: what might Joseph have gradually begun to apprehend about his relationship with people to whom he reports dreams or who report their dreams to him?

A sense of foreboding overtakes us as we read the introductory exchange between Joseph, the self-involved, naive, sexually mischievous, pampered tattletale, [15] and his brothers and father. Joseph plunges into disaster seemingly blindly (Gen. 37, 5-12):

> And Joseph dreamed a dream [*va-ya'ha'lom Yo'sef ha'lom*],
> and he told it to his brothers;
> and they hated him yet more.

> And he said to them: 'Hear, I pray you, this dream which I have dreamed.
> For, behold [*ve-hē'ney*], we were binding sheaves in the field,
> and, behold [*ve-hē'ney*], my sheaf arose, and also stood upright;
> and behold, your sheaves came round about, and bowed down to my sheaf.

> And his brothers said to him:

> 'Shall you indeed reign over us? Or shall you indeed have dominion over us?
> and they hated him more for his dreams, *and for his words*.

> And he dreamed yet another dream, and told it to his brothers, and said:

---

15   Rashi (R. Shlomo Yizhaki, d. 1105) *ad loc* refers to Joseph's childishness and narcissistic preoccupations, and the Talmud generally acknowledges that these where the very personality issues with which Joseph would need to learn to struggle in order to advance to leadership. As for his accusations regarding his brothers, opinion ranges from viewing these as outright untruths, exaggerations of minor differences, or projections of his own untamed conflicts (see Jerusalemite Talmud, *Pe'ah*, 1:1; Bab. Talmud, *Yoma*, 35b and *So'tah*, 13b, 36b).

'Behold [hē'ney], I have dreamed yet another dream: and, behold, the sun
and the moon and the eleven stars bowed down to me.'

And he told it to his father, and to his brothers;
and his father rebuked him, and said to him:
'What is this dream that you have dreamed?
Shall I and your mother and your brothers indeed come to bow down
to you to the earth?'

And his brothers envied him;
but his father kept the saying in his mind [ve-a'vēv sha'mar et ha-da'var].

Four items are conspicuous. One cannot ignore the phallic-oedipal
symbolism in Joseph's dreams. The reader will also learn that these sheaves
foreshadow the sheaves that feature in the Pharaoh's dreams, yet, as
I argued in the earlier paragraphs, symbolic cataloguing may not be the
deepest concern of the story.

More noteworthy is the fact that Joseph himself does not interpret
either of the two dreams he reports; these are interpreted by the brothers
and by Jacob. This process begins with the passing reference to a dream
(Gen.37:5) that is apparently not recounted in the text — a riddle yet to be
resolved — which stirs the brothers' anger. The purpose of this passage,
I believe, is to inform us that if the brothers already envied Joseph's
selective treatment at their father's own hand, their hatred grew *when
they began to notice that he alone shared their father's capacity for dreaming and
telling dreams!*

Joseph then (Gen.37:6) tells a dream to his brothers — this may have
been the dream alluded to in passage 5 or it is a new one — and their
wrath increases "for his dreams and for his words." In fact, Joseph
had shared his dream *but not* "his words," for he is not the one who
interpreted the dream. Thus, "his words" can only refer to the articulation
of the dream itself or are an allusion to the brothers' own words that they
experienced as Joseph's. The effect seems to have been a momentary sense
of dedifferentiation between what might have been on Joseph's mind and
what might have been on theirs; the dreaded sense of fate or "prophecy"

emanated from having projected their unconscious wishes onto Joseph. The brothers' wrath was fueled by projection; it is their interpretation that effectively gave narrative substance and emotional life to Joseph's word picture.[16]

The same phenomenon occurs when Joseph recounts his second dream (Gen.37:9-10). This time it is Jacob and possibly the brothers who invest it with meaning, and this creates the same atmosphere of dreadful fatedness and counter-introjected anger. But whereas the brothers are now inconsolable and must expel the toxic effect that Joseph's dreams have exerted upon their unconscious minds, Jacob's reaction is different: *ve-a'vēv sha'mar et ha-da'var*. I think this phrase means two things. First, though Jacob, too, expresses anger, he *contains* it until it can be better understood.[17] While the word *da'var* can metonymically connote "the saying" (as in *dēb'rot*) or "the matter," it also denotes any nondescript thing, thingness as such. This would allow us to read that Jacob may have tried to contain the not-yet-interpretable remainder or "residue" that is left by all dreams, since unconscious wishes and desire cannot ever be completely exhausted by symbolic forms. The same was no doubt true regarding Jacob's irrepressible love of Joseph, and could be traced further back to the insufficiencies and traumatic interruptions in his relationship with his father, Isaac. Had Jacob felt that these dreams were primarily prophetic revelations, of the kind that he himself had had, I believe the response to the dream message would have been far less explosive. And if Jacob sensed the uniqueness of the current situation, he may have sought to contain the entire episode in the intuitive effort to create an envelope for the fascinating but frightening phenomenon that he had just observed: *the effect of the dreamer on the listener, and the effect of narration upon the dream experience itself.*

---

[16] The traditional interpretation is that "his words" refers to his previous tale-bearing to Jacob, aside from his dreams.

[17] Had the text wished to convey simply that Jacob restrained himself, or was silent, it might more suitably have written *va-yēt'a'pek*.

In terms of intra-psychic development, then, this first episode portrays a deeply anxious, primitive state, where the regressive experience of a nocturnal image generates *a pressure towards immediately repeating the dream,* as opposed to a more aesthetically balanced desire to narrate the dream to an other and share the experience. The dream as such can be articulated, the dreamer's self is indirectly depicted, yet the dreamer seems stunned. In such states, the dim apperception of meaning cannot be fully located within the dreamer's own mind. The prototypic mind portrayed in the text seems completely untutored, unaware of the meaning of his dreams or their target, and does not quite sense that the ego itself is the central focus of the dream, even as it aspires to relate to the subjective world. There is naive anticipation of a "receptive audience" of narcissistic mirroring. *There is not yet a mature awareness that an external audience can only benefit from a dream to the degree that it has been dreamed by a mind that can contain a dream, by a mind that can interpret from within.* And yet this future development is hinted at. Alongside the fractious and fragmented reaction of the paranoid "brotherly" components of the mind, the paternal order, the system of lawful symbolization, attempts to quietly "save the thing."

V

The final important element in this chapter is the repeated appearance of term "behold," *hē'ney* ("and behold," *ve-hē'ney*). It is this little, much ignored yet very significant operative that alerts our attention to the fact that the speaker is attempting not simply to tell a story but to articulate in words an experience that is essentially pictorial.

The use of *hē'ney ha'lom* [חלם הנה] or *ve-hē'ney ha'lom* [והנה חלם][18] is established earlier during the experiences of Joseph's father, Jacob, during

---

[18] The term *ha'lom* [חלם] for dream has an interesting etymology. It seems to begin in pre-Hebrew times as a reference to power or strength (reflected in the term for "war," *mēl'ha'mah* [מלחמה]) in cultures where to be strong is to achieve puberty and sexual prowess, which culminates in the experience of sexual dreaming (see Bar, 2001, pp. 10-13; Brown, Driver & Briggs, 1906, p. 320).

his journey toward Haran. Reaching a certain place at sunset, physically exhausted, Jacob prepares his famous make-shift pillow of 12 stones, and dreams (Gen. 28:12-15):

> And he dreamed [*va-ya'ha'lom*], and behold [*ve-hē'ney*]:
> a ladder set upon the earth, and the top of it reached to heaven;
> and, behold [*ve-hē'ney*], the angels of God ascending and descending it.
>
> And, behold [*ve-hē'ney*], the Lord stood beside him, and said:
> 'I am the Lord, the God of Abraham thy father, and the God of Isaac.
> The land upon which you lie to you will I give it, and to your seed…

The word "behold" appears one more time during the dream (28:15). As the dream is completed, another important term appears (28:16):

> And Jacob awakened out of his sleep [*va-yē'kaz Ya'akov mē-shena'to*],
> and he said: 'Surely the Lord is in this place, and I knew it not.'

Key terms appear here that will reappear throughout the experiences of his son Joseph with Pharaoh: *va-ya'ha'lom, ve-hē'ney*, and *va-yē'kaz*. Importantly, these terms do not all appear when God himself, as it were, makes a direct or indirect appearance via a dream image.[19] So I will argue that when all three appear together we have evidence *that the speaker has been affected qualitatively by a unique psychological experience that he has been able to frame as a dream capable of being narrated, whether or not the content of the dream includes a divine message.* Further, when one of these three terms is missing or is utilized in an extraordinary manner, the biblical text is conveying that the speaker has experienced a flaw or disruption in the process of dream representation. In fact, this rule is broken in the episode of the dreams that Joseph shares with his brothers (Gen. 37:5-9) and in the dreams of his fellow prisoners in jail (40:5-18), but it holds, though in an odd way, in the dreams of the Pharaoh. We shall turn to this.

---

19   See Gen. 15:2-9, 20:3, 22:1-2, 9-19, 31:24; cf. 18:2 where *hē'ney* appears once, as in the 'burning bush" revelation at Exod. 3:2.

The *hē'ney* "rule" draws our attention to the finale of the episode of Joseph and his brothers described in Gen. 37:18. But before we treat this final episode, we need to comprehend a seemingly unnecessary *mise-en-scene*.

On the surface, it is a very brief and mysterious exchange. Following the angry confrontation with his brothers, Jacob charges Joseph to find his brothers who are tending their flock in She'hem. Joseph consents with a single word, *hē'ney'nē,* "I am here," or, to open up the contracted word: *hē'ney a'nē,* "Behold my presence!" This is a fascinatingly simple acknowledgement, and I would like to imagine that it bears a latent message — *"I am a beholder,* one who facilitates dreaming!"

After Joseph travels a while toward the city of She'hem, he becomes lost and seeks direction. The wording is critical (Gen. 37:15-16):

And a man found him [*va-yēm'za'eihu ēsh*]
And, behold, he was wandering in the field [*ve-hē'ney to'engh ba-sa'deh*],
and the man inquired of him, saying, 'what do you seek?'

This man, identified only as an *ēsh*, is described by rabbinic tradition as a divine power, the angel Gabriel,[20] but we may identify the anonymous *ēsh* as the essence of man, the wisdom of the deep unconscious. This, I think, is why the Bible states that the "man" found Joseph *before* it tells us, as would be logical, that Joseph was wandering or lost. This scene, I believe, is a self-inquiry, as Joseph, unconsciously abandoning direction and time, clarifies for himself exactly what it is that he is seeking. Joseph answers, "My brothers," and asks the "man" if he knows where they are located in a manner which implies that the speaker assumes his audience knows — *ha'gē'dah na lē.* Joseph's innermost self then correctly informs

---

[20] This tradition appears in *Pēr'key de-Rabē El'azar,* 38 and *Mēdrash Tan'hu'ma, va-Ye'shev,* 13, "*ein ēsh ha-a'mur kan ela Gavriel.*" *Targum Onkelos* translates *ēsh* simply as *gav'ra* whereas *Targum Yonatan ben Uziel* assumes it is the angel Gabriel. Interestingly, Joseph's father Jacob also struggled with a mysterious *ēsh* (Gen. 32:25) which tradition also identifies as an angel, the genius of Esau and not Gabriel, and here, too, one may say that the text describes an inner battle among split or not fully integrated aspects of a single personality.

him that they have traveled further beyond She'hem toward Do'tan, and that despite the fact that he had technically fulfilled his father's request, he knows that his destiny requires that he reclaim "lost objects."

Summarizing with an eye toward the intra-psychic model, the prototypic mind is depicted here in an interim state, lost and confused yet willing to confront the need to distinguish between the genetic brothers of external reality and the metaphor of "brothers" as representative of disorganized and conflicting self-states that must ultimately become organized. There seems to be an awareness that a *dreaming disposition* will be needed for this task and not mere intellection, an openness to the unconscious, to catastrophic change, potentially positive or negative, the resignation to let go of everyday perception and instead to pictorialize through the process of *hē'ney*. It is this willingness that enables the mind to move beyond concrete need satisfaction, to grasp destiny, and to balance former narcissistic self-interests against the creative surges of the death instinct and continue onward.

Returning to the text, as Joseph's brothers tend their flock, they spy Joseph emerging in the distance — their visual perception wavering unclearly in the desert heat but their fantasy image sharpened by fratricidal resolve (Gen. 37:18). A single, envy-drenched exclamation emerges from their mouths: *hē'ney ba'al ha-ha'lo'mot ha-la'zeh ba*, "behold *this dreamer* cometh," or "behold, this one, the master of the dreams, cometh." Indeed, it was the brothers who would soon declare (Gen. 37:20), "We shall *see* what will become of his dreams" [*ve-ner'eh mah ye'he'yu ha'lo'mo'taw*]. Rabbinic tradition sensed a subtle architectural ripple in the text and maintained that the 4 Hebrew words were not stated by the brothers — the words were either a divine subtext, or, as Naftali Zvi Berlin (d. 1893) suggested, the words emerged from their own mouths but without their awareness.[21]

---

[21] The Midrash (*Gen. Rabba*, 84, with vars. in *Ta'nhu'ma ha-Ya'shan*), cited by Rashi *ad loc*, opined that these words were uttered by a heavenly echo (*bat kol*): "You say, *Let us slay him*, but I say to you, *We shall see what will become of his dreams* — whose will prevails, yours or Mine!?" This motivated Berlin (*Ha'emek Da'var, ad loc*) to wonder how the brothers would have then dared to challenged a divine imperative, and offers instead that the thoughts occurred to them without awareness of their source.

"Behold," *the manifest image;* "we shall see," *the latent wish.* Here again, the brothers might have been grappling unconsciously with Joseph's unerring capacity to induce within them a mental state preparatory for the suspension of the concrete and the much more difficult task of representing and dreaming. Or, according to our parallel thesis, we have a portrait of mental part-objects in a paranoid state, fighting off the ego's tendency to coalesce fragmented images and to impose meaning, even if this requires the dismantling of the apparatus of dreaming itself.

VI

Joseph's next clinical experience concerns the dreams of others. Once again, textual subtleties and phonics indicate a change in internal dream structure.

After Joseph is brought up from the pit and sold to a series of traders, he is eventually sequestered in the house of Potiphar, captain of the guard of Pharaoh. Somehow, Potiphar is charmed and appoints Joseph majordomo "over his house and all that he had he put into his hand" (Gen. 39:1-4). The situation takes on paradoxical if not absurd proportions: a mere youth, an unsophisticated slave and an alien, is quickly regarded as an *ēsh maz'lē'ah*, a prosperous or fortunate man, and is soon granted additional trust (39:6). The circumstances are now ripe for disappointment or tragedy. Immediately the famous temptation scene unfolds; Joseph resists, yet falls from grace and is incarcerated.

The work of the repetition-compulsion quickly becomes obvious. Joseph again finds himself imprisoned in a dark pit, and is again regarded with disproportionate confidence. He is elevated to the status of assistant to the chief jailer, and a familiar description unfolds (Gen. 39:22-23):

> And the keeper of the prison committed to Joseph's hand all the prisoners that were in the prison;
> and whatsoever they did there, *he* was the doer of it.
>
> The keeper of the prison looked not to anything that was under [Joseph's] hand, because the Lord was with him;

and that which he did, the Lord made it to prosper
[*va-a'sher who o'seh a'do'nay maz'lē'ah*].

After we meet the two deposed royal ministers, the cup bearer (or butler) and the baker, both doomed to death (Gen. 40:5-8), we are presented with a powerfully alliterative text:

And they dreamed a dream, both of them,
each man his dream, that same night,

each man according to the interpretation of his dream,
the butler and the baker of the king of Egypt,
who were bound in the prison.

And Joseph came into them in the morning, and saw them,
And, behold [*ve-hē'ney*], they were sad.

And he asked Pharaoh's ministers that were with him in the ward of the master's house, saying: 'Why do you look so sad today?'

And they answered him:
'We have dreamed a dream [*ha'lom ha'lam'nu*],
and there is nobody to interpret it' [*u-po'ter eyn o'to*].

And Joseph said to them: 'Do not interpretations belong to God?
tell it to me, I pray you' [*sap'ru na lē*].

It seems obvious from the text that each minister had his own dream. Yet the text is repetitious and reemphasizes the singular *ha'lom* — "We have dreamed *a dream* and there is none to interpret *it!*" — so that it seems equally as if they might have *shared a single dream*. The ambiguous and superfluous phrase "Each man according to the interpretation of his dream" led one rabbinic commentator to deduce that each man dreamed his own dream *and also the interpretation of his fellow's dream* (*Tar'gum Yonatan ben Uziel, ad loc.*, Talmud, *Ber'a'hot*, 55b).[22] Yet another tradition deduced that Joseph himself

---

[22] This idea is deduced from the odd wording of the baker's exclamation (*Gen.*, 40:16): "And the baker saw that he interpreted well, and he said to Joseph, 'I, too, in my dream [i.e., since the baker had dreamed the interpretation that Joseph gave the first minister, the baker thus sensed that Joseph had interpreted

dreamed *their* dreams as well as the appropriate interpretation of each.

Note that before Joseph gathers additional facts or attends to the dreams, he empathically perceived that the two ministers were sad, and articulates this to himself with a by-now familiar adverb (Gen. 4:6): "and he saw them and, *behold,* they were vexed" [*va-ya'r o'tam ve-hē'nam zo'a'fēm*]. Only then does Joseph inquire *why* they are sad. Whether or not Joseph concretely dreamed their dreams or a very similar dream,[23] he seems *qua* psychoanalyst to have intuited that the two ministers were locked in a *folie a deux,* desperately attempting, like two men squabbling over a limited volume of air, to give representational form to an inexpressible dread of annihilation and to the wish to survive. The adverbial and adjectival percussion of the term *ha'lom* within the space of 2 small biblical passages conveys a single inexpressible fantasy: if there is not enough mental space to enable two men to each dream his own independent dream then surely one of them has ceased to be alive, or will soon no longer be.[24]

---

correctly]," and then clamors to report his dream, anticipating a similarly benevolent interpretation.

[23] The phenomenon of a psychoanalyst having a dream that is especially pertinent to a specific patient, or that seems almost identical to a dream that the patient has dreamed at the same time, has been reported in the literature (Brown, 2007; Lombardi & Rucker, 1998; Spero, 1984), and seems to be yet another of the unique contributions of the transference-countertransference matrix.

[24] This is akin to what Kohut's followers refer to as a self-state dream (Stolorow & Atwood, 1992). Perhaps Joseph imagined the situation in a manner similar to the way in which one resolves the infamous Prisoners' Dilemma riddle: It would be highly probable under the circumstances that each of them dreamed about what he suspected would happen to them both (*death*), and what he *wished* would happen optimally (both would be restored to freedom), *and* what he wished under less than optimum conditions (that *at least he* would be spared). That the cup bearer dreamed a dream that, through its symbols, implied life for himself made sense; that the baker dreamed a dream that implied death for himself truly indicated that he was a man who had given up hope of redemption. Even if Joseph did not know the truth via divine

In intra-psychic terms, the mind we have been studying now seems able to accept a certain kinship among its formerly fractious identifications. This prototypic mind does not *at first* actually need to know what a dream *means*; it needs primarily to appreciate that the germinating dream seeks a "locale" or object that can represent, absorb, and contain its existential anxieties. An empathic attitude toward internal emotions helps to create the anticipation that dreaming *could* take place and that the dream could take "good" form. The ministers, for example, knew nothing about Joseph experientially. They were essentially attracted to an object whose visage was a conglomeration of paradoxical idealizations: a former slave, risen and fallen, and yet an *ēsh maz'lē'ah,* a fortunate man, alien, uncanny, someone inherently "other." *Joseph* is not merely a man, it is not *as Joseph* that he helps dreamers. His function is that of an image or mirror reflection of the person who addresses him, an anonymous *ēsh* like the one he had discovered earlier within his own intrapsychic field, who somehow exudes apprenticeship with regression and survival, yet is always perceived as if in a distance, a man of *hē'ney* who incites the thinking process and marks the space suitable for transferring and preserving dream images.

VII

As the chapter continues, Joseph listens to the cup bearer's dream and interprets it as signaling redemption from prison. Then, twice emphasizing the term *ze'khar'ta'nē (Gen.,* 40:14), he entreats the cup bearer to remember him when this occurs. The cup bearer utters no such commitment. On the contrary, the narrator tells us, the cup bearer promptly forgets Joseph or, more to the point, actively denies and suppresses the memory (*ve-lo za'khar sar ha-mash'kēm et Yo'sef va-yesh'ka'he'hu* [Gen. 40:23]).

For all the frustration this turn of events engenders in the reader, it is crucial to the unfolding of the final episode. The story of the two ministers'

intervention, it made good sense to project his own desires into the dream (and possible future) of the cup bearer.

parallel and intersecting dreams and the cup bearer's attempted erasure of his moral debt to Joseph is a representational rendition of the manner in which memories, their negated avatars, and their reconstruction coexist in layers, each drawing in various ways on the autonomous functioning of the ego and superego (e.g., ingratitude led to memory "loss"). Each new accretion simultaneously anodizes previous levels of memory, enabling the reformulation of personal history.[25] As we know, hidden or repressed memories are often masked by screen memories (Freud, 1899; Greenson, 1958), or their absence may be marked by a sort of cusp or "hole" in the overall weave of historical continuity. In either case, it is the substitution, mask, or gap itself that attracts psychological attention.

It is very possible, then, from the intra-psychic perspective, that the chapter of the "dream interpreter forgotten" signifies a major effort at repressing the very process of internal dream interpretation that will soon reappear, in more mature form, in the next chapter of the Joseph myth. Pharaoh's dream, properly understood, *belongs* to the hole in memory that the cup bearer created; as we will see, it pictorializes the negation or swallowing that creates absence and holes. As the story has it, the cup bearer experienced Joseph as a representation of the inclination toward binding and preventing splitting, and as such his image evoked the constant threat of the restoration of repressed impulses and memories. The cup bearer dealt with this by massive denial. But it is more correct to say that it is not the cup bearer as such who "forgets" Joseph. If we are monitoring the development of a prototypical mind, expressed through the combined mental interaction of Joseph and Pharaoh, then we are observing the attempt to negate a basic transformative or interpretive dynamic by ceasing to dream.[26] *The ego's need to revise or totally occlude*

---

[25] Freud referred to this process as *Neiderschrift* or rewriting (see Freud, 1895).

[26] These intermediary mental processes are suitably screened by contrasting images of projecting stormy affect states and containing them, of being thrown into a pit, emerging, and again being thrown into a pit, enlightening other dreamers and then being forgotten, at turns the dreamer who dreams the dream and at turns the dreamer who interprets the dream (Grotstein, 1979, 2000).

its dreaming apparatus is what lies at the heart of Pharaoh's (the mind's) predicament, and the role of Joseph as the repressed internal dream interpreter who returns *will be crucial to the restoration of the dreaming apparatus.*

VIII

The final step in the biblical portrait comes in the form of the story of Pharaoh's fitful sleep and his dream experience. For ease of discussion, Appendices I and II, in Hebrew and English, provide both versions of the dream, as *'experienced'* (column 1) and as *narrated* (column 2), arranged to permit comparison of the critical segments and developments

Is Pharaoh simply in search of the "right" meaning for his dream symbols? While it is the case that *sometimes* the biblical dreamer — such as the ministers — seems preoccupied with concrete categorization and reading of the omina of the dream symbols (so-called "simple messsage" dreams [Jeffers, 1990]), Pharaoh seems not principally impressed by mere decoding or "stock" dream categorizations. In all likelihood, his *har'tu'mēm*,[27] occultists or wise men offered these, applying the standard oneirocritics.[28] Rather, Pharaoh's mind seems disturbed on a level that defied classical methods, *and would also have defied any effort on Joseph's part to merely decode the dream symbols (divine assistance notwithstanding) had it not been for the presence of additional developments.*

---

[27] Rashi posits that the word *har'tu'mēm* (pl.) is a contraction of the terms *ha-ne'ha'nēm be-te'me mey'tēm,* "men who are stirred by the bones of the dead." The original Egyptian quad-glyph term for these diviners is *hry hb hry tp* and in later documents we find reference to the profession of *hry 'tb* or *hyr tm* (now two syllables), "scribes of the House of Life," wise men who are able to "untie the knot" (Goedicke, 1996). This concept eventually became even more condensed. Brown, Driver & Briggs (1906, p. 355) consider the term to have evolved from the root *ha'rat,* denoting an engraver or writer. Thus, *har'tum* personifies the link between the concrete structure of hieroglyphic texts (Hirsch, 1870, p. 574) and the semi-concrete or so-called "presentational symbolic" character of dream imagery

[28] The Midrash fills the silent text at this juncture, and states that the wise men in fact suggested that seven daughters would be born to him and then would all die, or that he would conquer seven countries yet they would ultimately rebel against his rule, and so forth (*Mēdrash Genesis Rabba,* 89:7).

The secret to the final chapter resides in its use of an unparalleled literary device. The biblical text provides the reader with an "insider" or objective view of Pharaoh's dream experience as it occurred during his sleep, and then, following a significant middle scene, the repetition of the dream to Joseph. Often ignored is the fact that we do not know exactly how Pharaoh reported the dream to his wise men; we are informed only that Pharaoh dreamed and that he told the dream to his wise men. We can presume, as readers have for centuries, that Pharaoh repeated to them the very words that the text had used earlier in recording his nocturnal experience, but was this the case? We have a single but critical hint to what the magicians *heard*, as opposed to what Pharaoh himself believed he experienced![29] The text simply says (*Gen.*, 41:8):

> And he told them his dream, and none could interpret them to Pharaoh
> [*va-ye'sa'per la-hem et ha'lo'mo ve-eyn po'ter o'tam le-Fangr'oh*]

That is, Pharaoh reports a *dream* (*ha'lo'mo*), singular; the wise men attempt to interpret his *dreams* (*o'tam*, "them"). Evidently something went awry at this juncture.

The first item of interest is the Hebrew verb that introduces the episode, "and Pharaoh *dreamed*" (Gen. 41:1). The intransitive (objectless) verb *ho'lem*,[30] as opposed to Joseph's earlier *va-ya'ha'lom* (Gen. 37:5), conveys the sense of an ongoing and incomplete process "trapped" or suspended between past and present (see Leibowitz, 1972). This suggests that Pharaoh had slept and dreamt *unproductively, anxiously seeking to awaken* (*va-a'kēz*),

---

[29] Ron Pirson (2002, p. 59; see also Licht, 1978, p. 176) notes that Pharaoh appears as a subjective presence within his dream, as did already the deposed ministers in their dreams, but Pirson does not explore what this means psychologically. We do not know whether the ruler experienced his presence subjectively *while dreaming* or whether this awareness emerged only upon the telling. I shall take this up in the essay.

[30] Known in Hebrew as *a'var bil'tē nēsh'lam*, or past imperfect, such as *ve-Rev'kah sho'mang'at* (Gen. 27:5; and see gloss of *Avi ha-E'zer* ad loc.), *a'ra'me o'ved a'vē* (Deut. 26:5) and *u-De'vo'rah sha'fe'tah et Yēs'ra'el* (Judges, 5:4).

but upon experiencing a slight move toward wakefulness, longed to continue to dream![31] Let us hold this point for a moment.

Second, we notice that the initial dream text (see Appendix, column 1) is laden with the key term *hē'ney,* "Behold." Based on the analysis in section V, we know for certain that we are in the midst of a pictorial-representational effort, if an arduous one, as the mind stumbles over some disturbing element within the dream process itself.

Third, after the first dream installment we are informed that Pharaoh "awoke" and then that "he slept and dreamed a second time" (Gen. 41:4-5). The text does not declare after this first stage: "and, behold, it was a dream." The Hebrew — *va-yē'kaz... va-yē'shan va-ya'ha'lom shey'nēt* — actually tolerates two interpretations. It is possible that the dreamer awoke *fully,* with no sense of having dreamed, and returned to sleep and dreamed a *new* albeit similar dream. It is also possible that the dreamer's deep dream state (*i.e.,* perceptual apparatus oriented inward) was slightly altered, even arrested, permitting a slight movement toward perceptual consciousness *but without regaining full consciousness,* after which point the dreamer submerged again into the dream state already in process. A few classical commentaries anticipated the latter possibility. Shmuel ibn Hof'ne (*ad loc*), for example, emphasized that the single terse passage following the *second* stage of the dream (Gen. 41:7), "And Pharaoh awoke *and, behold,* [it was] *a dream,*" makes clear that only when fully awake did

---

31 Matters could have been worse. Compare Pharaoh's reaction here with the single similar event in the entire Bible: the dream of King Nebukhadnezzar (*Daniel,* 2). When Pharaoh awakens, we are told *va-tē'pang'em ru'ho* (Gen. 41:8), "his spirit was troubled," or, as the Aramaic translator Onkelos translates forcefully, *u-me'tar'fa ru'hey,* "he felt crazed." Still and all, Pharaoh recalled his dream, and struggled to understand what it meant. When the Persian king awakens, in contrast, the text states *va-tēt'pang'em ru'ho* — the key adverb now carrying a double reflexive 't' consonant even though it is translated the same way, as implying a troubled or crazed state. The text itself soon reveals the reason for the atypical emphasis. The Persian king summons his dream interpreters and states (*Daniel,* 2:4), "I dreamed a dream, and my spirit is troubled *to know the dream*" [*ha'lom ha'lam'tē va-tēt'pang'em ru'hē la-dang'at et ha-ha'lom*]. He then demands to know not only what his dream meant, but what it is that he actually dreamed (*Daniel,* 2:6). This was no mere test: as the rabbis interpret it, the Persian king awoke with no memory of what he had dreamed at all.

Pharaoh retrospect that he had been dreaming. The full emotional reaction follows after a further delay: "And the morning came, and his spirit was frightened."

This point is very significant because it is kindred to a related question: was it Pharaoh's reflective experience that he had dreamed a *single* dream or *two similar* dreams? Rabbinic commentary maintains that in fact the king was aware that he had dreamed a single dream, or at least understood — *at which point* is unclear — that the two dreams were significant as a unit and not as disparate events.[32] This is deduced from the brief and unsuccessful exchange between Pharaoh and his dream interpreters:

> And Pharaoh told them his dream
> [*va-ye'sa'per Pang'roh la-hem et ha'lo'mo*],
>
> but none could interpret them unto Pharaoh
> [*ve-eyn po'ter o'tam le-Pang'roh*]

Pharaoh tells his analysts *a dream*, yet they busy themselves with *dreams*. Again, confusion sets in, for it seems unlikely that the wise men would have heard a plurality of dreams had Pharaoh explicitly insisted upon a single dream.

Psychoanalytic work teaches that emotionally significant listening is not always autonomous or objective. Thus, following the text literally, it may be that Pharaoh reported one dream. But this *could* mean — as only the biblical text knows how to hint to the reader — that he *wished* to report a single dream. In reality, either two dreams emerged from his mouth, or he may actually have uttered a single dream in a manner that projected a conscious sense of plurality. The wise men, in turn, failed to know how exactly to develop their own double impressions! A third possibility is

---

[32] Some of the classical commentaries focused on this summary declaration. Rashi observed simply that the declarative *hē'ney ha'lom* emphasizes Pharaoh's experience of the special quality of this dream, but doesn't specify what that quality is. Ramban (R. Moshe ben Nahman Gerondi, d. 1270) felt that the second term, *ha'lom*, proves that Pharaoh was aware that the two dream scenes were in fact twin dimensions of a single dream (see also Hirsch [1867-1878]).

that Pharaoh *may have reported two dreams but emphasized one,* or spoke in a way that projected the experience of a single dream — especially if during sleep he never fully left one dream state. His wise men, however, clung to the concrete details as ancient oneirology dictated, and therefore wrongly pursued an interpretation of *two* dreams.

I will soon suggest a fourth possibility. But for the time being, we need only adopt the likelihood *that the matter was unclear to Pharaoh himself* and that is how we must experience the text. We need to accept that Pharaoh was not primarily concerned with the meaning of the dream symbols as such. He was much more deeply disturbed by the uncanny experience of hovering between a dream state and a non-dream state and between wakefulness and non-wakefulness, and by the peculiar combination of opposites that seemed to have taken additional expression through the unclear conviction of having dreamed one dream or two. The bungled analysis by the wise men only aggravated the king's latent impressions.

IX

Poised at the height of royal discomfiture, it is easy to imagine the hush cast over the court as the forgetful/forgotten cup bearer suddenly recalls his unheeded debt to Joseph and, at considerable risk to his own life, recounts the events in the prison. I have parsed the text in order to heighten the resonance that transports the main effect (Gen. 41:10-13):

Then spoke the cup bearer unto Pharaoh, saying,
'I make mention of my faults this day.'

'Pharaoh was wroth with his servants,
and put me in the ward of the house of the captain of the guard,
me and the chief baker.'

'And we dreamed a dream in one night,
I and he;
we dreamed each man according to the interpretation of his dream.'

[*va-na'hal'mah ha'lom be-lay'lah a'had*
a'nē ve-who
ēsh ke'fē pē'tron ha'lo'mo ha'lam'nu.]

'And there was with us there a young man;
a Hebrew,
a servant to the captain of the guard,
and we told him,
and he interpreted us our dreams;
to each man according to his dream did he interpret.'

[*ve-sham ē'tanu na'angr ev'rē*
e'ved le-sar ha-ta'ba'hēm
ve-na'sa'per lo
va-yēf'tar la'nu et ha'la'mo'tey'nu
ēsh ka-ha'lo'mo pa'tar.]

'And it came to pass, as he interpreted to us, so it was...'

[*va-ye'hē ka-a'sher pa'tar la'nu ken ha'yah...*]

Commentaries have pointed out (e.g., *Mēdrash Gen. Rabbah*, 89) that the minister's gratefulness is disingenuous: one certainly does not curry favor for someone in ancient Egypt by introducing the individual as "a young man," [*na'angr*] ignorant and inexperienced, "a Hebrew," a despised foreigner who may not even understand the national language, and "a servant," of semi-human status. Pharaoh nevertheless sends for Joseph, yet one wonders in what state of mind.

On one level, it is clear that the cup bearer's protestations created an ironic or "negative" attractiveness. Whatever the cup bearer's intentions, his devaluation, alongside the explicit acknowledgement that Joseph did correctly interpret dreams, tightened the analytic framework by denuding the interpretive field of distracting trappings, increasing the probability that Pharaoh's projective transference would be the most powerful factor to reverberate off the image of the *ēsh* standing before him. We are not *told* as much directly, but the latent psychological process is conveyed via the cup bearer's word play. He presents two people, simultaneously in time, sharing one dream (*ha'lom*), or two people dreaming two dreams, as well as the possibility, mentioned above, that each person dreamed his other's dream and even the dream's interpretation. And yet, the cup bearer hastens to add, none of this threw the alien interpreter! Eloquently repetitious, he adds, "and he interpreted to us our *dreams*; to each man according to his *dream* did he interpret."[33] Somewhere within this welter of terms, *Pharaoh's soul begins to re-experience the uncanny quality of his dream state of the previous night.* A variety of paradoxical states began to aggregate in Pharaoh's mind — dream, non-dream, many dreams, life and death, remembering and forgetting — and a combined image of the dreamer's self and the "other who knows" must have begun to coalesce within the dreamer's mind. It will not be Joseph as such who reveals the hidden desire of the dream but the dreamer himself. Joseph will prove right when he says that only God interprets dreams. That is, the deep unconscious is continuously speaking, whether we are awake or not, conscious of it or not; once the dreamer lessens his conscious restraints, he can know, to a large degree, what the conscious ego generally tries to not know.

X

The next dynamic step is Pharaoh's direct address to Joseph (Gen. 41:15):

And Pharaoh said to Joseph:
'I have dreamed a dream,
and there is none that can interpret it
[*ha'lom ha'lam'tē u-po'ter eyn o'to*];

and I have heard say of you,
that when you hear a dream you can interpret it
[*tēsh'ma ha'lom lēf'tor o'to*].

Subtle transformations have begun to take place. First, Pharaoh seems prepared to share an intimate secret with a most improbable, unidentified

---

[33] Ironically, the original comment of the ministers to Joseph when yet in the dungeon was: "We have dreamed a dream and none can interpret *it*" [*ha'lom ha'lam'nu u-po'ter eyn o'to*], which again indicates the singular even though each had his own individual dream

listener. Second, he hints to his impression of having had a unitary mental experience — "I dreamed *a dream*" and "none can interpret *it*" — despite the apparent repetition and despite the misguided impressions of his wise men. Third, Pharaoh reveals that he has learned from the cup bearer's story that the sense of overall unity of psychological dream experience derives from the quality of listening.

Joseph's response is not simply theological; it anticipates an analytic attitude that has remained basic from Freud to Lacan. The hub is a single term (Gen. 41:16):

> And Joseph answered Pharaoh saying: 'It is not in me [*bēl'ang'dē*];
> God will give Pharaoh an answer of peace'
> [*E'lo'hēm ya'angneh et she'lom Pang'roh*].

Strictly speaking, the simple Hebrew declaration *bēl'ang'dē* means "Not I!"[34] Through the sparse declaration — which semantically denotes utter exclusivity as well as utter insufficiency — Joseph posits a stunning paradox: I myself am singularly irrelevant and yet consequential. I am not that which I have been suggested to be and not whom you believe me to be. I am but a sign; I represent, just like dreams represent, an Other, God, the unconscious, and language itself.

By refusing to accept the imposed role of arbiter of the truth of dreams, Joseph effectively displaced the source of meaning outside of any standardized interpretive catalogue or code. Joseph preserved what Lacan calls the role of the "dead card" (*le mort*) or dummy, as in the game of bridge.[35] I have selected a statement by Lacan that clarifies his thinking on the matter (1955, pp. 288-289 [explications added, MHS]):

[34] Compare this with Abraham's similar statement (Gen. 14:24). The commentator Shlomo David Luzzato (d. 1865) opines that the term *bēl'ang'dē* is a portmanteaux which carries the latent injunctive command *bal ad* (two words in Hebrew), "no more" or "cease." A parallel is cast a few passages later when Pharaoh ultimately appoints Joseph viceroy and exclaims (Gen. 41:44): "I am Pharaoh, *but* [without] *your* [permission] [*bēl'ang'dekha*], no man shall lift his hand or foot in all of Egypt!"

[35] Lacan discusses this concept in great detail in his famous Rome Discourse, "The function and field of speech in language and psychoanalysis (1956 pp. 262; 1961, p. 499).

Indeed, by simply targeting the [imaginary] objects whose image is the subject's ego, that is, by targeting his [superficial] character traits [as analysts tend to do, in Lacan's view], the analyst *himself* falls under the sway of the illusions of his own ego, no less naively than the subject himself does. And the effect here is not so much to be engaged [trapped] in the mirages they produce as in the distance they bring about in his object-relation....In order for the transference relationship to escape these affects [i.e., narcissistic imaginary attachments and dependencies], *the analyst would have to strip the narcissistic image of his own ego of all forms of desire by which that image has been constituted,* reducing it to the only face that sustains it behind their masks: the face of the absolute master, death. It is thus here that the analysis of the ego finds its ideal terminus: that in which the subject, having refound the origins of his ego is an imaginary regression, comes, by the progression of remembering, to its end in analysis — namely, the subjectification of his death.

Naturally, the analyst often begins work in an empathic stance with the subject, but must pass as soon as possible to the role of dummy as stand-in for the Other, for the unconscious discourse within the patient's self that has not been heard or perhaps never before articulated. In this manner, the analyst brackets the imaginary character of the self, the misdirected weighting of its table of needs, and the paradoxical nature of its boundaries.

Lacan does not ridicule benevolent neutrality; he deems it insufficient for the task of symbolizing the paradox, loss, and falsity that characterize so much of our cultural tension, unachieved goals, and unrequited loves. "What must the analyst know in analysis?" Lacan famously asks (pp. 289-290): "How to ignore what he knows." Later, Wilfred Bion (1970, p. 34) and others would advocate a similar kind of professional negativization of our excess reliance on memory, desire, or saturated wisdom so that the patient can truly relocate the inner language of his soul that had been repressed or poorly signified over the years. The analyst is not simply another *subject* who happens to be more empathic and more knowledgeable. As an all-knowing "subject," Joseph would only be able to offer the dreamer more of the imaginary dimensions that the dreamer unconsciously wishes to relinquish (see Fink, 1995, pp. 74-87). Rather, the

217

analyst's subjectivity is muted so that he can represent sheer otherness and, thereby, the paradoxical nature of human libido or desire.

Joseph's power to arouse desire and induce meaning was enhanced by his refusal to don the mantle of desire cast upon him and by his willingness to *not know*. Like the psychoanalyst, Joseph answers Pharaoh's assumption by saying, "I am *supposed* to know. But it is not my ego, or yours, who knows, and it is not *my* knowledge you seek. I speak only in the name of the unconscious, or language itself, and it is to its wily and endless ways of disguising desire and anxiety within speech and imagery that you need to address yourself now."

While Joseph does eventually offer "manifest support" for Pharaoh's imaginary needs — the "wise" interpretation regarding the forthcoming famine — we shall now see that this is not Joseph's crucial contribution psychologically speaking. The successfulness of the process that Joseph initiates is testified to by the fact that Pharaoh does not simply *repeat* his dream but rather uncannily reenters the dreaming process.

XI

When Freud (1900) was perplexed by a dream that "resisted" interpretation he would ask the dreamer to repeat the dream since, Freud found, the patient rarely used the same words during the second telling. The parts of the dream that are described with different words reveal weak spots in the dream disguise, and signal the point at which the interpretation of the dream can be started. It is for this reason that the Bible's willingness to create a repeat account of Pharaoh's dream is so important,[36] for it draws the reader into the transformation of the dream experience.

---

[36] Several authors — such as Frieden (1990), Licht (1978), Pirson (2002), Rendsburg (1990), Schroeder (1972), Snedeker (1982) — have noted the changes in the second account, but all of them overlook the psychological significance of the items that I have emphasized here. Katz (1963, pp. 110-113) is the sole author to offer psychoanalytic significance to the altered portions of the second

The transformation is conveyed via five key alterations that are introduced in the second account. First, after describing the two contrasting sets of cattle Pharaoh suddenly emphasizes:

such as I never saw in all of the land of Egypt for badness.

This new comment seems to *replace* a detail from the original narrative (Gen. 41:3):

And [the lean kine] stood by the other kine upon the brink of the river.

Pharaoh then continues, but again reveals an additional detail not stated before:

And the lean and ill-favored kine did eat up the first seven fat kine. *and when they had eaten them up, it could not be known that they had eaten them; but they were still ill-favored as at the beginning.*

Pharaoh states that at this point he had partially awoken (*va-a'kez*), but he does not repeat the original words "and I slept and dreamed a second time." Finally, as he completes the "ears of corn" component of the dream, he does *not* repeat "and, behold, it was a dream," but simply adds:

And I told it to my magicians, and there was none who could *declare* it to me [*ve-eyn ma'gēd lē*].

Throughout this second narration, we are again subjected to the play of the plural against the singular form of the word *ha'lom* that we heard

---

telling, although he does not focus on the episode as a composite portrait of the development of the dreaming process as I do. According to Katz, Pharaoh's astonished denial, "Such as I never saw..." may have been a protest against his unconscious reconstruction of "The earliest impressions of cohabitation, conceivably viewed as the father, or the lean fleshed and ill favored kine, devouring or destroying the mother who is the fat fleshed and well favored kine. [Katz continues:] A youngster's reaction to mother's pregnancy and the subsequent birth could also be symbolically portrayed by the lean ill-favored kine not really changing in physical appearance in the end. The pregnant mother, despite the huge temporary protuberance [that might result] from seemingly engorging of such huge quantities, in the end reverts back to her old self and is as thin as ever."

before when the cup bearer introduced Joseph. At that point, by the time Pharaoh addresses Joseph he has clarified the confusion (Gen. 41:15):

And Pharaoh said to Joseph:
'I have dreamed a dream,
and there is none that can interpret it
[ha'lom ha'lam'tē u-po'ter eyn o'to];

and I have heard say of you,
that when you hear a dream you can interpret it
[tēsh'ma ha'lom lēf'tor o'to].

But by the time Pharaoh reaches the end of his second narration he is even more precise — the central object ha'lom has disappeared and must be inferred:

And I told [it] to my magicians, but there was none that could declare [it] to me.
[va-a'mar el ha-har'tu'mēm ve-eyn ma'gēd lē]

My impression is that Pharaoh is no longer primarily concerned with the pē'ta'ron or meaning (po'ter, lēf'tor) of the dream content, but rather with the articulation or hagg'a'dah (ma'gēd) of the dream/non-dream experience itself, the peculiar combination of opposites, contradictory representational states, and paradoxical states of awareness. Joseph is suited for this. Recall the earlier episode with the ēsh, which I interpreted as an internal self-representation, at which juncture Joseph taught himself to confront his desire by being prepared to representationalize — the hē'ney'nē resignation coupled with the demand: ha'gē'dah na lē. We also observed earlier that the Pharaoh-Joseph episode is introduced by the past imperfect verb, ho'lem, indicating incomplete action. The dream experience indeed remained incomplete until Pharaoh reentered the dream process in the presence of Joseph. Pharaoh initially did not experience his nocturnal fantasy as a dream until after the end of the "ears of corn" segment, and he only experiences terror or anxiety after he awoke fully in the morning. It is only when Pharaoh repeats his dream in front of Joseph, and begins to articulate the emotions and the subjective psychological experience that accompany the representational bits, that he fully integrates the nocturnal experience. *Nothing better confirms this than the fact that the king now seems to have no need to repeat the declarative statement "and I slept and dreamed a second time" nor, when finished, "and, behold, it was a dream."*

Taken as a whole, the alterations in the second narration reveal Pharaoh struggling with the unconscious embrace of negative experience — the lack of "no" in the unconscious — a dimension that the conscious mind can never fully experience yet which lies at the base of the possibility of symbolic thought. At the earliest stages of development, the mind is indifferent to the distinction between *inside* and *outside,* between *there is* or *there is not.* The unconscious — and later, dreams, art, etc. — fulfills wishful states via hallucination which militates against any such distinction *until* the incessant demands of biology, language, and maternal mirroring instate and insist upon this distinction. Yet throughout life, representation, symbolization, and negation exist side by side; hallucination helps prevent total enslavement by sensory perception while reality testing and judgment help prevent the concretization of hallucination.[37] The capacity to have a mind seems to be based on the capacity to maintain this duality. Thus, all reference to mental *representation* is always predicated upon the conditions in the mind that follow the differentiation between is and is not, internal and external.

This struggle is present in every dream as well, whether focal or not. Mental experience, overall, is a relationship between two major dimensions: the dimension of the unconscious which, absolutely or in its pristine state, is characterized by fully symmetrical experience — the

---

[37] That is to say, reality testing has to accommodate a crucial paradox. On one hand, hallucinatory satisfaction must often be surrendered to the demands of perception (i.e., "imagine what you like, dear child, but your electrolyte levels declare that you are still hungry for *real* milk); on the other hand, the concrete perception of an object has to be disavowed energetically so that *belief* can be maintained in the existence of an internal object that is "merely" representational. Whatever a psychic representation is *not,* it is the only thing that the mind really cathects, and it is completely private and immortal. Without this, the mind cannot feel that is has any control over the object, and the absence of the concrete object would cause excessive distress, that both the object and the subject himself might have disappeared. Every thought "murders" or detracts from the tyranny of the concrete object, but thought also prevents us from being devastated by the loss of perception because we have the capacity to represent, imagine, fantasize and think the object (see Botella & Botella, 2005, pp. 42, 90-91, 137).

domain where a thing can be the equivalent of its opposite (i.e., A = -A) and where no negation is conceivable — and the dimension of conscious experience that has been created by the establishment of asymmetrical logic — the domain which, thanks to language, outlaws the equivalence between a thing and its opposite (i.e., A ≠ -A) (see Matte-Blanco, 1975, 1988; Rayner, 1995, p. 120). While the conscious mind cannot ever imagine totally symmetrical thought without reverting to psychosis, it is capable of *enfolding* symmetrical-type elements within asymmetrical containers so as to create a richer, multidimensional experience of reality. After the advent of language, all sorts of experiences such as dreams, metaphor, symptoms, and art allow us lattices into the clash and merger between the symmetrical and asymmetrical dimensions, returning to the time when nothing was disjointed, where all desire could be playfully perceived as fulfilled, undisturbed by the necessary resignation to secondary process, logic, time, representation, and sublimation.

Pharaoh's dream is a classical example of the admixture of symmetrical and asymmetrical modes of thought. The disturbing, irrational images that the king "beholds" reflect the passionate lure of the symmetrical unconscious — a reality where small dimensions can readily and routinely incorporate large dimensions — alongside the asymmetrically-committed censorship apparatus of the ego, which declares "I have not seen such as this!" and protests the very experience that it had imagined: "it could *not be known* that they had eaten them" (for, after all, they *had* indeed!). Whereas Pharaoh's original record of the dream depicts cattle *standing* next to each other, and then one group eating the other, only his reiteration unveils the great and irrational mobility that was originally hidden behind a façade of stasis. Revealed now is the paradoxical fact that the only entity that *was not* were the rules of logic that would ordinarily have outlawed his hallucinatory perception. During the night, this dense vortex or nodal point was sufficiently disturbing as to awaken him, yet he returned to it with no awareness of what it was that frightened him.[38]

---

[38] Contemporary researchers Scalzone and Zontini (2001) refer to Freud's concept of the *dream navel* (*der Nabel des Traums* [1900, pp. 111n, 525]), a super-dense or opaque element in the dream which cannot be unraveled and points to the

Pharaoh's cloudy, not-fully-conscious description of a unified experience within what seemed like two distinct dreams confused his wise men. As Pharaoh warms to his own internal creativity, awakened by the presence of Joseph, he finally expresses his astonishment over seeing what he could not possibly have seen. It suddenly becomes clear that by dreaming the same idea twice — one dream segment alongside its fellow — Pharaoh had beheld an amazing psychic event: the effort by the eternal symmetrical black hole or "mouth" to negate asymmetry *alongside* the parallel effort of the asymmetry-oriented ego to reassert its dominion over symmetry.

As soon as Pharaoh completes his narration, Joseph wisely confirms the basic phenomenology of the experience (Gen. 41:25):

> And Joseph declared unto Pharaoh:
> 'The dream of Pharaoh is one;
> God has declared unto Pharaoh that which He is about to do.'

Regardless of how Joseph will soon monopolize upon the practical dimension of the prophecy, his emphasis first and foremost reinforces the successfulness of Pharaoh's experiment with symmetrization and the encounter with the ineluctable tendency of the unconscious — as "God" — to create the sense that past, present and future have overlapped, or swallowed each other, lending a profound sense of urgency to the experience.

XII

The impact of the powerful transformation in the presence of Joseph *qua* the other-who-interprets-not-by-knowing-but-by-tolerating-symmetry disposes Pharaoh to resonate with Joseph's political suggestion

---

unknown (*dem Unerkannten*) from which the dream sprung. They view the dream navel not merely as metaphor, but as a real chaotic link, or interface, between the unconscious wish — which constitutes an attractor — and the conscious thought. The attractor may be visualized as having an hourglass, the narrow mid-section being the navel, incorporating two dimensions in a super-condensed way. The dream's navel is the center of a turbulent vortex connecting the dream to the unconscious matrix that fuels it.

that a lack of expeditious planning could lead to the obliteration of the memory of Pharaoh. Yet the traditional focus upon Joseph's propitious recommendations to an unassuming Pharaoh neglects the likelihood that Pharaoh understood very well Egypt's dependence upon the Nile, the agronomic vicissitudes of the desert, and the pending socioeconomic disaster, and that he might have assessed and prepared for these without prompting. In any event, the biblical episode allows us to see how a deep-seated and universal struggle with the repressed desire to be enveloped, and also the dread of being enveloped and swallowed by the very breast upon which we feed gives life to all other conscious concerns, including socioeconomic crises. A monarch's fear of being forgotten, his name scratched off of the records and stele of Egypt's history, derives its motivating force from that area of the mind that never fully distinguishes between self and other, or between inside and outside, where a psychic "swallowing up" of the self would in fact lead to a sense of total oblivion. The ability to be the maternal sustainer of his "nursing" people, providing them with water and wheat (milk and semen), would require the capacity to contain and conserve and not fear being sucked dry by the needs and anxieties of hungry citizens.[39] Abandoned to a nameless dread during the early morning, the retelling of the dream in the presence of a more mature Joseph who has learned to swallow his own desire without disappearing, enabled Pharaoh to connect palpably with his own fantasies and consciously experience the swallowing up of desire.

These images in the king's dream are not pathological; they portray a mental experiment. The staccato emergence of representational images (*ve-hē'ney*) and the subsequent amazement upon learning that the "swallowing" is a purely mental phenomenon was the best expression possible of a budding awareness of *mental space*. For dreams to be experienced as dreams and not as quasi-external voices or divine

---

[39] Compare with Moses's direct expression of this kind of anxiety (Num. 12:12):
Have I conceived this entire nation?
Have I given birth to them, that Thou should say to me:
Carry them in thy bosom as the nursing-father [*ha-o'men*] carries the suckling child unto the Land.

communications the mind must carve out and safeguard a "volume" of dream *space* (Khan, 1976; Pontalis, 1974; Stewart, 1973) within which a dream can be experienced as a text emanating within the self. Such space is created as the individual becomes increasingly aware that dreams are expressions of the individual's own subjective interpretation of the interplay between symmetrical and asymmetrical modes of the mind. Under these circumstances, the semantically-founded representational images virtually widen the mind — cows swallowing cows, dreams swallowing dreams, the interpretive mind enveloping its dreaming self — so that the mind can find meaning through the subtle unfolding of the symmetrical mode of the deep unconscious.

REFERENCES

Aling, C. (2003). Joseph in Egypt. *Bible & Spade*, 16: 10-16.

Almoli, S. ben Jacob. (1516). *Dream Interpretation from Classical Jewish Sources* [*Pē'ta'ron ha-Ha'lo'mot ha-Sha'lem: Asu'fat Ma'ama'rēm al ha-Ha'lo'mot mey-ha'Re'sho'nēm ad ha-Aha'ro'nēm* (Amsterdam)]. trans. & ed. Y. Elman, Hoboken, NJ: Ktav, 1998.

Amram, N. (1901). *Se'fer Pēt'ron Ha'lo'mot*. Jerusalem: A. M. Lunts.

Anderson, J. W. (1981). The Methodology of Psychological Biography. *J. Interdisc. Hist.*, 11: 455-475.

Bar, S. (2001). *A Letter That Has Not Been Read: Dreams in the Hebrew Bible*. Cincinnati, OH: Hebrew Union College Press.

Berger, J. (1981). New Views on the Biblical Joseph. *Amer. J. Psychoanal.*, 41: 277-282.

Bion, W. R. (1962). *Learning from Experience*. London: Maresfield/Karnac.

--------. (1963). *Elements of Psycho-Analysis*. London: Maresfield/Karnac.

--------. (1965). *Transformations*. London: Maresfield/Karnac.

Bion, W. R. (1970). *Attention and Interpretation*. London: Maresfield/ Karnac.

Botella, C., & Botella, S. (2005). *The Work of Psychic Figurability: Mental States without Representation*. London: Routledge.

Brill, A. (2000). The Phenomenology of True Dreams in Maimonides. *Dreaming*, 10: 43-54.

Brown, F., Driver, S. R., & Briggs, C. A. (1906). *The Brown-Driver-Briggs Hebrew and English Lexicon*. Boston: Houghton, Mifflin & Co./ Hendrickson, 2004.

Brown, L. J. (2007). On Dreaming one's Patient: Reflections on an Aspect of Countertransference Dreams. *Psychoanal. Quar.*, 75: 835-861.

Chiel, H. J. (2005). Joseph, the Master of Dreams. *Tradition*, 39: 36-52.

Coats, G. W. (1992). Joseph. In *Anchor Bible Dictionary*. Vol. 3. Ed. D. N. Freedman. New York: Doubleday.

Cocks, G., & Travis, L. C. (1987). *Psycho/History: Readings in the Method of Psychology, Psychoanalysis and History*. New Haven, Conn.: Yale University Press.

de Mause, L. (1975). *The New Psychohistory*. Garland, NY: Psychohistory Press.

--------. (1982). *Foundations of Psychohistory*. Northvale, NJ: Aronson.

de Monchaux, C. (1978). Dreaming and the Organizing Function of the Ego. In: *The Dream Discourse Today*. ed. S. Flanders. London: Routledge (pp. 195-209).

Dennett, D. (1976). Are Dreams Experiences? In *Brainstorms: Philosophical Essays on Mind and Psychology* New York: Brighton, 1981 (pp. 129-148).

Erikson, E. H. (1958). *Young Man Luther. A Study in Psychoanalysis and History*. New York: Norton.

Fink, B. (1995). *The Lacanian Subject: Between Language and Jouissance*. Princeton: Princeton University Press.

Freud, S. (1895). Project for a Scientific Study of Psychology. In: *The Standard Edition of the Complete Psychological Works of Sigmund Freud*, Vol. 1, ed. & trans. J. Strachey, London: Hogarth, 1953 (pp. 281-391).

Freud, S. (1899). Screen Memories. In: *The Standard Edition of the Complete Psychological Works of Sigmund Freud*, Vol. 3, ed. & trans. J. Strachey, London: Hogarth, 1962 (pp. 301-322).

--------. (1900). *The Interpretation of Dreams*. In: *The Standard Edition of the Complete Psychological Works of Sigmund Freud* (Vols. 4-5), ed. & trans. J. Strachey, London: Hogarth, 1958.

--------. (1903). Three Essays on the Theory of Sexuality. In: *The Standard Edition of the Complete Psychological Works of Sigmund Freud*, Vol. 7, ed. & trans. J. Strachey, London: Hogarth, 1958 (pp. 135-203).

--------. (1920). A Note on the Prehistory of the Technique of Analysis. In: *The Standard Edition of the Complete Psychological Works of Sigmund Freud*, Vol. 18, ed. & trans. J. Strachey, London: Hogarth, 1958 (pp. 263-265).

--------. (1922). Letter from Sigmund Freud to Arthur Schnitzler, May 14, 1922. In: *Letters of Sigmund Freud 1873-1939*. Ed. E. L. Freud, New York: Basic Books, 1960.

--------. (1923). Josef Popper-Lynkeus and the Theory of Dreams. In *The Standard Edition of the Complete Psychological Works of Sigmund Freud*, Vol. 19, ed. & trans. J. Strachey, London: Hogarth, 1958 (pp. 261-263).

--------. (1923[1922]). Two encyclopedia articles: 'Psycho-Analysis,' and 'Libido-theory.' In: *The Standard Edition of the Complete Psychological Works of Sigmund Freud*, Vol. 18, ed. & trans. J. Strachey, London: Hogarth, 1958 (pp. 235-259).

--------. (1932[1933]). *New Introductory Lectures on Psycho-Analysis:* Lesson 29. Revision of the theory of dreams. In *The Standard Edition of the Complete Psychological Works of Sigmund Freud*. Vol. 22, ed. & trans. J. Strachey, London: Hogarth, 1958 (pp. 7-30).

--------. (1936). Letter from Sigmund Freud to Thomas Mann, November 29, 1936. In: *Letters of Sigmund Freud 1873-1939*. ed. E. L. Freud. New York: Basic Books, 1960.

Frieden, K. (1990). Dream Interpreters in Exile: Joseph, Daniel and Sigmund (Solomon). In: *Mappings of the Biblical Terrain: The Bible as a Text*. Eds. V. Tollers & J. Maier. Lewisberg, PA: Buckwell University Press (p. 193-203).

Gimani, A. (1997). va-Yē'kaz Pa'roh va-yē'shan va-ya'ha'lom shey'nēt. In mē-Pey'rot ha-E'lan al Par'shat ha-Sha'vua: Ma'ama'reēm me'et Hok'rey Une'versi'tat Bar-Ilan. Eds. J. Schwartz & D. Algavish. Ramat-Gan: Bar-Ilan University Press (pp. 132-133).

Goedicke, H. (1996). Hartummēm. *Orientalia,* 65: 24-30.

Greenson, R. R. (1958). On Screen Defenses, Screen Hunger and Screen Identity. *J. Amer. Psychoanal. Assn.,* 6: 242-262.

Grotstein, J. S. (1979). Who is the Dreamer who Dreams the Dream and Who is the Dreamer Who Understands It? — A Psychoanalytic Inquiry into the Ultimate Nature of Being. *Contemp. Psychoanal.,* 15: 110-169.

-------. (2000). *Who is the Dreamer who Dreams the Dream? A Study of Psychic Presences.* Hillsdale, NJ: Analytic Press.

Harris, M. (1994). *Studies in Jewish Dream Interpretation.* Northvale, NJ: Aronson.

Hirsch, S. R. (1867-1878). *The Pentateuch: Translated and Explained.* Trans. I. Levy. London: Judaica Press, 1976.

Izenberg, G. (1975). Psychohistory and Intellectual History. *Hist. & Theory,* 14: 139-155.

Jeffers, A. (1990). Divination by Dreams in Ugaritic Literature and in the Old Testament. *Int. Bible Stud., 12,* 167-183.

Kaltner, J. (2003). *Inquiring of Joseph: Getting to Know Biblical Characters Through the Qur'an.* Collegeville, MN: Liturgical Press.

Katz, J. (1963). The Joseph Dreams Anew. *Psychoanal. Rev.,* 50: 92-118.

Kelman, H. (1986). The Day Precipitate in Pharaoh's Dream. *Psychoanal. Quart.,* 55: 306-310.

Khan, M. M. R. (1972). The Use and Abuse of the Dream in Psychic Experience. In: *The Privacy of the Self.* London: Hogarth (pp. 306-315).

-------. (1976). Beyond the Dreaming Experience. In *Hidden Selves.* London: Hogarth, 1983 (pp. 42-50).

Klein, Y. (1997). *Yo'sef – Ba'al ha-ha'lo'mot*. In *mē-Pey'rot ha-E'lan al Par'shat ha-Sha'vua: Ma'ama'rēm me'et Hok'rey Un'ever'si'tat Bar-Ilan*, eds. J. Schwartz & D. Algavish. Ramat-Gan: Bar-Ilan University Press (pp. 125-126).

Lacan, J. (1955). Variations on the Standard Treatment. In *Écrits: The First Complete Edition in English*. Trans. B. Fink. New York: W. W. Norton, 2006 (pp. 269-302).

-------. (1955-1956). *The Seminar of Jacques Lacan: Book III: The Psychoses*. ed. J.-A. Miller, trans. R. Grigg. New York: Norton, 1993.

-------. (1956). The Function and Field of Speech in Language and Psychoanalysis. In: *Écrits: The First Complete Edition in English*. 7-268). Trans. B. Fink. New York: W. W. Norton, 2006 (pp. 197-268).

-------. (1961). The Direction of the Treatment and the Principles of its Power. In: *Écrits: The First Complete Edition in English*. Trans. B. Fink. New York: W. W. Norton, 2006 (pp. 585-642).

Lauer, C. (1913). Des Wesen des Traumes in der Beurteilung der Talmudischen und Rabbinishcen Literatur. *Int. Zeitsch. Artz. Psyscho-Anal.*, 1: 450-469.

Leibowitz, N. (1972). *Studies in Bereshit (Genesis) in the Context of Ancient and Modern Bible Commentary*. Trans. A. Newman. Jerusalem: World Zionist Congress.

Lévi-Strauss, C. (1958). *Structural Anthropology*, Vol. 1. Trans. C. Jacobson & B. Grundfest-Schoepf. Hammondsworth, UK: Penguin, 1968.

Licht, J. (1978). *Storytelling in the Bible*. Jerusalem: Magnes/Hebrew University Press.

Lombardi, N., & Rucker, N. (1998). Sounds of Silence: Parallel Dreaming and the Mutual Dream. In: *Subject Relations: Unconscious Experience and Relational Psychoanalysis*. London: Routledge (pp. 35-47).

Lorand, S. (1957). Dream Interpretation in the Talmud (Babylonian and Graeco-Roman period). In: *The New World of Dreams*. eds. R. L. Woods & H. B. Greenhouse. New York: Macmillan, 1974 (pp. 150-158).

Lowinger, A. (1908). *Der Traum in der Judischen Literatur*. Leipzig: M. W. Kaufmann.

Lurie, Y. (2000). *Cultural Beings: Readings of the Philosophers of Genesis.* Amsterdam: Rodophi.

MacKenzie, N. (1965). *Dreams and Dreaming.* New York: St Martin's Press.

Malcolm, N. (1959). *Dreaming: Studies in Philosophical Psychology.* New York: Humanities Press.

Matte-Blanco, I. (1975). *The Unconscious as Infinite Sets: An Essay in Bi-Logic.* London: Duckworth.

Matte-Blanco, I. (1988). *Thinking, Feeling, and Being: Clinical Reflections on the Fundamental Antinomy of Human Beings and World.* London: Routledge.

Meltzer, D. (1983). *Dream-Life: A Re-examination of the Psycho-Analytical Theory and Technique.* Perthshire: Clunie Press.

Niehoff, M. (1992). Do Biblical Characters Talk to Themselves? Narrative modes of representing Inner Speech in Early Biblical Fiction. *J. Biblical Lit.,* 111: 577-595.

Noegel, S. B. (2001). Dreams and Dream Interpreters in Mesopotamia and in the Hebrew Bible (Old Testament). In: *Dreams and Dreaming: A Reader in Religion, Anthropology, History, and Psychology* ed. K. Bulkeley. Hampshire, UK: Palgrave-St. Martin's Press (pp. 45-71).

Odelain, O., & Seguineau, R. (1981). Moses. In *Dictionary of Proper Names and Places in the Bible.* Trans. M. J. O'Connell. London: Robert Hale.

Ogden, T. H. (2003). On Not Being Able to Dream. In: *This Art of Psychoanalysis: Dreaming Undreamt Dreams and Interrupted Cries.* London: Routledge, 2005 (pp. 45-60).

Oppenheim, A. L. (1966). Mantic Dreams in the Ancient Near East. In: *The Dream and Human Societies* eds. G. E. von Grunebaum & H. Caillois. Berkeley: University of California (pp. 341-350).

Osman, A. (1987). *Stranger in the Valley of the Kings.* New York: Harper & Row.

Pirson, R. (2002). *The Lord of the Dreams: A Semantic and Literary Analysis of Genesis 37-50.* New York: Continuum International.

Pontalis, J.-B. (1974). Dream as an Object. *Int. Rev. Psycho-Anal.* 1: 125-134.

Raguse, H. (1996). Die Bible Zwischen Literaturinterpretation und Analytischem Prozess. *Psyche: Zeitsch. Psycho-Anal. & Anwend.,* 50: 817-935.

Rayner, E. (1995). *Unconscious Logic: An Introduction to Matte-Blanco's Bi-Logic and its Uses.* London: Routledge.

Rendsburg, G. A. (1990). Redactional Structuring in the Joseph Story: Genesis 37-50. In: *Mappings of the Biblical Terrain: The Bible as a Text,* eds. V. Tollers & J. Maier. Lewisberg, PA: Buckwell University Press (pp. 215-232).

Rice, M. (1999). *Who's Who in Ancient Egypt.* London: Routledge.

Rohl, D. M. (1995). *A Test of Time: The Bible from Myth to History.* London: Random House.

Rollins, W. C. (2008). The Bible and Psychology: New directions in biblical scholarship. In *Hearing Visions and Seeing Voices: Psychological Dimensions of Biblical Personalities sand Concepts,* eds., G. Glas, M. H. Spero, P. Verhagen & H. van Praag. Dordrecht: Springer (pp. 279-294).

Sand, R. (1999). *The Interpretation of Dreams:* Freud and the Western Dream Tradition. *Psychoanal. Dialog.,* 9: 725-749.

Sartre, J.-P. (1940). *Imagination: A Psychological Critique.* trans. F. Williams. New York: Philosophical Library, 1948.

Scalzone, F., & Zontini, G. (2001). The Dream's Navel: Between Chaos and Thought. *Int. J. Psycho-Anal.,* 82: 263-282.

Schroeder, F. W. (1972). *Visions and Renewal: Dynamic Dreams and Vitalizing Visions in the Bible.* St. Louis, MO: Eden.

Shupak, N. (2005). A Fresh Look at the Dreams of the Officials and of Pharaoh in the Story of Joseph (Genesis 40-41) in the Light of Egyptian Dreams. *J. Ancient Near East. Stud.,* 30: 103-138.

Smith, M. (1998). The Heart and Innards in Israelite Emotional Expressions: Notes from Anthropology and Psychology. *J. Bible Lit.,* 117: 427-436.

Snedeker, K. S. (1982). *Dreams in the Bible: A Depth Psychological Perspective.* Albion, MI: Albion College.

Spero, M. H. (1980). Dream Psychology in Rabbinic Thought. In: *Psychology and Judaism: Halakhic Perspectives.* New York: Yeshiva University Press/ Ktav (pp. 99-108).

——. (1984). A Psychotherapist's Reflections on a Countertransference Dream. *Amer. J. Psychoanal.,* 44: 191-196.

-------. (1992). *Religious Objects as Psychological Structures: A Critical Integration of Object Relations Theory, Psychotherapy and Judaism.* Chicago: University of Chicago Press.

-------. (1996). Original Sin, the Symbolization of Desire, and the Development of Mind. *Psychoanal. & Contemp. Thought,* 19: 499-562.

-------. (2010). *Repetition and Return: A Contemporary Psychoanalytic Investigation of the Judaic Concept of Teshuvah.* Northvale, NJ: Aronson/ Rowman & Littlefield.

Stewart, P. (1973). Changes in the Experience of the Dream and Transference. In: *Psychic Experience and Problems of Technique.* London: Routledge, 1992 (pp. 30-40).

Stolorow, R. D., & Atwood, G. (1992). Dreams and the Subjective World. In *Essential Papers on Dreams,* ed. M. L. Lansky. New York: New York University Press (pp. 272-294).

Turner, M. (1997). *ha-Ha'lo'mot be-sē'pur Yo'sef.* In: *mē-Pey'rot ha-E'lan al Par'shat ha-Sha'vua: Ma'ama'rēm me'et Hok'rey Un'e'versi'tat Bar-Ilan,* ed. J. Schwartz & D. Algavish. Ramat-Gan: Bar-Ilan University Press (pp. 123-125).

Vermes, G. (1973). *Scripture and Tradition in Judaism.* London: Brill.

Von Grunebaum, G. E., & Caillois, R. (1966). *The Dream and Human Societies.* Berkeley: University of California Press.

Wallace, E. R. (1985). *Historiography and Causation in Psychoanalysis: An Essay in Psychoanalytic and Historical Epistemology.* Hillside, NJ: Analytic Press.

Wax, M. L. (1998). Interpreting Dreams: Joseph, Freud and the Jewish tradition. *J. Psychol. & Jud.,* 22: 21-32.

Wax, M. L. (1999). The Angel of Dreams: Toward an Ethnology of Dream Interpreting. *J. Amer. Acad. Psychoanal.*, 27: 417-429.

Zeitlin, S. (1975-1976). Dreams and Their Interpretation from the Biblical Period to the Tanaaite Time: An Historical Study. *Jew. Quart. Rev.*, 66: 1-180.

Zeligs, D. (1974). *Psychoanalysis and the Bible: A Study in Depth of Seven Leaders.* New York: Bloch.

Zornberg, A. G. (1995). *Genesis: The Beginning of Desire.* Philadelphia: Jewish Publication Society.

-------. (2009). *The Murmuring Deep: Reflections on the Biblical Unconscious.* New York: Schocken.

APPENDIX

Column 1

*And it came to pass
at the end of two full years,
that Pharaoh dreamed:*

and, **behold,** he stood by the river.

And, **behold,** there came up out of the
river seven kine,
well-favored and fat-fleshed;
and they fed in the reed grass [swamp].

And, **behold,** seven other kine
came up after them out of the river,
ill-favored and lean-fleshed;

**and they stood by the other kine
upon the brink of the river.**

And the ill-favored and lean-fleshed kine
did eat up the seven well-favored and fat
kine;

*and Pharaoh awoke.
And he slept and dreamed a second time*

and, **behold,** seven ears of corn
came up on one stalk, healthy and good.

And, **behold,** seven ears,
thin and blasted with the east wind,
sprung up after them.

And the thin ears swallowed up
the seven healthy and full ears.

And Pharaoh awoke,
and, **behold,** it was a dream

Column 2

*And Pharaoh spoke unto Joseph:
'In my dream,*

behold,
I stood upon the brink of the river.'

And, **behold,** there came up out of the
river seven kine,
fat-fleshed and well-favored;
and they fed in the reed-grass [swamp].

And, **behold,** seven other kine
came up after them, poor and
very ill-favored and lean-fleshed,

**such as I never saw in all of the land
of Egypt for badness.**

And the lean and ill-favored kine
did eat up the first seven fat kine.

**and when they had eaten them up,
it could not be known that they had
eaten them; but they were still
ill-favored as at the beginning.**

So I awoke.

And I saw in my dream,
and, **behold,** seven ears
came up upon one stalk, full and good.

And, **behold,** seven ears, withered, thin,
and blasted with the east wind,
sprung up after them.

And the thin ears swallowed up
the seven good ears.

*And I told it to my magicians
but there was none that could declare it to me.*

234

מא : א
Column 1
1 ויהי מקץ שנתים ימים
2 ופרעה חלם
והנה עמד על-היאור

מא : ב
והנה מן-היאר עלת
שבע פרות יפות מראה
ובריאות בשר
ותרעינה באחו

מא : ג
והנה שבע פרות אחרות
עלות אחריהן מן-היאור
רעות מראה ודקות בשר
3 ותעמדנה אצל הפרות
על-שפת היאר

מא : ד
ותאכלנה הפרות רעות המראה
ודקות הבשר
את שבע הפרות יפת המראה והבריאת

5 וייקץ פרעה

מא : ה
6 ויישן ויחלם שנית
והנה שבע שבלים עלות בקנה אחד
בריאות וטבות

מא : ו
והנה שבע שבלים דקות ושדופת קדים
צמחות אחריהן

מא : ז
ותבלענה השבלים הדקות
את שבע השבלים הבריאות והמלאות

7 וייקץ פרעה והנה חלום

מא : יד
Column 2
1 וידבר פרעה אל-יוסף
2 בחלמי
הנני עמד על שפת היאר

מא : יח
והנה מן-היאר עלת
שבע פרות בריאות בשר
ויפת תאר
ותרעינה באחו

מא : יט
והנה שבע-פרות אחרות
עלות אחריהן
דלות ורעות תאר מאד ורקות
בשר
3 לא-ראיתי כהנה בכל-ארץ
מצרים לרע

מא : כ
ותאכלנה הפרות הרקות והרעות
את שבע הפרות הראשנות הבריאת

מא : כא
4 ותבאנה אל-קרבנה
ולא נודע כי-באו אל-קרבנה
ומראיהן רע כאשר בתחלה

5 ואקיץ

מא : כב
6 וארא בחלמי
והנה שבע שבלים עלת בקנה אחד
מלאות וטבות

מא : כג
והנה שבע שבלים צנמות דקות
שדפות קדים
צמחות אחריהם

מא : כד
ותבלען השבלים הדקת
את שבע השבלים הטבות

7 ואמר אל-החרטמים ואין
מגיד לי

235

'Let Me see That Good Land:' the Story of a Human Life

Avivah Gottlieb Zornberg

A tale of repudiated desire

In an individual human history, infancy, the condition of those who cannot speak, resolves into the competencies of language. But the fraught relations of word and desire remind us that the cross-over to language is, in a sense, always with us. The infant, 'cradled in tempests' in Shelley's phrase, is re-awakened in us when we stammer, when we hesitate, when words fail us. In any attempt to 'communicate impassioned feelings,' Wordsworth writes, there is 'a consciousness of the inadequateness of our own powers, or the deficiencies of language.' (Wordsworth, 1955, p. 236) In the world of biblical narrative, this moment of cross-over is most powerfully enacted in the words and wordlessness of Moses.

The relations between Moses, God, and the Israelites in the biblical narrative are often viewed through a prism of authoritative and manifest meaning. God speaks, Moses conveys His commands, and the people either obey or disobey. However, a closer reading of the text releases worlds of complex, even paradoxical meaning. Moses' voice intimates a profound personal life that questions its own ability to communicate. In the book of Deuteronomy, this voice is heard in a new way, speaking its own torment, reaching out to his listeners — and to his future readers — precisely through the disruption of its own knowingness. Skeptical of his own power to affect them, Moses acts out the reality of the unconscious.

If teaching is the 'impossible profession,' as Freud affirms, then it is through his implicated interest in that impossibility that Moses stages for his contemporary and future students new teaching possibilities that are born precisely of resistance. In the intensity of the transferential relation with his people, he speaks a language that says more than it knows. The poetical function of a language that is not entirely transparent to itself — that reaches through and beyond ignorance — comes to constitute the very possibility of teaching and of healing.

From the beginning of his life with God, Moses pleads a radical failure of voice: 'I am not a man of words.... I am heavy of mouth, heavy of tongue .... of uncircumcised lips ....' Despite God's reassurances — 'They *will* listen to you ....' — the Israelites indeed fail to hear his message of redemption: 'When Moses told the Israelites [God's message], they would not listen to him in the exasperation of hard labour.' (Exod. 6:9)

Against this background of conscious disability, the midrash ironically remarks on Moses' sudden flow of eloquence at the end of his life:

'These are the words that Moses spoke to the children of Israel:' Israel said: Just yesterday you said, 'I am not a man of words,' and now you have so much to say! R. Yitzhak said: If you have a speech-impediment, learn Torah and you will be healed! Moses had learned the whole Torah 'in the wilderness on the plains facing the Red Sea.' That is why it is written, 'Then the lame shall leap like a deer, and the tongue of the mute shall exult.' (Isaiah 35:6)

Come and see: When God told Moses, 'Go on my mission to Pharaoh,' Moses replied, 'You do me wrong! I am not a man of words! Seventy languages are spoken in Pharaoh's palace, so that wherever a visitor comes from he is addressed in his own language. Now, if I go on Your mission, they will interrogate me, and when they find that I claim to be Your emissary and yet I am unable to speak freely with them, will they not mock me: "Look at God's emissary who does not know how to discourse in all the seventy languages of the world!" You do me wrong! I am not a man of words! I am of uncircumcised lips!' Then God answered him: 'But how did Adam, who had no teacher, learn seventy languages? — as it is said, "He called them names" (Gen. 2:??) — not one name for each animal but *names* [seventy names]! And yet you say, "I am not a man of words!"'

237

Forty years after leaving Egypt, Moses began to interpret the Torah in seventy languages – 'He explained [*ba'er*] this Torah' (Deut. 1:5) The mouth that had said, 'I am not a man of words,' now spoke 'These [are the] words.' And the prophet cried out: 'Then shall the lame leap like a deer and the tongue of the mute shall sing aloud!' (Isaiah 35:6) Why? 'For waters shall burst forth in the desert, streams in the wilderness.' So, 'These are the words that Moses spoke....'[1]

Suddenly, it seems, Moses gains that access to language that was so long withheld from him. In the terms of the midrash, this means an ability to speak freely in all seventy languages – a minimum requirement for one who claims to speak for God! He can talk to everyone *in his own language*; he masters all possible codes of symbolic communication. He translates God's word into the terms of each human encounter. Like Adam, he discovers a primal genius for language; unprompted, like a spring in the desert, his voice resounds in the many words of Deuteronomy.[2]

The mysterious force of the analogy – language bursting forth like water in the wilderness – becomes more poignant when we consider the context and purpose of many of Moses' final speeches in Deuteronomy. These are, to a certain extent, re-tellings of Israel's forty year history of wandering in the desert and of laws already promulgated in the earlier volumes of the Torah. Other passages contain new material. But these speeches, which occupy a large portion of the Book, are understood, even by some of the traditional commentaries,[3] as bearing an unprecedently *personal* stamp. They are not simply mechanical transmissions of God's words, but the creation, to some extent, of the man Moses in the final months of his life. This assumption lies behind the midrash we have just quoted: the people are somewhat quizzically amazed at Moses' sudden

---

1   Tanchuma Devarim 2.

2   There may be a pun in the midrash on the word *be'er/ba'er* – 'a well'/ 'interpreting.'

3   See e.g. B. Megilla 31b; Maharal, *Tifferet Yisrael*, ch.43; the commentaries of Abarbanel, Or HaChaim and the Dubno Maggid (*Ohel Yaakov*).

eloquence, at the fertility of symbolic resonance that now characterizes him.

One tradition, cited by Rashi, places the opening speeches of the book under the heading of 'rebuke' (*tochacha*): as he revisits old rebellions and recriminations, Moses is inviting his people to a self-critical view of their shared past in the wilderness. In this reading, Moses has a rhetorical intention as he re-narrates these historical crises. In his own words, in his own voice, he is, I suggest, not only castigating his people but also making a demand on them. What is the nature of this implicit demand?

Of course, there is a peculiar pathos in the timing of these speeches. They are, in a sense, death-bed speeches. Central among these recountings is Moses' narrative of his own failure to achieve his life's desire — to enter the Holy Land. This brief autobiographical passage is uniquely personal in its content and in its timbre:

> 'And I beseeched God at that time, saying, "Lord God .... Let me, I pray, cross over and see the good land on the other side of the Jordan, that good hill country, and the Lebanon." But God was wrathful with me on your account and would not listen to me. God said to me, "Enough! Never speak to Me of this matter again! Go up to the summit of Pisgah and gaze about, to the west, the north, the south, and the east. Look at it well, for you shall not go across that Jordan. Charge Joshua with his instructions and imbue him with strength and courage, for he shall go across at the head of this people, and he shall allot to them the Land you may only see."' (Deut. 3:23-28)

Moses tells of a desperate plea to God, and of a cruel repudiation.[4] In a sense, he is telling the people of his failure to be heard by God, a failure that replicates his original failure of voice: 'And God *would not listen* to me ....' God cuts his plea short, and closes off any future pleas in this vein: 'Never speak (*dabber*) to Me of this matter (*davar*) again.' God seals off his language in words that exactly parallel the description

---

[4] See Rashi to 3:26: '"Enough:" so that people don't say, How harsh the teacher, how unruly the student!' The apparent cruelty of God's repudiation can be countered only by assuming that Moses' plea is in some way egregious. The more eloquent he is, the harder it is for the reader to avoid the dilemma of judgment.

of his outburst of language at the beginning of the book: 'These are the words (*devarim*) that Moses spoke (*dibber*).' With all the pathos he can command, Moses, the newly eloquent speaker, reports to his people how God interrupted his most passionate speech. As one to whom words come hard, Moses communicates his own frustration and humiliation.

Many questions arise from this poignant passage. This is, in fact, the only account we have of this encounter between Moses and God. There is no independent narrative of this painful moment. We know of it only because Moses chooses to tell the story to the people. Why does he do this? What would possess a leader, in his final speeches, to report such a crushing interaction with his God? What is his rhetorical purpose, the implicit demand he is making on his audience?

More concretely, *when* did Moses' prayer and God's denial occur? ' I beseeched God *at that time…*' The timing seems significant. Since there is no independent account of the moment, the midrash assumes that the prayer immediately followed on the conquest of Transjordan, just recorded. (2:26 — 3:22) Rashi finds in this sequence of events a hint of Moses' motivation:

> 'At that time:' After conquering the land of Sihon and Og, I thought that perhaps the decree [that I should not enter the land] had been annulled. 'To say:' This is one of three occasions when Moses said to God: 'I will not let You go till you tell me whether You will fulfil my request or not!'[5]

Rashi places Moses' prayer at the historical moment when Moses finds himself already, in a sense, inside the borders of the Holy Land. Having conquered the territories of Transjordan, he allows himself to hope that he will, after all, be permitted to cross the river and lead his people into their future. Perhaps the decree has been annulled? The moment of first conquest might plausibly have been a moment of personal hope for Moses; and this might well have issued in the prayer of extreme urgency that Rashi goes on to describe: 'I will not let You go until You tell me whether You

---

5   Rashi to 3:23.

will fulfil my request or not.' The assertive pressure of his desire elicits God's trenchant response: 'Enough!....'

Another clue to the timing and motivation of Moses's prayer lies in the mysterious speech that God makes to Moses in Num. 27:12:

> And God said to Moses: 'Go up to these heights of Avarim (crossing places) and view the Land that I have given to the children of Israel. You shall see it, and then you too shall be gathered in to your people, just as Aharon your brother was gathered in.'

This announcement of Moses' imminent death is strangely placed at the end of the book of Numbers, months before Moses' death. It occurs, in fact, immediately after the episode in which the five daughters of Tselofhad successfully plead their cause and gain the inheritance of their portion of the land. At this juncture, Rashi suggests, Moses sees a glimmer of hope in his personal case:

> 'Go up to these heights of Avarim:' Why is this passage placed here? When God said, 'You shall indeed give them [the daughters of Tselofhad] a hereditary holding, Moses thought, 'I was commanded to give them the inheritance — perhaps the decree has been annulled and I will after all enter the land?' Then God said,' My decree stands in place.'
>
> Another view: When Moses entered the inheritance of the children of Gad and of Reuben, he rejoiced: 'I think that the decree against me has been annulled.' This is like a king who decreed that his son would not enter the palace. He entered the gate, left it behind him, and then the courtyard, till it was behind him, then the main hall, till it was behind him; when he was about to enter the living quarters, the king said, 'My son, from here onwards you are forbidden to enter.'[6]

In two separate scenarios, Rashi tells his midrashic tale of repudiated desire. In the first scenario, Moses draws courage to pray from the wording of God's instructions: 'You (personally?) shall give them possession of their inheritance ....' He hears God's personal address as an invitation for prayer. Perhaps, too, he is inspired by being charged with an apparently

---

6   Rashi to Num. 27:17.

transgressive alteration in the iron decree of male inheritance.[7] Since one boundary has been shifted, perhaps this is a moment to press his own case?[8] God answers, 'My decree *stands in place'* — inexorably blocking Moses' movement of hopeful imagination.

In the second scenario, as in the passage from Rashi that we have already seen, it is the geographical reality of his conquests that fuels Moses' plea. In neither case, however, is any prayer explicitly narrated in the biblical text. Yet in both cases, the midrash detects a movement of irrepressible desire triggered by the historical event. The prayer, if it existed, is repressed. Perhaps it was never uttered, a silent prayer, or a murmur?

Whatever shape it assumed, it is answered by God's enigmatic words: 'Go up these heights of Avarim, of *transitions* ....' The mountain from which he is to view the land before he dies is here named *Avarim* — the peak of *going across,* of *seeing across* to the far side of his desire. This moment of seeing and dying is set in the future. But it is the essential response of God *now.* As Moses will later tell the people in his account of his prayer, God answered him: 'Raise your eyes and see with your eyes — for/that (*ki*) you will not cross over that Jordan.' (Deut. 3:27) Moses' vision will take in two things: the vista of the land and the fact that he will not cross over. His vision will be informed by the deep knowledge that he will not make this crossing.

When God addresses Moses in this enigmatic way, blocking his desire — *E'evra na* — 'Let me cross over and see ....' — yet cryptically offering him passage to some other form of vision, Moses replies by asking God to appoint an effective leader to succeed him. 'And Moses *spoke* (*Va-yidabber*) to God ....' (27:15) *Dibbur* expresses a forceful, even aggressive act of speech. This is, in fact, the only

---

[7]   See B. Baba Bathra 109b on Num. 27:8: 'You shall *transfer* his property to his daughter:' 'Rav said, 'Everywhere the word *give* is used, only here is *transfer* used. No-one *transfers* property from tribe to tribe but a daughter, since her son and her husband inherit her.' See also Rashi on this verse.

[8]   See Rashi to 27:16: 'The moment has come for me to plead my cause...'

occasion where the word is used when Moses addresses God. Rashi comments: 'He spoke trenchantly to God. This tells the praise of the righteous who, as they depart from this world, set their own needs aside and involve themselves in the needs of the community.' As the midrash puts it: 'Anyone who speaks for the needs of the community, it is as though he comes with force (lit. with the power of his arm).'[9]

The irony is striking. Precisely at the moment when his personal hopes have been dashed, Moses speaks to God with an unprecedented confidence that his voice *will be heard*. What is the emotional logic of this moment of passage? How does the frustration of his desire to 'cross over and see' the land metabolize into a new potency of language? 'And Moses *spoke* these words:' both in his speeches to the people and in his address to God, he who was not a man of words discovers a vein of powerful *dibbur*.

God's apparently ill-timed command ('Go up to the heights of Avarim') has, then, shifted the vector of Moses' desire. In the midrashic imagination, Moses has found an opening for hope and prayer. Then, harshly interrupted by God ('And God would not listen to me... "Enough! ..."'), effectively silenced by God, Moses turns his energy towards his people's needs. That is, silenced on one subject, he speaks, with unprecedented force, on another. Silenced in speaking to God ('Never speak *to Me* again....'), he speaks to the people with irrepressible power.

We have raised a number of related questions, about the new energy of Moses' language, as he engages both God and his people, about the ways in which this connects with God's interruption of his desire and of his attempt to speak it; about the timing of his prayer, its motivation, its mysterious absence from the text;[10] and, most radically, about his purpose in narrating this painful encounter with God to his people,

---

[9] See Bamidbar Rabba 21:15.

[10] The mystery diminishes if we assume, in the wake of Ramban, a principle of literary economy in the biblical text. See e.g. Ramban to Genesis 42:21.

as part of his last addresses. This last question — Why would he tell such a story of refusal and humiliation, which exists in the Torah *only* as part of his narrative? — evokes further questions about this uniquely autobiographical passage, its purposes, and its risks.

Crossing over

In thinking about these issues and in reading the text of Deuteronomy, we notice how often the motif of *crossing over* occurs. Particularly haunting is the way Moses repeats the refrain of 'You (Moses) shall not cross over …. He (Joshua) shall cross over ….' (Deut. 3:27-28)[11] Not only in relation to Joshua, his successor, is this counterpoint sustained,[12] but also in relation to the people: 'For I am to die in this land; I shall not cross over the Jordan. But you will cross over and take possession of that good land.' (4:22)[13] This is not simply an antithesis of (their) life and (his) death, but, precisely, of *crossing over* and *not crossing over*. ('I must die' is subsidiary to the main statement — *eineni over*: 'I shall not cross over.') It is striking that, in many cases, this expression is not completed by a reference to the Jordan river. It acquires a free-standing quality of metaphysical antinomy. The pathos of Moses' harping on this antinomy provokes the reader to wonder about *crossing over,* and about the enigmatic message that Moses may be conveying to the people. Once God has repudiated his desire, in some sense Moses lays his narrative at the door of his audience. What does he want of them? What anger, or sadness, or envy, or spurned love do his words limn forth?

One dramatic appearance of the *crossing over* theme occurs in the speech of the two-and-a-half tribes, Reuben, Gad and half Menasseh, when they lay claim to the conquered lands of Transjordan. They

---

[11] See also 31:2-3.

[12] Even before he tells the story of his prayer, Moses recounts how he charged Joshua with his future military role 'among the kingdoms, where you are crossing over.' (3:21)

[13] See also Num. 33:51; 35:10; and Deut. 4:14, 26; 6:1; 9:1; 11:8,11,31; 30:18; 31:13.

forcefully plead with Moses: '*Al ta'avirenu* — do not make us cross over that Jordan!' (Num. 32:5) These tribes want the conquered land for their cattle; but they just as strongly do *not* want to cross over the Jordan. They appeal to Moses, whose deepest wish is *E'ebra na* — 'Let me, I pray, cross over.' In contrast to the daughters of Tselofhad, who dare to speak beyond convention, staking their claim to ancestral lands on the far side of the Jordan — and drawing congratulations from God for their strong reading, their happy act of *dibbur:* 'They have spoken justly ...' (27:6) — these tribes speak for what they already hold in their possession, their *mikneh*, their cattle.[14] The word, with its root meaning of property or acquisition, stands in tension with the notion of *crossing over.* For them, *crossing over* is anathema. In his response, Moses excoriates them for demoralizing the people, precisely on this issue of *crossing over.*[15] He repeatedly refers to their *crossing* of the Jordan with the rest of the people to fight the wars of conquest: only on this condition may they inherit the pasture land on *this* side of the river. What precisely is implied in the tribes' reluctance to *cross over*, as it is played out against Moses' radical desire?

As Moses speaks, his desire to *cross over* becomes audible even in the prosaic context of his requests for safe passage through the territories of Transjordan. 'Let me pass through (*e'ebra*) your land ....' (Num. 21:22)), he begs Sihon, king of the Emorites; and in his last speeches to his people, he tells the story, repeating the word, *e'ebra* (2:27-28). Sihon's refusal leads to war. But for Moses the word and the desire it signifies hold a more than technical meaning. He is refused by Sihon, by Edom — and by God. And even among his own people, there are those whose language

---

14   The word *mikneh* opens and closes their first speech, and occurs seven times in its course.

15   They are re-playing, in a sense, the refusal of the Spies, their failure of desire, that made that crossing unthinkable. This is Moses' retrospective analysis of their rebellion: 'You had no desire to go up....' (Deuteronomy 1:26) It is striking that in Deuteronomy *crossing over* largely replaces *going up* (*aliyah*) as the verb used to describe the movement into the land. The latter was central to the story of the Spies; the former becomes the term of choice in Moses' parting speeches.

betrays a radical alienation from the structure of his desire: *al ta'avirenu* —
Do not make us cross over....

A heart to know?

In midrashic sources and in hassidic appropriations of these sources,
Moses' addresses to his people are informed by movements of implicit
disappointment, even bitterness, which are intimated even as they are
repressed in the biblical text. Covertly, he appeals to them to recognize and
support his desire. But they cannot hear his appeals. One such moment
occurs at the very beginning of Deuteronomy, in Moses' first speech to the
people. God has commanded them to move away from Sinai and begin the
journey into the Holy Land:

> 'And I said to you, I cannot bear the burden of you by myself .... Pick from
> each of your tribes men who are wise, perceptive, and experienced, and
> I will appoint them as your heads. You answered me and said, What you
> propose to do is good.' (1:9, 13-14)

Moses' expression, 'I cannot bear the burden of you by myself,' is
read by the 19th century hassidic master, Mei Hashiloah, as a plea to the
people to pray for him, to express their desire that Moses continue as their
leader. Without their solidarity, he cannot lead them into the land. Even
before the explicit decree at Merivah, he realizes that, alone, he will not
consummate the journey of exodus. Only if they *want* him to lead them
will his loneliness be mitigated.

However, he can communicate his desire only obliquely. On the
surface, he is telling them to appoint to judicial roles an auxiliary group
of 'wise, perceptive, and experienced men.' In fact, however, he is
appealing to them to reject his proposal and to declare their unequivocal
loyalty to him. But they, with magnificent obtuseness, respond: 'What
you propose to do is good.' They fail to understand his meaning; they in
fact declare their indifference to his leadership. For this reason, the new
appointees are later described as 'wise and experienced men,' omitting
the epithet, 'perceptive,' *nevonim*. 'Perceptive men he did not find,' says

Moses in a sardonic midrash. This is read by Mei Hashiloah as a sad comment on the people's lack of emotional intelligence. They might perhaps have helped Moses through their prayers; but they could not intuit his real meaning, the desire that wordlessly animated his appeal to them.

This radical reading, with its play of implicit and explicit meanings, has Moses, in the opening speech of Deuteronomy, remind his people of a past failure in *understanding*. The gap between his desire and God's decree might have been bridged only by their unforced prayer. They might have helped him across the Jordan. Now, he tells his story — reproachfully, wistfully, bitterly?[16]

Such a failed dialogue is already adumbrated in midrashic sources. One midrash, for example, focuses on the theme of 'You are crossing over — I am not crossing over ….:'

> Therefore, when they came to cross over the Jordan, Moses reminded them of every plea that he had made on their behalf, because he thought that now they would pray on his behalf, that he should enter the land with them. What is the force of 'You are crossing over'? R. Tanhuma said: Moses prostrated himself before Israel and said to them: 'You are to cross over, but not I.' He gave them the opportunity to pray for him, but they did not grasp his meaning.
>
> This can be compared to a king who had many children by a noble lady. The lady was undutiful to him and he resolved to dismiss her. He said to her: Know that I am going to marry another wife.' She replied: 'Yes, but will you not tell me whom it is that you intend to marry?' He replied: 'So-and-so.' What did the noble lady do? She summoned her children and said to them: 'Know that your father intends to divorce me and to marry So-and-so. Could you bear to be subjected to her?' They replied: 'Yes.' She then said to them: 'Know what she will do to you.' She thought that perhaps they would understand what she meant and would intercede with their father on her behalf, but they did not understand. As they did not understand, she

---

[16] See Rashi on 1:14: Moses ironically notes the enthusiasm of their response to the idea of delegating leadership. Their eager assent betrays their secret intention of corrupting the future judges who, unlike Moses, will be open to bribery

said: 'I will command you only for your own sake, be mindful of the honour of your father.'

So it was with Moses. When God said to him: 'Take Joshua the son of Nun ….(Num. 27:18); For you shall not cross over that Jordan ….' (Deuteronomy 3:27), Moses said to Israel, 'And it shall come to pass, when the Lord your God shall bring you into the land where you are going to possess it' (11:29); he stressed [the words], 'You are to cross over this day, not I;' he thought that perhaps Israel would understand. As they did not understand, he said: 'I will command you only for your own sakes, be mindful of the honour of your Father in heaven.' How do we know this?' For it is said, 'That you may fear the Lord your God ….' (6:2)[17]

In this poignant midrash, Moses simply tells the people the geography of his pain: 'You are crossing over — I am not crossing over.' Why can they not hear the appeal hidden within the words? Especially in the context of his many prayers of intercession for them? The parable of the noble lady sharpens and deflects the anguish of misunderstanding. Across the generation-gap, the lady probes her children's loyalty. They remain blithely insensitive to her need. Perhaps the prospect of a new mother has its attractions? In any case, they are incapable of realizing what the loss of their mother will mean. In the end, the lady darkly hints that it is their loss, rather than hers, that now concerns her. Where will they be without her intercession, without the dynamic family triangle of father, mother, children? But they cannot grasp their mother's crucial role in their lives. She can only warn them, somberly, 'Be mindful of your father's honour ….' So Moses warns his people about the future without his loving mediation: 'You are crossing over — I am not crossing over …. *Fear the Lord your God* — Be mindful of the honour of your Father in heaven.'

Midrashic sources offer many examples of explosive confrontations between fathers and sons. Here, the presence of the mother (Moses) displaces and diffuses some of the anger aroused by the unruly son. Without the symbolic complexity of this family triangle, such confrontations become dangerous. At first, Moses appeals to the people for his own sake;

---

[17] Devarim Rabba 3:12

ultimately, his concern shifts to their welfare. How will they, unruly as they are, survive their father's unaccommodated anger? Without the mother's softening influence, the effect of her double love, they can survive only by dint of extreme caution: by fear, not love.

Ironically, it is their incomprehension that triggers the shift in Moses' feeling, from narcissistic to altruistic concern. This obtuseness draws from Moses a final, devastating comment, shortly before his death: 'God did not give you a heart to know, or eyes to see, or ears to hear, until this day.' (29:3) The midrash reads this as a personal reproach directed by Moses at the people:

'God has not given you a heart to know:' R' Samuel b. Nahmani said: Moses said this with reference to himself. How so? The Holy One, blessed be He, made two decrees, one affecting Israel, and one affecting Moses. The one affecting Israel was when they committed the unmentionable sin [the Golden Calf], as it is said, 'Let Me alone, that I may destroy them' (Deut. 9:14). And the one affecting Moses? When Moses sought to enter the land of Israel, God said to him, 'You shall not cross over this Jordan' (3:27). Moses therefore entreated God to annul both decrees. He said to God: 'Master of the Universe, Pardon, I pray, the iniquity of this people according unto the greatness of Your lovingkindness' (Num. 14:19), and God's decree was annulled while his own prayer was fulfilled; as it is said, 'I have pardoned according to your word' (14:20). When he was about to enter the land, Moses entreated: 'Let me cross over, I pray, and see the good land' (Deut. 3:25). And God replied: 'Moses, on a former occasion you annulled My decree and I granted your prayer; I said: 'That I may destroy them,' and you prayed: 'Pardon, I pray;' and your prayer was fulfilled. On this occasion, I wish to carry out My decree and to refuse your prayer.' God added: 'Moses, you do not know how to behave! You wish to hold the rope at both ends. If you insist on "Let me cross over, I pray," then you must withdraw the prayer, "Pardon, I pray;" and if you insist on "Pardon, I pray," then you must withdraw, "Let me cross over, I pray."

R. Joshua b. Levi said: When Moses our teacher heard this, he exclaimed before God: 'Master of the Universe, let rather Moses and a hundred like him perish than that the finger-nail of even one of them [Israel] should be injured!' R. Samuel b. Isaac said: When Moses was nearing his end and Israel did not pray him that he should enter the land, he assembled them

249

and began rebuking them with the words: One man saved sixty myriads at the time of the Golden Calf, and yet sixty myriads cannot save one man!. This is the force of 'God has not given you a heart to know.'[18]

Moses makes a radical choice between the people's interests and his own. It seems that he can prevail over only one of God's two decrees. In a sense, there is nothing more natural than the desire to 'hold the rope at both ends,' as God puts it; and Moses in fact attempts to assert his will on both issues. But God interrupts him, as though some basic existential issue is at stake. Why, indeed, can Moses not save both himself and his people? Why is such a radical choice necessary?

The issue, I suggest, is one of language, of a combat of words between God and Moses: 'your word' against 'My word.' Moses has won the first round ('I have pardoned *according to your word*'); now he must yield to God's word. There is a cryptic and relentless logic to God's demand; it is an elemental *emotional* demand. He must choose, either his people or himself, either his literal, narcissistic fulfillment or the diffused, symbolic play of desire. He withdraws his prayer. Strikingly, in the midrash, God does not so much refuse his personal prayer as trigger a choice that is no choice: if the price of his own fulfillment is harm to even a finger-nail of theirs, then his course is clear. In withdrawing his prayer, he is reading quite literally God's words: 'Enough! Never speak to Me again of this matter!' God is telling him to *stop speaking*, to bite back his prayer, since the welfare of his people is inconsistent with it. There is a daring logic to this reading, since Moses has, precisely, asked God to withdraw His words of doom: 'Pardon, I pray ....' At its core, the choice is between two worlds of words; each is constituted by a victory and a defeat. In some sense, this represents a necessary structure of language, in which God educates Moses.

The climax of the midrash, however, comes in its final lines: when Moses is close to death, he gathers the people and *tells them the story*. The tone and purpose of the story is named as *tochacha* — rebuke. He confronts them with a radical reproach, in the form of a narrative of satiric grievance: One man could save 600,000, but 600,000 could not save one — 'God has

---

[18] Devarim Rabba 7:11.

not given you a *heart to know.*' He speaks about their insensitivity to his need, to his meaning. Presented in ironic, arithmetical terms, his speech creates an a-symmetric history in which his 'pleading for mercy' is set against their heartless obtuseness, their failure to find their own words of desire for his survival.

In other words, he is attacking their lack of imagination. He confronts them with this most radical reproach: they lack a knowing heart, they do not *understand* what is implicit, unspeakable. His narrative is, in essence, *tochacha* — rebuke — which evokes the notion of *presence* (*nocheach*). For this, I suggest, is what rebuke requires: the full presence of the speaker. If Moses is to reach them, if he is to achieve some lasting impact through his words, he must speak out of concern for them and their future. But he must also bring to bear the concentrated force of his own history. He must confront them with the movement of his desire.

Eros translated

So he tells them: 'I beseeched God .... "Let.... me cross over, I pray...."' What is it to *cross over*? I suggest that the word *avar* represents the very movement of desire, the movement to an *other* place, to an elsewhere.[19] Its definition is *not-here, not-now.* When, for instance, God tells the people that His commandments are 'not in heaven' — that is, not inaccessible, or mysterious — He elaborates: '....nor is it across — *me'ever* — the sea, that you should say, Who will go for us across — *ya'avor* — to that other shore — *el ever ha-yam* — and bring it back to us....?' The word *ever*, used three times in one sentence, comes to express the un-reachable terrain,

---

[19] Abraham, the father of the Jewish people, is resonantly described as *ha-ivri* (the Hebrew) (Genesis 14:13): the one who came from the other side of the river (Rashi). Another midrashic reading: 'The entire world was on one side of the divide, while he was on the other.' (Bereshit Rabba 42:13) This 'Hebrew' identification becomes the primal epithet for Joseph in Egypt, for the Hebrew slaves in Egypt, and, in legal texts, for members of the Hebrew nation, as opposed to Canaanite or other foreign nationalities. The Hebrew language, too, is referred to in talmudic and midrashic texts as *Ivrit*; this is, of course, the modern Hebrew word for the modern Hebrew language.

which is set against God's triumphant closing note: 'For it is very close to you, in your mouth and in your heart, to do it.' (30:13-14)

Here, the contrast is between the intimacy and concreteness of God's commandment, as against its alienation to ungraspable spheres. But Moses' desire — like all desire — is precisely for that place beyond place. To pass over, cross over is, essentially, to disappear from present space and present time. In temporal terms, the past is referred to as *l'she'avar* — that which is gone, lapsed, done with, over. (OED) The moment of *passing* is fleeting: 'My beloved slipped away and was gone — *avar* .... I sought him but found him not ....' (Song 5:6) The elusiveness of the lover is caught at the moment of his disappearance. Human life is compared to *tzel over* — a passing shadow. In the great epiphany, when God appears to Moses by dis-appearing, He responds to Moses' desire:

> 'Let me see Your presence!' And He answered, 'I will make all My goodness *pass* before you .... You cannot see My face, for man may not see Me and live.... See, there is a place with Me. Station yourself on the rock and, as My presence *passes by*. I will put you in a cleft in the rock and shield you with My hand until I *have passed by*. Then, I will take My hand away and you will see My back; but My face must not be seen.' (Exod. 33:18-23)

The 'place with Me' in which Moses is positioned — the crevice in the rock — is the spatial equivalent of the fleeting moment of God's passing before Moses' covered eyes. To witness that moment would be perilous: 'I will shield you with my hand *until I have passed by*.' Seeing God's *back* is witnessing the *pastness*, the aftermath of God's presence. In space and in time, Moses is to know God as One who has already been here. '"I will make all My goodness *pass* before you" .... And God *passed* before him ....' (34:6) The promise of the moment is withdrawn as it is given. To make His goodness pass in front of Moses is to remove it from his sight, to leave a space behind.

Here is the bitter-sweetness of Eros, which plays on the margin between the actual and possible. In her powerful meditation on Eros, Anne Carson describes the human desire that is 'wooer of a meaning that is inseparable from its absence.' (Carson, 1998, p.75) 'All men, by their very nature,' said

Aristotle, 'reach out to know.' (Carson, p.98) Moses reaches out to know God's glory and falls short. Desire makes a suitor of him, courting the unfathomable, eternally at the point of *ma'avar*, the crossing place to the unknown.

'Knowing and desiring entail the same delight, the same pain,' writes Anne Carson. (1998)

> Stationed at the edge of itself, or of its present knowledge, the thinking mind launches a suit for understanding into the unknown. So too the wooer stands at the edge of his value as a person and asserts a claim across the boundaries of another.... Something else. Think about what that feels like.' (p.71)

Eros is about boundaries and the desire to dissolve them: 'Infants begin to see by noticing the edges of things. How do they know an edge is an edge? By passionately wanting it not to be.' (p.30)

Eros becomes a verb, it acts. In a condition of acute tension, the mind moves into *meta-phor*, which *trans-fers* meaning from the familiar to the strange. By an act of imagination, we bring two incongruent things together and notice a new congruence. This requires a 'stereoscopic vision,' an 'ability to hold in equipoise two perspectives at once.' (p.73) The fusion we desire can be attained only through this *metaphoric* action, which *carries meaning across*.

'Space reaches out from us and translates the world.' (Rilke) Moses' desire to *cross over* involves this desire to fuse the near and the far. He reaches out to meanings not known, he woos that which must dissolve in his grasp. Unlike the two and a half tribes, for whom such reachings, such acts of poignant and joyful imagination are intolerable — *al ta'avirenu* — for whom *mikneh* — the bird in the hand — is the thing, Moses hungers for the play of transcendence, of transition, of transference, of translation. He keeps returning to this restless place — to God's edict, 'You shall not cross over,' and to his desire, 'Let me cross over....' His wings will not be clipped.[20] If he cannot cross over this Jordan river, he will trans-late,

---

[20]   The biblical word for 'wing' is *ever*.

trans-fer his desire to another extension of his being. At the very moment when God silences him, his soul grows new wings. Eros initiates a new metaphoric intensity.

Moses launches himself on a new movement of desire: to 'come across' to his people, to reach out from the known to the unknown that they now constitute for him. 'You are crossing over,' he tells them,' I am not crossing over.' 'You are going into the unknown, you are leaving me behind, I no longer have the possibility of leaving anything behind. I will be your past, you are moving out my sight.' This is the impassable gap that opens up between himself and the people. Moses stages for them his surrender to the knowledge of this difference.

This is what it means to die:

> Palomar does not underestimate the advantages that the condition of being alive can have over that of being dead: not as regards the future, where risks are always very great and benefits can be of short duration, but in the sense of the possibility of improving the form of one's own past. A person's life consists of a collection of events, the last of which could also change the meaning of the whole, not because it counts more than the previous ones but because once they are included in a life, events are arranged in an order that is not chronological but rather corresponds to an inner architecture. A person, for example, reads in adulthood a book that is important for him.... After he has read that book, his life becomes the life a person who has read that book and it is of little importance whether he read it early or late, because now his life before that reading also assumes a form shaped by that reading. (Calvino, 1986, pp.110-111)

In this description of learning 'how to be dead,' Calvino conveys the power of each moment to transform the relation between the elements of one's past, its 'inner architecture.' Moses is, I suggest, telling the people that, unlike theirs, his life is a closed book, with no further movements into the unknown. But, at the same time, by narrating the story of his desire to 'cross over this Jordan river,' he is launching both himself and the people into a new narrative, a new history of desire. Even as he describes the impassable gap between his people's future and his own, he is attempting, by indirection, to bridge that gap.

'I am to die in this land; I shall not cross the Jordan. But you will cross and take possession of that good land.' (4:22) Ramban and Seforno read this: 'Since I will not be crossing over with you, I need to warn you all the more powerfully about the dangers of disobedience.' Moses' concern for his people is sharpened by his imminent death. His vision of their future without him is pessimistic, or perhaps realistic. ('For I know that after my death, you will corrupt yourselves ....' [31:29]) *Therefore,* he gathers them together and speaks to them of his frustrated desire to cross over. His effort now is to *get through* to them, to *come across* to them in language. For they now represent his unknown, unreachable desire.

He urges them: 'But take utmost care and watch yourselves scrupulously, so that you do not forget the things that your eyes have seen and so that they do not fade from your mind as long as you live.' (4:9) But he knows that the people he is so passionately addressing, appealing to them to remember their own deepest experience, are a new generation. Only those who had been less than twenty years old at Sinai had actually seen it with their own eyes. A missing generation, numberless corpses fallen into the sand, now create a gap between Moses and his people that no sermons can bridge. As he speaks to them they are already 'dys-temporaneous' with him, they live in a different time zone. How, then, does he hope to *come across* to them?

In the future, he instructs them, they will gather together every seven years and publicly read the Torah in God's presence, in Jerusalem —

in order that they may hear and learn to revere the Lord your God and to observe faithfully every word of this Torah. Their children, too, who have not had the experience (lit., do not know), shall hear and learn to revere the Lord your God as long as they live in the land that you are about to cross over the Jordan to possess.' (31:12-13)

Before he dies, Moses instructs those who have had the experience (who *know*, who *have seen*) to transmit their experience to their children, so that those who *do not know* may learn. This will not be a mechanical matter of providing information. For those who will be the teachers of the future are now, in Moses' presence, the already unknowing successors of a past

255

generation that did know. How can Moses transmit to them the essential knowledge that can then be transmitted, generation to generation, into the future?

A poetic pedagogy

Here is the problem of education, of the teaching project — Freud's 'impossible profession' — in fact, one of three such professions (the other two being healing and governing). In Freud's words, in these professions, 'one can be sure beforehand of achieving unsatisfying results.' (Freud, *Standard Edition, XXIII*, p.248)

Shoshana Felman (1982) provocatively reframes the issue. Freud, she claims, has instituted a 'revolutionary pedagogy…[I]t is precisely in giving us unprecedented insight into the impossibility of teaching, that psychoanalysis has opened up unprecedented teaching possibilities.' (Felman, p.401) From a psychoanalytic perspective, it is precisely one's resistance to learning that sets the stage for a profound process of coming to knowledge. Paradoxically, what is transacted between patient and analyst or between student and teacher, disrupts knowingness. Reaching out beyond an ignorance of which one begins to take the measure, the student or the patient is possessed by an unnamable desire. Without this ignorance, or repression, or forgetting, there can be no passage, no crossing over.

'Come, *let yourself be taught….!'* Freud adjures his readers, '…*learn first to know yourself!'* (*SE*, XXVII, pp.142-3) The patient needs to reach out beyond her conscious intelligence. This new kind of knowledge is, in a sense, 'unlearnable.' Through 'breakthroughs, leaps, discontinuities, regressions,' and deferred action, the patient renews her understanding of what 'not to know' may really mean. (Felman, p.405) The analyst is to 'learn the patient's own unconscious knowledge' and to return it, as a surprise, to the patient. (p.409) Two partially unconscious speeches constitute a dialogue, in which 'both say more than they know.' (p.410)

It is, particularly, in the transference that the reality of the unconscious is acted out. 'As soon as there is somewhere a subject presumed to know, there is transference,' writes Lacan. (1973, p.210)

But the position of the teacher is itself the position of *the one who learns,* of the one who *teaches* nothing other than *the way he learns.* The subject of teaching is interminably — a student; the subject of teaching interminably — a learning. This is the most radical, perhaps the most far-reaching insight psychoanalysis can give us into pedagogy. (Felman, p.413)

From this perspective, 'the clear-cut opposition between the analyst and the analysand, between the teacher and the student' is radically subverted: 'what counts, in both cases, is precisely the transition, the struggle-filled *passage* from one position to the other.' (Felman, 414)

In this passage, knowledge is, in some important sense, 'not in mastery of itself.' Felman credits Lacan with understanding the radical significance of Freud's use of *literary* knowledge. This involves reading Freud as a literary text — which means that the author cannot exhaust the meaning of his own text. The poetic function of language becomes central, giving birth to genuine discoveries.

Ultimately, then, the Freudian pedagogical imperative is 'to learn from and through the insight which does not know its own meaning, from and through the knowledge which is not entirely in mastery — in possession — of itself.' Felman calls this a *poetic pedagogy,* which teaches 'with and through the very blindness of its literary knowledge, of insights not entirely transparent to themselves.' (Felman, 418)

Shoshana Felman's profound and brilliant discussion may serve us in reflecting on Moses' project in his last addresses to his people. I suggest that his aim is to overcome their active dynamic of negation, the active refusal that they have so often demonstrated. 'The pathological factor is not his ignorance in itself, but the root of this ignorance in his *inner resistances,*' Freud says of the patient in analysis. (*SE,* XI, p.225) There is a desire to ignore, a 'passion for ignorance,' a refusal to 'acknowledge *one's own implication in the information.*' (Felman, 407) If Moses is to deal with ignorance of this kind, he must engage with it in such a way that the ignorance itself becomes instructive.

He does this by speaking to the people from the site of his own ignorance, from the very place of unconscious conflict. He tells the story of his own repudiation by God. Pleading for his desire and being denied his desire, he plays out his resistance, the sadness, envy, hostility of his relation to the people. At least in part, the conflicts he stages are unconscious, as he allows them to learn from the process of his own unmeant knowledge. He tells an intimate life-story, which is poetically framed for *this* audience, and for *this* moment.

Perhaps we can even say that, as a teacher, he is, in some sense, like the *patient* in the analytic relationship. (Barthes, 1978, 194-6) He talks to a silent audience, which becomes the student of the patient's unknown knowledge. He who had begun life resisting language becomes a man who allows meanings beyond his conscious mastery to be released into the space between his audience and himself.

So great is his desire to reach out, to *cross over* to his people's inner world, that Moses puts on display, essentially, himself. Speaking beyond his means, by the poetic force of his language, he conveys to them the depths of his desire, its sheer humanity.

Making history

Kafka (1965) writes of Moses:

He is on the track of Canaan all his life; it is incredible that he should see the land only when on the verge of death. The dying vision of it can only be intended to illustrate how incomplete a moment is human life, incomplete because a life like this could last forever and still be nothing but a moment. Moses fails to enter Canaan not because his life is too short but because it is a human life (Kafka, 195-6).

A personal pathos is sublimated into a resonant demand in Moses' last speeches. His human life, eternally incomplete, inspires his words with intimations of an immortal desire. He teaches nothing other than the way he learns.[21] In a flood of language ('You said, *I am not a man of words*, and now you speak so much!'), his text endlessly evocative, he conveys a *literary* knowledge, of which he himself is not entirely aware.

---

[21] This is perhaps the meaning of the term *talmid chacham*, which refers to the ideal scholar who eternally teaches his ways of being a student of the text.

He remembers the past, he exhorts for the future. The implications of his meaning resound through the generations and between them. By re-telling the past, he moves across to his listeners, as he plays out the possibility of having a *history*, rather than merely repeating themselves for ever.

He narrates in order to integrate and transcend the traumatic effect of the facts of the past. The past, says Christopher Bollas, restricts our imaginative freedom, so congested is it with 'dumb facts,' that arrest the play of our minds. There is something *unthinkable*, even traumatic, about such facts of life. They create a momentary blankness; moving beyond this blankness, we may elaborate and interpret the facts. In this way, we may liberate our own specific idiom, that can counteract the intrinsically traumatic effect of the passing of time.

In the work of the historian, too, the narratives of the past, its great events and figures, need, in a sense, to be forgotten; the historian becomes absorbed in the minutiae of the texts and allows the unconscious work of organization to transpire. In a similar way, the psychoanalyst learns from the details, even from the apparently trivial minutiae, of the patient's past. This work 'surreptitiously defeats trauma and revives the selves that had been consigned to oblivion.' (Bollas, 1996, p.140)) The most profound secrets of a self or of an age are revealed. Here are the 'intensities of a lifetime, and history is the recovery of such moments.'

In relating his past to his people, Moses, like the historian, or the analyst, immerses himself in his material. He does not use the authoritarian language of the original biblical account but, in a sense, he *makes history*, by allowing unconscious meanings to liberate him from the 'bleakness of ordinary trauma.' (Bollas, p.141) And like the good historian or analyst, he is 'prepared for [his] own *undoing* each time [he] returns to the material .... [he] takes pleasure in the deconstruction of subjectivity ....if [he] values the work of the unconscious, [he] will find pleasure in this dismantling of self.' (Bollas, 142)

This deconstruction is particularly significant when Moses tells his own personal story and, by allowing imagination to work upon it, opens it to continuous revision. In this way, he transforms it into a history. Unlike the past, says Bollas, which sits in the self as a kind of lead weight, the work of making history 'transforms the debris into meaningful presence.' (Bollas, p.144)

If Moses is *rebuking* the people when he re-tells the story of personal desire and rejection, he is, at heart, creating himself as a meaningful *presence* (*tochacha, nocheach*) for them. On one level, he may be reproaching them for not 'asking for mercy' on his behalf — for ignoring, or resisting the knowledge of his meaning. But, more profoundly, he is staging for them his own life of aspiration, situated between knowing and not knowing: '*Let me cross over, I pray ....*'

When God asks him to withdraw his personal plea, a new energy is released in him: 'And Moses *spoke to God ....*' As his personal needs are sublimated, a language of unconscious force is liberated. In his speeches to the people, too, a personal voice reaches out from the debris of his desire. Implicitly, he is making a demand on them: that they find in themselves their own living process of *havana*, of imaginative understanding. This process is perhaps always unfinished, since it deals with something *else*, something essentially alien. In the past, they could not understand his private meanings, even as he pleaded with them to implicate themselves in his desire. However, like the children who cannot imagine the future, or the meaning of losing the mother, the people will come to understand his meanings. Or, at least to understand enough to ask: 'What did he mean when he spoke so many words, mysteriously opaque even to himself, before he died?' For them, Moses *will have spoken*.

That is Moses' final desire, transmuted, imaginatively re-worked from its original, literal form. Now, Moses wishes to traverse the gap that, more than ever, separates him from the people. His plea, *E'ebra na*, is displaced onto an unconscious plea to them. In narrating their past failure in understanding, he appeals to them to bring a transformed sensibility to bear on his silent desire. How effective is he in these last speeches? Does he indeed affect them at the depth he hoped for?

A whisper of an answer can be heard in the critical words with which he summarizes their history: 'God has not given you a heart to know, or eyes to see, or ears to hear, *until this day* ....' (29:3) They have always been unaware, insentient; but does 'this day' imply a shift towards understanding?

In a striking passage, the Talmud unpacks the implications of Moses' words:

> Yet Moses indicated this [their ingratitude] to the Israelites only after forty years had passed, as it is said:: 'And I have led you forty years in the wilderness.... But God has not given you a heart to know....' Said Rava: From this one can learn that it may take forty years to know the mind of one's teacher.[22]

Even as he takes leave of them, Moses can do no more than hint at the narrative of their 'ingratitude.' With regard to their various sins and shortcomings, he is quite explicit. But by ingratitude, the Talmud refers to the insensitivity, the absence of intuition or imagination, that is sketched in the verse: the unknowing heart, the blind eyes, the deaf ears. Moses is hinting that they have been incapable of receiving his transmissions, of registering the undercurrents of his desire for them to pray for him. But — 'It takes forty years to comprehend one's teacher,' says Rava. This means that, as he speaks, Moses is recognizing that they are, indeed, beginning to transcend their obtuseness to what is implicit within his words. He has, perhaps, begun to 'reach them,' to 'come across' to them. This is the hopeful turn in Rava's reading: 'till this day' opens up a possibility for a newly loving attentiveness.

Rashi translates: '"This day you have become a people:" this day, I understand that you do passionately long for God.'[23] The transformed consciousness that he now sees in them is the fruit of forty years' work, but, more specifically, it is the fruit of the concentrated work of Moses' many speeches in Deuteronomy. Rashi's expression may also suggest that Moses, too, is now in a state of evolved consciousness: *'Now, I understand* that you really do long for God.' Moses' consciousness of his people has undergone change in the course of forty years. The teacher,

---

[22] B. Avoda Zara 5b

[23] Rashi to 29:3.

too, has gradually grown in his appreciation of the student's potential understanding. Before he dies, he brings a loving intuition to bear on the past that has given birth to this present. Through his many words, something has transpired between them.

These words model for them a process of coming to the knowledge that holds ignorance at its heart. This process represents the new form of his passion to *cross over*, to achieve *'l'amour de loin,'* the 'love from a distance,' of which the troubadours wrote. This reach of desire — transition, translation, transmission, transference — creates a world of poetic language, retrieved after long resistance: *E'ebra na* in a new voice.

Translating the world

Strangely, painfully, one last time, at the very moment of death, God reminds Moses of His decree. At the summit of the Mountain of Transitions (*Avarim*), Moses is shown the whole vista of the Holy Land:

> And God said to him: 'This is the land of which I swore to Abraham, Isaac, and Jacob, "I will give it to your offspring." I have let you see it with your eyes, but *you shall not cross over there.'* And Moses the servant of God died there .... (34:4)

Why does God revert in His last words to the painful core of Moses' life? There is no practical force to the repetition of the decree at this moment. He shows Moses the land, and then tells him that He has shown it to him: why does He reiterate to Moses what has just happened and already been narrated — only to add the final words: 'you shall not cross over there'?

Perhaps we can say that God is appointing Moses, at this last moment, as a messenger, a bearer of words beyond the edge. The last words Moses hears on earth are not about the past, but about history — a transmission, a translation, to be *carried across* the gap.[24] Perhaps, the emphasis is on the

---

[24] See B. Brachot 18b; and Rashi to 34:4.

last word — *shamah* — 'You shall not cross over *there:*' geographically, you will not cross over to the land of your desire; but you will leave behind you a pedagogical poetry of desire.

Centrally, between Moses and his people, something significant, both personal and impersonal, has transpired. Moses' *tochachot*, his 'rebukes,' will leave their residue, will bear across to the people the interminable mystery of his presence. In the end, his love will reach through and beyond his anger, his rebukes will become songs, blessings.[25] The desert will burst forth in streams, the lame leap like a deer, the tongue of the mute will sing aloud. And Moses, not a man of words, will have spoken these many words. A space will reach out and translate the world.

---

25 The last two Portions of Deuteronomy centre on the Song in *Ha'azinu* and the blessings of the tribes in V*e-zot Ha-bracha.*

REFERENCES

Barthes, R. (1978). Writers, Intellectuals, Teachers. In *Image/Music/Text*. New York: Hill and Wang.

Bollas, C. (1996). *Cracking Up*. New York: Hill and Wang.

Calvino, I. (1986). *Mr. Palomar*. London: Picador.

Carson, A. (1998). *Eros*. London: Dalkey Archive Press.

Felman, S. (1982). Psychoanalysis and Education: Teaching Terminable and Interminable. In *Yale French* Studies, 63. In *Yale French Studies*, 63: 400-420.

Freud, S. *Standard Edition*, XI.

-------. *Standard Edition*, XVII.

-------. *Standard Edition*, XXIII.

Kafka, F. (1965). *Diaries 1914-1923*, ed. Max Brod, trans. Martin Greenberg and Hannah Arendt. New York: Schocken.

Lacan, J. (1973). *Le Seminaire, livre* XI. Paris: Seuil.

Shelley, P. B. *Prometheus Unbound*, II, I, 6.

Wordsworth, W. (1956). Note to 'The Thorn, 1800'. In: *Poetry and Prose*, selected by W.M. Merchant. London: Rupert Hart-Davis.

Rebecca's Veil:
A Weave of Conflict and Agency

Libby Henik

> There are four ways to write a woman's life: the
> woman herself may tell it, in what she chooses
> to call an autobiography; she may tell it in what
> she chooses to call fiction; a biographer, woman
> or man, may write the woman's life in what is
> called a biography; or the woman may write her
> own life in advance of living it, unconsciously,
> and without recognizing or naming the process.
>
> *Carolyn G. Heilbrun.*
> *Writing A Woman's Life*

The Book of Genesis is replete with stories that highlight the drama of the human experience. However, many Biblical women do not immediately resemble our modern concepts of self and other. In fact, when reviewing Rabbinic, as well as contemporary and feminist discussions of Biblical women, we find a strong tendency to regard these figures as either marginalized and written out of history by a patriarchal system, or as manipulative and deceitful personalities who, when needed to advance God's plan become powerful male constructs wresting authority from their male counterparts. When endowed with clarity and discernment they function simply as catalysts, who, by any means necessary, thwart the inaction of men who have failed to understand God's design.

This dichotomization robs Biblical women of complexity, subjectivity and agency and, therefore, does not adequately explain their behavior. Because they are portrayed either as victims or deceitful manipulators, we

265

do not know how to engage with them as subjects. Biblical women, to borrow from Virginia Woolf, need 'a reading of one's own,' which this paper intends to give the matriarch Rebecca by focusing on her story in Genesis 24-27. I introduce a different reading and understanding of Rebecca, wherein she emerges as a more variegated personality. Acting neither solely as an instrument of God nor as a victim or a victimizer, she is a woman self-authorized through conflict and choice and thus a full agent of her experience. I bring together the psychoanalytic thinking of Schafer, Greenberg and Hoffman, as well as Biblical hermeneutics founded on the tradition of Hidush, to understand Rebecca's life and our own.

Conflict, like love-hate (Schafer, 1993) and meaning-mortality (Hoffman, 1998), is ubiquitous to the human condition and inherent in all important activities and relationships. Born of tensions, ambivalences and alternatives, conflict demands a choice, and, as Greenberg (1991) points out, choice implies agency, i.e., self-authorization. However, in trying to comprehend, justify and/or rationalize Rebecca's deceit and betrayal in securing the birthright blessing for Jacob, Rabbinic interpretation avoids or mutes these inevitable conflicted experiences of being. Consequently, Rebecca remains an enigma, an instrument, rather than an individual who is conflicted, i.e., someone more recognizable to us as ourselves.

My approach to the Rebecca narrative follows the tradition of Hidush in Biblical interpretation which bears a remarkable similarity with the psychoanalytic method. Hidush (i.e. innovation, multiple meanings) is an interpretive act of the creation of meaning. Intersubjective, relational and non-linear, Hidush seeks neither factual truth nor a better understanding, but rather, understanding differently. In questioning Biblical text regarding not only the choice of words, but also their repetition, as well as gaps, silences and spaces between words, reader and text co-create different meanings in the same way that analyst and patient move out of fixed, 'either/or' polarity into a newly co-created understanding. In examining Biblical text from these perspectives, we find that preserved in the narrative are other narratives, a subtext of other meanings and stories. In Biblical exegesis these subtexts of other meanings and stories are called Midrash; in psychoanalysis, they are called the unconscious.

This paper proposes that Rebecca's conflict, and thus agency, are embedded in the Biblical text, and not unlike the unconscious, are awaiting an 'other,' a reader/analyst with whom to make new meanings. I must confess that it is daunting to approach a Biblical text whose narrative is so ancient, so well known, so examined. And yet, in being an often-told story, it is strikingly similar to the life stories that patients bring into therapy, which they have told themselves consciously or unconsciously thousands of times, where the players and dynamics are fixed and well known. By listening to the Rebecca narrative as we would listen to a patient, exploring words, silences, repetitions and inconsistencies, allowing past and present to illuminate and use each other, we view Rebecca, as we might a patient, in a different light. She is no longer the typical Biblical woman cast as either an instrument, a victim or a manipulator. She is, instead, an individual who, in the face of ambivalence, existential trauma and disappointment, chooses and is thus self-authorized, with all of the inherent power, guilt and anxiety. As Avivah Zornberg states: "[In detecting] the intimations of disorder within order...we are assured to find ourselves, with our most radical dilemmas, reflected in these ancient texts" (Zornberg, 1996, p. xv).

As previously noted, Biblical hermeneutics, interpretation of inconsistencies, choice of words, repetitions and puzzling narrative constructions allow multiple levels of meaning to emerge. Time is fluid, with past and present informing and illuminating each other. "Thus, even in traditional Rabbinic discourse, authorial voice and intent become muted and irrelevant before the sovereignty of the text and the dynamics of its dialogue with the readers of subsequent generations" (Klitsner, 2006, p. 23). Meaning is co-created by 'a meeting of the minds' (Aron, 1996) between reader and text just as with analyst and patient. However, unlike the narrative of patients or narratives in literature, in Biblical narrative "there are virtually no 'free motifs'...Whatever is reported...can be assumed to be essential to the story" (Alter, 1981, pp. 79-80). Therefore, those words or phrases that do appear take on a special significance, particularly when they are repeated. Alter (1981) raises an interesting question: How is it that from the compressed narrative style of Biblical text, where few indicators of individuality (in the way of motive, feelings,

267

attitudes and intention) are offered, have such "indelibly vivid individuals [become etched] in the imagination of a hundred generations" (p. 114)? For Alter, the resolution of this paradox lies in the dominant role of the verb in Biblical text: "Verbs tend to dominate this biblical narration of the essential, and…sudden dense concentrations or unbroken chains of verbs, usually attached to a single subject…indicate some particular intensity, rapidity, or single-minded purposefulness of activity" (Alter, 1981, p. 80).

According to the principles of Biblical hermeneutics, the complexity of the individual is to be gleaned from the verb. Intentions, conflict, wishes, motives and feelings are revealed in the nature of the action as expressed (e.g., in its absence or presence) or by the quality of the action (e.g., active or passive, hurried or measured). Repetition of verbs and phrases, whether appearing in one story or in different stories, is intended to create connection and association of motivation. Textual anomaly is indicative of subtext, and subtext is indicative of internal struggle and psychological complexity. As Klitsner notes, "We suggest that the relationship between text and subtext often mirrors the interplay of the conscious and the subconscious of biblical characters" (Klitsner, 2006, p. 40).

Roy Schafer's (1993) new language of action, with its emphasis on verbs, is particularly suited to a psychoanalytic understanding of Biblical narrative that almost exclusively uses action and sparse dialogue to suggest the internal struggles and psychological complexities of its main characters. Schafer himself considered his re-conceptualization of psychoanalytic theory "a hermeneutic version of psychoanalysis" (Schafer, 1993, p. 255) in that narrative is a construction and all understanding is a "radically new" (Schafer, 1993, p.219) co-created, jointly authored product of narrator and hearer/reader. The fact that

> no history [narrative] is the single and final one does not mean that each history is a mythic creation…[Multiple] life histories are versions of the truth…They are new, never before possible versions of the truth and therefore new truths; on this account, they may be said to enhance the life that is being examined (Schafer, 1993, p. 206).

Schafer rejected Freud's deterministic model of a mind controlled by opposing forces and impulses leaving no room for freedom and responsibility. In his reformulation of conflict within a new language of action, Schafer (1976, 1993) argued for a psychoanalytic model that reclaimed the individual as a unitary agent of his experience, responsible for choices and actions which are inherently conflicted, contradictory and at times destructive. In action language, unconscious conflict is re-conceptualized as paradoxical actions. Schafer (1993) cast a wide net in defining action as "human activity of every sort," (p. 83), including "every kind of emotional activity" (p. 83).

Schafer insisted that verbs were the descriptors of conscious and unconscious human activity. Active verbs within narratives signify agency through the embrace of conflict's disclaimed actions and intent. His insistence on the action language of verbs returned subjectivity, the "I," to the individual and established the person as agent of one's experience. Schafer argued that "the chief business of clinical interpretation...is to define how and why each person...makes the life that he or she does" (1993, p.142).

With Schafer's questions of how and why in mind, I turn to Rebecca. Can we think of Rebecca as a case study? She is not my patient, sitting in my office, or lying on my couch. However, from the point of view of Biblical hermeneutics, there is no time linearity in the Torah, nor is there temporal distance separating the interpreter from the text (Ouaknin & Brown, 1998). Likewise, in Schafer's hermeneutic approach to interpretation, "the past is used to make the present more intelligible and the present is used to make the past more intelligible, which is to say more coherent, continuous and convincing...until past and present seem as one or timeless" (1993, p. 188). Interestingly, Schafer (1993) considered psychoanalysts to be "re-tellers" (p. 241) or re-contextualizers of narration.

Rebecca and I, like patient and analyst in psychoanalysis, engage in an "ongoing dialogue" (Schafer, 1993, p. 239) of discovery, transformation, and creation of meaning (Schafer, 1993) of narratives. Similarly, Biblical interpretation is not about uncovering meaning, but rather, invites interpreters and text to

"meet and shed light on each other so that the interpreter, in order to reveal the text in its entirety, must grasp it in one of its particular aspects, and

269

conversely, a particular aspect of the text must await the interpreter capable of perceiving it....[I]nterpretation is not just perception; it is the creation of meaning." (Ouaknin and Brown,1998, p. 173-174).

Rebecca's story is related in Gen. 24-27. Her story is unique amongst the matriarchal stories in its length and detail. Eliezer, Abraham's trusted servant, is sent by Abraham to find a wife for Isaac. Isaac, the son of Abraham and Sarah, whom Abraham bound on the altar as a sacrifice to God, was saved from death at the last minute by an angel of God. Eliezer is sent to Abraham's birthplace to find a fitting wife for Isaac. Upon reaching his destination, Eliezer asks God for a sign as to which woman would be worthy as Isaac's wife. The sign will be that the "maiden to whom I shall say, 'Let down thy pitcher, I pray thee, that I may drink'…shall say, 'Drink, and I will give thy camels drink also'" (24:12-14). It is at this point that Rebecca enters the story. In four short verses (Gen. 24:16,18-20) she is the subject of 11 action verbs (Alter, 1981): going down to the well, drawing water from the well, giving water to the servant, on her own initiative offering to draw water for Eliezer's ten camels, refilling her pitcher, pouring, giving drink. Again on her own initiative, she invites Eliezer to her brother's house, she runs to her mother's house to tell of the visitor and his gifts (Gen. 24:15-28). Her rapid, bustling activity is reinforced by the repetition of two verbs: 'rutz' (run) and 'maher' (hurry).

Rebecca is also portrayed as a self-confident and decisive young woman. When asked by her mother and her brother, Laban, if she wishes leave home with "this man (Eliezer)", her response, "I will go" (Gen. 24:58), is concise and unequivocal.

The Bible tells us that Isaac was 40 when he married Rebecca (25:20) and that he was 60 when the twins, Jacob and Esau were born (25:26). During this period of time, we hear nothing from Rebecca or of any conversation between husband and wife. The woman who was a whirlwind of activity, who negotiated her own marriage arrangements, who set her own course, is silent for 20 years. Most striking is that Rebecca, unlike other childless women of the Bible, does not actively seek to become pregnant, nor does she seem anguished by her infertility or worry that her position is threatened by it. Unlike Sarah, she does not resort to giving her servant as a concubine to her husband (16:2), nor does she admonish her husband for failing to give her sons, as Rachel did (30:1). She does not persistently plead and negotiate with God, as Hannah did (Samuel 1:11), nor does she seek out love potions, as Leah did (30:14). What we know from the text regarding the relationship between Rebecca and Isaac is that it was monogamous, sexually intimate (26:8) and silent.

What can we understand about Rebecca from her silence of 20 years? Is there a narrative in the silence? Reik (1948) talks about the power of words and the power of silence. "The patient himself comes into the psychoanalytic situation...out of silence. He has been silent about certain experiences, emotions, and thoughts" (p. 123). In psychoanalysis, Reik (1945) states, "what is spoken is not the most important thing. It appears to us more important to recognize what speech conceals and what silence reveals" (p.126).

The Rabbis, too, were aware of this enormous gap in the narrative and sought meaning in it. The last words spoken by Rebecca prior to her 20 years of silence are in the form of a question to the servant Eliezer upon her first sighting of Isaac: "Who is that man walking in the field toward us?" (24:65). The question follows a most puzzling piece of narrative. The Bible tells us that Isaac went out walking in the field toward evening (24:63). However, the word used in the narrative for walking is not from the conventional verb root l'ch't but 'su'ach,' meaning to meditate, a meditation that our Rabbis understood to be the evening prayer. When, from a distance, Rebecca sees Isaac wrapped in meditation, the Torah relates "and she fell from her camel" (24:64). The text, so dramatic and cryptic, invites interpretations. A traumatic reaction troubled the Rabbis and some attempted to disclaim it. Many sought to interpret the Hebrew va'ti'pol (from the verb root n'f'l — clearly meaning to fall) as "alighted" or "slipped down" so as to minimize the impact of her shock implicit in the text. The Ibn Ezra does not negate that she fell off her camel, but states that she did so out of her own volition, and interprets the use of the verb va'ti'pol as in the Hebrew expression for prostration ("va'tipol al panav"), indicating an act of respect. Avivah Zornberg (1996), however, retains the

271

full impact of the scene: "Rebecca…meets Isaac in the field and her whole body falls" (pp. 158-159).

What did Rebecca see that would cause such a collapse, such a striking loss of presence? Rashi (26:64) explains Rebecca: "She saw him majestic and she was dumbfounded in his presence," thereby saying that she was awe-struck by Isaac's majestic bearing. Avivah Zornberg (1996) focuses instead on Isaac's psychic reality, the imprinting of "the deep death-knowledge of his Binding…darkly narrating his story to God" (p. 163).

> What Rebecca sees in Isaac is the vital anguish at the heart of his prayers... Too abruptly perhaps, she receives the shock of his world. Nothing mediates, nothing explains him to her. 'Who is that man?' (24:65), she asks, fascinated, alienated. What dialogue is possible between two who have met in such a way?" (Zornberg, 142-143).

When the servant responds to Rebecca's question, "That is my master" (24:65), Rebecca is emptied of words. Her response, no longer finding shape in words, is expressed in her action: "And she took her veil and covered herself" (24:65).

Many Rabbinic commentators have questioned this action. Why did the Torah relate this seemingly minute gesture at such a momentous meeting? Typical of Torah narrative, Rebecca's emotions and thoughts are not revealed and must be understood from the action itself. Many Rabbinic commentators have stated that it comes to teach us of Rebecca's trait of modesty. However, the Netziv (1817-1893), in his commentary on the Torah known as *Ha'amek Davar*, understands the veiling as an action full of intra-psychic and relational meaning, a non-verbal expression of her diminishment and of her future relationship with Isaac:

> Rebecca looked up and saw Isaac while he was in prayer. He looked like an angel of God; fearful in appearance. And she fell off the camel: from fright! She did not know who he was…When she heard he was her husband, she covered her face with a veil: From fear and embarrassment, as if with a realization that she was not worthy to be his wife. From that moment on, there was always a sense of trepidation in her heart (24:64-65).

The Midreshet HaRova commentary recognizes in the Netziv's interpretation two important aspects of the encounter: "The first is Isaac's spiritual intensity. Isaac in prayer is a fearful sight...He always had some of that fire of [the Binding] with him throughout his life" (Midreshet haRova, 5760). The second aspect is the impact of this state of being on Rebecca: "The self-assured Rebecca loses confidence in the face of this spiritual whirlwind. In the Netziv's reading here, Rebecca cannot communicate with Isaac. She is in awe of him" (Midreshet haRova, 5760).

I am proposing that the veiling is an action revealing and expressing conflict, a conflict so unmentionable as to be rendered unconscious. This unconscious conflict, according to my hypothesis, is internalized and expressed in 20 years of silence and barrenness. In Schafer's action language, Rebecca's narrative would be retold in the following manner: *Rebecca became frightened when faced with Isaac's spiritual appearance and intensity. She began to doubt the sureness of her decision. Fearful of openly revealing her conflict and disappointment, she took her veil and covered/masked herself.* In this imagined retelling between analyst and patient, reader and text, a new and more complex account emerges. In the retelling, "certain features are related to others in new ways or for the first time" (Schafer, 1993, p. 219). In this co-authored narrative of personal agency and self-reflection, Rebecca's 'veiling' is newly understood as a symptom of conflict.

The introduction of conflict into the story opens new possibilities of understanding of future choices, actions and relationships. Rebecca is now the agent of her 20-year silence and of the sequestering of her vitality and subjectivity. "A fatal seepage of doubt and dread affects her, so that she can no longer meet [Isaac] in the full energy of her difference" (Zornberg, 1996, p. 143). The veiling is now understood as a sequestering of subjectivity, a receding of self to the inner recesses of one's being.

What follows in the unfolding of the story of Isaac and Rebecca and their twin sons, Esau and Jacob, is a family drama of existential anguish, deceit and betrayal. The bewilderment of such an unraveling of family relations is expressed poignantly by Shmuel Klitsner in *Wrestling Jacob* (2006) when he asked the question: "How does a family reach the depths of dysfunction in which a wife enlists her son's compliance in deceiving her blind husband (his father) in order to rob her own son (his brother) of his blessing?" (p. 51). Schafer (1993) would ask the question as follows:

"What is this person doing? And why is...she doing it and doing it just this way?" (p. 101).

We may begin looking for an answer by referring back to the Biblical commentaries of the Netziv and Avivah Zornberg, who located conflict in the quality of relatedness between Rebecca and Isaac. In this, Biblical commentary finds common ground with Greenberg's position that it is one's conflicts that shape how one experiences their world and their relations (1991). This repositioning of the origin of conflict places the individual at the center, and thus as agent, in the act of organizing their experience and actions, and, invests them with personal choice.

Greenberg (1991) understands conflict as embedded in personal striving. It is the inherent tension resulting from two innate motives or desired states of being: safety and effectance. Safety refers to our need for human relatedness within a secure environment. The desire for feelings of safety can lead to " a surrender of our vitality...We are constantly moved to renounce not only competence, but autonomy itself" (pp. 137-138). In contrast, effectance is characterized by a sense of self-sufficiency and agency, and "the experience of being alive and active" (p. 130). As such, it can account for the difficulties in relatedness. Greenberg (2005) conceptualizes the tension between safety and effectance as the struggle between restraint (i.e., being the object of the intentions and reactions of others) on the one hand, and desire/strivings (i.e., being the subject of one's conflicted intentions) on the other. Because of the difficulty in holding the tension of being both subject and object, Greenberg posits, we rid ourselves of the awareness of one or the other aspect of our experience by experiencing ourselves only as either subject or object, victimizer or victim, doer or done-to, "thus limiting what we are able to know" (2005, p. 112).

Greenberg's understanding of the nature of conflict opens up a new way to understand why a patient, or Rebecca, experiences and reacts to events in a particular way. Similarly, Schafer states, "By introducing the new, one may throw much previous knowledge and understanding into a new light...The life history keeps being rewritten" (1993, p. 87). Rebecca's story becomes more complex and subjective. Alongside the story of a woman chosen to be an instrument of God's plan is another story, the personal story of a woman who, full of the exuberance and vitality of life chose to leave home, who desired a "life of consequence" (Rotenberg, 2002, p. 58) and who, upon being confronted with the reality of her husband's withdrawal from life, gave expression to her conflict between safety and effectance, restraint and striving, by concealing her subjectivity with her veil. She understood immediately that this cannot be a relationship between two subjects (Benjamin, 1990). Conflicted by her own strivings, she empties herself of desire, even for children, and is silent for 20 years, becoming the object of her husband's needs for comfort and mothering/ soothing (24:67). In Schafer's action language, one cannot empty one's "self," as there is no such spatial space. For Schafer, this expression needs to be re-conceptualized for the patient/Rebecca as reflecting unconscious feelings of profound helplessness and hopelessness and fears of being robbed of one's contents.

For Greenberg and Schafer, as well as the Netziv and Zornberg, the "timelessness of the unconscious" (Schafer, 1993, p. 196) of the narrative is actualized in the analysis/reading. Rebecca's veiling herself is re-contextualized and interpreted as an action expressing the collapse of her subjectivity, content and strivings. Consciously or unconsciously, by her action, she chooses to disclaim her effectance and autonomy in order "to carry out renunciations or develop compromises" (Schafer, 1993, p. 142) to the dilemma facing her. She is no longer the woman we met in Gen. 24. Her disappearance from the narrative is inconsistent with her original assertiveness, sense of self-possession and intention.

Rebecca's 20-year silence is broken with a cry of existential anguish during her pregnancy: "If so, why then I?" *(translation: Zornberg, 2007)*. Since these are the first words we hear from her following an extended period of silence, they require special attention.

Pregnancies in the Bible are usually briefly noted ("and she conceived and she gave birth"). However, the account of Rebecca's painful pregnancy is singular in its length and detail. This change in narrative format called for Rabbinic interpretation. We learn (25:22) that Rebecca's twins "struggled within her" ("va'yit'ro'tzezu ha'banim b'kirbah"), but the nature of the struggle is left undefined. In this 'space,' Rabbinic commentary sought meaning. The verb "va'yit'ro'tzezu" is often translated as 'they struggled.' The word originates from the root r't'z which means 'run,' and most Rabbinic commentary interprets the struggle as reflecting the opposing characters of the two yet-unborn sons. Zornberg (2007), however, turns the focus to Rebecca and her subjective experience of the pregnancy. "Va'yit'ro'tzezu" can also be understood to come from the root r'tza'tz, which denotes the act of crushing. The statement about the pregnancy now has other meanings. In this retelling, "Va'yit'ro'tzezu" becomes about Rebecca. Her inner world is in turmoil. In this new narration, Rebecca is "the first portrait of a [Biblical] woman who becomes aware of the difficulty in knowing what one wants" (Zornberg, 2007).

Rebecca's response to her anguish ("If so, why then I?") breaks her silence of 20 years and takes the form of an existential 'why' question (25:22). Subjective experience, according to Schafer and Greenberg, is always influenced by personal interpretation. For Schafer, all experience is a constructed experience. 'Why' questions uncover the reasons for actions, and "reasons are the way of stating actions in terms of their meaning or directedness" (Schafer, 1993, p.90). In analytic interpretation, patient and analyst recover the reasons for "construing certain events in a certain way, for responding to them in certain emotional modes" (Schafer, 1993, pp. 89-90).

How can we understand Rebecca's anguished questioning of life, so striking a reversal from the self-confident and determined woman who engaged both Eliezer and her family? The Maharal (1525-1609) took the interpretive position that the word "Anochi" ("I") in Rebecca's 'why' question (25:22) refers to an individual in solitary conversation with herself, taking responsibility for her own actions (Gen. 25: p.9, comment 84). Similar to the action language later proposed by Schafer, the Maharal describes Rebecca as wondering why she has chosen to remain idle in making meaning of her situation. Zornberg (1996) elaborates on the interpretation of the Maharal: Rebecca's years of silent, empty, passive existence have shattered her sense of "I," of will. She is despairing of a life of "otherness" when confronted by Isaac's impenetrable, mysterious psychic world. In Greenberg's perspective, Rebecca's wish for harmony conflicts with her desire for consequence. The Maharal understands the 'why' question of life as a decisive moment for Rebecca, one in which she decides to act. Her loss of "otherness" is "counteracted by an energy generated by absence and longing" (Zornberg, 1996, p. 160).

Once more daring and independent, Rebecca decides to seek (or, alternatively, demand) answers directly from God (25:22), and then shapes the ambiguous oracular response to her own decision of how she will live her "otherness."

Can we interpret, then, that Rebecca's 'why life' question is the cry of anguish at having to choose and, in so doing, lift the veil from disavowed strivings for substance and consequence as well as disclaimed ambition and aggression? What is suggested here is that a narrative of a woman's subjectivity has been sanitized and idealized by repressing her aggression. Aggression in women either is split off to another (in this case, Esau) or devolves her into a male construct, a patriarch (Rotenberg, 2002), thereby robbing her of an essential aspect of agency.

This erasure of aggression is preserved in the perplexing structural imbalance in the following passage: "Isaac loved Esau because of the game he fed him, and Rebecca loved Jacob" (Gen. 25:28). Isaac's reason for preferring Esau is given a causal explanation, while the passage is silent as to Rebecca's reason for loving Jacob. The glaring absence of cause and textual symmetry required Rabbinic commentary. Following their idealization of Rebecca, the Rabbis explained her partiality to Jacob as reflecting her capacity to recognize his righteousness (Rashbam) or her recognition of Esau's wickedness (S'forno). However, Alter (1981), by staying closer to the text in seeking meaning in this gap in the narrative, reveals a darker, aggressive side: "Rebecca's maternal solicitude, however, is not without its troubling side, for we shall soon see a passive and rather timid Jacob…maneuvered about by his mother" (p. 44).

In accepting the many-sidedness of oneself, the patient/Rebecca "becomes readier to experience and contain the tension of opposites within a unified self-presentation" (Schafer, 1996, p. 60). One does not feel the need to resort to veiling, but instead can begin to feel safe "to become a whole person engaged with whole others" (ibid.).

277

Rebecca's existential quandry is multi-determined and permeates the entire narrative, overtly and covertly, from the first moment we engage with her until the last. The 'why' question of life appears again at the end of her story: "What good will my life be to me?" (26:47). As noted above, repetition in Biblical narrative requires examination and association. And so, there is still another storyline, another history. "One action may be analyzed into several or even many as we return to it again and again in many different contexts" (Schafer, p. 86). Similarly, Biblical interpretive study requires of the reader to take the text and "turn it over again and again." (Pirkei Avot, 5:24)

Hoffman (1999) places existential tension at the center of the human experience. "The dialectic of our sense of being and our sense of our mortality is superordinate to all others because it is the paradoxical foundation for our sense of meaning" (p. 19). This perspective adds another dimension, or storyline, to Rebecca's conflict. Constructing meaning in the face of mortality, and, a sense of being in the anticipation of non-being, demands choice. According to Rotenberg (2002), Rebecca "conceived of a life lived on a heroic scale and…she conceived of it even before she met the servant. For while it was his wish that she water his camels, the offer was born of her desire (p.5 8)." From Hoffman's (1999) perspective, Rebecca's existential cry: "If so, why then I?" places her in the crosshairs of our universal striving for significance and meaning, and thus, agency, and our knowledge that we stand "in the teeth of the constant threat of nonbeing and meaningless" (p. 16).

Our first and last encounters with Rebecca are with a woman in constant motion. In the opening scene at the well, the Rabbis laud her prodigious activity, comparing her actions to the chesed (kindness) of the patriarch Abraham. However, there is also a disturbing affect to the rapidity, even frenzy, embedded in the compiling of one verb after the other. Is Rebecca's behavior an act of kindness or a manic defense to be interpreted, according to Schafer (1993), as a constructive experience designed "to reduce the possibility of responding depressively to a situation that otherwise would be viewed as ruined and barren" (p. 90)? Again, if we listen to the Biblical narrative, as we would to a patient, do we find traces of this existential ennui in our first meeting/session with Rebecca?

The absence of attachment to her immediate family is implicit in the text by what is said and what is missing. Again, repetition appears in separate occasions (24:15,24,47) where Rebecca presents herself and is presented as the granddaughter of Milkah, never mentioning her mother. The text continues to suggest distance by relating that Rebecca runs "to her mother's house" (24:28), but not to her mother, to tell the news of the visitor. Through repetition and specificity of detail, the narrative conveys distance between mother and daughter.

Many have commented on Rebecca's response to her mother and brother Laban's asking if she will leave with "this man" (Gen. 24:58). Even in the English translation, her response is a quick, terse and decisive "I will go" (Gen. 24:58), but in Hebrew this essence of her answer is even more striking because it is expressed in one word "Ay'lech." The scene is very brief and the dialogue minimal.

Because Laban and her mother do not tell Rebecca of "this man's" request to take her away immediately, a detailed inquiry might wonder how she knew what had been discussed? Was she listening at the doorway to overhear the conversation in the same way that she eavesdropped on the conversation between Isaac and Esau (Gen. 27:5)? Do we already have a glimpse at Rebecca's ambition to shape life and determine her own destiny? Was she already packed and ready to go? Was she ready to take matters into her own hands now, as she does later on? Is her hasty leave-taking motivated by her wish to be the wife of a righteous man, as the Rabbis understood, or is she acting conflictedly towards a mother and devious brother from whom she feels alienated and towards whom she harbors grandiose and aggressive feelings? After all, "some degree of love-hate ambivalence characterizes every important activity and relationship" (Schafer, 1993, p. 8).

Like Reik (1945), I wonder, is "this my own unconscious mind acting as an instrument of perception?"(p. 133). Reik continues, "The analyst can achieve some psychological insight into a patient even before the beginning of treatment if he will only trust his impressions as soon as he becomes aware of them" (p. 151). Whereas the Rabbis have praised Rebecca for her "chesed" (kindness) towards the servant Eliezer, I note that this kindness and sensitivity never surface to any of her family members, her beloved Jacob included. Rashi may have also sensed this undercurrent of aggression in the narrative when in his commentary to "I will go," he adds: "On my own, by myself, even if you object."

In approaching Biblical textual ambiguities, repetitions and lacunae as "subtle and purposeful indicators of meaning" (Klitsner, 2006, p.17), and patient narratives as changing and more insightful constructions of subjective experiences of conflict, analyst and patient retell and reshape the story so that the end result is "an interweaving of texts" and a "jointly authored work" (Schafer, 1993, p.219). Multiple storylines "unveil" Rebecca's subjectivity as a conflicted construction of the complexity of love, desire, aggression, strivings and existential dread.

Having established Rebecca's conflicts, can we now establish her as the full agent of her life? Having engaged in contradictory actions, does she recognize and claim them as such? Does she nevertheless choose, and thus take responsibility for life as her own construction, along with the pain, regret, guilt and fear that she creates in her life and others'? Can we find this in the narrative? "When a tradition is rejected by [the Biblical] writers, it still has a life. It finds its way of reappearing in Rabbinic literature" (Zakovitch, 2007).

Rebecca wants to understand the meaning of her difficult pregnancy. She turns to God, directly, and receives an ambiguous response: "Two nations are in thy womb, and two peoples shall be separated from thy bowels. And the one people shall be stronger than the other people, and the elder shall serve the younger" (25:23).

Due to the syntax of the Hebrew language, the oracle is open to personal interpretation.[1] It is never revealed to Rebecca how she is to

---

[1]   The Radak (13th century, Provence) states: "although the Torah states that 'the great [the elder] the small [younger[shall serve' (ve-rav ya'avod tza'ir), it does not make use of the particle 'ET' that is used to mark the direct object. Thus, the matter is left doubtful as to who will serve whom. Will the great serve the small or will the small serve the great?" In other words, had the original text stated:

understand God's explanation, nor is she instructed by God or told that it is her responsibility to actualize God's plan or by what means. To understand Rebecca's acts of betrayal and deception as a means of being God's instrument is to rob her of all agency. Claiming to receive legitimacy directly from God negates the very idea of personal agency by ascribing authority not to oneself, but to God (Hollywood, 2004). In Schafer's (1993) action language, the performer of the action, the action itself and the external forces do not split to create a relational polarity of victim/victimizer, doer/done-to. One is self-authorized by assuming responsibility for previously conscious, unconscious or preconscious disclaimed intentions/actions, all the while recognizing that agency does not imply the absence of conflicted or contradictory actions (p. 142).

> "If a similarity between the psychoanalytic enterprise and the biblical narratives emerges from the texts themselves, it would seem to be found in the biblical hero's struggle to achieve identity and autonomy. This seems to occur, much as in the therapeutic model, by courageously confronting our own masquerades and evasions" (Klitsner, 2006, p. 38).

The ambiguity of the oracle reawakens in Rebecca her desire for a "sovereign self" (Klitsner, 2006, p. 53), even in her relationship with God. It is Rebecca who interprets the oracle and who chooses which son to elevate (see Radak, note 1, above), and it is she who chooses the action to be taken when her ambition appears threatened.

Placing Rebecca, and not God, as agent of the narrative, her contradictory, destructive course of action allows her to "retell' the story of the deceit and betrayal in terms of her disavowed desire and conflict. What emerges is a more complex account of at times, parallel storylines, and at times, conflicted storylines, "in which the analysand [Rebecca] is portrayed as more or less unconsciously taking several roles at once — hero, victim" (Schafer, 1993, p. 229), passive, active.

Rebecca's action can now be clarified in terms of a reaction to an unconscious danger situation in which she will not be able to shape life. The

---

've-rav ya'avod ET tza'ir" the identity of the subject and object would have been obvious. In the absence of 'ET' one may just as easily render "the great shall be served by the small. Hebrew syntax leaves subject and object unclear.

deception itself can be understood as to its origins (perhaps a regression, in the face of danger, to the culture of deceit of her brother Laban) and its multiple meanings of love, ambition and acuity. Rebecca is no longer merely a vehicle, but rather the center of motive and its concomitant paradoxical or contradictory actions.

Does Rebecca ever claim the human experience of conflicted subjectivity in her passion to "create destiny out of fate" (Klitsner, 2006, p. 37), or does she remain an epic heroine of idealized proportions? Is it true, as Esther Fuchs (1999) claims, that Biblical female characters are essentially functional, lacking depth and complexity and "move in a single direction... no conflict, pain or regret" (p. 83)?

As in psychoanalytic narrative, Biblical narrative is the conveyer of agency in language. As pointed out earlier, because of its economy of language, repetitions and word choices are considered covert indicators of subtext, motivation and meaning. Therefore, it did not go unnoticed by Biblical commentators that, following the pregnancy narrative and the act of betrayal, there appears the seemingly superfluous statement that Rebecca is the "mother of Jacob and Esau" (28:5). In addition, the Rabbis paid close attention to Rebecca's choice of words in explaining the necessity for sending Jacob away: "Why should I be bereaved of you both in one day?" (27:45).[2]

Nehama Leibowitz (1976) explains that the intent is to show Rebecca's attachment to and concern for both her sons. Sending Jacob away is not only for his protection, but also is motivated by her concern to protect Esau from his murderous intentions in the heat of the moment. Rebecca gives voice to her own despair that the possible consequence of her actions may be to suffer the same fate as Eve (Gen. 4) and be "bereaved of both [sons] in one day" (27:45) because both the victim and the perpetrator will be lost

---

[2] That Rebecca is referring to being bereaved of both sons on one day, rather than, as some have posited, to losing her husband and Jacob in one day, is based on the interpretation of the word 'eshakel' which in Hebrew refers solely to bereavement that results from the death of children, not spouses. Unfortunately, the expression in Israel of 'Ima shakulah' (a mother whose child has died') is too well-known.

to her: Whichever son is the victim will die, and the perpetrator will have to be shut out of her mind forever.[3]

We have here a picture of a woman, a mother, determined in her choice to have history be of her own making. The narrative is now one of an agent, claiming responsibility for her decisions, contradictory and perplexing though they may be, and taking responsibility for their consequences. Instead of the woman described above by Esther Fuchs, we find a woman conflicted and in pain.

A relationship between Rebecca and Esau, erased in the manifest text, is preserved in a seemingly minute piece of narrative. We are told that Esau's garments, used to masquerade Jacob, were in Rebecca's house. Rotenberg (2002) points out that Esau was already a married man with two wives. What were his garments doing in Rebecca's house? "Whatever we might speculate, it should not escape our attention that Rebecca and Esau had some kind of relationship...This detail and the fact...that she does not wish to be 'bereaved of both her sons in one day' (27:45) indicates that she is not without feelings for Esau" (Rotenberg, 2002, p. 56). Although he is not her preferred son, Esau is not a spiritual stranger to Rebecca. His response to Jacob when asked to sell his birthright, "I am going to die, of what use is my birthright to me?" (25:32) echoes Rebecca's questions as to the value of life during her difficult pregnancy and at the end of the narrative, when she learns that Esau intends to kill Jacob.

Esau and Rebecca are both filled with "the immenence of death" (Zornberg, 1996, p.160) and share the questioning of life. They speak the same language and share the same angst. "Psychologically, Esau has inherited...his mother's pregnancy-related gloom" (Chessler, 1999). Thus, Rebecca's "ruthlessness is not born of thoughtlessness, and once again we see Rebecca portrayed as a complex figure" (Rotenberg, 2002, p. 56).

---

[3]   As Alter (1997) points out: "...although a physical struggle between the two would scarcely be a battle of equals, in her maternal fear she imagines the worst-case scenario, the twins killing each other, and in the subsequent narrative (28:10) the sedentary Jacob does demonstrate a capacity of unusual physical strength" (p. 144, n. 45)

The final words of Rebecca's narrative are a repetition of a prior statement, again beckoning close attention as to association and meaning. In the end, Rebecca repeats the same existential question 'why life?' (27:46) that she voiced during her pregnancy. Like bookends to her story of the ambivalences in human relatedness between striving and safety, meaning and mortality, Rebecca is not soothed by answers. Left with questions and with the existential fear that pervaded her life, that colored the nature of her relationships, that directed the choices she made, Rebecca is no longer a victim or a manipulator. Through a non-linear reading between Rabbinic exegesis and psychoanalytic theory, the narrative strategy (Schafer, 1993) has shifted to 'unveil' another story, one of Rebecca as the agent of intention engaged in a dialectic with the 'other,' including God, with all its inherent tensions of opposites, contradiction and ever-changing, multiple narratives of one's life. Psychoanalytic interpretation and Biblical exegesis have enabled the integration of disclaimed feelings into a whole person, a whole woman, albeit not a perfect one, but someone with whom we can engage.

REFERENCES

Aron, L. (1996). *A Meeting of the Minds: Mutuality in Psychoanalysis,* Hillsdate, NJ: The Analytic Press

Alter, R. (1981). *The Art of Biblical Narrative.* New York: Basic Books, 1983

Benjamin, J. (1990). An Outline of Intersubjectivity: The Development of Recognition. *Psychoanalytic Psychology,* 78:33-46

Chesler, P. (1999). Phyllis Chesler's Second Dvar Torah on Vayishlach, www.phyllis-chesler.com

Fuchs, E. (1999). Status and Role of Female Heroines in the Biblical Narrative. *In Women in the Hebrew Bible.* Edited by Alice Bach, Routledge: London, UK

Greenberg, J. (1991). *Oedipus and Beyond: a clinical theory:* Cambridge, MA: Harvard University Press

Greenberg, J. (2005). Conflict in the Middle Voice. *Psychoanalytic Quarterly,* 74:105-120.

Hoffman, I.Z. (1998). *Ritual and Spontaneity in the Psychoanalytic Process*: Hillsdale, NJ: The Analytic Press.

Hollywood, A. (2004). Gender, Agency and the Divine in Religious Historiography. *The Journal of Religion* 84 (4): 514-528.

Klitsner, S. (2007). *Wrestling Jacob: Deception, Identity, and Freudian Slips in Genesis*, Urim Publications, Jerusalem, Israel.

Leibowitz, N. (1976). *Studies in Bereshit, Third Revised Edition*, Alpha Press, Jerusalem, Israel.

Midreshet haRova, (5760). Toldot 5760, www.harova.org

Ouaknin,M. & Brown, L. (1998). *The Burnt Book: Reading the Talmud.* Princeton University, Princeton, NJ.

Reik,T. (1948). *Listening with the Third Ear: The Inner Experience of a Psychoanalyst.* New York: Grove.

Rotenberg, M. (2002). A Portrait of Rebecca: The Devolution of a Matriarch into a Patriarch. *Conservative Judaism*, 54: 46-62.

Schafer, R. (1993). *The Analytic Attitude*, London: Karnac Books.

-------. (1976). *A New Language for Psychoanalysis*, Yale University Press.

Zakovitch, Y. (2007). Jewish Book Week: Yehuda Amichai Evening, www.jewishbookweek.com

Zornberg, A. (1996). *The Beginning of Desire: Reflections on Genesis*: New York, Doubleday.

-------. (2007). Jewish Book Week: Yehuda Amichai Evening, www.jewishbookweek.com

4 Theoretical Papers

"Demand a Speaking Part!": The Character of the Jewish Father

Lori Hope Lefkovitz

Popularly, the Jewish father — though to date less vividly rendered in critical analyses than, say, the Jewish Mother or the Jewish American Princess — is also a cultural type with distinctive characteristics. He may be devoted and indulgent; patriarchal, authoritarian, and bossy; gentle, temperate, learned, a model for other ethnic groups; domesticated, alienated, psychologically compromised, in need of liberation, among other competing stereotypes, some of which overlap with constructions of Jewish masculinity generally and others of which are particular to the relational qualities of Jewish fatherhood *per se*. What I have noticed is a pattern of nostalgic representations in modern Jewish literature of the Jewish father who, perhaps in part as a response to crises of immigration, fashions outspoken daughters to supplement his compromised Jewish and gender identities and finds gratification and consolation in his child's capacity to speak out, speak up, and speak well, even as her successes carry the textual traces of his own losses. At this essay's conclusion, I will root this pattern of the Jewish father whose compromised power and masculinity is supplemented by a strong, loyal daughter in the story of Antigone and Oedipus, extending Sigmund Freud's analysis of the family romance and Oedipal drama to a father-daughter relationship that

289

seems to me is particularly evident in the Jewish family story, with its stereotypically compromised men and strong women.[1]

The founders of Jewish cultural studies have focused special attention on the feminization of Jewish men in the European imagination, and Sander Gilman isolates the Jewish man's speech as one indicator of Jewish difference (on a list that includes his nose and his feet).[2] Whether his use of voice makes him too Jewish (like Jackie Mason) or, on the contrary, appropriates high culture in the kind of colonial mimicry described by Homi Bhabha (1994), such that the Jew's linguistic prowess becomes a feature of his characteristic identity passing, speech and pitch are implicated in the making of Jewish masculinity. Voice, pitch, accent, prolixity, tone, and silence are also marked — if confused — features of The Jewish Mother and the Jewish daughter, the American Princess.[3] Ann Pellegrini (1997), attending to Jewish women's dramatic self-enactments and freedoms of speech, explores the consequences to Jewish women produced by the cultural construction of feminized Jewish men and Freudian efforts to re-describe sexuality so as to recuperate Jewish masculinity. She finds that Freud undermines the very gender divisions that he labors to create. My own conclusions, which find ambivalence in the engendering of outspokenness, will also return us to Freud, extending the classic reading of the oedipal drama.

The subject of the Jewish father as he is characterized in Jewish literature is a convergence of multiple Jewish and gender identities and performances.[4] Although the challenge of working this knot can not entail a hope of finding anything definite in Jewish fatherhood, it participates in a larger interdisciplinary effort to untangle aspects of identity production

---

[1]   For an interesting discussion of Freud's own distress at his father, Jakob Freud's "unheroic conduct," see Salberg (2007).

[2]   Gilman, pp. 10-37. See also Daniel Boyarin (1997).

[3]   See Riv-Ellen Prell (1993); also: Aviva Cantor (1995), pp. 249-253; and Joyce Antler (2007).

[4]   An earlier and briefer consideration of this topic, which includes a slightly fuller discussion of Paley's short story, appeared in *Bridges* (2009).

within cultural systems. My plan here is to look at a small constellation of modern Jewish stories and trace a single pattern among many, asking what this example contributes to conversations about the intersections of gender and ethnicity and the interplay of racial, class, and social performances in the composition of identity.

The narrator of "The Loudest Voice," Grace Paley's triumphant 1959 short story about a first-generation American Jewish family's confrontation with the public school Christmas pageant begins by locating us in a time and place characterized by its noisiness. The story opens: "There is a certain place where dumb-waiters boom, doors slam, dishes crash; every window is a mother's mouth bidding the street to shut up, go skate somewhere else, come home. My voice," the narrator tells us matter-of-factly — even proudly — "is the loudest." The narrator remembers her mother's effort to excuse Shirley's volubility to the grocer: "'Ah, Mr. Bialik,' my mother replies, 'if you say to her or her father 'Ssh,' they say, 'In the grave it will be quiet.'" And Shirley herself invokes one of her father's refrains: "'From Coney Island to the cemetery,' says papa. 'It's the same subway; it's the same fare'" (Paley, pp. 34-40).

We see in this opening scene that Shirley's strength rests in her identification with her father, as Shirley's exasperated mother meets the grocer's accusation with the lament that Shirley's other parent sets the difficult example of refusing to be shushed himself. The narrator sums up the meaning of the whole scene: "In that place the whole street groans: Be quiet! Be quiet! But steals from the whole chorus of my inside self not a tittle or a jot." By the time we actually meet her father, Misha Abramowitz, Shirley has been rewarded for her loud voice — as well as for her intelligence, leadership capacity, and organizational talents — with the part of narrator and teacher's assistant for the school Christmas play, honors that delight her.

Paley uses a narrative trick of pulling the reader out of the deep past and into that later time when the narrator's parents are hopefully "resting in peace" to keep the story sepia-tinted, a nostalgic evocation of parents who played their parts in the obvious happiness of this narrator's childhood, a childhood that yielded a woman who could narrate this story so lightly and well. Paley makes this move impressively when after prolonged days in preparation at school for the Christmas play, with her mother's resistance to Jewish families "making tra-la-la for Christmas" still evident, Shirley's father gives a little lesson in comparative religion that, for all of its expansive historical sweep, turns out to be entirely in the service of his personal, paternal interests: "'Christmas. What's the harm? After all, history teaches everyone. We learn from reading this is a holiday from pagan times also, candles, lights, even Chanukah. So we learn it's not altogether Christmas. So if they think it's a private holiday, they're only ignorant, not patriotic. What belongs to history, belongs to all men. You want to go back to the Middle Ages? Is it better to shave your head with a second hand razor? Does it hurt Shirley to learn to speak up? It does not. So someday she won't live between the kitchen and the shop. She's not a fool.'"

The narrator steps into the light of perfect hindsight and speaks with warmth: "I thank you, Papa, for your kindness. It's true about me to this day. I am foolish but I am not a fool." And then immediately following this reflection, the narrator yanks us back into the past: "That night my father kissed me and said with great interest in my career, 'Shirley, tomorrow's your big day. Congrats.'

Shirley says her prayers confident that God will hear her because her voice is the loudest, and this faith that she commands God's privileged attention has been inspired by the male teacher who directs the pageant and repeatedly tells Shirley that he doesn't know what he'd do without her, and by her father, whose own optimism is rooted in his aspirations for the daughter whom he admires ("she's no fool"), who identifies with him ("in the grave it will be quiet"), who knows that it doesn't hurt for her to learn to speak up, and for whom he has expectations of a better professional future than his own, one beyond the space between the kitchen and the shop, expectations that the reader has every reason to suspect are amply justified by Shirley's alter-ego, Grace Paley.

In another story, "Conversation with my Father," Paley's represents an adult daughter, a writer who develops a fictional story dialogically and dialectically, in reaction against her father's values and literary standards in a process of affectionate disagreement, and respectful, intimate, and playfully contentious banter with the older man. These fathers, in the tradition of Tevye, Sholom Aleichem's renowned father of daughters, share something (however parodically) with popular, if unsubstantiated, folk traditions about the idealized medieval scholar, Rashi, who — perhaps imagined to be frustrated by the fact of having had only daughters — reputedly indulged his daughters with education and afforded them ritual privileges and authority ordinarily reserved for boys, until he married them off to scholars and acquired worthy sons-in-law.

Poor, pious, Tevye feels the burden of beautiful, smart daughters, for whom he too only wishes pious scholars (with money) for husbands.[5] But Tevye — for all his attachment to tradition — betrays his author's attraction to those secular values that might advance his children's ambitions for, minimally, independence and maximally, effective political power. One after another, Tevye's daughters persuade him to compromise on the tradition that invests him with authority over their futures. Had Tevye wanted to justify his vulnerability with a Scriptural prooftext, he need have gone no further than the first patriarch, another quarreler with God, noting that at a moment of domestic crisis, the great Abraham was told to "listen to the voice of Sarah." Indeed, when Shirley **Abram**owitz, that Americanized daughter of Abraham, expresses her faith that God would listen to her loudest voice, I found myself wondering if Shirley's Jewish name might have been Sora or if a more unconscious foundation for her confidence might not have come from Hebrew School stories that betray matriarchal privilege in claims on God's attention.

Whether it is Tevye's old world ambivalence about his daughters' self-assertion or Misha Abramowitz's unqualified new world encouragement of Shirley learning to speak up, the persistent indulgence of the Jewish father of daughters meets with reader approval. Against what he suspects is his better judgment, Tevye's habit of listening to his wife and daughters, and his helplessness in the face of his daughters' tears, is endearing, for all of its tragic consequences. When Lazer Wolf presents himself as a candidate

---

[5]   See Sholem Aleichem, *Tevye the Dairyman and the Railroad Stories.*

293

for Tseitel's hand in marriage, Tevye knows that he must first consult with both his wife Goldie (who, when it comes to such matters is matriarchal, no "schmatah") and with Tseitel, who also has to be asked. "Tell her! Don't ask her!" Lazer insists, mindful of the prerogatives of fatherhood that Tevye can rarely bring himself to exercise. Even Goldie, well pleased with the match, cannot be told that it is Tseitel's resistance that makes Tevye go back on his handshake. Instead, Tevye contrives to recuperate his patriarchal authority by inventing a supernatural communication to reverse the arranged marriage. The ploy may succeed with Goldie, but Tevye himself, his daughter, and the reader know differently. Ruth Wisse's summary of this aspect of Tevye's character contains the suggestion that his weakness for his wife and daughters engenders in him the tenderness of womanhood. Wisse writes of Tevye: "He cries when he sees his daughters wolfing down their first abundant meal, and he cannot live without the approval of the wife whom he mocks as his inferior" (p. 45). Operating in an unarticulated calculus of virility, the Jewish father tenderly weeps as his daughters are transformed into wolves.

These Jewish fathers of daughters, ambitious on their behalf, vulnerable to their wants, and devoted to them and to their mothers, with whom they live in endless verbal battle, earn our sympathy even as we witness the erosion of the pride of place once guaranteed by their patriarchal status. Rather than conferring the secure generosity of paternalism, these fathers — who each mark a place of insecurity in the history of the Jewish people — depend upon the strength of their daughters to prop up the Jewish future in the modern era. Paley's portraits of these fathers are meant to be unqualified, but characterization always has a subterranean gender dynamic. Misha Abramowitz, a latter day Abraham who listens to Sarah, a latter day Rashi, who empowers girls who are not fools, and a new Tevye, who also breaks traditional rules to listen to Goldie and satisfy his girls' ambitions, is decidedly a *Jewish* man, carrying that particular tragic-comic history and our conditioned judgment that the phrase "Jewish **man**" itself may be an oxymoron, or contradiction in terms.

Wisse puts it this way: "Hodl and Chava have no trouble outarguing their father — precisely because they talk right to the point without any need for prooftexts. Tevye knows that his power is invested in his speech and that it, like Samson's hair, can be cut off by women." Her metaphor is well chosen. In Hebrew Scriptures, the strongest man on earth may be able rip a lion with his hands or single-handedly defeat an army, but female sexuality brings sure defeat. Psychoanalytic theory makes explicit that the shorn hero has been symbolically castrated, just as Isaac, with his compromised vision, like that of Oedipus himself, or the stammering Moses, or the circumcised race more generally are men who have had their power clipped. But Tevye does not fall prey to female sexuality like those paradigmatic Scriptural heroes who discover too late that the bedroom is that battlefield where men always lose. Instead, Tevye's voice is cut off by his daughters. He might have cited that classic Talmudic statement of cosmic paternal pride: "my children have defeated me" (*Baba Mezia*, 59, ab) except that these victories are not only girls' victories but they are hardly worthy of celebration.

The distance between and shifts from Sholem Aleichem to Grace Paley are from Europe to America and from a male writer to a female one. In the American Jewish story the father's ethnicity is expressed as loving ambition even as it entails compromise with and rationalizations of assimilation. Abramowitz tolerates Christmas because America (that "creeping pogrom") will enable a better life for his daughter. If Tevye's heartbreaking losses teach him otherwise, his creator — by contrast — sees a future for his own children that leaves behind all that Tevye stands for. Wisse writes movingly that "the broken heart at issue here was the author's: Sholem Aleichem knew that he could not hope to satisfy the new Morrises and Zacharys and Clementis, because he himself was speaking and writing Russian to his children. So that they might have access to everything that emancipation had to offer, he weaned them from the language to which he was devoting his creative genius. Tevye is the expression of this tragic paradox. The father knows that in addition to letting his children go, he will abet their defection so that they might enjoy a better life" (p. 48).

I would add that it is not unremarkable that Tevye is the father of only daughters. The future for Jewish daughters in emancipated times or more importantly, places, most notably America, represents both a more exaggerated example of what will be new for Jews in the new world and magnifies what will be lost from the old. If once Goldie had a special authority in the family — on the model of Sarah, Rebecca, and Rachel — tradition kept her from asserting her advantage in the schul or the schoolhouse. American stories liberated the Jewish daughter, with her father pushing at her back and fanning wind in her sails, as she gets herself an education at the expense of old-world Jewish traditions. Shirley's success entails tolerating Christmas. And if Tevye's Chava lives to regret her intermarriage, once she is reincarnated in *Fiddler*, reversing that intermarriage would have been unthinkably un-American. Born in the era of optimism about progress, the play promotes the advancement of daughters as one modern way to be Jewish, with a regrettable, but necessary cost to Jewish traditions and the Jewish masculinity that had long been privileged by traditional Judaism.

One can detect that regret in Isaac Bashevis Singer's derisive reaction to Barbra Streisand's comparable transformation of the ending to his 1961 story, "Yentl, the Yeshiva Boy" in her 1984 movie, *Yentl*. *Yentl*, like *Fiddler*, also projects a sentimentalized vision of America as that place that can accommodate the Jewish daughter whose old world father indulged her gender-bending need for learning. Singer objected, among other more convincing reasons, on the absurd grounds that Yentl's singing violates the *halachic* prohibition of "*kol isha*" (literally, "a woman's voice," the phrase refers to the dubious legal prohibition against hearing a woman sing).[6] Although the audience knows that Barbra/Yentl/Anshel (the boundaries among them blur) may not satisfy her need for Talmud study in the new world, she will escape the old world's strictures on her sex and exercise her vocal chords to her heart's content. What Shirley Abramowitz and Barbra Streisand have in common is the loudest voice.

Singer's story, which begins with the words "after her father's death," is conditioned by Yentl's orphaning. Her bedridden father, Reb Todros,

---

[6]   The information on Singer's reaction to the movie comes from the discussion in Stephen J. Whitfield (1998/1999), esp. p. 158. On *kol isha*, Whitfield refers us to Hadda (1997), pp. 199-200. Singer published his reaction to the movie in the *New York Times*: January 29, 1984.

who had secretly studied with her as if she were a son, is dispensed with summarily. We are told that on the evidence of her textual talents "her father used to say, 'Yentl, you have the soul of a man.'" When Yentl asked why she was born a woman, her father allowed that, "Even heaven makes mistakes." And indeed this story is about the consequences of one such mistake, the cascade of *aveyros* (sins) that follow from Yentl's yielding to the impulses that heaven's error inspires. The story resolves, according to Marjorie Garber (1992), with the transvestite's escape, though she "returns powerfully and uncannily as 'the loved boy,'" in the shape of Hadas' and Avigdor's infant, with whose bris the story ends, Avigdor revealing to a shocked assembly that the baby's name is "Anshel" (p. 83).

The reader must imagine that the memory of Yentl works as a Lilith in the young couple's marriage bed, a shared fantasy of a heavenly error, which — perhaps like all heavenly errors — carries blessings: in this case, a marriage and baby that were meant to be and if not for Yentl would not have been and a new kind of marriage at that, one improved by knowledge of the possibility of more flexible gender roles. At very least, the anomalous Yentl generates our sympathy for a girl who prefers study to darning socks, and who, like Lilith and Antigone, prefers to live without a man to surrendering her independence or having her rights limited by the accident and arbitrary delimiting of her gender.

Streisand's *Yentl*, which had been playfully received as *Funny Boy* or *Tootsie on the Roof*, departs from the spirit of Singer's story not only in Yentl's habit of breaking into heartfelt song but most importantly in the changed frame imposed on the story. Here, the loss of Yentl's father is represented as a grievous tragedy to the daughter, who wails, at some length, in "Papa, Can you Hear Me?" just as the boat-trip ending allows Yentl the possibility of having a satisfying career without needing to masquerade as a man. Singer's facetious response in the *New York Times* to Streisand's removal of Yentl to America betrays, to my ears, a sympathy for the daughter who needs to learn that is stronger than the story itself represents and a regret — his own regret — for the traditions that were abandoned for the sake of America's freedoms. Singer wrote in the Sunday *Arts and Leisure* section: "What would Yentl have done in America? Worked in a sweatshop twelve hours a day when there is no time for learning? Would she try to marry a salesman in New York, move to the Bronx or Brooklyn and rent an apartment with an icebox and dumbwaiter?" And: "Weren't there enough yeshivas in Poland and Lithuania where she could continue to study?" (p. 1).[7] One might almost suspect that Singer believes that there was even one yeshiva in Poland or Lithuania where Yentl could have studied.

But Streisand, herself a kind of "Funny Girl" whose extraordinary voice and intense drive helped her effect her escape from Brooklyn poverty, nowhere evidenced her own ambition more than in her long effort to get *Yentl* produced. Stephen J. Whitfield reports that fully a decade after Streisand began to pursue this goal, she received new energy from what she took to be a communication from her own father from beyond the grave. Visiting him at Mount Hebron cemetery in Queens, Streisand felt directed to notice the "rather rare name Anshel" on a neighboring tombstone.[8]

Both Garber and Whitfield present evidence that *Yentl* was widely understood as an expression of Streisand's Jewish feminist ambitions, ambitions that received a decidedly mixed response. Garber quotes one makeup artist, who observed that Streisand, unlike most actors who willingly cut or even shave off their hair when required to do so by a role, wore a wig to avoid parting with the "Medusa hair" that Streisand so loved. Garber invokes Freud's analysis of the Medusa myth — whose phallic snakes cause men to stiffen — to emphasize the makeup artist's ambivalence toward Streisand herself. Although Freud finds the Medusa monster ultimately consoling to men (their stiffening is reassuring), the makeup artist's association probably intends that the larger-than-life, pushy, Jewish Streisand, with her big hair and her big voice, has a paralyzing effect on men.

I want to emphasize that the Jewish father, even in his absence, holds a kind of responsibility for his daughter's confidence that she will be heard and her prayers will be answered. Breaking rules to study with his daughter, the Jewish father, because of the limitations imposed on him

---

[7]   Quoted in Whitfield, pp. 160-161.

[8]   Whitfield, p.156 cites James Spada (1995), pp. 401-405.

as a Jew, identifies with the daughter who finds herself limited by the gender norms of Judaism. If America holds the promise of some liberation for both Jewish father as Jew and Jewish daughter as woman, the price for such liberalization is literally the price of admission to rabbinical school. Whitfield, who defends Streisand's choice of putting Yentl on a boat at story's end, on the grounds that "the United States was neither eccentric nor senseless for a woman who seeks a wider sphere for her own piety than what the Old Country appears to offer," suggests that when Streisand's Yentl says, "learning is my whole life," she might have been speaking for Henrietta Szold, who "had to assure Solomon Schechter that her sole intention in seeking admission to the Jewish Theological Seminary of America (JTS) was to study and not to become a rabbi."

Although I don't share Whitfield's obvious pleasure in Streisand's version of Singer's story, I agree that it "provides an entrée into the conditions under which American Jewish culture has manifested itself." What I think is particularly significant, however, is that once more the path to the new world begins at the place where an old world father learns with his daughter and sets her on a journey that ultimately leads Henrietta Szold to study at JTS — and which carries the anxiety that she might take her ambition too far, on the model of Yentl, and might even wish to be a rabbi! Measuring the affect in Singer's reaction to the film, we can also detect some ambivalence to the Yentl of his own creation, whose need to claim a place in the beit midrash inspired a next generation woman (Streisand) to have the chutzpah to stand in his authorial stead and change his story.

Whitfield's association of Yentl with Szold, both of whose expressed devotion to *Torah lishma* apparently trumps (or compromises) the heroine's more usual dream of a happy ending in marriage signals a struggle between competing goals to which the privileged Jewish daughter seems especially susceptible (evidenced in the ongoing controversy that still surrounds Herman Wouk's *Marjorie Morningstar*).[9] I find a precedent

---

[9]   See discussion of the controversy over remaking the film of this novel and the history of feminist debate in Alana Newhouse (2005).

for the Jewish girl's romantic fantasy of a *hevruta* partner (the traditional Talmud study partner) on the model of her father in Mary Antin's 1911 story, "Malinke's Atonement," a story that I read as a fairytale in which the Jewish Cinderella's prince comes in the form of a surrogate father who will teach her Torah. No picture of want could be sadder than Antin's rendering of Polotsk, the shtetl from which Antin herself immigrated to America as a child. Malinke, the fatherless heroine of the story, is as lonely and industrious a Cinderella as one might imagine, burdened by hunger, hard work, long days of isolation, her mother, Breine Henne, a well meaning egg woman whose ignorance and fears can make her cruel to her daughter, and Malinke's older brother Yosele, who lords it over her because he is a boy, though he does not come close to being Malinke's intellectual equal.

In spite of everything that conspires to reduce her, Malinke is characterized by the exuberance of her devotion and the vitality of her mind. Malinke's endless questions and the idiosyncratic logic of her religious practice exasperate her poor mother, who fears that the child's ideas may be heretical, and the reader is treated to one of Yosele's memories as he wonders why his sister is "such a queer little girl": "Yosele knew no one who asked such strange questions as Malinke, and no one who could satisfy her. His own teacher, a pious scholar, caught in the coils of one of her impudent inquisitions, was obliged to silence her by the only argument that ever made Malinke hide her head in submission. 'You are only a girl,' the rebbe had reminded her. 'Girls don't need to know things out of books.'"

On the day of the story, Breine Henne has made a Yom Tov (a holiday) of an ordinary day by her unlikely decision that her little family will eat the chicken that has proven too pathetic to sell at market. Antin spares no prose in her descriptions of the children's excitement and the details of anticipation and days of preparation. When Breine Henne discovers a wire in the chicken and Malinke is sent to the rav for his judgment as to whether the chicken is kosher, we are treated both to the shortsighted rabbi's deliberations and Malinke's equally complex cogitations. After some hesitation, and no attention to the hungry child before him, Reb Nossen tentatively declares the chicken treif (unkosher). By the time Malinke has run home, during which time she has a good communication with God, the chicken had been declared kosher.

Malinke chokes, confesses — to the stunned horror of all of Polotsk — decides that God requires a sacrifice, and secretly throws her only possessions of any value, her worn Shabbos dress and cherished hand-me-down Shabbos boots, into the river. The extraordinary gossip about Malinke's unthinkable sin (allowing her family to eat treif) reaches Reb Nossen. The interview that Reb Nossen conducts with the child, his dawning spiritual vision, and the feeding of her body and soul make for a stunningly moving encounter. Breine Henne, who intrudes on the scene, begs for the rav's leniency on the strength of Malinke's having grown up without a father. The story ends with Reb Nossen's atonement, his determination that this child's Jewish education has been inadequate, and his offer to pay tuition for her to learn on condition that he can name her teacher. Here, Malinke expresses the hope that her teacher will be a rebbe and not a rebbetzin because "the rebbetzins don't know so much," and while Breine Henne bursts into apologies, the rav (in stark contrast with Yossele's less capable teacher) simply observes that "if the rebbe knows more than the rebbetzin, it is because he has spent more time in study." He now offers himself as Malinke's teacher, and as the gossiping town escorts Malinke home, the rumor in Polotsk blazes that Reb Nossen is going to adopt Malinke and make of her a great scholar. Malinke's own conclusion is more theological: "The Lord had accepted her atonement. In compensation for her blindness that had led her into error, God had sent her a teacher."

The intertext for "Malinke's Atonement" is George Eliot's autobiographical novel *The Mill on the Floss*, with details so similar that I am convinced that Mary Antin had the novel in mind when she composed her story. Malinke and Maggie Tulliver are similarly — even identically — constituted; each has a mother ill-equipped to appreciate her daughter; each has a loved brother with a teacher unequal to the girl's questions and who stifles her with a truism about the limits of her sex. Both heroines are irrepressible, outspoken children, who make great mistakes because their exceptional intelligence is untutored. Each story has the character that Eliot calls "The World's Wife," the determining power of local gossip and judgment. Maggie, however, has a father who indulges her and loves her, though he regularly laments that God played a nasty trick on him by giving his daughter cleverness and his son conventionality. When Mr. Tulliver dies, however, Maggie's story turns tragic. She, like Malinke after her, appears to have committed an unspeakable sin that results in social ostracism, and in what may seem like divine judgment, Maggie drowns while attempting to rescue her brother in a flood.

Antin's story reverses this tragedy by restoring the absent protecting father through a classic Jewish paternal substitution: a worthy teacher. On reflection, however, the reader must conclude that "Malinke's Atonement" communicates a tragedy after all. The poverty, hunger, and ignorance are realistic enough but the redemptive ending whisks us out of realism and into fantasy. Not only is it more than unlikely that the rabbi in so poor a shtetl could be so generous and progressive as Reb Nossen turns out to be, but there is no possibility that the Jewish Cinderella would find her happily ever after in being adopted by the rav who will make of her a great scholar. Redeeming a family from poverty and hunger by educating its daughter could only happen in America, and it is to America, where Antin becomes a writer and imaginatively returns to her childhood home, that the story points. If the moral of the story is that the Jewish girl's Prince Charming is an adoptive father-teacher with a progressive approach to Jewish law and traditions, then the place where this fairytale can come true, as it did for the author, is in America. Implicitly, the American advantage for Jewish daughters is once more distinguished by a loving, paternal man who will break with tradition to facilitate the daughter's learning.

The Jewish father in this constellation of texts invests in the New World by investing in his daughter, and as we have seen, the compromise entailed in this investment is to both time-honored religious norms and to male privilege. Reb Nossen believes the rebbetzin to be as capable as the rebbe, and he speaks for his author when he regrets her comparative lack of education. A sadder corollary to this pattern of father-daughter relationships also finds early example in the youngest of Tevye's daughters, the one who finally fulfills Tevye's dream of marrying well and, in so doing, teaches Tevye, whose life is nothing if not a series of hard lessons, "beware what you wish for because you might get it." If Tevye spends his life praying for wealth so as to be able to be a better Jew, this son-in-law exemplifies the ambition that comes to dominate the modern era, the ambition to climb up and out of Jewish traditions. More painfully, Tevye, the dairyman, whose main characteristics are his underdeveloped textual skills and his exaggerated love for his daughters, ends up as an embarrassment to his youngest child and her husband, who plan to send him off to Palestine (after he rejects their offer of America, though they, ironically, end up there, and he never makes it).

Anzia Yesierska's 1923 story "Children of Loneliness," captures this gulf between generations, as Rachel, newly graduated from Cornell, finds herself disgusted to the point of illness by her parents' slovenly lower east side apartment, terrible table manners, and uneducated speech. Rachel is ashamed. Her father Yankev, embittered, declines to take lessons from her, declaring that all his teachers died in the old country. Yankev Ravinsky is roused to rage, first goaded by his wife, and then shushed by her as she fears that all of Essex Street, indeed all of New York, will be convinced that there are no fights like those "by us." Yankev is unstoppable because his daughter's insistence on knife and fork "spelled apostasy, anti-Semitism, and the aping of the Gentiles." "*Pfui* on all your American colleges!" he screams, lamenting American morals that have no respect for Torah or old age. He curses the new generation that it "should sink in the earth like Korach."

Mrs. Ravinsky ends the tirade by reminding Yankev to *daven mincha*, and Rachel finds herself thinking that "a chasm of four centuries could not have separated her more from them than her four years at Cornell." Rachel flees home, as if for her life, and overcome with loneliness invests in a fantasy of Frank Baker, whose pretentious self-absorption turns out to be a crushing disappointment to her, expressed ironically in his admiration for the "social types" of the lower east side. While he admires the gentle Talmud scholar, Rachel responds with scorn that she'd rather have "a plain American who supports his wife and children" than "all of those dreamers of the Talmud."

Earlier in the day, Rachel, spying on her parents at home but unable to bring herself to see them or express love, remembers her early childhood, "often waking up in the middle of the night and hearing her father chant his age-old song of woe. There flashed a vivid picture of him, huddled in his corner beside a table piled high with Hebrew books, swaying...." The narrator tells us that the memory made him seem "like a mystic stranger from a far off world and not a father. The father of the daylight who ate with a knife, spat on the floor, and was forever denouncing America and Americans was different from this mystic spirit stranger who could thrill with such impassioned rapture."

This story — set in the same screaming lower east side of Paley's fiction — but written more than a generation earlier, characterizes the Jewish father as helplessly stuck in his Jewish past as his daughter strains to loosen herself from its reins. The reader is impressed by the irony of how much Rachel and her father share: both are passionate, desperate, and enraged, and Yezierska subtly directs our attention to the similarities in their behaviors and in the quality of their souls. Yankev's piety becomes her passion for American gentility and university learning. But father and daughter are fixed in their respective textual positions, and if Rachel, in her youth, can hope to find other first-generation Americans, a community of peers who will help pull her from her loneliness, her father is depleted and silenced by America itself, which may have advantaged his child but has stolen her from both him and his beloved Judaism. Like Tevye, this Jewish father and Judaism share in being victims of the daughter's ambition. Misha Abramowitz, by contrast, is more liberal than his wife Clara, as he can forgive the "tra-la-la of Christmas" if it means that his Shirley, who is no fool, can transcend the space between kitchen and shop.

Just as the father in Paley's story wants to empower Shirley to have her voice be heard not to secure her a husband who will take her out of her class but so that she can do so through the force of her own voice, so too Mary Antin's Cinderella, Malinke, dreams not of a Prince to rescue her from poverty but of a teacher so she can make her own way. Uninterested as Emma Lazarus's father ostensibly was in his Jewish identity, or that of his daughters, he may have unwittingly expressed his Jewishness in his parenting. Lazarus' illustrious writing vocation began with — to lift a phrase from Paley's story — her father's "interest in" her "career."[10] Lazarus's family valued her talent and professional success but thought her affinity with Jews was a phase. Perhaps the assimilated father's Jewishness shows up as a symptom in his promotion of his daughters.

These Jewish fathers suggest a kind of deep cultural explanation for Jewish difference highlighted in more recent sociological studies. In 1995, the National Commission on American Jewish Women cites studies conducted between 1987 and 1993 that showed that Jewish women believe that working women make more interesting marriage partners and are equally good mothers, and that significantly fewer non-Jewish women hold those views. "Jewish men," the report continues, "apparently agree. They tend to marry women who are their 'equals' and they encourage their wives' endeavors; 90% of married Jewish women say their husbands are supportive of their aspirations." A 1986 Boston study showed that "81% of Jewish fathers who are professionals have daughters who also became professionals. That is about the same level as for Jewish sons, but significantly higher than for non-Jews." These data suggest that educated women find approval for their successes in Jewish men to a greater degree than from non-Jewish men and that both Jewish mothers and fathers communicate educational ambition to their daughters without prejudice while non-Jewish men are less likely to do so (p. 28).

The old canard that "Jewish men make good husbands" and the idea that women and girls are encouraged to speak up in Jewish households is balanced by stereotypes that Jewish sons are less ambitious for themselves than their mothers are on their behalf, and have fathers who set less than a perfect example of strength and ambition. The stereotype of the silenced Jewish family man is evidenced in a joke so classic that a version of it finds

---

[10]   The editors of *The Norton Anthology of American Jewish Literature* introduce the entry to Emma Lazarus with a brief biography that includes the following: "Lazarus's ambitions as a writer began when she was young. In 1866, when Lazarus was 17, her father privately printed her first book..." (p. 101).

its way into *The Norton Anthology of American Jewish Literature* (p. 323). It's the one about the Jewish boy who comes home and announces that he got the part of the Jewish husband in the school play, at which information the mother screams that he must go back to the teacher and demand a speaking part! This joke, ostensibly at the expense of the Jewish husband, manages to slander wife, mother, and son as well. If the Jewish husband is so henpecked that he stands on the line in heaven for non-henpecked husbands because that's the line his wife told him to stand on, if Jewish men are versions of Bontshe Shvayg and Gimpel the Fool, quiet and accepting in the face of every indignity, schlemiels like Woody Allen, and weak by comparison with non-Jewish men, the clear implication of the joke is that one explanation for his silence is that the Jewish wife fills all the air space with her voice.[11] The Jewish boy in the joke is paradoxically pushed by his mother to get a speaking part because the example of his own father is one of a silenced man. The son is doubly silenced by the joke: first, by the example of the father whom he is presumably destined to become when he himself becomes a Jewish husband (a worse fate perhaps than playing the role in a school drama) and second by his mother who responds to his boast by telling him what to say to his teacher, overpowering his voice with her own. The implication too is that the Jewish mother, and not the Jewish father, sets the bar for Jewish masculinity.

His own masculine power compromised by history, the Jewish father of sons cannot bequeath to them what is not his to pass on. Elsewhere, I have interpreted the biblical episode of Jacob masquerading as Esau as one origin story of Jewish gender ambiguity and performative masculinity (Lefkovitz, 2002). Jacob, the son who is allied with his mother, dresses in animal skins to pass as Esau, and so, to pass as the kind of man who can inherit the patriarchy. Reading backwards from our own cultural moment — by which time the categories of "Jew" and "woman" have an overlapping history — the deception that earns Jacob the patriarchy reads as a story of his ability to fool his old blind father into believing that he

---

[11] Bontshe Shvayg is the long-suffering Jewish hero in I. L Peretz's classic story of "Bontshe Shvayg"; Gimpel the Fool is I. B. Singer's creation (*Jewish American Literature: A Norton Anthology*, pp. 614-623).

possesses the requisite virility, signified by a metaphoric assumption of animalism, to be a patriarch.

From our own historical vantage point it is hard not to see Jacob's masquerade as a kind of "camp." This foundation myth can be read as that version of the Freudian family romance that has become both a caricature of the Jewish family and a formula for the production of homosexual men: a manipulative mother, a blind (read castrated) father, and the son whose confused identity emerges out of this family dynamic. And one can read this story, like other stories of the Hebrew patriarchy, as a victory of the more feminine domestic son over his more masculine rival brethren. The son who inherits the narrative future is younger, and this relative youth in their families (Isaac, Jacob, Joseph, Moses, David, Solomon) is represented through greater attachment to or dependence on the mother, greater vulnerability, and comparative smallness; the younger son is also less hairy and less wild and therefore has features that would in later generations — the nineteenth century in particular — be identified as feminine, contributing to the anti-Semitic characterization of the Jews as a feminized people. The victorious son, in myths with virtually no daughters, is a kind of daughter by comparison with the stronger, older brother who is less favored by mother and God.

The patriarchy itself is thus built on the foundation of radically destabilized identity categories. Although the term "patriarchy" has since come to signify the grounding origin of masculinity and male privilege, the stories that establish the binary terms "matriarchy" and "patriarchy," themselves represent an always already feminized, insecure, and undermined patriarchy. Because of the divine alliance with the matriarchs whose barrenness God — and not the human father — ends, the human father is required to surrender authority over his sons' futures, and in these Jewish myths, the human father is twice the loser in adulterous and Oedipal triangles: first, to conspiring God and wife and second, to wife and the younger son who becomes an Oedipal victor, in a psychologically unhealthy triumphing over the bond between mother and father. Freud is at something of a loss when it comes to girls, recognizing the inadequacy of the symmetry he posits. I wonder if Freud, a Jewish father himself, could not quite bring himself to see how the Oedipal story extends beyond Oedipus' punishment for sexual crimes.

As the Oedipal story is re-presented by Freud, the boy wishes to kill his father and sleep with his mother, and he fears punishment for sexual transgression with castration (loss of limb and eyes being symbolic forms of castration).[12] Sophocles' story, however, does not end where Freud's story ends, indispensable as that reading has been for understanding the symbolic castrations of a long list of emasculated heroes, from Samson to Edward Rochester, in narratives that punish the hero for sexual crimes by diminishing masculine excess. But there is more to the story that Freud read with such attention.

Oedipus loses eyes and limb — symbolic castration, Freud explains. The story continues beyond these losses, and Antigone, Oedipus' daughter, leads her father around, specifically and relentlessly identified as her father's "eyes, staff, and support." The logic is clear: if loss of limb and eyes are representations of lost phallic authority (which Freud later casts as every boy's fear of castration), the daughter who becomes his eyes, staff, and support, supplements his lack.

This version of the Antigone story finds repeated representation in our narrative tradition: the supplemental daughter of an absent, inadequate, or somehow incapacitated father, the daughter who assumes the paternal function and is imagined to have to sacrifice the natural pleasures of womanhood, just as Antigone insistently transgresses the law so that the tomb becomes her marriage bed, explicitly preferring death to the fate of wife and mother. Other features of the story include the urgent need that the king, Creon, feels to destroy this emasculating woman — not so much because she breaks his law as because he explicitly feels his masculinity threatened. Also a feature of this plot is Haemon, Antigone's betrothed, whose masculinity is vigorously assaulted by his father King Creon, the Law itself. ("Are you a man?" the father asks, when Haemon defends the unwomanly woman.) Antigone's brothers are similarly tainted, called by

---

[12] I have described what I call "Antigone Anxiety" (by which I intend to point to a cultural anxiety about Antigone's phallic authority) in Lefkovitz (1990 and 1993).

their father, Oedipus, "homeloving girls" by comparison with the daughter Antigone, who is his best son. If Antigone incarnates the phallus, all of the men connected to her are tainted and fear for their masculinity. JAP jokes about "daddy's girl" fit hand in glove with jokes about the silenced Jewish husband.

What I am suggesting is that the most influential writer of modern Jewish fiction may be Sigmund Freud himself, who may resort to Greek myth for articulating the psychodynamics of the modern family but who analyzes a paradigmatic family that looks peculiarly biblical, on the model of the matriarchy and patriarchy. Moreover, Freud stops in his tracks before he gets to Antigone, though his own daughter Anna — having received privileged training from her father — picks up the pen that the father hands her, taking over responsibility for the future of psychoanalytic theory, extending his voice, and speaking for him after he is gone.

Please do not mistake me: I do not believe that there really is such a thing as "the" Jewish father, and I am not asking us to subscribe to the truth claims of Freudian theory or my playful invention of what I call "Antigone anxiety." Nor do I think that the Antigone character is uniquely Jewish. We find her in Jane Austen's Elinor Dashwood and Elizabeth Bennet, in Eliot's Maggie and Dorothea Brooke, in Louisa May Alcott's Jo March, and in Katherine Hepburn's version of Tess Harding in Joseph Mankiewicz's 1942 film *Woman of the Year*. She is evident in the biographies of Austen, Eliot, and Alcott, all unmarried, productive writers, who like Antigone, have relatively feminine sisters, and each of whom is promoted by and supplements a weak father.

Rather, I am inviting us to notice that there is a Jewish stake in this construction of one type of father and daughter with implications for the special constructions of Jewish femininity (not so feminine) and Jewish masculinity (not so masculine). I invite us to notice that if masculinity has one set of connotations, the adjective "Jewish" qualifies those connotations to the point of virtually reversing them. If patriarchy has one set of preferred meanings, the patriarch who parents girls looks differently patriarchal and more dependent than he does otherwise. Gender performances and Jewish performances — when enacted on the same stage of the cultural imagination — qualify one another nearly out of existence, happily adding to the exposure of gender itself as an empty category.

If the Jewish mother demands of her son that he demand a speaking part on stage because the Jewish husband does not play such a part in life, the Jewish daughter speaks up and speaks out because off-stage her father develops in her an internal megaphone. The boundary between stage and life is of course never a simple one to negotiate. There are gains and losses in this model. The consequence of exploring Jewish and gender identity relationally creates kaleidoscopic effects, complicating the meaning of these words nearly out of their senses.

I presume that any effort to define the Jewish father will result in contradictions comparable to those that emerge from efforts to define Jewish literature... or Jewish mothers... or Jewish beauty or, for that matter, "man" or "woman," terms, which — to borrow Judith Butler's formulation — are "ontological phantasms" (1993, p. 313). Butler (1990) concludes *Gender Trouble* with the question: "What ...local strategies for engaging the 'unnatural' might lead to the denaturalization of gender as such?" (pp. 148-149). The "Jewish father" is one such locale, and the range of significations and the particular contradictions that attach to the noun "father" when qualified by the adjective "Jewish" carries the baggage of connotations that have traveled with these words to the point at which we encounter them, at the same time that each characterization intervenes in that history, adjusting both future instantiations and past mythologies.[13]

---

[13] Because literary analysis cannot be disinterested, it behooves us to admit that we may have very different investments in gender identity and Jewish identity, respectively. Whatever "Jewish" may mean, many of us have an existential stake in its perpetuation, whereas I, for one, delight in gender's destabilization. I dedicate this exploration to the memory of my own beloved father, who had only daughters, and to the father of my daughters, neither of whom could be more paternal or more Jewish, though the very differences in the details of their enactments of those qualities only deepen my uncertainty about what those adjectives "Jewish" and "paternal" mean.

REFERENCES

Antin, M. (1990). Malinke's Atonement. In *America and I: Short Stories by American Jewish Women Writers*, ed. Joyce Antler. Boston: Beacon Press, pp. 27-56.

Antler, J. (2007). *You Never Write, You Never Call: A History of the Jewish Mother*. New York: Oxford University Press.

Bhabha, H. K. (1994). *The Location of Culture*. New York: Routledge.

Boyarin, D. (1997). *Unheroic Conduct: The Rise of Heterosexuality and the Invention of the Jewish Man*. Berkeley: University of California Press.

Butler, J. (1990). *Gender Trouble: Feminism and the Subversion of Identity*. New York: Routledge.

-------. (1993). Imitation and Gender Insubordination. In *The Lesbian and Gay Studies Reader*. Eds. Henry Abelove, Michele Aina Barale, and David M. Halperin. New York: Routledge, pp. 307-320.

Chametzky, J. et al. (2001). *Jewish American Literature: A Norton Anthology*. New York: Norton.

Cantor, A. (1995). *Jewish Women/Jewish Men: The Legacy of Patriarchy in Jewish Life*. New York: Harper Collins.

Garber, M. (1992). *Vested Interests: Cross Dressing and Cultural Anxiety*. New York: Routledge.

Gilman, S. (1991). *The Jew's Body*. New York: Routledge.

Hadda, J. (1997). *Isaac Bashevis Singer: A Life*. New York: Oxford University Press.

Lefkovitz, L. (1990). Her Father's Eyes, Staff, and Support: The Sage Author as Phallic Sister in Nineteenth-Century Fiction. In: *Victorian Sages and Cultural Discourse: Renegotiating Gender and Power*. Ed. Thais Morgan. New Brunswick: Rutgers Univ. Press, pp. 225-245.

-------. (1993). Antigone Anxiety: Manly Girls, Emasculated Men and the Transcendence of Gender. In: *Gender, Race, and Identity*. Eds. Craig Barrow et al. Southern Humanities Press, pp. 111-118.

Lefkovitz, L. (January 2002). Passing As a Man: Narratives of Jewish Gender Performance. *Narrative*, 10 (1): 91-103.

Lefkovitz, L. (2009) "Does it Hurt Shirley to Learn to Speak Up?": Tevye's New World Legacy in the Jewish Daughter's Father. *Bridges: A Jewish*

Feminist Journal special issue on "Jewish Feminists and Our Fathers." Ed. by Rebecca Alpert and Laura Levitt (spring).

The National Commission on American Jewish Women (1995). *Voices for Change: Future Directions for American Jewish Women* (sponsored by Hadassah and Brandeis University), p. 28.

Newhouse, A. (2005). *Marjorie Morningstar*: The Conservative Novel that Liberal Feminists Love, posted to *Slate.com*, September 14: http://www.slate.com/id/2126022/

Paley, G. (1994). *Grace Paley: The Collected Stories*. New York: Farrar, Straus, and Giroux.

Pellegrini, A. (1997). Interarticulations: Gender, Race, and the Jewish Woman Question. In: *Judaism Since Gender*. Eds. Miriam Peskowitz and Laura Levitt. New York: Routledge, pp. 49-55.

Peretz, I. L. (rpt. 2002). Bontshe Schvayg. In: *The I. L. Peretz Reader*. Ed. Ruth Wisse. New Haven: Yale University Press, pp. 146-152.

Prell, R.-E. (1993). Why Jewish Princess Don't Sweat: Desire and Consumption in Postwar American Jewish Culture. In: *People of the Body: Jews and Judaism from an Embodied Perspective*. Ed. Howard Eilberg-Schwartz. Albany: SUNY Press, pp. 329-360.

Salberg, J. (2007). Hidden in Plain Sight: Freud's Jewish Identity Revisited. *Psychoanalytic Dialogues*, 17 (2): 197-217.

Aleichem, S. (1987). *Tevye the Dairyman and the Railroad Stories*, Library of Yiddish Classics. New York: Schocken Books.

Singer, I. B. (1961; 1983). Yentl the Yeshiva Boy. In *The Collected Stories of Isaac Bashevis Singer*. Trans. Marion Magid and Elizabeth Pollet. New York: Farrar, Straus, Giroux.

-------. (1984). I. B. Singer talks to I. B. Singer about the Movie "Yentl." *New York Times,* January 29, sec. 2, p.1.

Spada, J. (1995). *Streisand: Her Life*. New York: Crown.

Whitfield, S. J. (fall 1998/winter 1999). Yentl. *Jewish Social Studies: History, Culture, and Society* 5 (1-2): pp. 154-176.

Wisse, R. R. (2000). *The Modern Jewish Canon: A Journey through Language and Culture*. New York: The Free Press.

Yezierska, A. (rpt. 2001). Children of Loneliness. In: *Jewish American Literature: A Norton Anthology*. Ed. by Jules Chametzky et al. New York: Norton, pp. 234-244.

The Problem of Desire: Psychoanalysis as a Jewish Wisdom Tradition[1]

Seth Aronson

In Havah Tirosh-Samuelson's extensive monograph "Happiness in Premodern Judaism: Virtue, Knowledge and Well-being", she argues that from ancient times onward within Judaism, the achievement of happiness, the eudaemonia so ardently sought by the wisdom and philosophical traditions of antiquity, became inextricably linked to the Torah. The Torah was seen to provide the blueprint, the basis, for a happy and fulfilling life. She writes, "the ancient Israelite Wisdom tradition (whose prime exemplar was the Biblical book of Proverbs) was practical and pragmatic. Based on the observation of nature and human conduct, it was concerned with ordering life so as to maximize success and prosperity. Its teachings enabled the learner to master his environment and cope with the dangers and vicissitudes of life" (Tirosh-Samuelson, 2003, p. 58). Self discipline was thus not only a command, but a virtue, with the goal being the individual's mastery of desires and impulses.

Seen in this light, the Ten Commandments came to represent the highest catalogue of virtues (Tirosh-Samuelson, p. 94). By following these commandments, wrote the Jewish philosopher Philo (15 BCE-50CE), one

[1] I wish to thank Jonathan Fishburn, Rosh Kehilah Dina Najman, and Dr. Jill Salberg to directing me to some of the sources cited. My deep gratitude to Rabbi Dr. Yehudah Mirsky for his careful reading on comments of an earlier draft. A version of this paper was presented at the Shavuot retreat, Isabella Friedman Center, Falls Village, Conn., June 2008.

313

"ought to be free from all unreasonable passions"(as quoted in Tirosh-Samuelson, p. 94). If one followed the commandments, happiness could be achieved via the required, implicit self discipline.

The curbing of desire is, Philo says, specifically addressed in the Tenth commandment. Desire was seen as a "fountain of evil" and Philo proscribed "discarding this passion, detesting it as the most disgraceful thing" (as quoted in Tirosh-Samuelson, p. 96). Little, if any regard, was given to the individual's internal life. The proscription was clear — if you follow the commandments and steer clear of unruly passions and desires, you are assured of a happy, prosperous and peaceful life.

However, with time, the interiority of experience began to be more recognized and valued. What once constituted Wisdom in Judaism changed over time and history. With increased attention paid to the individual's internal life, it was no longer tenable to believe that the simple proscription of behavioral acts could lead to the curbing of desire and to happiness and fulfillment. We see a steady parallel evolution in both the range of Wisdoms that will lead to the human being's flourishing, and in the complexity of the human and his or her motivations.

Tirosh-Samuelson describes the evolution of the Wisdom tradition in Judaism: "Wisdom became the pursuit of truth accessible to all human beings by virtue of their being rational. Under that rubric, Jews have acquired knowledge about the world and about God from a variety of sources and traditions....the pursuit of truth transcends ethnic and cultural boundaries" (p. 447). By widening the concept of Wisdom — which itself drew from a well of ideas and traditions circulating in the ancient Mediterranean world — to include other areas of study and discourse, truth gleaned from philosophical, scientific and other forms of study could be used to understand, expand and elaborate Jewish ideas and values, as seen perhaps most vividly in the extraordinary works of Maimonides and other medieval philosophers. This exchange has, in turn, allowed Judaism to evolve and exhibit "a remarkable elasticity without losing its unique identity" (Tirosh-Samuelson, p. 5). I would like to argue that psychoanalysis may, in this historical moment, function as a further step in the evolution of the Wisdom tradition and propose to do so by looking at how we might we use psychoanalytic wisdom to understand the Tenth commandment against desire today. More specifically, given psychoanalysis' value of the individual's subjective life and experience and the interpersonal relationship, how might a modern psychoanalytic approach help in understanding the difficult, ubiquitous problem of coveting?

The Tenth Commandment

"You shall not covet your fellow man's house, wife, or his male slave, or his female servant, or his ox, or his donkey, or anything that your fellow man has" (Exod. 20:17). In keeping with the ancient, pre-modern view, the Tenth commandment is clear in its proscription- coveting, desiring what another has, is forbidden.

Rene Girard underscores the unique character of this commandment: "in a place of prohibiting an act, it forbids a desire" (Girard, 2001, p. 7). Girard argues that the preceding commandments gradually are related to the tenth; "if we ceased to desire the goods of our neighbor, we would never commit murder, adultery, theft or false witness" (Girard, 2001, p. 12). The desire prohibited by the Tenth commandment, said Girard, "must be the desire of *all* (italics mine) human beings" (Girard, 2001, p. 8). This natural inclination to envy and desire is at the very heart of human social interaction.

This unusual mitzvah, which prohibits a feeling, raised the question for Biblical commentators (more so, incidentally, than other mitzvot involving feelings, such as honoring one's parents) — can one, in fact, legislate feelings such as desire, covetousness, and envy? If so, how? The modern Biblical scholar Robert Alter explains that the verb "hamad" in this commandment ('Lo tahmod') "exhibits a range of meaning from 'yearn for,' 'desire,' even 'lust after' to simply 'want.' But here......it clearly suggests wanting to possess something that belongs to someone else and so the King James version rendering of 'covet' still seems the best English equivalent" (Alter, 2004, p. 432).

The Biblical Commentaries on Desire and Coveting

Many of the Biblical commentaries were clearly troubled by this injunction against desire. Some recognized the need to operationalize such an elusive concept in keeping with the ancient tradition, while others took a more behavioral approach, and a select few focused on the subjective experience in understanding the dynamics of desire.

Ibn Ezra

The major medieval Biblical commentator, Abraham Ibn Ezra (1092-1167), in an uncharacteristically lengthy exposition, provides a sensible, rational, and ultimately somewhat implausible answer to the question— can one legislate desire?

As Ibn Ezra wrote,

> "Many men have raised questions about this mitzvah (referring to the prohibition against coveting). How is that a man will not have desire in his heart for something desirous and beautiful that he sees?"

Ibn Ezra goes on to provide a parable:

> "A peasant who sees a beautiful princess will not have any sexual desire for her. Because he knows this can never come to be. And don't think this peasant is one of the delusional, unrealistic types who may wish to grow wings so as to fly. Similarly (in an unexpected pre-Freudian nod to the incest taboo), a man will never wish to sleep with his mother, even though she is beautiful, because he has become accustomed from his youth that she is forbidden to him" (Ibn Ezra, Exod. 20: 17).

Ibn Ezra proclaims (perhaps too confidently, says Robert Alter) that a person will never desire anything beyond his reach, because he realizes how utterly implausible his desires and fantasies are. He will condition himself, as he does with Oedipal desires, to simply do away with such feelings. It is important to note another factor — that of class. Ibn Ezra was living in a world in which social and class distinction were hard and inescapable facts (as reflected in the example he uses).

Ibn Ezra's approach is a hyper-rational one, and one which seems to proscribe behavior, more in keeping with the ancient Jewish, pre-modern view of not giving credence to the interior life (e.g. what might contribute to such strong passionate feelings). Ibn Ezra acknowledged desire's place in the Decalogue and yet, dismissed the power of affects that drive an individual's desire. Bott Spillius, in her discussion of 'varieties of envious experience', notes how envy has the distinction of being recognized in the Ten Commandments and the seven deadly sins, and yet, is often "rapidly dismissed" (Bott Spillius, 1993).

Maimonides

The great 12th century philosopher and legal scholar Maimonides (Rambam) (1135-1204) attempted to operationalize the prohibition in his quintessentially rational manner. His explanation is found in his great legal code, the *Mishneh Torah*, in the section dealing with the laws of Theft and Loss.

There he wrote,

> "Whoever covets his neighbor's servant- male or female, house, possessions or anything that he may purchase from his neighbor, and covets them so much so that he coerces his neighbor to allow him to purchase it — even if the neighbor is compensated well- is guilty of "Lo Tachmod" (You Shall Not Covet)." (Maimonides, *Mishneh Torah*, Laws of Theft and Loss, 1,9-11)

For the Rambam, one isn't guilty until one takes action and actually takes possession of the coveted object. The feeling, in essence, is meaningless; it is the action that is critical. Maimonides, then, is separating feeling and desire on the one hand, from action on the other. Jimmy Carter, according to the Rambam, was not guilty of anything because, as he told *Playboy* magazine in a famous interview, he did not act on the 'lust in his heart"; he only harbored it. Carter's merely feeling lust rather than acting on it makes him innocent, according to the Rambam, of breaking this commandment.

In the next section, the Rambam goes further:

"Desire may lead to theft because if the owners don't wish to sell, even at a great price, it may lead him to steal the object. And if the owners attempt to prevent the theft, it may lead the one who covets to murder the owners to gain possession of the desired object" (Maimonides, Mishneh Torah, Laws of Theft and Loss, 1, 9-11).

Ultimately, the transgression is not due to the feeling, but to the actions set in motion by the desire.[2]

Benno Jacob

Maimonides' approach in which he is seemingly unconcerned with the person's internal, psychological world, is in stark contrast to the 20th century German commentator Benno Jacob (1862-1945). Jacob, a 20th century scholar, an interesting mix of traditionalist and modern who engaged in dialogue with the intellectual currents of his time, wrote during a historical period, when, unlike, Maimonides, the inner life of the individual was much more accepted as a force to be reckoned with.

"It is totally wrong to state that the Hebrew Bible and its God were not concerned with inner motivation and only judges the resulting action" (Jacob, 1992, p. 575).

Jacob, in contrast to the Rambam, is more psychological, focused more on the inner life of the individual, in his interpretation of the Tenth commandment. For Jacob, the inner life of the individual is integral to understanding this mitzvah.

However, a notable exception to the lack of acknowledgement of the inner world can be found in the writings of Rabbeinu Yonah Gerondi (1210-1263), a Spanish Talmudist, moralist and exegete of the 13th century.

---

[2]   The Rambam's emphasis on the act, rather than the desire, introduces intriguing questions such as whether Judaism is based on a behavioral or depth psychology as well as the role of kavannah (intent) (Aron, personal communication). Space does not permit the elaboration of these questions.

Rabbeinu Yonah

Jacob's concern with the inner life finds early echoes in the work of this 12th century Spanish commentator, Rabbeinu Yonah. In his discussion of the Tenth commandment, he wrote:

> "...even desire that does not come to action falls in this category (emphasizing the inner life)."

Rabbeinu Yonah takes issue with the Ibn Ezra's pragmatic, common sensible approach. He then wrote:

> And whoever covets and hates the individual who appears to have good bestowed upon him, thinks that it as if this goodness belonging to the other was stolen from him. And for the one who covets, all his days are filled with pain, as if the fire of his desire burns in his heart every day and he knows no peace" (*Rabbeinu Yonah*, Exod. 20: 17).

This is an extraordinary psychological observation. Whoever covets a desired object and comes to believe that the object rightfully belongs to him, believes that the object was in fact, stolen from him and he is entitled to its rightful return. The projection of his desire allows him to assume rights over it, as it were, and this tie to the object consumes him, like 'a fire burning in his heart' and consumes his every waking moment. He becomes obsessed with the perverse morality (it was stolen from him) and his desire represents his inability to relinquish ties to an object belonging to someone else. Indeed, in this linkage of thwarted desire with hatred for the one possessing the object of our desire, Rabbeinu Yonah foreshadows (by some seven centuries!!) Melanie Klein. Her ideas offer a psychoanalytic point of entry into the Jewish Wisdom tradition as regards the temptations and pitfalls of envy and desire.

> "The infant's feeling seems to be that when the breast deprives him, it becomes bad because it keeps all the milk, love and care associated with the good breast all to itself" (Klein,1957, p. 183).

In a similar vein to Rabbeinu Yonah's thinking, Bott Spillius, a contemporary Kleinian, further developed nuances of envious

319

experience. She describes the person whose envy is "impenitent"; this person "does not suffer from conscious guilt and a sense of responsibility for his envy; he thinks it is the envied person's fault that he, the envier, feels so wretched" (Bott Spillius, 1993, p. 1203).

Melanie Klein on Envy

The universal struggle against desiring, coveting, and envying what is not ours is a central feature of the work of Melanie Klein (1882-1960). The underlying premise for Klein is that all experience is related to the relationship with the object. Klein believed that the infant is born with a rudimentary ego, which essentially gets built up from birth through the process of relating to the object. Through interaction with a (good) object, the infant can rid itself of bad experiences, experiences that are characterized by pain and discomfort. Initially, for the infant, these experiences are bodily based. Because Klein believed in the ubiquitousness of unconscious phantasy, the way the infant rids itself of these experiences is directly related to corporeal experience. Thus, for example, if the infant is hungry, the infant feels as if a 'bad' object has inflicted this painful hungry state on (into) the infant. By crying, the infant's unconscious phantasy is such that the bad feelings can be expelled and projected into the object via its tears and screams, who is there to receive it. Hopefully, the object responds by ministering to the infant, feeding it, changing the baby if necessary and in this way, demonstrating a good object response to the infant's distress. The infant then introjects the resultant good feeling and in this way, acquires a positive, good object. Through accrual of these positive experiences, the infant gradually develops a good internal object and ego that allow the baby to withstand times of pain and distress.

The contemporary Kleinian Robert Caper has explained good internal objects as "our states of mind". "For example, 'containing a good internal object' is a vivid way of expressing what we would otherwise call feeling love. We do not feel love for our good internal object, or because we contain a good internal object; the feeling of 'having a good internal object is our feeling of love" (Caper, 1999, p. 56).

Such love is undermined by hatred and envy, the kind associated with coveting and desiring what is not ours. Our good internal object, our good, loving feelings and states of mind allow us to weather the inevitable times of despair, hate and envy we all experience.

Klein underscored the universal quality of envy. The infant requires milk/food to survive and via unconscious phantasy, covets the breast, which appears to have an inexhaustible supply of the very stuff the infant needs to exist.

> "My work has taught me that the first object to be envied is the breast, for the infant feels that it possesses everything he desires and that it has an unlimited flow of milk and love which the breast keeps for its own gratification. This feeling adds to his sense of grievance and hate." (Klein, 1957, p. 183).

This grievance leads the infant first to covet the desired object as a possession. When the infant realizes he cannot possess the object, he attacks it (in unconscious phantasy) in an effort to spoil and destroy it. Rather than tolerate the existence of such a powerful object beyond its control, the infant phantasizes attacking and spoiling the breast via assaultive projective attacks. If I can't have it, no one can.

The person overwhelmed by envy can never be satisfied, says Klein (much like Rabbeinu Yonah's description of knowing "no peace"), because his envy stems from within.

Klein goes on to offer her own proscription for the problem of envy — the building up of a secure, good internal object. With such a good object, one can "withstand temporary states of envy, hatred and grievance," (states which Klein feels are natural and inevitable), "which arise even in children who are loved and well mothered" (Klein, 1957, p.187).

The universality and acceptance of such desire also seem to be expressed in a story in the Babylonian Talmud Chagigah, 16a:

> Rabbi El'ah the Elder said, "If a man sees that his desires overwhelm him, he should travel to a place where no one recognizes him, don black clothing and enwrap himself in these clothes, and do what his heart desires so as to not profane the name of God in public [in front of those who know him]."

The author of this Talmudic passage (which may be the source for the title of Nathan Englander's short story "For the Relief of Unbearable Urges") seems to understand that desire and coveting cannot be controlled through simply forbidding them, but rather must be dealt with. In Englander's story, a young Talmudic scholar is instructed by his rebbe to travel to another town to visit a prostitute and relieve his intense sexual urges.

Rabbi El'ah appears to be sympathetic to one whose desires are overwhelming. He, much like Klein, acknowledges the universality of dark feelings and desires, desires that must be reckoned with and cannot simply be behaviorally conditioned away (in the style of the Ibn Ezra). The steps outlined by Rabbi El'ah represent various deterrents, as Rashi (1040-1105), whose range and depth of commentaries are breathtaking, pointed out. Rashi explains that by suggesting travel, purchasing unfamiliar clothing, donning these clothes, enveloping himself in them, the person overwhelmed by desire will rouse himself and not act on his feelings and desires. However, ultimately, Rabbi El'ah, although sympathetic to the idea that desires may rule the human heart, in keeping with wisdom of his time proscribes a behavioral approach (travel, donning unfamiliar clothing, etc.).

The fact that one of the Ten Commandments is directed against the problem of coveting and envy indicates that such dark feelings and desires were clearly felt to be universal. The wisdom then was for the individual to exercise self control and simply curb these 'disgraceful' feelings. Klein's descriptions underscore the ubiquity of these feelings today. However, what Klein underscores is the interpersonal matrix in which envy and desire occur. How, then, may we use a modern psychoanalytic approach to proscribe an approach to the problem of desire?

A Psychoanalytic Approach
to the Problem of Desire and Envy

This psychoanalytic-wisdom on the proscription of envy shifts the emphasis from the individual trapped in his envy and desire: Man alone cannot conquer covetousness and envy, rather it is via relationship.

The Diary of Anne Frank is an extraordinary document. Anne Frank's perceptiveness, empathy and humor — especially remarkable at a time of horror — all underscore what promise her life might have held. In the diary, she wrote,

> "It's really a wonder that I haven't dropped all my ideals, because they seem so absurd and impossible to carry out. Yet I keep them, because in spite of everything I still believe that people are really good at heart. I simply can't build up my hopes on a foundation consisting of confusion, misery, and death. I see the world gradually being turned into a wilderness, I hear the ever approaching thunder, which will destroy us too. I can feel the suffering of the millions and yet, if I look up into the heavens, I think that it will come all right, that this cruelty too will end, and that peace and tranquility will return again" (*Diary of Anne Frank*, 1952, p.237).

How is that, during World War II, at a time of intense hatred, envy, and covetousness, Anne Frank was able to write this passage and to have such conviction of feeling? I would like to suggest that it was the presence of a good internal object ("yet if I look up into the heavens") that allowed her to have the faith she did. As Klein wrote, "Hope and trust in the existence of goodness, as can be observed in every life, helps people through great adversity, and effectively counteracts persecution" (Klein,1957, p.194). Those with strong capacities for love and gratitude due to a deep-rooted relationship to a good internal object can withstand such destructive attacks .This is a result of a positive relationship with an other, a loving relationship that allows for the accrual of positive experiences, and the development of the good internal object. Anne Frank clearly benefited from a relationship with a good internal object. This relationship was one in which her mind was met with another's, one who cared for and about her, thought about her with love, and allowed her to develop the unusual reflectiveness and empathy evident in the Diary. Such a nourishing relationship provided Anne Frank with a foundation that allowed this remarkable young woman to demonstrate and express hope and optimism at a time when the external world was filled with hateful aggression and destructive covetousness.[3]

I believe we can find traces of such relationships in the Talmud. In the Babylonian Talmud, Brachot, 3a-b, the Talmud discusses three precautionary reasons why one should not enter an abandoned, dilapidated building alone. The first reason is that there may be undesirable people loitering there. The second is that the building may collapse and the person may be injured or killed. The third reason is due to the presence of "mazikkim" (demonic spirits). In the course of the discussion, the Talmud says that if the person is accompanied, we don't worry about the demonic spirits because they will not make their presence known if there are two people present, but will appear only if the person is alone.

I would like to suggest that these 'mazzikim' (alternatively called 'sheddim') represent projections of an internal world. These mazzikim are mentioned throughout the Talmud and I believe represent rabbinic efforts to make sense of internal, psychological experience by establishing external (projected) forces. These projections, which are demonic, evil, aggressive, hateful, not unlike the infant's first experience of pain, are felt to be inflicted (in unconscious phantasy) by the aggressive other. With the introjection of the other, an other who ministers to the infant and contains the projections, these dissipate. The caregiver who meets and contains the infant's projections is not perfect, but a "good enough mother" (Winnicott, p. 145, 1960). (In fact, Likierman cautions against painting a picture of an idealized mother, "a being who is mentally 'sanitized' of all primitive impulses" (Likierman, p. 31, 1988).This caregiver who helps the child

---

[3] From her writing, it is clear that Anne Frank struggled with other issues, such as conflict, competitiveness and adolescent sexuality and aggression. For purposes of this essay, I am focusing on her ability to build up a good internal object which allowed her to withstand the wartime experience, in part due to her positive relationship with her father (cf. Dalsimer, 1986). In addition, adolescents' use of diaries and journals often allows them to forge a relationship with an other, who 'listens' to their innermost thoughts and feelings.

build a good internal object contains the child's phantasied destructive projections and metabolizes them (Bion, 1962), making sense of them and re-presenting (and representing) them to the baby in understandable, usable form. In this way, the child gradually builds up an internal world populated by good, responsive caregivers and a good self worthy of such care.

This process is not unlike Fonagy et al (2002)'s ideas regarding mentalization. In order for the child's mind to grow and develop, the child requires another mind to think about the child with love. This is what Winnicott referred to as "the mother's [mirror] role of giving back to the baby the baby's own self" (Winnicott, 1971, p.118). It is via relationship — the interpersonal interaction — that hatred, aggression, envy, covetousness and the darker feelings and desires can be made sense of. We need no longer be scared of the 'mazzikim' dwelling in the shadows if there is a benevolent other there with us along for the journey.

Conclusion

What, then, might be a modern proscription for the individual who covets? The ancient categorical — and seemingly behavioral — prohibition of desire, coveting, and envy does not seem to make sense, given our modern sensibilities. What we can do is to proscribe a good internal object relationship for the individual plagued by destructive envy, a relationship in which projected hateful, envious, destructive experiences are contained, made sense of, and transformed, ultimately being returned to the individual in more palatable form. Ultimately, this allows the person to withstand the temporary bouts of envy and hatred, and recover and regain his equilibrium (temporarily lost in these dark moments). Intense coveting can be mitigated and managed with the help of a good internal object.

We cannot wish away envy and covetous desire-it is there in all of us, throughout our lives. But, if we value relationship and prize interaction with an other, we can (hopefully, optimally) build an internal world populated with good objects that allow us to withstand the hatred, envy and aggression first identified in the Tenth commandment, that each and everyone of us, as human beings, is prone to.

REFERENCES

Alter, R. (2004). *The Five Books of Moses: A Translation with Commentary.* New York: W.W. Norton.

Aron, L. (2008). Personal communication.

Bion,W. (1962). *Learning From Experience.* London: Maresfield.

Bott Spillius, E. (1993) "Varieties of envious experience." *International Journal of Psychoanalysis,* 74(6): 1199-1213.

Caper, R. (1999). *A Mind of One's Own.* London: Routledge

Dalsimer, K. (1986). *Female Adolescence.* New Haven: Yale University Press.

Fonagy, P. et al (2002). *Affect Regulation, Mentalization and the Development of the Self.* New York: Other Press.

Frank, A. (1952). *The Diary of Anne Frank.* New York: Simon and Schuster.

Girard, R. (2001). *I See Satan Fall Like Lightning.* Maryknoll: Orbis.

Girondi, Rabbeinu Yonah. *Derashot and Payrushim.* Vagshul: Jerusalem.

Ibn Ezra. In: Mikraot Gedolot- Torah. Shulzinger: New York

Jacob, B.(1992). *The Second Book of the Bible: Exodus.* New Jersey: Ktav.

Klein, M. (1957/1997). *Envy and Gratitude.* London: Vintage.

Likierman, M. (1988). "Maternal Love and Positive Projective Identification." *Journal of Child Psychotherapy,* 14(2): 29-46.

Maimonides. *Mishneh Torah.* Friedman: New York.

Tirosh-Samuelson, H. (2003). *Happiness in Pre-modern Judaism: Virtue, Knowledge and Well-Being.* Cinncinati: Hebrew Union College Press

Winnicott, D. (1971). *Playing and Reality.* London: Tavistock..

-------. (1960). *The Maturational Processes and the Facilitating Environment.* New York: International Universities Press.

"Going Out to Meet You, I Found You Coming Toward me"

Transformation in Jewish Mysticism and Contemporary Psychoanalysis

Lewis Aron, Karen E. Starr [*]

"Also from above will come help." Just when I felt a desperate need, a strong voice from the Heavens called out under special, magical, emotionally loaded, transitional, luminal, even Holy circumstances. Not imaginary, not just in my head, but a real voice, a strong but distant voice. But I did not believe in heavenly voices and so felt stunned, confused, for a split second even transported beside myself, outside of myself, dissociated, split, transported and transformed at least momentarily, just for a second, but in a way that I have never forgotten, even now, almost four decades later.

It was 1970 and I was a boy of 17 living, and as we would say, "learning" for a semester in a yeshiva in Israel. It was our last night of the semester and we — my friends, dorm mates, all young men — were to fly home the following morning. We had been busy packing and saying our goodbyes, preparing to leave what had been a remarkable few months. Many of us were deeply ambivalent about returning home, "descending" from the

---

[*] Much of the material in this chapter was adapted from *Repair of the Soul: Metaphors of Transformation in Jewish Mysticism and Psychoanalysis*, Routledge, 2008, by Karen E. Starr, Foreword by Lewis Aron. Although written primarily in the first person, this chapter was co-authored collaboratively by Drs. Aron and Starr.

Holy Land. Some in fact stayed on to "learn" in yeshiva for several more years, as I planned to do. Some remained to join the Israeli army. And some were returning to begin college.

By now it was late in the evening, probably later than it should have been when we realized it was time for evening prayers. We decided that rather than pray at the school we would walk to the Western Wall in the Old City. It wasn't a far walk from our school in Rechavia and we had all walked there many times. In fact every Friday evening we would walk with groups of other yeshiva students, marching, almost dancing together to the Wall to say our prayers, welcoming the Sabbath. Walking together, in our open-collared white shirts as we sang and chanted religious hymns, to pray on Friday nights at the Holiest site of Judaism, joined together. It was exhilarating, moving, and inspirational; a group experience, a spiritual and yet bodily activity powerful enough to last a lifetime. We all knew the way through the Old City, even some of the short cuts.

In 1970 we could walk through the Old City at night without fear. Only just recently, following Israel's victory during the 1967 Six-Day War had the Western Wall come under Israeli control. In those days, not long after the war, Jews were heady with victory and full of pride, and there was hope for a lasting peace. The markets of the Old City were busy with business and shopping, filled with tourists, and seemed safe. And so off we went in the dark through the Old City, through the Jewish Quarter and to the Wall.

It was a beautiful night and we were all in good spirits, but our mood was bittersweet. We were feeling mournful about the end of our stay and ambivalent about our return to parents and home and whatever would come next. We were all struck by just how quiet it was at the Wall. The Wall was usually busy with visitors, tourists, guides, families, students, soldiers; people taking photos, saying their prayers or placing slips of paper with prayers into its cracks. But this was late on a June evening and we were surprised to find it silent, with very few people there.

Jewish sources, including the Zohar, the foundational text of the Kabbalah, suggest that the Divine Presence rests upon the Western Wall. It is the place where the great Jewish sages, including Isaac Luria, the famous sixteenth-century mystic of Safed, are said to have experienced revelations of God. The Wall itself, The *Kotel*, is a remnant of the Second Temple, which was built on the foundations of the destroyed First Temple, thought to have been built by King David. Sometimes known as the "Wailing Wall" because it is where Jews have historically wept for the lost Temple, it is adjacent to the Temple Mount, the holiest site of Judaism. None of us had ever actually gone up to see the Temple Mount area as it is forbidden for Jews to set foot on such holy space. It was the site of the Holy of Holies, the innermost sanctum of the Temple where only the High Priest, the priest of priests would set foot, and then only on the Holiest of Holy Days, and even then, even he was at risk for his life to enter such a holy space. This was the very spot, the very rock upon which Abraham prepared to sacrifice his son Isaac and where he heard a voice cry out to him.

So here we were in need of a *minyan*, by tradition and religious law a quorum of ten men, the minimum number needed for public prayer. We asked whatever other men were there to join us but there were only nine of us altogether at the Wall that night. And so we waited. We were sure that it would only be a matter of moments for someone to come along, just one more Jewish man to join us to constitute a quorum so that we could begin some quick prayers; it would take just a few minutes. But on that crystal clear night, for some strange reason we could not fathom, no one came. We waited but began to feel rushed. We were leaving the next morning and besides, it was late, and our dorm counselor must by now be anxious and annoyed that we had not returned. We'd have to get up early to leave for the airport. We really couldn't, shouldn't wait much longer. But we couldn't pray together without a tenth man.

I was emotional, deeply ambivalent about returning home. It had been my first extended stay away from my family and it wasn't easy for me. Yet my plan was to come home just for the summer and then to return to Israel to study in Yeshiva for another year or two. I didn't know what it would be like to come home, and then, whether I'd really want to return to Israel. Would I stay as religious as I had become? Would I be corrupted by my return to a secular world? And beneath my conscious concerns I must have been anxious about rejoining my family, but also anxious anticipating further separations from them, as well as moving out of an all male environment and back to some pressure I felt about dating. Anxious about college and career choices, worried about my temptations to rejoin my friends experimenting with drugs; it was after all 1970 and I was 17. I was still three years away from beginning my own personal analysis; it might as well have been eons. But now we were late and needed a tenth man.

"*Gam me'lemalah ya'azor*": "Also from above will come help." We all heard this voice. I knew it wasn't just me because we all looked up, each of us stunned. A strong voice, a man's voice, loud and clear. And then silence for a brief moment. We looked up but there was nothing and no one. The voice seemed to come from the night sky, way up above us, but there was nothing up there. We glanced at each other; was it a mistake, an illusion? And then a second time. The same words in the same certain tone. "*Gam me'lemalah ya'azor*": "Also from above will come help." This time I was shaken. Absolutely beside myself. There was not enough time for me to actually process my thoughts; it was much too quick for that. But I have no doubt, and have never doubted in all of these years since, that for at least one moment in my life I was certain that I had heard a Heavenly Voice, a "*Bat-Kol*." Was it miraculous? Would God Himself help us constitute a *minyan*? Had God sent an angel, a Heavenly agent to join us on this night?

I had been raised in a modern Orthodox home and community. We were not taught to expect voices from the Heavens. The Rabbinic tradition had been very conservative about direct communications from God. Rabbinic Judaism developed at a time of religious and political upheaval. Within the span of about a century the Jews had to cope with the loss of political sovereignty, a series of military defeats, the loss of their capital and their homeland, the destruction of the Temple, and the rise of Christianity and Gnosticism, as well as the crisis of faith initiated by all of these catastrophes. In the biblical era, God's law had been mediated by prophets and oracular devices that were assumed to provide unambiguous signs. For the rabbis, prophecy was exceedingly dangerous. Who, after all, could be certain of who was a true prophet?

And, furthermore, if one were to follow prophets — or, more accurately, if the entire community were to follow a prophet — then the law could be subject to change or abrogation at any time and hence prophecy could lead to radical change and legal chaos. The rabbis argued that after the destruction of the first Temple, God's will was no longer made known through prophecy. Instead, the rabbis claimed, God's will was determined through their interpretation of God's Torah. Since the text was ambiguous and interpretations were often contradictory and incompatible, they developed a legal system based on majority rule. They then took the authority that had been vested in the prophets and judges and claimed it for rabbinic interpretation. They discouraged attending to direct Divine communication because they anticipated that these mystical experiences would destabilize normative legal authority. Heavenly voices were suspect. Mysticism was always potentially antinomian.

So I was not raised to expect to hear Heavenly voices. I repeatedly heard as a child that when you pray you speak to God, but when you learn, God speaks to you. Learning, a passionate, engaged, spiritual activity, the deep study of texts, was as close as I ever expected to come to hearing God's voice.

There were some lights shining on the Wall. It was not completely dark, and the lights may have made it harder for us to see. But we soon recognized that the voice was that of an Israeli soldier who was stationed far above on the Temple Mount as a guard. It was this soldier who must have been paying attention down below to a group of boys looking for a tenth to pray. He was offering to have us count him in. It turned out that our Heavenly Voice was in fact a young soldier, Uzi in hand, ready as he stood guard this night, to be counted for a *minyan*.

Truly, to my astonishment, and quite literally, I lived the realization of the words of the eleventh-century Jewish mystical poet Yehuda Halevi, "Going out to meet You, I found You coming toward me" (quoted in Ostow, 2007, p. 57).

***

Perhaps it makes sense to begin this study of psychoanalysis and Jewish mysticism with the recognition that both psychoanalysis and the

331

mainstream Rabbinic Jewish tradition were rationalistic traditions; both were deeply skeptical of irrationality and mysticism (see Aron, 2004). Nevertheless, the bifurcation of normative religion with Kabbalah and the Jewish mystical tradition has been overstated. Back in the 1970s, Abraham Heschel disagreed with the then dominant modern scholar of Jewish mysticism, Gershom Scholem, who emphasized the antinomian nature of Jewish mysticism. That is, Scholem had suggested that Jewish mysticism deemphasized normative Rabbinic law. Heschel argued to the contrary, that mysticism was part and parcel of the Rabbinic and Hasidic tradition and that mysticism was deeply rooted in and tied to Jewish theology and religious practice. The current dominant scholar of Jewish mysticism is Moshe Idel, and Idel, like Heschel before him, challenges Scholem on this issue, arguing that Jewish mysticism and the great historic Jewish mystics were all deeply embedded in and loyal to Jewish religious observance and practice (see Sherwin, 2006). Thus the polarized split between rational religion and irrational mysticism does not seem to accurately reflect or do justice to the historical development of the Jewish mystical or religious tradition.

Among Freud's greatest achievements was his bringing together enlightenment rationality with romantic subjectivity, the influences of the Greek and the Jewish (Salberg, 2007), Athens and Jerusalem. Freud, however, brought rationality and irrationality together only by splitting them between the method and the object of investigation, between analyst and patient. The psychoanalytic method was meant to be scientific and rational. Fenichel (1941) institutionalized this understanding better than anyone when he declared regarding psychoanalysis that, "The subject matter, not the method, of psychoanalysis is irrational" (p. 13). In other words, Freud took from Romanticism the object of his study, irrationality, the unconscious, dreams, femininity, sexuality, the dark depths of the human spirit, but he devised a method and a theory based on Enlightenment rationality that he liked to think of as objective and scientific (see Aron, 2007). Gay (1987) described Freud as "the last of the philosophes" (p. 41).

Just as mainstream Rabbinic or Orthodox Judaism, especially as it had been affected by the *Haskalah*, the Jewish Enlightenment, had tried to create a rational religion, freed of superstitious, irrational and mystical elements, so too had psychoanalysis attempted to be a rational, scientific psychology. Freud's Enlightenment ideal of science saw it as liberating the individual from the illusion of religion. Psychoanalysis offered Truth as replacement for regressive fantasy. Religious belief was "a lost cause," a "childhood neurosis" (Freud, 1927, p. 53), and Freud paid homage only to "Our god Logos — Reason" (p. 54). But as modern psychoanalytic thinkers and philosophers of science have pointed out, "a more contemporary and nuanced view of science challenges any strict dichotomy between natural science and all other fields, including psychoanalysis and religion" (Jones, quoted in Spezzano & Gargiulo, 1997, p. x). Freud's worship of the god Reason is ironically not supported by the contemporary empirical sciences, which challenge a unitary conception of rationality. Both science and rationality on the one hand and religion and spirituality on the other are more complex and multidimensional than Freud envisioned (Spezzano & Gargiulo, 1997).

Stephen Mitchell's (1993) synthetic integration of relational psychoanalysis offered a strong critique of the dichotomizations of fantasy and reality, illusion and rationality, religion and science. For him, "What is inspiring about psychoanalysis today is not the renunciation of illusion in the hope of joining a common, progressively realistic knowledge and control, but rather the hope of fashioning a personal reality that feels authentic and enriching" (Mitchell, 1993, p. 21). With its goal as the enhancement and revitalization of human experience, and in its primary concern with felt meaning, significance, purpose, and value, the sharp division between religion and psychoanalysis diminishes.

But for most of its history, this has not been the attitude of mainstream psychoanalysis. And even in recent years psychoanalytic scholarship, even when deeply sympathetic to religious and mystical experience, has viewed it with suspicion as childish and illusory, irrational and regressive. (See Wolfson, 1997, who argues against the psychoanalytic reduction of the phenomenology of religious experience in general and mystical experience in particular, to the dichotomy of rational vs. irrational). Among the most sympathetic of psychoanalytic scholars of Jewish mysticism was

Mortimer Ostow, whose final book *Spirit, Mind, and Body: A Psychoanalytic Examination of Spirituality and Religion* (2007) affirmatively argued that religion was compatible with psychological health. Ostow tried not to diminish the value of the spiritual journey. One might say that his motto was borrowed from Albert Einstein, whom he quoted approvingly: "Science without religion is lame, religion without science is blind" (cited in Ostow, 2007, p. 4).

Nevertheless, while recognizing its value, Ostow brings an attachment based psychoanalytic perspective to his understanding of religious and spiritual experience that consistently analyzes its origins in the earliest mother-infant relationship. Experiences that we call spiritual are thought to be "re-activations" of affects from our earliest childhood. I want to remind you of my adolescent experience at the Western Wall where I looked up and heard the voice from the Heavens. Ostow writes, "The classic prayerful posture is eyes toward the heavens, often with hands held upward as well...The basis for this behavior can only be the child's upward gaze and upward reach toward the mother, when the child needs to be picked up, rescued. Help comes from above." (p. 79). I looked up upon hearing, "Also from above will come help."

Ostow writes: "In the ancient world, religious sites were often set up on hills, for example the Acropolis and the Jerusalem Temple. These places seem to be endowed with an immanent spirituality, often awesome. I believe the reason is that the small child always needs to look up to the mother's face and cries to be lifted in her arms to her shoulder. Above, for the child, is the source of salvation. Demons lurk in the chthonic depth, as the child on the floor is vulnerable to strangers and animals" (p. 100). "What is now the mountain of the Lord was once the mother's shoulder" (p. 107).

Ostow argues that "Spirituality reflects and retrieves the baby's feeling of attachment to his mother; religion recapitulates and retrieves the older child's feelings and modes of relating to his family" (p. 203). Ostow has moved beyond Freud in several ways. Unlike Freud, he is much more sympathetic to the value of religious experience and much less disdainful. Unlike Freud, he traces religious and spiritual experience to the child's earliest attachment to the mother, instead of focusing almost exclusively on the child's Oedipal relationship to the father. His analysis of religious and spiritual experience is largely compelling, insightful, and deeply respectful. Nevertheless, in his use of such language as "retrieving," "recapitulating," and "re-activating," he remains in the paradigm of "regression," a return to childish and infantile mental states.

Ostow frames his central question as: Is spiritual experience connected to something "real," in other words, a "supernatural external influence," or is it "generated only by intrapsychic dynamics" and therefore an illusion? (pp. 8-9) Embedded in the classical psychoanalytic tradition, Ostow is primarily concerned with the distinction between reality and illusion, a concern that inevitably shapes his perspective. Following the drive model, Ostow concludes that the function of spiritual experience is illusory, serving only to gratify the instinctual need for attachment. He views awe, spirituality, and mystical experience as expressions of infantile longings, activated during periods of loneliness or depression. In line with the traditional psychoanalytic understanding of religious experience as illusory, Ostow identifies the dynamics of mysticism as a "disturbance of the ego," a "regressive step backward, to hallucination and full loss of reality testing." (p. 45)

What is unfortunately lost in Ostow's focus and particularly in the use of such terms as "infantile" and "regressive step backward" to describe the mystical experience, is an appreciation of the transformative possibilities of illusion, the potential for enrichment and enlargement throughout the life cycle described so beautifully by Winnicott, Loewald, and others. In his preoccupation with the dichotomy of reality vs. illusion, Ostow places little emphasis on "transformation." Yet it is transformation that is a vital concern of both the Jewish mystical tradition and contemporary psychoanalysis (see Starr, 2008). Drawing upon the contemporary relational approach to psychoanalysis, including the work of Stephen Mitchell and others in the relational tradition, spiritual experience in general and Jewish mysticism in particular can be viewed in an affirmative spirit: not reduced to something infantile, childish, primitive, or pathological, but a transformation of these experiences into something new and something significant.

335

For Freud, who drew his analogies from the natural sciences, change was quantitative, a matter of degree. The ego could be strengthened and its control over the instincts improved, but only partially. "Portions of the old mechanisms remain untouched by the work of analysis" (Freud, 1937, p. 229). Yet long before Freud, transformation was associated with religious experience, with a connotation more qualitative than quantitative. Individuals were said to be transformed by encounters with the divine, emerging with a sense of a reality greater than themselves, a more expansive perspective of life's possibilities, and a sharper perception of their own unique purpose. In the Torah, such transformation is often marked by a change in name: at the moment of entering into relationship with God through His covenant, Abram becomes Abraham and his wife Sarai, Sarah, signifying that the elderly, childless couple will be patriarchs of a great nation.

The night before he is to meet with his estranged and presumably hostile brother Esau, Jacob wrestles with a mysterious figure until dawn. From the narrative, it is never clear whether it is a man, angel, God, or an aspect of Jacob himself; the text is ambiguous and open to interpretation. Jacob's conflict does not leave him unscathed, but it does leave him richer for the experience. Jacob emerges from his encounter with a wound in his thigh and a life-long limp, but also with an expanded perception of himself and his relationship with his brother. He is given the name Israel — "wrestles with God" — to mark the struggle as well as the suffering that is the turning point of his transformation.

Jacob's new name also signifies the manner in which he has changed. When we first meet Jacob, he is characterized as a simple man, a tent-dweller, a man who, at the moment of his birth, grabbed on to the heel of his twin brother Esau, and then in later years proceeded to steal his brother's birthright through deceiving his elderly, blind father. His name, Yaakov in Hebrew, has as its root the word "heel;" the Zohar interprets its meaning as "deceiver." (Matt, 2004, p. 270) Because of his treachery, Jacob lived in fear of being killed by Esau, who was much stronger and more aggressive than he. But on this day, Jacob set out toward Esau, prepared to meet his brother face to face, not knowing what the outcome would be — whether he would live or die. The name Israel signifies an added dimension to Jacob's identity, encompassing a newfound willingness to come to terms with his prior actions, to grapple with their consequences, and to tolerate the unknown of a new way of relating. He is different, somehow larger, than he was before. Interestingly, it is the agent of Jacob's transformation, the mysterious figure who struggles with him, who gives Jacob the name Israel. By naming him, he helps Jacob to grasp the emotional essence of what he has just gone through and to understand that he has been changed by it.

In turn, Jacob puts words to his ineffable experience by giving the scene of his transformation a name. He calls the place Peniel — "I have seen God face to face." By naming it, he acknowledges the revelatory nature of his experience and seeks its affirmation through linking his changed inner reality to the concrete outer reality of place. In psychoanalytic terms, naming is Jacob's way of processing an experience that was most certainly traumatic — painful, but also numinous; putting his experience into words helps him not only to understand it but also to assign it a transformative meaning, enabling him to go forth a changed person. Through his struggle, Jacob has come face to face with God and, in the process, face to face with a heretofore-unexpressed aspect of himself. Or perhaps it is the reverse — through Jacob's knowing himself more deeply, God is revealed.

The Kabbalah identifies a yearning for personal transformation, speaking of the divine spark clothed within a person's soul, veiled from conscious awareness, yet longing to be perceived and enflamed. In psychological terms, the divine spark may be read as the intimation of one's authenticity, which emerges within the intimacy of the analytic relationship. However, the Kabbalah does not limit authenticity to the genuineness of a person in a given interaction, nor does it posit a static core self; rather it formulates the divine spark as the unique and indispensable creative potential of a particular individual and no other. As potential, it can be manifest only when it is brought down to the level of reality — lived-out through a person's actions and relationships in daily living. The divine spark is a singular manifestation of God, capable of being articulated only by the human being in the material world. Hence the living-out of

337

one's authenticity in a life of meaning and purpose has not only personal but cosmic reverberations: it is an aspect of God that can find expression exclusively in the life of that person, and no other.

Quite movingly, the Zohar attributes the motivation for Creation itself to God's longing for recognition by and connection with humanity – the desire to be perceived by His own creation and to enter into relationship with it. In turn, the individual seeks out God in relationship through his striving toward self-understanding, toward perceiving the divine spark clothed within his own soul. Through being sought out and recognized by the human being, God's aspects are brought into balance, facilitating the flow of divine plenty earthward. This interplay of mutual recognition and connection is said to sustain the world, whose existence relies on the reciprocal flow of influence between the human and the divine, the individual and the universal. At-one-ment with the truth of one's being is not a static achievement, but an ephemeral moment that may occur throughout one's lifetime, resulting in ever-deepening levels of awareness. It is conceived as a mutual encounter in which both parties, the human being and God, are transformed.

Contemporary psychoanalytic scholarship has paid increasing attention to humanity's spiritual and aesthetic yearnings, recognizing that the task of transformation involves not only coping with reality, but also transcending familiar modes of being – living in and appreciating the moment, knowing the self deeply, and entering into a new relationship, a truer and more meaningful one, with one's self, with others, and with the universe of which we are a part (Mitchell, 1993). More and more, illusion is linked with imagination and vitality, rather than with the satisfaction of drives and the avoidance of reality, a shift that can be traced to Winnicott's (1967) reconsideration of cultural experience as an extension of transitional phenomena.

Asking the question, "What is life about?" Winnicott concluded that what makes human life human and therefore worth living is not merely instinctual satisfaction, but the richness of experience of the transitional realm. He reframed illusion as a vehicle for attaining emotional maturity, a way to *relate* to reality rather than to defend against it. Through her use of the "transitional object," the child relates her subjective reality to a shared reality that can be objectively perceived by the external world. The capacity for illusion is thus a necessary step toward relationship with others. Artistic creativity and religious feeling are manifestations of transitional experiencing, characterized by the growth-enhancing ability to enter into shared illusions, to relate inner and outer reality. "The potential space between the baby and the mother, between the child and the family, between the individual and society or the world...can be looked upon as sacred to the individual in that it is here that the individual experiences creative living." (p. 372)

Loewald (1978) also roots the experience of the sacred in the *being* of the maternal-infant matrix. He translates Freud's "Wo Es war, soll Ich warden," as "where id was, there shall ego *come into being*," holding that psychic transformation is a matter of the ego's renewal by the dynamic unconscious. What makes human life human is the interplay between the dynamic unconscious and the ego, a reciprocal shaping of different levels of mentation. Irrational forces have the potential to enrich and transform the rational. Loewald uses the term "conscire," knowing together, to describe the intersection of unconscious with conscious knowing, explicitly connecting this form of knowing with mysticism. Inherent to the knowing of the unconscious is a sense of unity and timelessness, rooted in the infant-maternal relationship that exists before the development of ego boundaries, and before the capacity to make distinctions develops. Echoing Heidegger, Loewald terms this state "being." From this unitary state, mental processes differentiate, enabling a complex, mutual relationship between different levels of mentation, and potentiating conscire, the knowing together.

Mitchell (2000), building on and explicating Loewald, suggests that fantasy and reality not be thought of in opposition to each other, but rather as mutually interpenetrating. "There is a sense of enchantment in early experience, and an inevitable disenchantment accompanies the child's growing adaptation to the consensual world of objective reality" (p. 23). For Loewald, and following him, for Mitchell, the objective world of consensual reality is not the only true reality. "Adult reality that has been wholly separated from infantile fantasy is a desiccated, meaningless, passionless world" (p. 24).

Mitchell (2000) highlights the significance of Loewald's theoretical contributions in radically transforming the basic values that guide the psychoanalytic undertaking. Rather than the victory of the rational over the irrational, the goal of the analytic project becomes the ability to move fluidly from one realm of experience to the other. Central to this paradigm shift in psychoanalytic thought is an increasing concern with how meaning is created in the context of human relatedness. Drawing upon Loewald's vision of mind as embedded from the beginning in an interactive field with other minds, and further developing from these interactions, Mitchell proposes a system of mutual influence between the individual and the larger relational matrix, in which each, the microcosm and the macrocosm, the intrapsychic and the interpersonal, shape and transform one another, "on and on in an endless Mobius strip in which internal and external are perpetually regenerating and transforming themselves and each other." (p. 57)

In contrast, for Ostow, the unit of study is the individual. We are self-contained creatures, and our experience of connection with others is illusory. He writes,

> Ultimately, of course, we are alone, confined within our bodies and the limitations of our minds. We entertain and encourage the illusion of "contact" with others. Our communication may include touch, speech, music, exchange of smiles and other facial expressions, exchange of gestures and actions, and exposure to the visible presence and the bodily warmth and scents of others. All of these create the illusion of contact, even union, not being alone. It is the illusion of lovers that their spirits are united; of the religious that they achieve some form of communication with God at some variable remove; of all of us that we are literal members of our community. But in fact, we live within the limits of our skin and our brains. A communication of minds, and metaphorically of hearts and souls, is illusory... (p. 30)

In the Kabbalah, the foreground and background are reversed, and it is our perception of boundary and separation that is illusory, although a necessary pre-requisite for living in the material world of reality. Creation, both cosmic and personal, begins in primal unity and develops outward into complexity, toward the experience of individual identity and separate existence. Although we experience ourselves as separate, we have intimations of being but one aspect of a greater whole; hence our deeply felt longing for connection and (re)union.

The Kabbalah insists that the search for the other, the central motivational force that underlies human relatedness, is a microcosmic reflection of the life force that animates all being and is the basis of all existence. Revelation requires encounter: the one who is revealed needs a recognizing other in order to fully come into being. In locating the divine within the human, and in placing relationship at the heart of the soul's fulfillment, the Kabbalah suggests that the point of meeting between self and other potentiates an experience of a deeper level of reality, of union and deep connection, in which God Himself is revealed.

In Genesis, we are told that Jacob dreams of a ladder, its base rooted solidly on the ground, its top reaching toward the heavens. On it, angels ascend and descend, moving heavenward from earth, and earthward from heaven. While Jacob dreams, God stands beside him. Jacob wakes from his dream and exclaims, "God is in this place, and I didn't realize it!" The Zohar interprets Jacob's ladder as the conduit through which the divine plenty flows, the channel of mutual influence that links the human and the divine, and which relies on relationship to remain open and sustain life. Further, the Zohar identifies Jacob as the personification of this conduit. He represents the human capacity to move between different dimensions of being and levels of awareness. Significantly, God is encountered not in heaven, but on earth, standing right beside Jacob all along, longing to be recognized, and thereby, revealed.

The imagery of Jacob's dream serves as a vivid illustration in spiritual terms of Loewald's psychological vision of "conscire," the "knowing together" of primary and secondary process that has been further developed by contemporary relational theorists. In the relational framework, mind is comprised of a mutual relationship between different levels of mentation. Although primal unity is the original state from which consciousness

341

emerges, it does not disappear, but continues to exist alongside higher modes of organization, serving as a source of renewal and vitality. The capacity for self-reflection is based on the mind's transcendent function, the ability to oscillate between and to bridge these different levels of awareness (Aron, 2000). In both the relational and kabbalistic paradigms, cultivating open channels between foreground and background, union and separateness, imagination and reality, makes the creation of new meaning possible, and potentiates the transformative experience of the sacred.

Referring to awe, spirituality, and mystical experience, Ostow writes, "For reasons that I do not quite understand, accounts of experiences in the three categories considered here are seldom reported in psychotherapy or even in psychoanalysis." He concludes, "Perhaps the truly Spiritual life does not invite psychotherapy." (p. 47) If one takes into account the historical animosity between psychoanalysis and religion in general and psychoanalysts and religious belief in particular, this should come as no surprise. One may argue that in fact, it is the other way around--that because of its traditionally reductive interpretation of religious experience, psychoanalysis has not invited the truly Spiritual into the room. Undoubtedly, the frequency with which this type of experience is reported in psychoanalysis is directly related to the patient's perception of how the analyst is likely to perceive and interpret such experience.

For a richer understanding of transformation, we must not "explain away" spiritual experience in psychoanalytic terms, nor discard psychoanalytic formulations in favor of spiritual metaphors, but rather be willing to play in the possibilities created by opening a dialogue between them. In considering our patients' experience-spiritual or otherwise--it is crucial that we be keenly attentive to the ways in which our own subjectivities, including our relationship to theoretical models (whether they be psychoanalytic or theological or both), shape our understanding of what our patients bring to us, and equally as important, the questions we choose to ask of them, of ourselves, and of our profession as a whole.

On that quiet night in Jerusalem, standing next to the Western Wall, is it best to think of Lew's experience hearing a Heavenly voice as only or predominantly a regressive, re-activation of an infantile experience? Or (while not ignoring its childhood origins) is it also useful to think of it as a significant transformation that allowed him for at least one moment to re-enchant his world and to infuse it, for ever after, with the meaning and passion of the High Priest, the Holiest official, entering the Holiest space at the Holiest moment of time? Do we view this moment best by reducing it to something earlier or do we understand it better by also recognizing it holistically, as making whole, wholesome, and thus holy?

REFERENCES

Aron, L. (2000). Self-reflexivity and the therapeutic action of psychoanalysis. *Psychoanalytic Psychology*, 17: 667-689

-------. (2004). God's influence on my psychoanalytic vision and values. *Psychoanalytic Psychology*, 21: 442-451.

-------. (2007). Freud's ironically Jewish science: Commentary on paper by Jill Salberg. *Psychoanalytic Dialogues*, 17(2): 219-231.

Fenichel, O. (1941). *Problems of Psychoanalytic Technique*. New York: The Psychoanalytic Quarterly.

Freud, S. (1927). The future of an illusion. *Standard Edition*, 21:1-56. London: Hogarth Press, 1961.

-------. (1937). Analysis terminable and interminable. *Standard Edition*, 23: 215-253. London: Hogarth Press, 1964.

Gay, P. (1987). *A Godless Jew*. New Haven, CT: Yale University Press.

Loewald, H. (1978). *Psychoanalysis and the History of the Individual*. New Haven, CT: Yale University Press.

Matt, D. (2004). *The Zohar: Pritzker Edition. Volume II.* Stanford, CA: Stanford University Press.

Mitchell, S. A. (1993). *Hope and Dread in Psychoanalysis*. New York: Basic Books.

-------. (2000). *Relationality*. Hillsdale, NJ: The Analytic Press.

Ostow, M. (2007). *Spirit, Mind, and Brain*. New York: Columbia University Press.

Salberg, J. (2007). Hidden in plain sight: Freud's Jewish identity revisited. *Psychoanalytic Dialogues,* 17(2): 197–217.

Sherwin, B. L. (2006). *Kabbalah.* Lanham, MD: Rowman & Littlefield.

Spezzano, C., & Gargiulo, G. J., eds. (1997). *Soul on the Couch.* Hillsdale, NJ: The Analytic Press.

Starr, K. E. (2008). *Repair of the Soul: Metaphors of Transformation in Jewish Mysticism and Psychoanalysis.* New York: Routledge.

Winnicott, D. W. (1967). The location of cultural experience. *International Journal of Psycho-Analysis,* 48: 368-372.

Wolfson, E. R. (1997). *Through a Speculum that Shines: Vision and Imagination in Medieval Jewish Mysticism.* Princeton, NJ: Princeton University Press.

'Foreignness is the Quality Which the Jews and One's Own Instincts Have in Common':
Anti-Semitism, Identity and the Other *

Stephen Frosh

It is clear from the history of psychoanalysis that its Jewish connections are more than just a historical accident. The conditions under which psychoanalysis arose were strongly marked by shifts in modern identity generally, and Jewish identity specifically, occurring at the end of the nineteenth century in Europe. As well as determining the make-up of the early psychoanalytic movement, the marginalised and ambiguous status of Jewish identity lent psychoanalysis acuity of perception, a sharp, ironic and iconoclastic interpretive facility. Whilst this proved to be an immensely creative legacy, the price of this Jewish heritage was also great. It meant that anti-Semitism was programmed into the new discipline: psychoanalysis always embodied the mixed pride and prejudice of being a 'Jewish science', provoking erratic emotions amongst its adherents and opponents, Jewish and non-Jewish alike (Frosh, 2005). This 'virus', carried by psychoanalysis throughout its early history, burst into activity in Germany when the Nazis came to power, with effects that have been visible ever since.

If psychoanalysis provoked and at times *enacted* anti-Semitism, one might also ask that it should be capable of *understanding* it. After all,

---

* This chapter is based on material in S. Frosh, *Hate and the 'Jewish Science': Anti-Semitism, Nazism and Psychoanalysis* (London: Palgrave, 2005)

anti-Semitism has many of the attributes of the excessive, self-damaging, irrational and yet persistent psychopathological complexes that are the meat and drink of psychoanalysis' clinical and theoretical activity. Few other social phenomena are better set up for psychoanalytic exploration, because the intensity of anti-Semitism, its perseverance over generations, its continued operations even in the absence of Jews and its characteristic failure to be in tune with reality, all have the hallmarks of a phenomenon saturated with unconscious emotion. Add to this the particular relevance of anti-Semitism for understanding psychoanalysis itself and this seems a research seam of such potential richness that it could not be missed. However, whilst there have been creative attempts to theorise anti-Semitism from a psychoanalytic perspective, the work overall has been disappointingly limited, leading one to ask whether there is something in psychoanalysis itself that creates a systematic blind spot in this area.

It is curious to note, given how explicit Freud was about anti-Semitism and how powerfully Nazism impacted upon the psychoanalytic movement, that relatively little has been written about anti-Semitism from a psychoanalytic perspective, and that whilst there was some notable work by European Jewish émigrés after the war, by the 1960s psychoanalytic explorations of anti-Semitism had dried up (Bergman, 1988). Mortimor Ostow (1996a, p.4) comments on this,

> Aside from Freud's many references to antisemitism in a number of papers, psychoanalytic literature was relatively silent about the matter until the Nazi period. When European psychoanalysts reached safety, a few of them undertook an essay, or in a few cases even a book, on the subject. For the most part, these offered explanations based upon the common defence mechanisms of displacement and projection, yielding the scapegoat theory and Oedipal determination. Some spoke of the influence of Christian mythology, especially the charge of deicide and the symbolism of the mass. Others attempted an approach via group psychology.

However, at least until the stirring events of the 1985 Hamburg congress of the International Psychoanalytic Association let various cats out of the bag (Chasseguet-Smirgel, 1987), this work on anti-Semitism was desultory at best and in general failed to develop a set of concepts attuned to the pervasiveness of anti-Semitic phenomena. Indeed, Freud's own work in this area — as in many other areas, one might suggest — remained well ahead of that of his followers, despite advances in historical and cultural theory that meant they had much better explanatory resources upon which to draw. Ostow (1996a) is of the opinion that the early analysts' avoidance of contestation of anti-Semitism alongside their active repudiation of religion represented more than just a statement about scientific priorities.

> With respect to the early generations of analysts, if we consider their general derogation of the Jewish religion and its practitioners; their failure to express an interest in Jewish affairs and Jewish destiny until the confrontation with Nazism made these issues unavoidable; their reductionist and simplistic efforts to 'analyze' Jewish religious ritual and liturgy with which they were barely familiar, while simultaneously taking no psychoanalytic interest in antisemitism with which they were very familiar, we are forced to infer the existence of a degree of Jewish shame and self-hatred. (p. 24)

Such a psychological reading of the early analysts' behaviour is supported by consideration of their cultural context, which provoked them to try to distance themselves from the East European stereotypes of the Jew as part of their own assimilationist strategy for coping with anti-Semitism. Even Freud was not immune from this dynamic (Gilman, 1993); and the psychoanalysts' appeasement policy towards the Nazis during the 1930s might be seen as the extension of an attitude that anti-Semitism would cease if the Jews would only hide. Non-Jewish analysts also bought into this attitude, with Ernest Jones exemplifying the ambivalence surrounding their involvement with the 'Jewish science'. As late as 1951, in his paper, 'On the Psychology of the Jewish Question', Jones could locate a source of anti-Semitism in Jewish separatism and their 'superiority complex', as well as, following Freud (1909), in circumcision and castration anxiety. The most likely solution to anti-Semitism, according to Jones — failing to learn from the recent history of Nazism — was assimilation into the surrounding community.

Freud's (1939) account of anti-Semitism is rather more thorough, focusing on how the Jew represents elements in the anti-Semite's psychic constitution that are uncomfortable or threatening, and are consequently repudiated, yet are also objects of fascination. Because of the history of Christian anti-Semitism, which laid the important mythological groundwork for the pervasiveness of anti-Semitic beliefs in Western culture, the Jew is the chosen carrier of these unwanted yet seductive projections. In addition, there are real attributes of Jews and Judaism (such as circumcision, monotheism, and the idea of the 'chosen people') that fuel this set of compelling myths. In the limited bibliography of psychoanalytic studies of anti-Semitism, this generally Freudian account has continued to hold sway. Characteristic themes in this work include: 'displacement, projection, scapegoating, castration anxiety (as linked to circumcision), latent homosexuality, sibling rivalry, intolerance of small differences, rejection of dark pigmentation because of its association with feces, Jewish disavowal of the murder of the father, Jewish masochism, psychopathy, paranoia, and envy of the Chosen People' (Knafo, 1999, p. 36). These 'themes' have helped to fill out the possible dynamics of the anti-Semitic state of mind, but also reveal something of the limits of psychoanalysis when faced with such a complex, emotive, psychosocial phenomenon.

The relative silence of psychoanalysis on anti-Semitism is especially noticeable in reports on clinical work with anti-Semitic patients, where there are very few studies and where those that have been carried out have been concerned mostly not with cases of strong anti-Semitic belief or activity, but with patients (several of them Jewish) who have expressed some anti-Semitic sentiments in the course of the work. Thus, Ostow (1996a,b) presents a lengthy account of the work of a large group of analysts plus a couple of academic specialists, who spent nine years in regular seminars on anti-Semitism, yet dealt only with ten case histories 'in some depth' and four cases 'less intensively' plus five others who were 'mentioned briefly' (Ostow, 1996a, p. 43). The thinness of their clinical material is thus remarkable given the effort they expended. What they did note was that when anti-Semitic comments occurred, analysts were very reluctant to take them up. Other widely referenced and important studies, such as those deriving from the work of the Institute of Social Research in the 1940s (e.g. Ackerman and Jahoda, 1948; Adorno et al, 1950) similarly used relatively 'mild' instances of anti-Semitism or studied people who were rarely expressive of very strong anti-Semitic sentiments. Even the useful paper by Knafo (1999), set up to redress the silence about anti-Semitism in the clinical setting, is based on only three cases, one of them Jewish and one half-Jewish. Some authors have argued that this does not matter: for example, Loewenstein (1952, p. 38) states that psychoanalysis is so strongly thought of as 'Jewish' that, 'At some point in the course of analysis almost all non-Jewish patients will manifest varying degrees of anti-Semitism,' whether or not the analyst is actually Jewish; that is, *all* analysts are Jewish in the minds of their necessarily anti-Semitic patients. For most 'classical' psychoanalysts, the analyst, representing authority, automatically takes on the attributes of the father; what is added here is the idea that there is a psychic equivalence between the Jew as represented in social discourse – in particular, in Christian-influenced ideology – and the father, so that the working-out of Oedipal conflicts in the transference brings anti-Semitic impulses to the fore. Additionally, as castration fears emerge so the 'superstitious horror' (p.40) produced by the Jew's circumcised state becomes manifest; more generally, anti-Semitic patients experience their own 'inadmissible instinctual drives' (p.39) as placed inside them by the analyst, whose own 'dirty Jewish imagination' is responsible for corrupting their minds. Finally, some anti-Semitic patients show very clearly how sadistic impulses towards the Jews arise:

> Neurotics who suffer from an intense sense of guilt and who live in anticipation of punishment protect themselves by projecting their faults onto the Jewish analyst or onto Jews in general. They would like to see the Jews tortured and punished in order not to feel guilty themselves. To avoid punishment they would like to assume the punitive role themselves. (p. 40)

This is the 'classic' anti-Semitic dynamic linking the transitory manifestations of anti-Semitism that occur during all analyses with the characteristic state of mind of those who are truly and stably anti-Semites.

Knafo (1999) notes the reluctance of most analysts to engage with anti-Semitism and attributes this to a discomfort that has countertransference roots: 'Our personal oversensitivity and defensiveness with regard to this issue, I believe, frequently results in silence or avoidance, which too often is rationalized as analytic neutrality' (pp. 37-8). This is especially true for Jewish analysts, in her view. But if the failure to engage fully with anti-Semitism arises in part or whole from unresolved traumatic responses on the part of analysts, the effect of this failure is to blame the victim, to see the sources of historical and continuing anti-Semitism as lying in the provocations of the Jews themselves. That is, failure adequately to theorise what might be the dynamic origins and phenomenology of anti-Semitic beliefs and actions directs interrogation towards places where it does not belong; it states, 'if we can say nothing of the perpetrators, then we are left only with the psychology of the victims.' Here, in a parallel argument, is a bitter outburst from Kijak (1989, p. 217).

> Over the twenty years during which I have participated in the psychoanalytic world, I have frequently read and heard variations on the theme of the participation of the victims in their own destruction. The causes of this participation may be found, according to these psychoanalysts, in the predominance of Thanatos, in the masochism of the Jews, in unconscious guilt, in submission to castrating parents, in the fact of generating the hatred of their neighbours through their behaviour and habits, in the use of pathological defences to impede the perception of danger, and many other like explanations. All these opinions express a common ignorance of the historical context in which the events occurred and also express the desire to apply theories taken from individual psychopathology to phenomena of such complexity as the Holocaust.

Where an honest attempt to articulate the murderous form of anti-Semitism embodied in Nazism failed, recourse to blaming the victim followed.

Projection and the Foreigner Within

Freud's analysis of anti-Semitism as arising out of Christianity's sibling rivalry and displaced guilt for parricide is a theme taken up strongly in the post-Freudian literature. For some earlier writers, there is a direct relationship between the emotional ambiguities of Christianity itself and the construction of an anti-Semitic vessel to 'hold' these antagonisms in place. Simmel (1946), for instance, proposes that deicidal wishes are provoked and expressed by the Christian ceremony of eating the holy wafer (devouring the Lamb of God), but such wishes are untenable, and hence are projected outwards. The projection finds as its historically-constructed target the Jew, to whom this murderous inclination becomes attributed. Thus, anti-Semitism arises from the guilt feelings of Christians due to their own ambivalence.

This idea that the Jews as a separate and historically denigrated 'out-group' serve as suitable cultural recipients for the split-off, unacceptable elements of the anti-Semite's psyche is a pervasive one in psychoanalytic theorising on the subject. Under some circumstances, such as personal or social trauma, those impulses that are most disturbing to the individual are experienced as powerful enough to threaten the person's stability, leading to impending fragmentation and breakdown. Preserving the psyche becomes urgent, a matter of life and death, and extreme measures are often taken to accomplish it, including projecting the unwanted impulses into some form of outside carrier. This process constructs a useful enemy out of what is available in the outside world; in the case of anti-Semitism, the Jew is thus made into the carrier of what is hated and threatening to the integrity of the anti-Semite's psychic life.

What, however, might be the exact contents of these destructive urges and the mechanisms for managing them through anti-Semitism? For some writers, taking their lead from Freud, the key issue is the threat posed by castration, the sense that what is most precious is also most at risk. Glenn (1960), for instance, arising from a study of two patients (the generation of grand theories from small numbers being a characteristic of psychoanalysis), argues that 'the anti-Semite may harbour contradictory attitudes towards Jews. Because the Jew is circumcised, he is held to be castrated and effeminate. For the same reason, he is feared and envied as being virile, aggressive and castrative' (p. 398). Building on some proposals from Fenichel (1946, p. 27), who suggests that circumcision gives the anti-Semite the idea that the Jews might seek sexual retaliation against non-

Jews, Glenn argues that the male Jew is seen as feminine and deficient, but that this also arouses the idea that the Jew is threatening and seeking revenge, making him potentially aggressive and virile, and thus a source of envy. Thus it is sexual anxiety that is at the core of the anti-Semite's discomfort; and the Jew, because of circumcision/castration, is the vessel into which this anxiety is poured.

Fenichel (1946), in one of the last papers he wrote, offers a powerful account of both the social and personal dynamic of anti-Semitic feeling. Fenichel takes the common psychoanalytic position that anti-Semitism arises in periods of social stress: the anti-Semite, immersed in confusion and led astray by ideological forces, 'sees in the Jew everything which brings him misery — not only his social oppressor but also his own unconscious instincts, which have gained a bloody, dirty, dreadful character from their socially induced repression' (p. 29). Why the Jew? Because 'with his unintelligible language and incomprehensible God' the Jew appears 'uncanny' to the non-Jew, yet recognisable in continuing to hold to 'archaic' customs that were once part of the non-Jew's repertoire: 'rejected instincts and rejected ancient times are revived for them in these incomprehensible people who live as strangers in their midst' (p. 22). Jews are the ideal object for projection of disturbing unconscious urges 'because of the actual peculiarities of Jewish life, the strangeness of their mental culture, their bodily (black) and religious (God of the oppressed peoples) peculiarities, and their old customs' (ibid.), which remind the anti-Semite of 'old primeval powers' which non-Jews have given up (p. 18). Linked to this is a more profound identification between the Jew as foreign and uncanny, and the site of foreignness within: 'It can be expressed in one sentence: one's own unconscious is also foreign. Foreignness is the quality which the Jews and one's own instincts have in common' (p. 20). Jews as foreigners and preservers of archaic customs can be the recipients of projection of what is feared and hated within oneself, the 'foreign' unconscious; they thus carry the sense of destruction and desire, of 'what is murderous, dirty and debauched' (p. 19), and racist hate is magnified by the anti-Semite's terror of these inner urges. The disturbing awareness of the existence of something strange inside one's own self is made tolerable by projecting that strangeness into the outsider, the desired and despised other.

A more systematic account of the splitting processes endemic to anti-Semitism is provided in a powerful and now classic paper by Wangh (1964), focused on the Holocaust. Wangh proposes that the degree of anti-Semitism expressed by an individual will depend both on her or his own characteristics and on aspects of the social situation, such as the possibility of sharing these ideas with others and the power of the external situation. In the case of the followers of Nazism, he suggests that they 'were young men affected by the [historical] events of their childhood and early adolescence in such a way as to promote a fixation on sado-masochistic fantasies and on specific defences directed against them; and that under the renewed external crisis regression to this fixation level occurred' (p. 391). These young men saw their fathers go to war and come back defeated, and then saw these same fathers as unable to protect them against the ravages of the economic depression of the early nineteen-twenties, with the concomitant impact on mothers who would be in a state of long-term heightened anxiety. Under such conditions, the mother's anxiety and the father's weakness produces an internal state of boundary loss and fragile identity, which is kept at bay only by increasingly strong defensive operations, specifically splitting and projection. It also made these youngsters (specifically young *men*, it would appear from the article), prone to regression and sado-masochism, so when the renewed troubles of the nineteen-thirties arose, and with it the Nazi promise of safety and revenge in the mass, the response was immediate and powerful.

> The external calamity of the thirties rekindled the anxiety of the war and post-war years and at the same time reawakened the magic, illogical, sadistic defensive methods of childhood. The former wartime enemy, while denounced, was, in fact, for the time being unassailable. Instead, the stranger within, the Jew, was substituted for him and all aggressive methods against fear could be applied to him with impunity. (p. 394)

The notion of the 'stranger within' has particular resonance here, acting on both the social and the psychological level. The Jew is the culturally given 'stranger' within European society and hence readily available as

353

the recipient of projections and sadistic impulses; the Jew also represents the unconscious, the 'strangeness' within the psyche, with its femininity and fluidity that is such a threat to the insecure fascist, the one who cannot face the breakdown of boundaries that such fluidity entails.

The Narcissistic Universe

The emphasis on splitting and projection in this material has linked anti-Semitism with psychosis or at least borderline phenomena — the 'borderline' here referring to a kind of half-world in which the self is shadowy and somehow incomplete, requiring for its survival manipulation and externalisation to a degree that verges on the psychotic. The Jew is selected as the object for projection because of the specific cultural history of anti-Semitism; the Jew's function in this is to hold onto these projections and act as the collecting point for paranoid fantasies. The closest one can get to a formal psychoanalytic theory here is to suggest that paranoid-schizoid mechanisms are at work, and that the specific failure of the anti-Semite's consciousness is the failure to come to grips with ambivalence and consequently to be able to integrate the psyche, including its destructive aspects.

There is another element that can be introduced here to sharpen the account. Once again, this builds on an argument of Freud's, here that what Judaism represents is an affiliation to the father. One suggestion from various authors is that Christianity represents a repudiation of the father, a return to a more 'maternal' mode of comforting and service. Anti-Semitism, therefore, is driven in part by repugnance at Judaism's constant reminder that the father has been Oedipally displaced, with the attendant guilt that act promotes. That is, anti-Semitism is seen by some authors as a reflection of hatred for the father, represented by the Jew, and a regressive urge to disavow Oedipal reality with its injunction to deal with difference and instead take refuge in a state of primordial oneness with the mother, in which no outside otherness needs to be faced.

Narcissism, repudiation of the father and anti-Semitism are drawn together most powerfully in the work of Béla Grunberger, especially in his 1964 article, 'The Anti-Semite and the Oedipal Conflict'. Grunberger's account is based on two linked propositions. The first is that anti-Semitism is characterised by regression to preoedipal levels of functioning, and hence is associated with a wish for a narcissistic solution to the problems of reality, in which everything will be 'at one' with the self and no challenging differences will exist. Oral and anal — that is, regressive and preoedipal — components dominate the mind and are revealed vividly in the accusations that the anti-Semite produces against the Jews. Thus, for example, oral aggression is witnessed in the accusation of the blood libel, effectively the claim that Jews drink the blood of Christians; Grunberger also notes, 'the time-worn accusation which turns up in different guises, but always has the same significance: "The Jews have poisoned the wells"' (p. 381). Anal fantasies are most evident in the association of the Jew with the devil: 'As we know, the devil represents anal components which are endowed with guilt and whose home is the lower regions of the body... The anti-Semite prides himself on his ability to smell a Jew a hundred miles away' (ibid.). All the fantasies of dirt, disgust, poison and weakness with which the anti-Semite is afflicted are put into the Jew. This ensures that the narcissistic ego is protected from the damage that could be caused it by having to acknowledge and resolve internal contradictions, especially 'unacceptable' desires.

> The anti-Semite's profound satisfaction flows from the fact that his ego is in perfect harmony with his ego-ideal. Having made his projection onto the Jew, he has found his Manichaean paradise: all that is bad is thereafter on one side — the side of the Jew — and all that is good on the other side where he himself is. (p. 382)

Once again, the Jew is the principle of evil in this split psychic world, the Jew is to blame for all the badness the anti-Semite feels welling up inside.

Grunberger's second theme is based on Freud's proposal that Jewish monotheism was a move away from the more sensual and material 'mothering' kind of religion towards a more austere, distanced and rule-bound set of beliefs and practices that represented the Oedipal and super-egoic mode of functioning: restrictive, prohibitive, moralistic.

Christianity is a partial rebellion against the harshness of this situation, a return to a more mother-centred religious structure, albeit with some element of distance as the aspect of the mother as virgin shows. For the narcissist, however, the Judaic reminder that the father exists, that there are prohibitions and restrictions laid upon the extent to which one can have what one wants, is an irritant or even, at the extreme, an unbearable assault. More broadly, Grunberger's argument is that anti-Semitism is a characteristic expression of narcissism in a certain kind of social world, which happens to be the social world of the West over hundreds of years. Narcissists cannot tolerate difference and otherness, yet this is precisely what constitutes reality, which asserts the impossibility of the wish for oneness with the mother, of a place in which there will be no contradiction and no restriction on pleasure, in which no-one will say 'no'. Because the narcissistic wish for omnipotence is so strong, scapegoats are needed to hold the projected otherness, to be to blame for the inevitable entry of contradiction into the system. 'And,' writes Grunberger (1989, p. 87), 'because it was the Father, with his laws, prohibitions and reminders about reality, who drove them out of the paradise in which they merged with the Mother, *they attack the first herald of that strict authority, namely the Jew.* No matter who committed the offence, it is the Jew who is held responsible.' This is the legacy of thousands of years of hostility. What is hated is the paternal order itself; all narcissists, whether non-Jewish or Jewish, hate this, and for all of them the Jew is the cultural category that is available to carry the hate — hence the phenomenon of Jewish anti-Semitism, to which Grunberger, in common with many psychoanalysts, pays perhaps undue attention. Anti-Semitism is a social phenomenon only in the sense that it is the social expression of a pervasive psychological structure: an inability to deal with reality accompanied by a wish to 'return' to the fantasised state in which nothing disruptive or restrictive impinged on the mind.

The Social Other

Most psychoanalytic theories thus follow Freud in arguing that the roots of Western anti-Semitism lie at least in part in Christianity, and that this has at its source hatred of the restrictive nature of monotheism, which is identified with the father. Rebelling against the father's constraints, Christianity was marked by repudiation of guilt and revulsion towards the Jews, who were experienced psychically as carrying the message of the father forwards, when what was wished for was to escape his wrath. Building on this, Judaism and the Jews became Christianity's scapegoat, and a powerful cultural category was constructed that continues into the (mainly) post-Christian world as a useful repository for hatred, narcissistic rage, and unmanageable negativity. There is general agreement amongst these theorists that anti-Semitism is not a specific psychopathology, but rather the culturally amenable expression of various troubled psychological states, with projective mechanisms characteristic of preoedipal functioning being the dominant defences. Psychotic and borderline type functioning is proposed, and some powerful work rests on the idea that anti-Semitism can be understood as a socially valorised expression of regressive narcissism, with the Jew standing in both for the father and for difference or otherness in general. Hatred of the Jew is hatred of otherness, of anything that threatens to disrupt the hard-fought-for unity of the psyche; the other, the stranger, the outsider all introduce difference and potential conflict, all remind the anti-Semite of uncontrollable elements in the unconscious, and all, therefore, are to be opposed.

Much of what has been described here seems phenomenologically correct, in that it portrays a set of experiences and attitudes that are recognisable in anti-Semites, and psychodynamically interesting in postulating possible unconscious mechanisms. It is also mostly respectful of the social component of anti-Semitism, in that it allows that anti-Semitism is historically produced by a specific culture that has just happened to be dominant, and as such is a *contingent* phenomenon. That is, anti-Semitism is not 'hard-wired' into the psyche, but rather is the culturally available vehicle for the expression of certain psychic conflicts that are themselves more likely to occur under some social circumstances (such as those which prevailed in Germany after the First World War) than others. This partially protects psychoanalysis from the criticism of psychological reductionism (i.e. the tendency to treat social phenomena as if they were purely

357

psychological), although it is still the case that, as one would expect, the psychoanalytic emphasis is on the psychodynamics of anti-Semitism at the individual level rather than in relation to its social causes. This is in important respects simply a statement of what psychoanalysis does: it is an approach to psychology, not sociology (despite its historical application to social phenomena), so it legitimately asks questions about what anti-Semitism 'means' at the psychological level, and how it takes hold of individuals.

There are a number of strands of thought here, however, which need to be disentangled. Psychologising explanations of systemically social phenomena such as anti-Semitism need to be placed within a context in which, at the very least, there is acknowledgement of the power of the social; the 'blaming the victim' school of (avoidance of) thought fails to do this, but many psychoanalysts have been scrupulous in setting their attempts to theorise anti-Semitism in its broader context. Simmel (1946, p. xx), for example, introducing the volume of essays that arose out of a symposium on anti-Semitism commissioned by the San Francisco Psychoanalytic Society in the aftermath of the Second World War, asserts that 'It is only through psychoanalysis that we can hope to shed some light on [the anti-Semite's] obscure entanglement of irrational hatred and neurotic misery,' but then goes on immediately to make this subordinate to social forces.

> However, anti-Semitism cannot be understood merely through an understanding of the anti-Semitic individual. It is his problem, to be sure, but beyond this it is a social problem involving political groups, classes and nations.

The general agreement amongst psychoanalytic investigators is that anti-Semitism is the expression of a more generic type of pathological prejudice, taking the specific form it does because of the way in which anti-Jewish stereotypes and beliefs are endemic in western society. Psychoanalysis, because it is a method of investigating the minds of *individuals* is appropriately limited in its contribution to what Fenichel (1946, p. 11), writing in the same volume as Simmel, calls 'the psychoanalysis of the anti-Semite, not of anti-Semitism'. As he phrases it, 'The question is what can the comparison of psychoanalyses of many anti-Semites contribute to an understanding of the social phenomenon of anti-Semitism?' Fenichel has a clear account of what it *cannot* do: 'After a study of the influences determining the structure of the anti-Semitic personality and of how this structure functions, the questions of the genesis of these influences and of the social function of the anti-Semitic reaction still remain unanswered' (p.12). In essence, the restricted claim of these politically highly sophisticated analysts is that psychoanalysis can offer accounts of the internal dynamics of the anti-Semitic individual — a crucial component of any complete theory — but that anti-Semitism itself, as a social phenomenon, requires explanation at a different level. For Fenichel, drawing on his background in Marxist theory, this is a primarily economic level of explanation: given a situation of social disorder, the misery experienced by people is matched by a lack of clarity as to the causes of this misery, 'partly because the underlying causes are too complicated, and partly because the existing ruling class does everything in its power to obscure the true causes' (p.15). Under these circumstances, the victim of this social disorder seeks 'someone in the environment' who can feasibly be seen as the cause of the misery. 'For centuries,' writes Fenichel (ibid.), 'it has been the Jew, in his role as money lender and as tradesman, who has appeared to those confronted with financial need as the representative of money, regardless of how much Jewish poverty there prevailed at the same time.'

Ackerman and Jahoda (1948, pp. 243-4) express a similar idea about the relationship between individual pathology and social hatred as follows.

> The common denominator underlying an anti-Semitic reaction in our cases is, thus, not a similarity of psychiatric symptoms, or total character structure, but rather the common presence of certain specific emotional dispositions. These trends are not in themselves specific for the production of anti-Semitism. They may as well be the dynamic basis for other irrational group hostilities. Undoubtedly, they can exist without anti-Semitism. But in the culture in which our patients live, anti-Semitism does not develop without these character trends. They represent, therefore, an emotional

predisposition, a necessary though not sufficient cause of anti-Semitism. In a different culture these character traits may be released in some other hostility reaction.

Thus, the 'emotional predisposition' for irrational group hostilities is laid down through particular developmental experiences and becomes part of the character structure of the individual; their expression as anti-Semitism is due to the 'culture'; a different culture would produce different types of 'hostility reaction'. Ostow's (1996b, p. 15) view is similar, albeit couched in a more extended historical analysis; he too places weight on the social ('stereotypical myths') as overriding what he terms 'individual dynamics'.

After the definitive secession of early Jewish and Gentile Christ followers from the Jewish community at the end of the first century Common Era, the Jews were stigmatised and demonised by them and by the early Church fathers and labelled as a principle of evil, along with Satan, that was to blame for all Christian misfortune. The many antisemitic myths that evolved throughout the history of the Christian West all concurred in this theme. Apocalyptic thinking required such a principle as the source of the death phase, so that the elimination of Jews became the condition for the rebirth phase. In the presence of a sense of disorganisation and chaos, societies congeal into fundamentalist groups that require a mythic enemy. These groups tend to cultivate apocalyptic paranoia. Under those circumstances, anti-Jewish sentiment and discrimination become active persecution.

What is particularly interesting about this analysis is that anti-Semitism is viewed as the product of many centuries of Christian myth-making, interpreted according to psychodynamic principles. Ostow holds that Christianity needed an enemy in order to create its own mythology of death-and-rebirth, and the Jews were selected as such because of the fact that Christianity had begun as a 'secession' from Judaism and thus benefited from heaping abuse on its progenitor. The explanatory structure here reads cultures much as it reads individuals: just as the psychic equilibrium of a person might be maintained by the 'myth-making' propensity to project hostile urges into an outside other, so Christian culture as a whole maintained its own organisation by the construction of Jews as the despised other. When external pressures are particularly hard, individuals project more strongly and with more extreme content to their projections; the same is true of cultures: 'In the presence of a sense of disorganisation and chaos, societies congeal into fundamentalist groups that require a mythic enemy' and persecution follows.

Despite the emotional power of this kind of historical conjecture, one has to ask whether it really solves the problem of welding together social and psychoanalytic perceptions. It seems rather to reduce the social to the individual, treating an entire (and very complex) culture as if it has the kinds of feelings and disturbances that can be observed in analytic patients. Nevertheless, Ostow's account is interesting in its implication that the 'stereotypical myths' promoted by the culture may be best viewed not as empty vessels into which individual psychopathology is channelled (the disturbed person becomes anti-Semitic because culture makes available that route for expression of the disturbance), but rather as forces that construct forms of consciousness, that is, that make subjects in their image. Put more simply, the social inheritance of anti-Semitism is so powerful that it serves as one of the building blocks upon which western subjectivity is built. This is the case despite Christianity's relative loss of power in the past two hundred years: as many scholars have shown (e.g. Gilman, 1991), the Christian heritage of anti-Semitism has been passed down very firmly through biological, racial and social theories to retain considerable hold amongst those in the west, even if the traditional imagery of what Ostow terms the 'principle of evil' is no longer as widespread as it was. This kind of heritage is not just a channel for expression of emotional disturbance, though it can be useful as such; it is, rather, a way in which the unconscious dynamics of each person's psyche are marked. Jews and non-Jews of all kinds have a connection to anti-Semitism, are 'positioned' in relation to it, and its expression in an individual therefore needs to be understood as a manifestation of a social force. There is no magic here, nor does it require an appeal to a Jungian 'collective unconscious'; rather, anti-Semitism is so embedded in the culture that it can be understood as one of the taken-for-granted kernels of meaning out of which each western subject is constructed. Žižek (1997, p. 76) comments, 'The (anti-Semitic figure of the) "Jew" is not the positive cause of social imbalance and antagonisms: social antagonism comes first, and the "Jew" merely gives body to this obstacle.' Culture's investment in this figure of the Jew produces it as an element in the unconscious, and with it arises the widespread nature of anti-Semitism itself.

This leads to another way of looking at things. An assumption running through most of the theories dealt with here is that the machinations of the individual psyche produce certain problems (for example, an inability to manage ambivalence, narcissistic regressive fantasies) that are 'solved' through the use of categories (the 'Jew') that are available from within the culture. However, perhaps this is not strong enough in terms of its theorisation of the social. For one thing, it reflects a set of ambiguities to be found within psychoanalysis itself, centring especially on a lack of clarity about the gendered elements in anti-Semitic thinking. For the majority of psychoanalytic theorists, the Jew represents the father and is hated by the anti-Semite because of this, either as a residue of unresolved Oedipal conflicts or as an expression of revulsion against the Oedipal order in total. Yet in much anti-Semitic imagery, the Jew is seen not as masculine but as *feminine*, and this is an aspect of the representation of the Jew that, it is plausibly argued, had a powerful impact on the construction of psychoanalysis itself. It may in fact be the case, as Boyarin (1997) hypothesises, that Freud's representation of Judaism in *Moses and Monotheism* as a religion of the father — and hence superior to Christianity because more abstract and intellectual and therefore more culturally 'advanced' — was not just a way of theorising anti-Semitism, but was also a reflection of his own *internalised* anti-Semitism. That is, in distancing himself from the 'feminine' components of Judaism and Jewish culture — for example, its representation of ideal masculinity as scholarly and meek (like Freud's actual father) rather than soldierly and physically strong (like Hannibal) — Freud might himself have been embracing the anti-Semitic discourse that disparages such 'effeminacy'. The psychoanalytic theorists following in Freud's wake have not redressed the balance here with a more sophisticated understanding of the gender complexities of Jewish culture, which has indeed both 'paternal/masculine' and 'maternal/feminine' components. Instead, with their own rather unquestioning acceptance of the idea that Judaism is a quintessentially paternal religion, they can be seen to have reproduced a certain kind of anti-Semitic and misogynistic ideology: the feminine (traditionally associated with Jews) is bad; the masculine, good; therefore, to reclaim the Jews from the place in which Western culture has placed them, only the 'masculine' elements of Judaism will be stressed. The transparent gender stereotyping of several post-Freudian theories, in which 'regressive' narcissism is associated with the mother and opposed to the Oedipal/paternal capacity to face reality, shows even more explicitly how the failure of psychoanalysis to explore its own ideological and political investments can result in theories that obscure as much as they explain.

The widespread psychoanalytic assumption that the primary function of the social world is to offer beliefs and practices that can serve as carriers or containers for split-off individual projections is also problematic, notwithstanding the care with which some theorists have argued for the significance of anti-Semitism as a social phenomenon. An alternative framework of at least equal viability is one in which, rather than running parallel to the individual, culture is understood to *construct* subjectivity: that is, one might argue that anti-Semitism, and racism in general, is a key category in the making of the Western citizen. Everyone, whether Jew or non-Jew, has to deal with anti-Semitism if they are to deal with society at all, and in so doing they take up 'positions' in relation to anti-Semitism that enfold psychic processes within them. Put more strongly, one might suggest that the contradictions in society are not simply accompaniments of, or accidental parallels to, the contradictions of the unconscious; they actively *produce* them, through all the micro — and macro-social processes (parental interactions and anxieties; socialisation practices; familial beliefs; gendered and 'racialised' institutional practices, etc.) out of which each person is made. In all this, the figure of the Jew is a particularly powerful instance of the figure of the 'other' in general. Through its historically-derived cultural pervasiveness it is perpetuated as a representation of that which is needed yet despised, that which holds in place the otherwise potentially intolerable destructiveness of a social system founded on inequality and alienation. Such systems *create* their own psychic structures and psychological disturbances; thus, given the organisation of Western society, anti-Semitism is as much an element in the unconscious of every subject as is any other psychosocial state — love, loneliness or loss, for example. The Jew, and more generally the figure of the 'other', is a constitutive feature of Western consciousness, an element out of which subjectivity is made.

The key psychoanalytic issue here, then, is the relationship between the other of society and the other of the unconscious. Whilst there are several forms that exclusionary othering takes, including vicious modes of anti-Black and other colour racism, anti-Semitism has been and remains a potent signifier of the underside of Western culture. The Jew is a *principle* of otherness for the West, articulating (through contrast) what is safe and unitary by embodying difference. The two-thousand year history of Christian anti-Semitism has created a figure that is more than a symbol of the splits in Western society; the Jew is rather a kernel of otherness, that which is always found everywhere, yet is never to be allowed in. Inchoate fantasies of purity opposed by Jewish corruption, of secret societies and conspiracies, of trickery and poison ('poisoning the wells', as Grunberger (1964) remarks) show that the Jew is a materialisation of that otherness which is most feared and least understood. 'In' the unconscious, this means that otherness itself has a 'Jewish' feel to it; the hidden recesses of sex and aggression are easily identified with anti-Semitic paradigms. It is not, then, that the Jew is just a convenient scapegoat upon whom these inner urges can be projected; it is rather that just as psychoanalysis is 'Jewish' in important ways, so is the unconscious that it has discovered and invented.

If this is an extreme formulation, then this is because what has to be thought about is an extreme phenomenon: the recurrent, never-ending, barely even cyclical reiteration of anti-Semitic ideology and practices. Freud offered some ways into understanding this, although these were undermined by his own cultural ambivalence about Jews and his powerfully motivated wish to sublimate the Jewish stereotype. Post-Freudian analysts have supplied only limited additional insights, though they have shown how anti-Semitism works to preserve psychic integrity in many people, and they have also offered some plausible accounts of what allows mass anti-Semitic movements to take hold. As psychoanalysis has often shown, however, in dealing with real irrational material, it is often necessary to push things to the limit, to embrace 'excessive' thoughts in order to counter 'excessive' emotional intensity. So despite it being easily shown that otherness in the West has many components — misogyny, for one crucial example, colonialist thought for another — I want to finish with the bald statement that anti-Semitism is precisely such a modality of excess, legitimised, institutionalised and naturalised over centuries and now deeply internalised in a coding of the Jew as both enticing and dangerous, both alluring and disgusting. This is not just a parallel phenomenon to how people feel about their unconscious desires — alluring and disgusting too; it is *the same thing*. The unconscious is the materialisation of otherness, and in a society historically constructed on the basis of the Jew as other, then social otherness and psychological otherness entwine, feeding off each other and carrying anti-Semitism with them wherever they may go.

REFERENCES

Ackerman, N. & Jahoda, M. (1948). The Dynamic Basis of Anti-Semitic Attitudes. *The Psychoanalytic Quarterly, 17*: 240-260.

Adorno, T., Frenkel-Brunswick, E., Levinson, D. & Sanford, R. (1950). *The Authoritarian Personality.* NY: Norton.

Bergman, W. (1988). Approaches to Antisemitism Based on Psychodynamics and Personality Theory. In: *Error Without Trial: Psychological Research on Antisemitism,* ed. W. Bergman. Berlin and New York: Walter de Gruyter, pp.9-20.

Boyarin, D. (1997). *Unheroic Conduct.* Berkeley: University of California Press.

Chasseguet-Smirgel, J. (1987).'Time's White Hair We Ruffle': Reflections on the Hamburg Congress. *International Review of Psycho-Analysis, 14*: 433-444.

Fenichel, O. (1946). Elements of a Psychoanalytic Theory of Anti-Semitism. In: *Anti-Semitism: A Social Disease,* ed. E. Simmel. NY: International Universities Press, pp.11-32.

Freud, S. (1909), *Analysis of a Phobia in a Five-Year-Old Boy.* London: Hogarth (SE10, 1-145, 1955).

-------. (1939). *Moses and Monotheism.* London: Hogarth Press (SE23, 1-137, 1964).

Frosh, S. (2005). *Hate and the Jewish Science: Anti-Semitism, Nazism and Psychoanalysis.* London: Palgrave.

Gilman, S. (1991). Reading Freud in English: Problems, Paradoxes, and a Solution. *International Review of Psycho-Analysis 18*: 331-344.

-------. (1993). *Freud, Race and Gender.* Princeton: Princeton University Press.

Glenn, J. (1960). Circumcision and Anti-Semitism *Psychoanalytic Quarterly, 29*: 395-399.

Grunberger, B. (1964). The Anti-Semite and the Oedipal Conflict. *International Journal of Psycho-Analysis 45*: 380-385.

-------. (1989). *New Essays on Narcissism.* London: Free Association Books.

Jones, E. (1951). *Essays in Applied Psycho-Analysis.* London: Hogarth Press.

Kijak, M. (1989). Further Discussions of Reactions of Psychoanalysts to the Nazi Persecution, and Lessons to be Learnt. *International Review of Psycho-Analysis, 16*: 213-222.

Knafo, D. (1999). Anti-Semitism in the Clinical Setting. *Journal of the American Psychoanalytical Association*, 47: 35-63.

Loewenstein R. (1952). Anti-Semites in Psychoanalysis. *Error Without Trial: Psychological Research on Antisemitism*, ed. W. Bergman (1988). Berlin & New York: Walter de Gruyter, pp. 37-51.

Ostow, M. (1996a). *Myth and Madness: The Psychodynamics of Antisemitism.* New Brunswick: Transaction.

-------. (1996b), Myth and Madness: A Report of a Psychoanalytic Study of Antisemitism. *International Journal of Psycho-Analysis, 77*: 15-31

Simmel, E. (1946). *Anti-Semitism: A Social Disease.* NY: International Universities Press.

Wangh, M. (1964). National Socialism and the Genocide of the Jews — A Psychoanalytic Study of a Historical Event. *International Journal of Psycho-Analysis,* 45: 386-395.

Žižek, S. (1997). *The Plague of Fantasies* London: Verso.

A Burning World, An Absent God: Midrash, Hermeneutics, and Relational Psychoanalysis[1]

Philip Cushman

> "The distance that separates the text from the reader is the space in which the very evolution of the spirit is lodged"
>
> *Ira Stone*

Following the terrorist attack on 9/11, a pervasive suspicion and unresolved grief has undermined the capacity of the United States to tolerate ambiguity, subtlety, and uncertainty. In religion, in particular, one sees a flight from the awareness of uncertainty, limitation, absence, and vulnerability into forms of mantic and mystical experiences linked to

---

[1] An earlier and more detailed version of this chapter was published in *Contemporary Psychoanalysis*, 2007 along with a commentary by Lewis Aron and a reply by Philip Cushman. Our appreciation to *Contemporary Psychoanalysis* for permission to reprint.

The interested reader is referred back to the journal for the full exchange. References are as follows:

Philip Cushman (2007), "A Burning World, An Absent God: Midrash, Hermeneutics, and Relational Psychoanalysis." *Contemporary Psychoanalysis*, 43: 47-88.

Lewis Aron (2007), "Black Fire On White Fire, Resting On The Knee Of The Holy And Blessed One." Discussion Of Philip Cushman's "A Burning World, An Absent God: Midrash, Hermeneutics, And Relational Psychoanalysis." *Contemporary Psychoanalysis*, 43: 89-111.

Philip Cushman, Ph.D. (2007), Response to Lewis Aron. *Contemporary Psychoanalysis*, 43: 113-120.

visions of presence and apocalypse. In other words, fundamentalisms of all sorts seem to be on the rise.

In this paper I describe and discuss *midrash*, a Jewish interpretive practice of Biblical commentary that originated in late antiquity. I argue that midrash 1) is a good example of an ontological hermeneutic tradition; 2) has characteristics in common with contemporary forms of relational psychoanalysis; and 3) embodies understandings, processes, and commitments antithetical to fundamentalist beliefs and practices.

Fundamentalist thinking, whether in the realm of religion, politics, or psychotherapy, usually clusters around several qualities (see e.g., Ali, 2002; Altemeyer, 1988; Ammerman, 1991; Barr, 1977; Carpenter, 1997; Edel, 1987; Marty & Appleby, 1993; Reichley, 1987; Strozier, 1994). Some of these qualities are:

1) a binary conception of reality;
2) authoritarian, literalist, hyper-concrete patterns of belief;
3) a sense of a divinely ordained, universal, immediate mission;
4) an intolerance of dissent.

This pattern culminates in a belief that the one, simple, unambiguous truth has been revealed, that it applies to all humans for all time, and that it emanates from a superhuman source whose will is made known and triumphant (either through direct communication with humans or direct intervention in human events). Fundamentalists have no need for human interpretation: the truth is perfect and complete in itself, needing no clarification or emendation. For them, interpretation will always, necessarily, be the enemy.

Hermeneutics As Political Resistance

To my mind the most philosophically sound opposition to fundamentalism is ontological hermeneutics, a branch of what some have referred to as the interpretive turn (see e. g., Hiley, Bohman, & Shusterman, 1991). Hermeneutics features ideas such as the belief that

a. Human being is historical and perspectival;

b. Historical traditions are "inescapably" moral traditions that are embodied by individuals and are thus constituted by them;

c. Therefore human action, explicitly or implicitly, revolves around trying to determine and then act in accordance with the good;

d. However, human perception is problematic, and therefore the most central and primordial human activity is interpretation;

e. Interpretation is inevitably and inextricably entangled with history, language, culture, and power;

f. Humans not only interpret actions and speech but also texts;

g. Texts can embody truths;

h. There can be more than one truth in a text;

i. To explore the truths in a text one must actively engage with the text;

j. To actively engage with and interpret the text one must turn to other texts, and contextualize those texts;

k. The concept of "dialogue" is thought to be an interpersonal process through which two or more persons recognize their differences, develop the capacity to place their own opinions and moral understandings into question by contextualizing them, comparing them to the understandings of others, seeing the limitations of their own beliefs, and then modifying or changing them accordingly.

Hermeneuticists value historical vision, engaged process, intellectual honesty and self-reflection. But they don't furnish a ready-made, detailed moral code that can be used to resist the coercions and seductions of one's time and place. Instead, they recognize the constitutive power of historical traditions, and by implication encourage us to plumb the depths of the traditions into which we have been thrown at birth — respecting, exploring, questioning, historically situating, critiquing, and modifying them. Each of us lives at a point of intersecting traditions, and hermeneuticists suggest that it is our job as humans to sift through those traditions and choose ways of living that fit with our best, evolving understandings of the good. Hermeneutics can best be understood as a challenge to the political arrangements and overall sociocultural framework of the early 21st century — it is a kind of political resistance.

Midrash

Midrash is a type of Jewish storytelling (see e.g., Holtz, 1984; D. Stern, 1991). Midrashim (plural) are found in three types of rabbinic literary collection: legal, homiletical, and exegetical. They were developed first in oral traditions in the centuries surrounding the beginning of the Common Era and then slowly compiled and committed to writing in stages. The first major collection and redaction of post-biblical Jewish law, the Mishnah, was finished toward the end of the second century C.E., and was organized according to subject categories.

Biblical exegesis or commentary is composed of various types of rabbinic stories, conversations, and debates organized by chapter and verse of the biblical texts they attempt to understand and explain. Although Judaic scholars date the compilation and redaction of the first wave of biblical commentary during the years 400-650 C.E. (see e.g., Holtz, 1984, p. 188), midrash continues to be written and published to this day. The two sets of midrashim discussed in detail in this article are found, respectively, in a first wave compilation, Genesis Rabbah (commentary on Genesis, 400-650 C.E.), and a third wave, Exodus Rabbah (commentary on Exodus, 900-1000 C.E.).

I have noticed that there are points in common between hermeneutic ideas about interpretation, historical traditions, and the good, and some of the concepts and processes that inhere in midrashic interpretive traditions.[2 & 3]

---

[2] There were other Jewish literary genres in late antiquity, such as those found in Qumranic, prophetic, and mystical traditions, as well as the Christian Gospels, that do not follow the above hermeneutic practices. They emphasize the possibility of a direct communion with God, especially during ecstatic states of prophetic possession and apocalyptic visions. They are distinguished by the belief that there is only one truth — certain, complete, and perfect — in the text (D. Stern, 1996, p. 23)

[3] Of course, it goes without saying that some similarities between a culture in late antiquity and early 21st century U.S. society do not — and cannot — mean that the two societies are alike, or that the authors of, say, Exodus Rabbah, understood the self, literary work, or fundamental life questions in the same ways we do today. Michel Foucault (e.g., 1977), for one, often noted that historical eras are

Although hermeneuticists are fond of discussing the history of their movement, they make little or no mention of midrashic traditions, either as ongoing interpretive practices or a body of interpretive theory. And yet, careful examination of midrashic texts and later iterations of Jewish biblical commentary indicates that some forms of Jewish midrashic tradition are among humankind's better examples of an ongoing, self-consciously interpretive hermeneutic tradition.[4]

Furthermore, I found some of the central moral understandings and commitments featured and especially enacted in the everyday process of studying midrash to be valuable today, faced as the United States is with the ever-increasing power of right-wing fundamentalist movements. I have come to realize that some midrashic practices can be understood, among other things, as the opposite of fundamentalist practices, as are hermeneutic practices. The two aims of this article are to encourage a more fitting recognition of Jewish interpretive practice as an early ontological hermeneutic tradition[5] and to apply some of its insights to relational psychoanalysis in particular and contemporary politics in general. Midrash in late antiquity was a literary form and social practice that, among other things, struggled with the meaning of God's absence in the world both as a power that intervenes and as an immanent, intimate presence in the experiential lives of believers. As such, midrashic practices may serve as an encouragement for current attempts to create meaning in a world struggling with similar absences.

---

marked by disjunction and difference. However, similarities among cultural artifacts and sociopolitical ideas or structures are not impossible, just unlikely, and usually have somewhat different functions and meanings.

[4] This is an assertion commonly accepted by several contemporary Judaic scholars. See e.g., Boyarin (1990), Fishbane (1993), Goldenberg (1984), Ochs and Levene (2002), Rojtman (1998), Rosenberg (1987, 1989, in press), D. Stern (1991, 1996).

[5] For a good explanation of the distinctions between epistemological and ontological hermeneutics, see Woolfolk, Sass, & Messer (1988).

Midrash as Interpretive Process

For the last 2000 years, Jewish interpretive traditions have been at the center of Jewish communal life; they have had a profound effect on the identities and moral understandings of Jewish communities across time and around the world. One way of understanding the millennia of Jewish literary production is to think of it as a continuous process of rewriting and extending the Hebrew Bible, which is usually — and mistakenly— thought of by non-Jews as the one, and unchanging, Jewish text. Instead, there are literary forms that have grown up in response to the Bible — commenting on, telling stories about, making law out of and gaining inspiration from it. Some of them can be thought of as elements of a fully-embraced, self-conscious, intertextual, process-oriented, ambiguity-embracing hermeneutic tradition that has continuously reframed and reinterpreted the Bible and thus, much of Jewish life. Precisely *because* the Bible was thought to be the word of God, midrashic rabbis believed that it required interpretation.

Through the process of studying, interpreting, and interpreting the interpretations, some Jewish traditions developed a prolonged and tenacious commitment to certain values (e.g., engagement, historicity, interpersonal interaction, the dialectic of absence and presence, the prohibition against idolatry). They also developed a process of study and authorial creation that seems structured to encourage community members to engage with and enact those values, which are among the most important concepts in Jewish thought. Some of the values are remarkably similar to processes and commitments implicit in contemporary hermeneutic practices. Importantly, one of the qualities that can make psychotherapy so promising, frustrating, and elusive, is this same sort of dual function.

The Historical Context of Midrash

Pre-Pharisaic Judaism, (up to approximately the 2nd century B.C.E.) was focused in part on festivals and on the sacrificial rites that, over time, came to be confined to the Temple Mount in Jerusalem. The centralization of sacrificial practices and ceremonies in Jerusalem was helpful to the emerging nation in several ways (Kaufmann, 1960). However, centralization and the resultant strengthening of the priestly class also brought on certain vulnerabilities, chief among them an inescapable dependence on the relatively hierarchical and static processes of religious practices and the singular location of the Temple Mount. If deprived of the Temple, Judaism would have been at risk of receding into irrelevance and then death. And, indeed, that is what the Jews faced when the Temple was destroyed by Rome in 70 C.E. However, historians such as Ellis Rivkin (1971) argued that a new political party called the Pharisees, composed of scribes, judges, and intellectuals, had created or at least influenced an alternative understanding of Judaism. They slowly gained respect and power in the decades following the triumph of the Maccabees (165 B.C.E.) and before the destruction of the Temple. They modified Judaism and prepared the people for a life without the sacrificial system by inventing or at least recasting and building upon the concept of a continuously modifiable oral tradition.

Pharisaic tradition was based on the belief that, simultaneous with the giving of the Ten Commandments, God also communicated to Moses an oral tradition of commentary and law, which Moses then relayed to Joshua, and Joshua to the elders, etc.[6] (see Avot 1:1). One of the distinguishing marks of this oral tradition, from a 21st century perspective, was its inherent flexibility and thus its capacity for change and innovation. We could say that it functioned to make the development and especially the warranting of new laws and customs possible. There is a question as to whether or not a coherent oral tradition existed before the Pharisees. But either way, an ongoing oral literature that created and justified a new, self-conscious body of laws and customs had materialized in the cultural terrain of late antiquity.

Deprived of both their geographical and spiritual place by the destruction of the Temple, loss of national sovereignty, and finally exile,

---

[6] "Moses received the Torah on Sinai, and handed it down to Joshua; Joshua to the elders; the elders to the prophets; and the prophets handed it down to the Men of the Great Assembly."

the Jews needed a way of living that could accompany them wherever they dwelt. Without the concrete relation embodied in the smoke of the Temple's animal sacrifices, they desperately needed a new way of understanding and then enacting their relation with God. The Pharisees accomplished both through the creation, systematic collection, and arrangement of small, everyday social practices and customs that were necessitated by the ever-new challenges brought on by new historical circumstances in both Judaea and the diaspora. They came to warrant, describe, and explain their practices and customs through biblical commentary and legal texts.

Because the rabbis believed that their religious practices originated in and were determined by God's word as contained in the Bible, they had to develop ways of linking cultural and ideological innovations to biblical sources. Over time they achieved this by developing the idea that the Bible "contains endless levels of meaning that inhere, implicitly, in the biblical text" (Peters, 2004, p. 16; see also Holtz, 1984). These meanings, they argued, could be drawn out by skillful reading and interpretation, and were then committed to memory as oral tradition, which eventually was written down, studied, and continuously added to. Then, in time, the newly written compendia were subjected to newer textual study and examination, which would discover new gaps and puzzles that in turn justified the development of new interpretations that allowed the rabbis to address new cultural, political, and religious dilemmas.

As a result of strategic necessity, Judaism became a critical practice, and rabbinics in part became a training in critical thinking and textual analysis. Rabbis and their students learned how to notice gaps in the texts and how to address questions to them. As the centuries turned, living in unfamiliar cultures and changing historical eras profoundly influenced Jewish ways of being. In some locales, Jews became affected — even partially constituted — by the social world of the dominant culture; they had to adapt to it and yet not lose sight of their own commitments and gifts. They did so in part by developing the capacity for self-criticism and, in some cases, even the ability to evaluate their beliefs and practices in relation to those of neighboring traditions. These textual skills also included the ability to appreciate literary and historical context, maneuver through and draw upon the ideas, events, and images of different Judaic texts from different time periods and different cultures, and use them to understand problematic biblical texts. These processes were made possible in part by intertextuality, the way Jewish texts from various historical eras are thought to be entangled and interdependent; they allude to, comment upon, and, through the literary activity of the rabbis, mutually interpret one another. Through intertextuality, Boyarin argued (1990, p. 78), midrashic texts affirm the "complexity and polyphony of the Torah."

The rabbis recognized the importance of relying on human social practices — in the form of literary production — rather than unmediated divine revelation.[7] Above all, they came to shape new understandings about human being, the good, God, and God's relation to the Jewish people. They brought all this about through the crafting and telling of stories explaining textual gaps, the debating and arguing over their implications, the interpreting and re-interpreting of the sacred texts.

The rabbis revered the Hebrew Bible and knew it remarkably, astoundingly well; their intellectual and spiritual life revolved around it to an extreme degree. And yet they developed an orientation toward the written word that is the opposite of the deification and worship of sacred texts characteristic of many fundamentalist movements of the late 20th and early 21st centuries. In a paradox emblematic of a prominent stream of Jewish thought throughout the last 2000 years, the rabbis' love for and attention to the Bible did not at all stop them from noticing its many gaps, puzzlements, annoyances, contradictions, paradoxes. In fact, their unswerving attention to those gaps became the mark of their devotion, the vehicle through which the Pharisees and the rabbis who inherited the Pharisaic tradition breathed new life into Judaism. To realize the paradox inherent in a tradition that is given by God and yet continuously reinvented by mortals is to begin to understand the heart of Diaspora Judaism.

A particular characteristic of the midrashic texts of the first several centuries C.E. is that the rabbis proceeded with the painful understanding

---

[7]   Or, as they might have thought of it, the rabbis relied on human relations and literary creativity as the principle *medium* of divine revelation.)

that God had ceased to intervene directly in human events. Especially given the Jewish nation's defeat and exile, the rabbis were acutely aware of God's absence in their world. Both Jews and Christians seem to have been affected by the experience of absence: Jews yearned for the messiah, Christians for the second coming. About the time of the first of the midrashic collections, the Christian philosopher Augustine of Hippo experienced a revelation: his self-loathing revealed an immense personal emptiness that could only be filled by the presence of God. But for the Rabbinic Judaism of late antiquity, there was no such comfort available in the form of an unmediated presence. A limited solution was achieved, in part, through the learned capacity to tolerate absence through everyday rituals, the beginnings of group prayer, and the communal study of the texts. The tension between absence and presence, and the subsequent development of what appears to be a different understanding of God's presence, permeates midrash.

Unpacking the Process

Reading about the process of learning midrash might be similar to reading a description of how a sweet, juicy orange tastes on a hot, dry day, or trying to dance without the music: there is simply no substitute for the experience itself. Studying biblical commentary in a traditional setting is a dyadic or group project. The text is read, questioned, and debated aloud, and the dyad or group does not move on to the next biblical verse until all parties are for the moment satisfied they understand the issues involved. Although there is usually someone who guides and facilitates, everyone gets to be involved. It might appear to be chaotic to an outsider, because the texts are read and debated in a rhythmic, idiosyncratic way that sounds as much like singing as reciting. The method is a remarkable mix of obsessiveness combined with an imaginative, flowing style in some ways similar to psychoanalytic free association. It is a kind of poetry, a kind of singing, and yet always with an eye to interrogating the text. After witnessing it, one could never again unquestioningly think of Judaism as a Western religion, nor could one utter the phrase Judeo-Christian and believe the two were one.

Midrash is structured according to the chapters and verses of the Bible, and it is initiated by a textual problem that needs to be solved. It begins with a puzzlement in the text: an unusual spelling, an incorrect choice of words, a contradiction or an incoherence, an action outrageous on its face (such as when Jonah the prophet tries to run from God) or a statement that makes no sense (such as God's response when asked by Moses for His name). Midrashim sometimes begin interrogating the text or developing a solution to a problem by telling a story, called a *mashal*. However, often the mashal itself needs an explanation (usually an analogy sometimes, not surprisingly, in the form of another story) in order to become part of the solution rather than the problem. This second level story or saying, brought in to clarify the mashal or summarize its message, is called a *nimshal*. It is usually shorter, less complex, and the meaning more directly stated.

Some midrashim are fairly simple narrative fragments often used for homiletic purposes. Some possess straightforward story lines revolving around the explanation of a grammatical abnormality. Other midrashim are complex, featuring several stories and rabbinic interpretations that contrast and conflict with one another, illustrating different theological concepts and forming different textual solutions.

In studying midrash one enters a process fraught with puzzles, mysteries, and competing opinions. It seems true that the rabbis distributed clues so as to entice the reader down paths of understanding, but they are not easy to find or decipher. As one wades into the process, though, it is possible to discern reason in the chaos. For instance, the rabbis are playing with the texts; the Bible is where they live, and they have fun in it and with it. Also, they are intimately familiar with and knowledgeable about it; they allude to it, use one text to illuminate, debate, disprove, reinterpret a second text, and a third to speak to the first. The Bible, in tandem with the rabbis' respect for and love of it, is also their field of play.

Also, although they were profoundly committed to the ideas expressed in the Bible, they were not simply preaching a doctrine in some removed, authoritarian way. By the way they shaped and taught midrash, they created study situations in which they and their students were maneuvered into <u>enacting</u> those values as well. The gaps, puzzles and mysteries the text provides are not only present in the Bible, they are also — and perhaps even more so — present in midrashim. As students of history we can hypothesize that at least sometimes the rabbis consciously placed puzzles and gaps in their texts. And so, close textual reading, critical thinking, historical awareness, participation in group study and debate, the ability to tolerate confusion and uncertainty, and the capacity for engaged learning and dialogue must have been important values to the rabbis, because they designed midrashic texts so as to influence readers to enact those values and develop those skills.

Genesis Rabba 39:1

Let us study together. In the commentary about the following short but famous verse from Gen. 12:1 we can see many aspects of midrash that are characteristic of the genre. Due to the limitations of space, this will be the only midrash we will study in this much detail.[8]

> And God said to Avram: "Go, you, from your land,
> and your birthplace and your father's house to the land
> that I will show you."

Genesis Rabba 39:1 comments:

(1) And God said to Avram: Go, you, from your land. ...

(2) R. Yitzhak opened: (Psalms 45:11) "Listen, daughter, and see and turn your ear and forget your people and your father's house."

(3) R. Yitzhak said: This may be compared to one who was passing from place to place and saw a fortress (bira) illuminated/burning (doleket).

(4) He said, 'Will you say this fortress has no governor (manhig)?

(5) The master (baal) of the fortress peeped out (hetzitz) at him.

(6) He said to him, "I am the master of the fortress."

(7) Thus, because our father Avraham would say, "Will you say this world has no governor?"

---

8 The translation is from Peters (2004, pp. 37-38)

(8)   The Holy One Blessed be He peeped out at him and said to him, 'I am the Master of the world.'

(9)   (Psalms 45:12) 'And the king will desire your beauty' — to beautify you in the world;

(10)   "because he is your master and bow to him," that is, "And God said to Avram. ... "

That is the way midrash reads; it is dense, cryptic, formulaic, and full of quotations or partial quotations from or allusions to other books of the Bible or other commentaries. There are many problems and gaps in this text, and only a few are discussed here. The first and most obvious problem, of course, is the difficulties encountered when translating one language to another. *Doleket* (line 3) is a Hebrew word that scholars seem unable to agree on; they cannot tell us for certain whether in this particular situation it means illuminated or burning. Here we have, then, a good lesson about the uncertainties of interpretation: because human being is historical and linguistic, learning about another era or culture through a text is always problematic and fraught with unsolvable quandaries such as the degree to which differing social worlds are commensurable with one another.

In the structure of this midrash, line 1 is the opening quote; line 2 is the opening verse, in this case from Psalms, that serves as a kind of epigraph for the midrash; lines 3-6 constitute the *mashal* (the primary story); lines 7-8 make up the *nimshal* (the secondary analogy, which usually starts with "Thus"); and lines 9-10 furnish a concluding verse from Psalms, including commentary.

I would like to interpret one particular issue. What seems important about this story is Abraham's critical, almost confrontive, stance toward God. If we adopt the translation of *doleket* as burning rather than illuminated, then we could read the midrash as portraying Abraham as saying something like, "What is happening here? The fortress, our refuge, is burning, and God, its owner, is nowhere to be found! I know you are there, God, so show yourself, and do something before our protection is destroyed."

This interpretation fits well with the characterization of Abraham in later chapters in Genesis (e.g., 18:16-33), when Abraham is explicitly portrayed as questioning or arguing with God over whether God should destroy Sodom and Gomorrah.

Remember that the midrash in question was developed in the centuries following the destruction of the Temple in Jerusalem, the despoliation of the land, and the exile of the Jewish people from their ancestral home. The fortress of the Temple had, quite literally, burned, and the focal point of the nation had been destroyed. For the rabbis, it was not an ancient event but a current, immediate issue. In lines 7 and 8 of the midrash, first Abraham and then God drop the poetic conceit of the "fortress" analogy and say directly that they are discussing the fate of "the world." It must have seemed as though the world continued to burn, both because of the long-ago destruction of the Temple and because of the less monumental, everyday injustices they witnessed in a social world not of their own making.

But there is more to my interpretation: Abraham's critical question not only complains about God's absence, it also provokes a response from the fortress' owner, who in the *nimshal* (line 8), is identified as God. Importantly, it is *after* Abraham complains about God's absence through a rhetorical question (line 4) that God appears and identifies Himself as "the Master of the world." Abraham was not content to ignore the problem; he noticed and commented on the scene and asked a question that was calculated to confront God gently and thereby prod him into action. Abraham's behavior in this midrash echoes biblical stories that narrate Abraham's relationship with God, such as the Sodom and Gomorrah confrontation. In the midrash we are studying, Abraham provokes God into relating to him and into taking His rightful place in the world. Abraham is pictured as critical, outspoken, and related. He insists that God be present in the world and do something about the destruction that Abraham witnesses. And God is willing to show himself and accept His responsibility, as soon as he has a related, engaged partner. In his complaint, Abraham thereby becomes an active force for good by engaging with — and enlivening — God.

This midrash seems to be prescriptive: that is, just as Abraham engages with God through awareness, criticism, and relatedness, so too is the student of midrash encouraged to engage with the text through awareness (a careful reading), criticism, and relatedness (with the text and with his or her colleagues). It is difficult for students to understand this midrash without actively engaging with it and with one another; it is too complicated and cryptic to be understood in isolation and disengagement. When students do engage, thoughtfully, critically, and caringly with the text and with one another (as Abraham did with God), they prod or provoke the text into showing itself, relating, being responsible — revealing its meanings. And, by implication, we might say that students also provoke God out of His hiding place and evoke a new understanding of God's presence in the space between student and text or student and student. This is a story about the indispensable nature of interpretive, compassionate moral engagement and political activism that demands, and finds, relationship.

Exodus Rabba (3:4)

According to the rabbis, Moses also had a critical conversation with God. It happened during the episode of the burning bush (Exod. 3:6-10). It is worth noting that once again something is burning and God's absence is revealed and (as we shall see) challenged. There is a saying that the primordial Torah, God's writing, was "Black fire on white fire" (Tanhuma, Genesis 1). The letters of the Torah, just as the midrashic fortress, the world, and the bush (which we are about to study), are aflame with the relational paradox of silence and speech, inaction and action, negative space and the written word, God's absence and presence, hopelessness and the wish for a repaired, just world.

Moses stops before the burning bush and hears God speaking to him, telling him to return to Egypt and lead the Israelites out of slavery. Moses responds by saying *mi anokhi?* (i.e., "who am I?") in a sentence usually translated as "Who am I, that I should go to Pharoah, and I should take the children of Israel out of Egypt?" (Exodus 3:11). The midrash of *Exodus Rabba*

(3:4) presents three different readings of the phrase *mi anokhi*? by three different rabbis, each interpretation suggesting a different punctuation and thereby a different meaning. Only the text from one rabbi will be discussed below, but it is important to note that the text included three interpretations. This is often the case — the student is free to decide which of the interpretations is persuasive, although the order and presentation of the interpretations might also hold clues as to which were favored by the rabbis or by the editors. As usual, midrash welcomes ambiguities, contradictions, and multiple truths.

R. Yehoshua ben Levi compared Moses' complaint to a king's daughter who was promised an excellent lady-in-waiting when she was wed, but who received instead a common servant. R. Yehoshua implies that Moses was saying to God, "Look, you promised the Israelites that you would lead them out of Egypt, ["'And I (*anokhi*) will surely bring you up' (Gen. 46:4)], but then you gave them me instead, a poor substitute." Moses' point revolves around emphasizing the word *anokhi*, which is an archaic or highly poetic form of the word *ani*, I or me. The rabbis were disturbed by God's absence in the proposed exodus, as well as puzzled by the use of the unusual form *anokhi*, and explained them both in order to understand the verse and to argue for a particular moral value.

According to Peters (2004, p. 148), R. Yehoshua ben Levi's story suggests that the punctuation of the phrase *mi anokhi*? should be changed to read *mi 'anokhi'*? Instead of meaning "Who am I to accomplish this feat," Moses could be understood as saying to God "Hey, wait a minute — *who* is the 'I' in this phrase? It's not me, because I never promised to lead the Israelites out of Egypt. The only person who uses *anokhi* is you, God, as in Genesis 46:4, when *You* promised to free them by saying 'And I [*anokhi*] will surely bring you up.'"

This is a long and involved midrash, with many twists and turns. But for the purposes of this article it is sufficient to note the way the rabbis play with the grammar, use narrative expansions to explain their point of view about the passage and better understand the passage, use one part of the text to illuminate another part, and especially to highlight once again the moment of challenge and critical meeting between an important historical

383

figure and God. In this midrash Moses is thought to be challenging God to remember His promise to the Israelites and realize He is not living up to His part of the covenant. In God's plan for the Israelites, criticism and an appeal to justice intensify and deepen the relationship. Moses' engagement draws God out, as it did with Abraham. As a result of Moses' challenge, God promises several things to the Israelites and to Moses to help them on their journey; again, the dynamic between absence and presence, and their link to justice, is highlighted. Midrashic interpretation became a vehicle for both respecting and challenging a text, thereby simultaneously revering and yet continuously updating the tradition.

In the midrashim about Abraham, Moses, and God, the prescriptive element of midrashic texts as a whole seems obvious: engagement with the text reveals a God who thrives on relationship and responds positively to honest, critical dialogue and to a reminder of His part of the covenant. This is a God who is relational and just, and the social practices of critical and communal study evoke a new understanding of the presence of God in the room. "The object of midrash," Judaic scholar David Stern (1996 p. 31) wrote,

> was not so much to find the meaning of Scripture as it was literally to engage its text. Midrash became a kind of conversation the Rabbis invented in order to enable God to speak to them from between the lines of Scripture, in the textual fissures and discontinuities that exegesis discovers.

The world of the rabbis was burning, and it was difficult to find God — especially the covenantal God who had agreed to protect and watch over them — amidst the rubble. They found God, and a new understanding of God's presence, in the gaps of the text.

In light of all that the Jews were experiencing during the early centuries of the Common Era — the serial wars against Rome, continuing devastation and loss, Bar Kochba's failed revolution[9], and finally an exile without end — the rabbis were faced with several difficult tasks that were historical, political, psychological, emotional, spiritual. Their response to this job is

---

[9]   132-135 C.E.

inscribed in the books and chapters and paragraphs and lines of midrash. In their hands, midrash became an instrument of religious experience, political resistance, and communal salvation.

> The Rabbis' conception of Torah as a figurative trope for God . . . expresses both their sense of alienation and their attempt to overcome that alienation intellectually. . . . [T]he text of the Torah became for the Rabbis the primary sign of the continued existence of the covenantal relationship between God and Israel, and the activity of Torah study — midrash — thus became the foremost medium for preserving and pursuing that relationship. (D. Stern, 1996, p. 31)

The midrashim that we have studied in this section seem to comprise a rigorous training program in critical, historical, and imaginative interpretation. The rabbis' work seems framed in a fascinating mix of both a genuine reverence for and a playful relation with the text. Above all, these interpretive practices seem to me to embody the most important of all Jewish commitments: the fight against idolatry. In this case, it is the opposition to the idolatry of the written word. This interpretation of midrashic tradition stands against authoritarian uses of the written word. It opposes the demand that a text — even a sacred text, thought to be the word of God — be seen as hyper-concrete, immutable, the one truth. It opposes the idea that the meaning of the text is the same for all time and all people, that it is transparent to and thus unproblematically understood by those in power, and that their singular understanding should be imposed through a unilateral, disengaged, authoritarian process.

Engagement and Paradox

Over time, and continuing even today, some of the activities that inhere in interpretive process came to be understood as the quintessence of Jewish life: engagement — both textual and interpersonal — as spiritual practice. You can't have texts without people to write them, and you can't have people writing them without a sense of community and mission. These texts can't be studied, learned about, debated and discussed, new stories and new ideas can't be developed and applied to everyday life, without one's fellow students. As the tradition says, "Torah is acquired only in community." And of course the converse is also true. Engagement with one's colleagues, neighbors, friends, and family, through the living out of the ever-changing oral tradition applied to the everyday (*halacha*), became the foundation of Jewish communal life.

But Jewish engagement wasn't — couldn't be — a heavy, overly serious activity, because of the paradox lurking quietly in the background. It is true that the myriad interpretations in midrashic texts are thought to be worthy of learned rabbinic dispute because they are attempts to explain God's word. And yet, shockingly, for every interpretation there are several more, each with its own biblical prooftexts and each with its engaging story and thoughtful reasoning. How can all these interpretations, sometimes confusing, contradictory, or incoherent, be considered correct interpretations? How can a custom be the correct custom in one historical era or culture, and a forgotten custom in a new setting? How can one understanding of God be embraced by the Jewish people in one era or setting and another, different understanding be embraced in a new era or setting? How can the prescribed content and manner of prayer change from era to era?

In other words, the rabbis were playing with fire; to work on such demanding philosophical challenges you have to be light on your hermeneutic feet. You have to be capable of tolerating paradox; thinking that there can be more than one truth in the text; realizing that textual engagement is generative and therefore readers coauthor the text; facing the fact that human understandings are always uncertain and incomplete; accepting that to some degree the shape of truths and the good change with the shape of the cultural terrain, and that the terrain provides helpful, but imperfect, moral guidance.[10]

Above all, one must come to the understanding that God is not only in the product, but also in the process; that it is in the space between persons, between persons and texts, and between one text and another,

---

[10] There are other, more historical, explanations for multiplicity (D. Stern, 1996, pp. 31-33).

between one word and another, that God resides; that the activity of engaged communal searching and study and care and critical thinking is, somehow, a way of relating to or being a partner with God; that even when new stories are made up to justify new ideas or new customs, they are not exactly made up — in some way, the texts are speaking us, and in some way God is thought to have spoken or inspired the texts. So, in other words, participation in the activity of engaged, compassionate study and interpersonal interaction is a kind of relation with God.

Midrashic texts require a conception of a text that is something not so much penetrated into as opened outward from within (Rosenberg, personal communication, August, 2005).

This highlights one of the major paradoxes with which Jewish interpretive tradition wrestles. Humans must develop ideas, make decisions, live in a social world with others, all of which necessitate taking stands about the good in everyday life. These decisions require a knowledge of and a commitment to a particular historical tradition. But, in order to make these decisions, we also have to be critical of and creative with the tradition as well as committed to it. How can we do both at the same time? One way is to develop a stream of the tradition that values change, that by its very nature understands that change is a necessity and a virtue; to define God as ever-changing[11] and humans as made in His image; to live in and encourage a way of being capable of change — change that is framed and profoundly influenced by particular ideals and values, but change nonetheless; to worship a God that is invisible, that has no name, and is always becoming.[12] This is a God that has no name because it is alive, not an inert idol of stone or wood; it is the verb "to be," third person singular in the imperfect tense (see Exod. 3:14); it is *YHVH* — that which is becoming — the Jewish God.

A God that is ever-reinterpreted requires a human tradition willing to tolerate the awareness that human truth is always historical: new truths

---

[11] "Just as a single verse may have many meanings," David Stern wrote while discussing Pesikta de-Rab Kahana 1:223, "so God, too, is said to possess many countenances" (1996, p. 27).

[12] See Fromm, 1966, pp. 29-32.

come to light at different times for different reasons. Midrashic practices provide those interpretive understandings.

It is not easy to live with that paradox. To be involved in a stream of tradition dedicated to critical but playful thought and ongoing historical and cultural change is to be challenged to face the power, fragility, and imperfection of human interpretation. It is to realize how much and how little humans are capable of. It is to understand — and thus reject — the desperation that drives people to cling to belief systems and practices that claim the one, indisputable, perfect truth, and to warrant their truth by claiming a direct experience of God's presence. Ultimately, it is to reject the fundamentalist fantasy of a concrete, unquestionable, unproblematic, perfectly knowable truth, be it a set of practices, a system of belief, a scientific method, or the doctrine of a charismatic leader. Human traditions, in other words, are always historically contingent, contestable, available for examination and debate, in need of additions, subtractions, or sometimes even a complete reconfiguring. They are beautiful and imperfect, inspirational and incomplete — always in question. Human being, Heidegger scholar Hubert Dreyfus (1991, p. 25) once noted, is interpretation "all the way down." When this hermeneutic vision gets too much to bear, human thought collapses into fundamentalism.

Although the hermeneutic paradox at the heart of midrash has played a large part in the shape of Jewish culture, the paradox's influence both waxes and wanes historically. The capacity to hold both sides of the hermeneutic paradox, human history demonstrates, is fragile indeed. Absolutist, authoritarian claims, especially during times of turmoil and trauma, are powerfully seductive as an anesthetic of last resort. So a people's capacity to tolerate the paradox and do something creative with it is necessarily fragile.

Therapeutic Implications

During my study of midrash, similarities between Jewish interpretive processes and various ideas from relational psychoanalysis and relationally-oriented psychotherapy began to emerge. Processes central to the learning of midrash emphasize, among other things, the importance of intertextuality, interpersonal engagement, the absence-presence dynamic, and the prohibition against idolatry.

Intertextuality

The concept of intertextuality is used to describe the relation between the many Jewish texts that appear in midrash: how texts refer to, inform, echo, mirror, oppose, reinforce and modify, contrast and dispute and engage with, intertwine and repel one another (see especially Boyarin, 1990). Intertextuality implies that, in a certain sense, texts are all we have to turn to when learning about the world. In the social world the rabbis inhabited, direct experiences of God, such as a witnessing of miracles or a direct communication or mystical communion with God, did not usually happen. Because they only knew God through the interpretations they compiled about God, there was no way to turn to some putatively unproblematic and unmediated experience of or text about God. Humans, they thought, learn about the world through imperfect, historically contingent, human-made sources and tools. These sources are always reflections of their time and place, products of the inescapable moral frameworks of their historical traditions and the power relations of their political terrain. "A midrashic exegesis," D. Stern (1996, p. 30) explained, "always returns to the text, not to God."

Similarly, although it is comforting for therapists to believe our favorite psychotherapy theory (or teacher, supervisor, or mentor) delivers a perfect, universal truth about human being, no such truth exists. What we have to work with — and it can be a lot — is the thoughtful, imaginative interpretations of our colleagues and teachers, captured in the writing and the personal interactions of supervision or consultation. Those gifts — not unlike midrashic texts — are imperfect and incomplete, always open to new interpretations that are necessitated by challenges that appear in an ever-changing historical terrain, and that flow from the textual problems and flaws sometimes discovered through group effort, but they can also be helpful, insightful, at times even brilliant.

Primarily, of course, therapists have the opportunity to learn about a particular patient from interacting with that patient. But again, a hermeneutic interpretation of midrashic process teaches us not to believe that our impressions about patients are the one truth about them, unproblematically discovered and perfectly understood. In fact, just as midrash turns to a second text in order to learn about the first, Louis Sass (1988, p. 250) has cautioned that humans are not texts, and we ought not claim a privileged, unquestioned ability to read them. Instead, Sass suggested, when we learn about patients we are not reading them, we are reading over their shoulder the cultural text from which they themselves are reading. And let us remember that when we read over a patient's shoulder we use other texts, especially the cultural texts about the good that have brought us to light, in order to interpret the texts from which the patient is reading.

In this way, the midrashic emphasis on intertextuality suggests that therapists exercise caution in relation to the claims of the teachers, professional celebrities, and theories that we admire, and to our own opinions and evaluations. Our job, as was the job of the rabbis who created midrash, is not to use a text unquestioningly, but instead to question, historically situate, critically appraise it. Our job is to find the gaps and problems and puzzles in texts and try to make sense out of them by using other texts to compare and contrast. Of course we don't want to see the problems in a cherished theory or its practices, we want to believe that we have found the one perfect psychotherapeutic truth. But just as the rabbis couldn't do that with their sacred texts, neither can we do that with ours. In other words, this interpretation of midrash reinforces hermeneutic commitments about the value of critical reading, dialogue (see below), and humility in one's work as therapist, teacher, supervisor. (e.g., see Fowers, 2005; Richardson, Fowers, & Guignon, 1999; Sass, 1988; D.B. Stern, 1991, 1997).[13] There are truths in a text, and similarly there are truths achieved in personal meeting, and we should cherish them when they appear. But

---

[13] These midrashic and hermeneutic values have many implications for clinical practice that fit well with the work of interpersonalists and relationalists such as Aron, 1996; Hoffman, 1998; Ehrenberg, 1992; Layton, 2002, 2005; Leary, 1997, 2000; Levenson, 1991; Mitchell, 1988, 1993; Stern, 1997; and those published in Mitchell & Aron, 1999, Aron & Harris, 2005, and Suchet, Harris, & Aron, 2007).

that does not mean a truth forecloses further interpretation, exploration, even disagreement.

Interpersonal engagement

The rabbis' emphasis on intertextuality will also lead us to the concept of interpersonality. By that I mean a recognition of the importance of depending on our fellow humans, turning to them in order to learn about and affect the world. As in intertextuality, understanding one person through another sheds light on both. The rabbis mined the spaces between letters, words, and concepts, explored the gaps and puzzles in their texts, and turned to other texts and their study partners in order to explain those gaps. Similarly, therapists can mine the spaces between them and their patients, explore the gaps and puzzles of the other (and themselves), and turn to the impressions and opinions of their patients and colleagues — and the intersections they have with those impressions and opinions — in order to better discuss the gaps and puzzles from which they are trying to understand and make meaning.

In this respect, aspects of relational psychoanalysis seem to be similar to aspects of the stream of Jewish interpretive traditions emphasized in this article. The profound insistence on communal activity — interpersonality — reflects the main mode of literary study — intertextuality — and both activities reflect and live out one of the strongest of Jewish values: the commitment to respect the cultural, historical space between persons, to recognize the existence and importance of the other as other, and to encourage a meaningful engagement with the other. It is the space between that is the terrain in which meaning is made. As much as the content of its ideas, it is the process of engaged, critical, compassionate, respectful involvement that heals texts, souls, psyches, and communities.

Above all, a belief in the healing nature of genuine human engagement, beyond particular technical theory and strategic technique, is a concept that is at the heart of both relational psychoanalysis and the study of midrash. What Martin Buber called "meeting" has similarities to what the hermeneuticist Gadamer (1975) called "genuine conversation" or "dialogue" and to how Donnel Stern (1991, 1997) applied Gadamer's "fusion of horizons" to the practice of psychoanalysis. The concept

391

of the fallacy of the blank screen and the importance of a two-person psychology[14] — a cornerstone of relational psychoanalysis — are ideas the practitioners of midrashic tradition would intuitively understand.

The Absence-Presence Dialectic

In the social world of the early mishnaic rabbis, unlike that which was recorded by the biblical texts they studied and interpreted, God neither intervened directly in the affairs of humans, nor did He communicate directly and personally with them. The contrast, one might imagine, must have been difficult for them to come to terms with. However, over time, the ability of the rabbis to face the fact of God's absences, while still remaining in relation with Him, helped them shape a new understanding of presence. The tension between the two poles of absence and presence appeared to open up a space in which neither hopeless despair over God's absence nor a defensive inflation or exaggeration of His presence prevailed.

In that dialectical space emerged the literary practices of midrash. The rabbis held on to presence in the face of absence in two ways. First, they drew forth new stories and meanings from a text that, to the untutored eye, contained little to none of what was subsequently developed. And second, through the process of communal study and ongoing artistic creativity, the rabbis created a new way of being with one another and with God in a social world that, to the untutored eye, contained little or no precedent for what was then developed. By relying on one text to interpret another and by relying on a group of study partners to support, encourage, challenge, and care for one another, the rabbis created a way of enlivening and relating to a God who, to the uninitiated, must have seemed removed and weak. They created a way of being that brought presence into an otherwise absent space.

Similarly, patient and therapist hold onto presence in the face of absence in two ways. First, they create new stories out of a conversation that, to the untutored eye, initially contained few of the memories, ideas, or especially meanings that are then developed. And second, through the process of mutual, cooperative, honest interpersonal involvement and care, patient

---

[14] See e.g., Racker, 1968; Levenson, 1983, 1991; Gill, 1983; Hoffman, 1983, 1998.

and therapist shape a new way of relating that, to the untutored eye, initially contained little possibility for what is then developed. They come to live out a way of being that brings the presence of meaning into an otherwise absent space.

Patient and therapist accomplish this in a way similar to the rabbis: by relying on the generative processes of textual interpretation and moral discourse. In both the 1st century C.E. rabbinic academy at Yavneh and the contemporary analytic dyad, new meanings are developed through a process of interpretive relations. The rabbis turned to the text because that was all that was available, just as patient and therapist turn to the narrative they develop because it is all they have: they cannot revisit the past in some direct, materialized way, they cannot make the past a presence. Similarly, they can't materialize life outside the consulting room during the clinical hour. They can only tell stories about the past or life outside the office, and from that process recognize and develop new meanings out of the presence that was given to them from their traditions and over time develops between them.

Relational analysts have written extensively on the healing qualities of relational processes. For instance, Rachel Peltz (1998), drawing from philosophers and analysts, including Irwin Hoffman (e.g., 1998) and Thomas Ogden (e.g., 1994), argued that the dialectic between presence and absence, when both poles are held in a dynamic tension, has the potential to open up a generative space in which new meanings come to light. Presence and absence, she suggested,

> represent overarching terms that, when held in relation to each other, help sustain the tension between other binary pairs like certainty and uncertainty, permanence and temporality, stasis and transformation, reality and fantasy, communication and noncommunication, immortality and mortality. (p. 387)

The degree of the parent's presence or absence, most psychoanalysts believe, has a constitutive effect on the (take your pick) internal object relations, regulatory selfobject functions, or relational patterns of the individual throughout the life span. Similarly, the continuing negotiation over the presence and absence of both patient and therapist during the course of treatment will have a significant effect on its outcome. And, as I (2005b) have argued, the sense the patient has about the overall degree of safety and meaningfulness of the social world (i.e., the degree of absence and presence) is thought to have an impact on the quality of his or her relational life and sense of wellbeing.

In other words, there must be enough of a sense of presence to produce relatedness, and enough honesty to face and complain about the inevitable and necessary absences of everyday life. The move from stuckness or deadness during moments of impasse or enactment in treatment, Peltz thought, are generated when the dialectic collapses and the dyad is trapped in one pole or the other. Too much presence — usually in the form of grandiosity or overidealization — causes a defensive reliance on ecstatic communion with a fantasized omnipotent other that makes the generation of new meaning impossible. This is parallel to the spate of mantic experiences and mystical communion with God in late antiquity from which the mishanic rabbis diverged. Conversely, being caught up solely in absence causes an obsession with betrayal and loss and the continual reenactment and re-experiencing of painful feelings and rage that make the generation of new meaning impossible.

Finally, the rabbis' characteristic quality — the belief that engaged textual reading, combined with communal study, will bring to light new meanings potentially available but previously unseen — seems similar to the recent analytic belief that the unconscious is best thought of not as a kind of archeological site, but rather a process in which, to use Donnel Stern's (1997) important words, that which previously has been "unformulated" can become "formulated" when the patient's perspective shifts. Just as the rabbis seemingly brought new stories and meanings out of God's silence, so too does the dialectical moment in the clinical hour open up a space — an absence — in which new memories, ideas, and feelings can be formulated and then explicitly interpreted in order to make meaning — a kind of presence. The particular content of inflated and intoxicated fantasies about presence and the betrayals and rages produced by loss and absence vary, of course, depending on the historical terrain in which they appear. But the struggle with absence and presence in which the rabbis were engaged might well shed light on the struggles patients and therapists go through during the contemporary clinical hour.

The Prohibition Against Idolatry

The prohibition against idolatry brings together and concentrates many of the hermeneutic understandings and Jewish values discussed in this paper. It is ironic that the fight against idolatry is usually thought of as either an antiquated issue long-since dispensed with or one too obvious to be important in modern Western society. However, Erich Fromm (1955, 1966) applied the concept of idolatry to the political and psychological struggles of contemporary life in an insightful and creative way.

Fromm argued (see e.g., 1955, pp. 111-137; 1966, pp. 41-49) that idolatry is the process by which certain qualities become de-identified from or disavowed by an individual or society, and are then projected onto another — either a particular person (e.g., a charismatic leader or celebrity), a type of person (e.g., a person of color), or an object (e.g., a commodity such as a car). The disavowed quality is then worshipped from afar either positively (as in placing the movie star "on a pedestal"), or negatively (as in believing African American males are naturally hostile, Jews dishonest, Latinos lazy). Worship takes on the quality of complete submission to idolatrous processes, an inability to question the dynamic or resist its power. Either in the positive or negative varieties, this dynamic of disavowal and worship is alienating and highly destructive for both the one who is projecting and the one projected upon.

The main point is that the dynamic of either positive or negative idolatry is a kind of deadening process. It freezes human creativity because it stops critical thought and meaningful engagement with oneself and with the other. It is alienating because it prevents the one who projects from confronting and integrating the quality that is being disavowed. It locks the disavowed quality into a trap from which it cannot escape. And of course it does equal or worse damage to the one upon whom the quality is being projected. To be the object of over-idealizing admiration or hatred is a horrible (sometimes life-threatening) experience, bound to end in disaster. One thinks immediately of Marilyn Monroe or Medgar Evers as examples of the deadly force of either positive or negative forms of the dynamic.

The most prominent aspect of idolatry, according to Fromm, is the alienation of the individual from his or her human qualities, foremost among them the quality of intelligent, critical thought. Submission to the idol is complete and uncompromising. When one gives up the ability to think for oneself, to question and doubt and resist, Fromm thought, all is lost. That is an awful kind of slavery, the most dangerous way of "escaping" from freedom (Fromm, 1941).

One way of understanding midrashic process is to realize that it is the antithesis of idolatry. To embody midrashic process is to have the capacity to hold both sides of the hermeneutic paradox: to question rigorously and thoughtfully within a historical tradition of moral understandings deeply held. It is both to refuse to accept texts or authority without interrogating and exploring their inconsistencies and contradictions, and to be aware that critical activity is achieved only by virtue of a set of moral commitments and beliefs framed by the historical tradition one lives within and modified by those of neighboring traditions. Midrashic study is a kind of training in critical thought, moral discourse, political resistance; from it we learn that no text, person, or idea should be exempt from being evaluated according to the tradition's highest standards of social justice, compassion, and personal respect.

Midrashic process, in Fromm's terms, is preparation for the fight of a lifetime: the fight against idolatry. It inspires us to develop a way of life that features intellectual honesty, flexibility, and an openness to difference always informed, necessarily, by the historical traditions that value and enable these qualities. It is a definition of the good in Jewish life.

The application of this Jewish concept to psychotherapy seems obvious. Regardless of a patient's particular presenting problem, from a hermeneutic perspective therapy can be thought to help a patient be less involved with an old social terrain that contains certain limited, contradictory, destructive (or in Kleinian terms, perverse) moral understandings about the good and the self-images that fit with and enable them (see Cushman, 1995, chapter 9). But humans cannot simply substitute one understanding of the good for another, because during the course of living, the good becomes embodied by us in various complex and unconscious ways, and because we cannot live without some understanding of the good that is linked to the historical traditions in which we live. The good, according to this interpretation, encompasses much that current therapists refer to as character structure, object relations, self-state regulation, identity, Jungian complexes, the subject positions of gender, race, and class, or what Lynne Layton has recently called "the normative unconscious" (2005). Understandings of the good may differ in content, but not in location: they are central to human being. Traditions about the good are not clothing we can take on or off. They come to constitute us.

So therapeutic change is difficult and usually time-consuming; it cannot happen until therapist and patient develop a meaningful (although usually covert) encounter about the good with one another, and begin — both drawing on their understandings of the good — to argue and dispute and question and care for one another. It takes time to settle into a rhythm that allows for the living out of one's moral terrain, the inevitable enactments that are produced, the growing awareness of how we reproduce the very cultural terrain and personal relations that in part cause our suffering and the suffering of others, the questioning and disputing of our moral understandings, the slow encounter with the other's perspective, and the openness that allows the other's perspective to influence our own perspective. It is important to remember that the understandings and identities of patient and therapist do not materialize out of thin air; they are not wished into being, created out of fantasies, created solely in the therapy office, or just adopted impulsively from someone else — first and foremost, they are products of historical traditions. The traditions can be questioned, modified, and reworked — in fact, that is the essence of a hermeneutic approach — but they can never simply be dismissed, wished away, or magically transformed. It is in that type of moral discourse — more a dance than a discussion — that some hermeneuticists think therapeutic change comes about.

This hermeneutic way of thinking about the process of psychotherapy has points in common with the process of midrashic study. They both require the capacity to think critically and discuss the good. They are predicated on both the freedom to question and the freedom to be part of a larger tradition; the capacity to resist that which one thinks is bad, and the capacity to have a place to stand, to know what one stands for, and who one stands with; the freedom to know incompletely and uncertainly. These qualities are the products of a life less influenced by idolatry.

When texts, belief systems, leaders, psychotherapy theories, or therapists lose sight of the simultaneous power and fragility of human interpretation, they lose touch with an essential aspect of humanity. When a text becomes an idol, God becomes a thing (visible, named, and known), and human creativity and relatedness become deadened. The less people believe in their ability to be engaged and effective in the world, the more they look toward — and begin to depend on — a magical figure (or, in psychology, a disengaged method) to save them. Subservience follows idolatry and leads to apocalyptic visions and inflated fantasies. In our desperation, God is thought to be intimate and immanent, a presence who stands ready to intervene whenever needed, to provide a sign, a touchdown, a remission for cancer, or an irrefutable justification for war.

An idolatrous dynamic and its products run counter to the strategies midrashic traditions developed. "To really understand the concept of the coming of the Messiah," a wise old rabbi once told me, "you must realize he will never come." An important Jewish understanding is that, contrary to the Christian Bible,[15] the word is not made flesh. It remains the word, and the word, as always, remains contingent, imperfect, incomplete. "Midrash refuses," David Stern (1996, p. 29) taught, "to make the identification between God and Torah literal." Psychoanalysis, Freud often reminded us, refuses to equate God's word with the analyst's interpretations. Words are surrounded by gaps, puzzles, inconsistencies, self-contradictions. Readers, therapists, and patients fall into those textual gaps, engage with their interlocutors there, wrestle with God there. We live in those gaps, we are our best selves there.

---

[15] See John, chapter one.

Conclusion

From my perspective, one of the most important features of midrashic practice is its grasp of the primordial entanglements between moral understandings, communal activity, and personal well-being. Because of this vision, as well as its intellectual content, the interpretive midrashic tradition of 1st millennium C.E. can be identified as an early form of an ontological hermeneutic tradition, and can be understood to offer something valuable to current psychotherapy theory. In particular, the valorization of intertextuality, engaged understanding, the dialectic of absence and presence, and the prohibition against idolatry suggest the kind of psychotherapy we now refer to as relational psychoanalysis. As I recently argued (2005, a & b), a robust hermeneutic vision recognizes and builds from an understanding of the entanglements of moral and political meanings and recognizes them as central constituents of the self.

Ours is a social world that in recent years increasingly has adopted the processes and commitments of fundamentalism — religious, political, and intellectual. Religious fundamentalism is apparent in Jewish, Christian, and Muslim communities, and whether it is combined with terrorism (as in radical Islam), geographic imperialism (as in the Israeli ultra-orthodox *haradim*), or political power (as in the Christian far right), it constitutes a threat to thoughtful, cooperative, peace-loving people throughout the world.

Fundamentalisms of all kinds believe that the one perfect truth has been revealed to the proper authorities, and one's only task is to comply with it. Some streams of Jewish interpretive traditions — and I'm sure aspects of other traditions as well (e.g., Sufism, Zen Buddhism, Mennonite interpretive traditions) — are built on a different understanding: texts are the works of mortals, regardless of the source of their inspiration, and must be questioned in a playful but conscientious manner, and according to standards, in order for the tradition to shift, allowing its various truths to come to light.

For some Jewish interpretive traditions, argument is as valued as agreement, and compliance is worthless — or worse, dangerous —

399

unless first the belief or custom has been contested and, for the moment, found worthy. It is the space between that makes possible the engaged, interpersonally related life some streams of Jewish interpretive traditions, ontological hermeneutics, and relational psychoanalysis value.

Engaged, related moral discourse, in occasional moments, has the potential to evoke the dialectic of presence and absence. This evocation is possible, even though the world continues to burn, and evidence of God's absence is all around us. Struggling with the world as it is, not as we would wish it, learning to live a life forever east of Eden, realizing that the messiah will come only after we don't need him — these might give us, like the midrashic rabbis, the opportunity to develop a different understanding of presence. This would be an understanding that would identify interpersonal, communal, interpretive practices as a medium for pursuing the relationship between God and humans, locate God's voice in the spaces between words and between people and in the puzzles and uncertainties and multiple meanings of people and texts, and place into question the claim of a privileged, unmediated experience of God. This in turn, might help us face up to our responsibilities to one another, including the necessity of making thoughtful, persuasive political arguments that do not rest on the claim that God has spoken the one truth (but only into the ears of a privileged few). By facing God's absences, we might better turn our attention to our responsibilities to one another, as did the rabbis of late antiquity. This, in turn, might help us become slightly better human beings who work to make the world a slightly better place. Although couched in language unusual for the clinical hour, that is a description of what some of us might call a crucial aspect of a good therapeutic outcome.

REFERENCES

Ali, T. (1988). *Enemies of Freedom: Understanding Right-wing Authoritarianism.* San Francisco: Jossey-Bass.

----- (2002). *The clash of fundamentalisms.* London:Verso.Altemeyer, B.

Altemeyer, B. (1988). *Enemies of Freedom: Understanding Right-Wing Authoritarianism.* San Francisco, CA: Jossey-Bass.

Ammerman, N.T. (1991), "North American Protestant Fundamentalism." In: *Fundamentalisms Observed,* eds. M.E. Marty and R.S. Appleby. Chicago: University of Chicago Press, pp. 1-65.

Aron, L. (1996). *A Meeting of Minds: Mutuality in Psychoanalysis.* Hillsdale, NJ: The Analytic Press.

Aron, L. and Harris, A. (2005). *Relational Psychoanalysis, Volume II: Innovation and Expansion.* Hillsdale, NJ: The Analytic Press.

Barr, J. (1977). *Fundamentalism.* Philadelphia: Westminster Press.

Boyarin, D. (1990). *Intertextuality and the reading of Midrash.* Bloomington, IN: Indiana University Press.

Carpenter, J.A. (1997). *Revive Us Again: The Reawakening of American Fundamentalism.* New York: Oxford University Press.

Cushman, P. (1995). *Constructing the Self, Constructing America: A Cultural History of Psychotherapy.* Reading, MA: Addison-Wesley.

-------. (2005a). Between arrogance and a dead-end: Psychoanalysis and the Heidegger/Foucault dilemma. *ContemporaryPsychoanalysis,* 41: 399-417.

-------. (2005b). Clinical implications: A response to Layton. *Contemporary Psychoanalysis,* 41: 431-445.

Dreyfus, H.L. (1991*). Being-in-the-World: A Commentary on Heidegger's Being and Time, Division I.* Cambridge, MA: MIT Press.

Edel, W. (1987). *Defenders of the Faith: Religion and Politics From the Pilgrim Fathers to Ronald Reagan.* New York: Praeger.

Ehrenberg, D.B. (1992). *The Intimate Edge: Extending the Reach of Psychoanalytic Interaction.* New York: W.W. Norton.

Fishbane, M. ed. (1993). *The Midrashic Imagination: Jewish Exegesis, Thought, and History.* Albany, NY: SUNY Press.

401

Foucault, M. (1977). *Discipline and Punish: The Birth of the Prison*. New York: Random House.

Fowers, B.J. (2005). *Virtue and Psychology: Pursuing Excellence in Ordinary Practices*. Washington, D.C.: American Psychological Association.

Fromm, E. (1941). *Escape From Freedom*. New York: Holt, Rinehart & Winston.

-------. (1955). *The Sane Society*. New York: Holt, Rinehart & Winston.

-------. (1966). *You Shall Be As Gods: A Radical Interpretation of the Old Testament and Its Traditions*. New York: Holt, Rinehart and Winston.

Gadamer, H.-G. (1975). *Truth and Method*, trans. & ed. G. Barden & J. Cumming. New York: Seabury Press. Originally published in 1960.

Gill, M.M. (1983). The distinction between the interpersonal paradigm and the degree of the therapist's involvement. *Contemporary Psychologist*, 19: 200-237.

Goldenberg, R. (1984). Talmud. In *Back To the Sources: Reading the Classical Jewish Texts*, ed. B.W. Holtz. New York: Summit Books, pp. 129-176.

Hiley, D.R., Bohman, J.F. & Shusterman, R., eds. (1991). *The Interpretive Turn: Philosophy, Science, Culture*. Ithaca, NY: Cornell University Press.

Hoffman, I.Z. (1983). The patient as interpreter of the analyst's experience. *Contemporary Psychoanalysis*, 19: 389-422.

-------. (1998). *Ritual and Spontaneity In the Psychoanalytic Process: A Dialectical-Constructivist Approach*. Hillsdale, NJ: The Analytic Press.

Holtz, B.W. (1984). Midrash. In: *Back to the Sources: Reading the Classic Jewish Texts*, ed. B.W. Holtz. New York: Summit Books, pp. 177-211.

Kaufmann, Y. (1960). *The Religion of Israel: From Its Beginnings To the Babylonian Exile*. Chicago: University of Chicago Press.

Layton, L. (2002). Cultural hierarchies, splitting, and the heterosexist unconscious. In: *Bringing the plague: Toward a postmodern psychoanalysis*, eds. S. Fairfield, L. Layton, and C. Stack. New York: Other Press, pp.195-223.

-------. (2005). Notes toward a nonconformist clinical practice: Response to Philip Cushman's "Between arrogance and a dead-end." *Contemporary Psychoanalysis*, 41: 419-429.

Leary, K. (1997). Race in psychoanalytic space. *Gender & Psychoanalysis*, 2: 157-172.

-------. (2000). Racial enactments in dynamic treatment. *Psychoanalytic Dialogues*, 10: 639-654.

Levenson, E. A. (1983). *The Ambiguity of Change*. New York: Basic Books.

-------. (1991). *The Purloined Self*. New York: Contemporary Psychoanalysis Books.

Marty, M.E. and Appleby, R.S. eds. (1993). *Fundamentalism and the State*. Boston: Beacon Press.

Mitchell, S.A. (1988). *Relational Concepts in Psychoanalysis: An Integration*. Cambridge, MA: Harvard University Press.

-------. (1993). *Hope and Dread in Psychoanalysis*. NY: Basic Books.

Mitchell, S.A. and Aron, L. (1999). *Relational Psychoanalysis: The Emergence of a Tradition*. Hillsdale, NJ: The Analytic Press.

Ochs, P. and Levene, N. (2002). *Textual Reasonings: Jewish Philosophy and Text Study at the End of the Twentieth Century*. Grand Rapids, MI: William B. Eerdmans.

Ogden, T. (1994). *Subjects of Analysis*. Northvale, NJ: Aronson.

Peltz, R. (1998). The dialectic of presence and absence: Impasses and the retrieval of meaning states. *Psychoanalytic Dialogues*, 8: 385-409.

Peters, S. (2004). *Learning to Read Midrash*. New York: Urim.

Racker, H. (1968), *Transference and Countertransference*. New York: International Universities Press.

Reichley, A.J. (1987). The evangelical and fundamentalist revolt. In: *Piety and Politics: Evangelicals and Fundamentalists Confront the World*, eds. R.J. Neuhaus and M. Cromartie. Washington, D.C.:Ethics and Public Policy Center.

Richardson, F.C., Fowers, B.J., and Guignon, C.B. (1999). *Re-Envisioning Psychology: Moral Dimensions of Theory and Practice*. San Francisco: Jossey-Bass.

Rivkin, E. (1971). *The Shaping of Jewish History: A Radical New Interpretation*. New York: Scribners.

Rojtman, B. ed. (1998). *Black Fire on White Fire: An Essay in Jewish Hermeneutics, From Midrash to Kabbalah*. Berkeley, CA: University of Califonia Press.

Rosenberg, J. (1987). Biblical tradition: Literature and spirit in ancient Israel. In: *Jewish Spirituality: From the Bible through the Middle Ages,* ed. A. Green. New York: Crossroad, pp. 82-112.

-------. (July, 1989). *Notes on midrash.* Unpublished address delivered at the Midrash Institute, Reconstructionist Rabbinical College, Wyncote, PA.

-------. (in press). *When midrash is right: Rabbinic exegesis and Biblical literary criticism.* Prooftexts.

Sass, L. A. (1988). Humanism, hermeneutics, and the concept of the human subject. In *Hermeneutics and Psychological Theory: Interpretive Perspectives on Personality, Psychotherapy, and Psychopathology,* eds. S. B. Messer, L. A. Sass, and R. L. Woolfolk. New Brunswick, NJ: Rutgers University Press, pp. 222-271.

Stern, D. (1991). *Parables in Midrash: Narrative and Exegesis in Rabbinic Literature.* Cambridge, MA: Harvard University Press.

-------. (1996). *Midrash and Theory: Ancient Jewish Exegesis and Contemporary Literary Studies.* Evanston, IL: Northwestern University Press.

Stern, D.B. (1991). A philosophy for the embedded analyst. *Contemporary Psychoanalysis,* 27:51-80.

-------. (1997). *Unformulated Experience: From Dissociation to Imagination in Psychoanalysis.* Hillsdale, NJ and London: The Analytic Press.

Strozier, C.B. (1994). *Apocalypse: On the Psychology of Fundamentalism in America.* Boston: Beacon Press.

Suchet, M., Harris, A., & Aron, L. (2007). *Relational Psychoanalysis: New Voices.* NY: Routledge.

Woolfolk, R.L., Sass, L.A., & Messer, S.B. (1988). Introduction to hermeneutics. In: *Hermeneutics and Psychological Theory: Interpretive Perspectives on Personality, Psychotherapy, and Psychopathology,* eds. S.B. Messer, L.A. Sass, and R.L. Woolfolk. New Brunswick, NJ: Rutgers University Press, pp. 2-26.

CONTRIBUTORS

Lewis Aron, Ph.D. is director of the New York University, Postdoctoral Program in Psychotherapy and Psychoanalysis. He has served as President of the Division of Psychoanalysis of the American Psychological Association; founding President of the International Association for Relational Psychoanalysis and Psychotherapy (IARPP); founding President of the Division of Psychologist-Psychoanalysts of the New York State Psychological Association (NYSPA). He holds a Diplomate in Psychoanalysis from the American Board of Professional Psychology and is a Fellow of both the American Psychological Association and of the Academy of Psychoanalysis. Dr. Aron is author and editor of numerous scholarly articles and books including *A Meeting of Minds*. He was one of the founders, and is an Associate Editor of the journal, *Psychoanalytic Dialogues* and is the co-editor (with Adrienne Harris) of the *Relational Perspectives* Book Series, Routledge. He is the author of the forthcoming book, co-authored with Karen Starr, *Defining Psychoanalysis: The Ego and the Yid*.

lew.aron@nyu.edu

Yehoshua Arnowitz, M.D. graduated from Yeshivah University in New York City and completed medical school at the Albert Einstein College of Medicine in the Bronx, New York. He trained in Adult Psychiatry at Albert Einstein College of Medicine and afterwards completed a fellowship in Child Psychiatry at Tufts New England Medical Center in Boston,

405

Massachusetts. He has lived in Israel since the early 1980's. He was a staff member at the Hadassah Hospital Medical Center in Jerusalem, Israel, first in the Department of Child Psychiatry and later in the Department of Adult Psychiatry. He completed his psychoanalytic training at the Israel Psychoanalytic Institute and is presently a Training and Supervising Analyst within the Israel Psychoanalytic Association. Currently he is in private practice in Jerusalem, Israel.

Seth Aronson, Psy.D. is Fellow, Training and Supervising Analyst, Faculty at the William Alanson white Institute, New York. He is Supervisor and Faculty, Manhattan Institute for Psychoanalysis and Northwest Center for Psychoanalysis, Seattle and Portland.At Yeshivat Chovevei Torah, he is a member of the faculty.

Celia Brickman, Ph.D. is a faculty and clinical staff member at the Center for Religion and Psychotherapy of Chicago, where she is also the co-director of the Education Program. She is the author of *Aboriginal Populations in the Mind: Race and Primitivity in Psychoanalysis*, nominated for the Gradiva award by the National Assocation of for the Advancement of Psychoanalysis, and has published other essays and reviews concerning the intersection of psychoanalysis, race and religion.

Philip Cushman, Ph.D. is core faculty in the Psy.D. program at Antioch University in Seattle, Washington. He is the author of *Constructing the Self, Constructing America: A Cultural History of Psychotherapy* (Addison Wesley, 1995) and many articles on the history, theory, and practice of psychotherapy and on interpretive, hermeneutic approaches to psychology. He has practiced as a psychotherapist since 1977.

Stephen Frosh, Ph.D. is Pro-Vice-Master, Head of the Department of Psychosocial Studies and Professor of Psychology at Birkbeck College, University of London. He was previously Consultant Clinical Psychologist at the Tavistock Clinic, London. He is the author of many books and papers on psychosocial studies and on psychoanalysis, including *Hate and the 'Jewish Science': Anti-Semitism, Nazism and Psychoanalysis* (Palgrave, 2005), *For and Against Psychoanalysis* (Routledge, 2006), *After Words* (Palgrave, 2002) and *The Politics of Psychoanalysis* (Palgrave, 1999).

David Goodman, Ph.D. is a Clinical Fellow at Harvard Medical School/Cambridge Hospital, a Research Fellow at Boston University, and an adjunct faculty at Regis College and Lesley University. He has a Ph.D. in Clinical Psychology and a Masters in Theology. In addition to clinical work with underserved populations, Dr. Goodman has written several articles on Levinas, Jewish philosophy, social justice, and psychotherapy. He has a forthcoming book that explores the Jewish philosophy of Levinas as it pertains to constructs of the self in modern psychologies. He and his wife, Priscilla, currently reside in Cambridge, MA.

Libby Henik, LCSW is in private practice in New York and New Jersey. She is a graduate of the Wurzweiler School of Social Work of the Yeshiva University and a graduate in Psychodynamic Psychotherapy of the American Institute for Psychoanalysis of the Karen Horney Psychoanalytic Center. She also holds a Master of Arts in Hebrew Literature from Hunter College. Ms. Henik studied biblical exegesis and Hebrew literature with Nechama Leibowitz at Bar-Ilan University and with Professor Milton Arfa at Hunter College. She has taught ulpan in Israel, the United States and the former Soviet Union.
lhenik@hotmail.com

Lori Hope Lefkovitz is the Sadie Gottesman and Arlene Gottesman Reff Professor of Gender and Judaism and director of Kolot: The Center for Jewish Women's Studies at the Reconstructionist Rabbinical College. Her most recent book is In Scriptures: First Stories of Jewish Sexual Identities (Rowman and Littlefield, 2010).

Tuvia Peri, Ph.D is a clinical psychologist and supervisor in the Clinical Psychology residency program, Psychiatric Department and Center for

Traumatic Stress, Hadassah Medical Center, Jerusalem. He also serves as Head of Education and Psychology Studies at the Yaacov Herzog College.

Jill Salberg, Ph.D. is Clinical Associate Professor at the New York University Postdoctoral Program in Psychotherapy and Psychoanalysis, Faculty, Stephen A. Mitchell Center for Relational Psychoanalysis and has taught at the JCC in Manhattan and Skirball Center for Adult Jewish Learning. She is in private practice in Manhattan.

Joyce Slochower Ph.D., APBB is Professor of Psychology at Hunter College & the Graduate Center, CUNY, faculty and supervisor at the NYU Postdoctoral Program, the Steven Mitchell Center, the National Training Program of NIP and PPSC in New York, and the Psychoanalytic Institute of Northern California in San Francisco. She is on the American Editorial Board *of the International Journal of Psychoanalysis, Psychoanalytic Dialogues, Ricerca Psicoanalitica* and *Perspectives in Psychoanalysis.* The author of over 50 articles and two books: *Holding and Psychoanalysis: A Relational Perspective* (1996) and *Psychoanalytic Collisions* (2006), both by The Analytic Press.

Moshe Halevi Spero, Ph.D. is Elie Wiesel Professor and Director, Postgraduate Program of Psychoanalytic Psychotherapy, School of Social Work, Bar-Ilan University; Senior Clinical Psychologist, Weinstock Oncology Day Hospital, Shaare Zedek Medical Center and Department of Psychiatry, Sarah Herzog Memorial Hospital; Scientific Associate, American Academy of Psychoanalysis and Dynamic Psychiatry; author, *Religious Objects as Psychological Structures* (University of Chicago); co-author, *Hearing Visions and Seeing Voices* (Springer).

Karen E. Starr, Psy.D. is Adjunct Faculty and Supervisor at Long Island University, Clinical Psychology Doctoral Program, and maintains a private practice in New York City. She is the author of *Repair of the Soul: Metaphors of Transformation in Jewish Mysticism and Psychoanalysis*, Routledge 2008. Dr. Starr is the co-author, with Lewis Aron, of the forthcoming book, Defining Psychoanalysis: The Ego and the Yid.

Avivah Zornberg holds a **Ph.D.** in English Literature from Cambridge University. She is the author of three books: *Genesis: The Beginning of Desire* (JPS), which won the National Jewish Book Award in 1995; *The Particulars of Rapture: Reflections on Exodus* (Doubleday); and *The Murmuring Deep Reflections on the Biblical Unconscious*, published by Schocken in March 2009. Zornberg has grown to world acclaim through her writing and teaching of biblical commentary on the books of the Torah.

INDEX

LaVergne, TN USA
08 June 2010
185327LV00001BA/16/P